DATA, ARCHITECTURE AND THE EXPERIENCE OF PLACE

The notion of data is increasingly encountered in spatial, creative and cultural studies. Big Data and artificial intelligence are significantly influencing a number of disciplines. Processes, methods and vocabularies from sciences, architecture and the arts are borrowed, discussed and tweaked, and new cross-disciplinary fields emerge. More and more, artists and designers are drawing on hard data to interpret the world and to create meaningful, sensuous environments. Architects are using neurophysiological data to improve their understanding of people's experiences in built spaces. Different disciplines collaborate with scientists to visualise data in different and creative ways, revealing new connections, interpretations and readings. This often demonstrates a genuine desire to comprehend human behaviour and experience and to – possibly – inform design processes accordingly. At the same time, this opens up questions as to why this desire and curiosity is emerging now, how it relates to recent technological advances and how it converses with the cultural, philosophical and methodological context of the disciplines with which it engages. Questions are also raised as to how the use of data and data-informed methods may serve, support, promote and/or challenge political agendas.

Data, Architecture and the Experience of Place provides an overview of new approaches on this significant subject and is ideal for students and researchers in digital architecture, architectural theory, design, digital media, sensory studies and related fields.

Anastasia Karandinou is an architect and senior lecturer at the University of East London in the area of Architecture and Design. She has taught at the University of Portsmouth and at the University of Edinburgh and conducted research in the areas of architectural design, urbanism, digital media, interactive design, architecture and neuroscience. She represented Greece in the 11th Venice Biennale of Architecture as the main curator/architect of the 'Athens by Sound' project, exploring the non-visual aspects of architecture. She recently co-led the 'Cities in Transition' project, funded by a British Council Newton grant, examining the political and social role of public space in cities of rapidly changing demographics.

DATA, ARCHITECTURE AND THE EXPERIENCE OF PLACE

Edited by Anastasia Karandinou

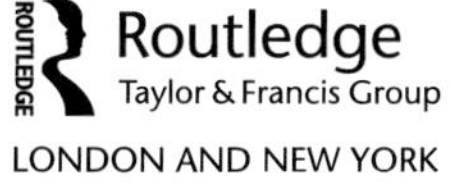

LONDON AND NEW YORK

First published 2019
by Routledge
2 Park Square, Milton Park, Abingdon, Oxon OX14 4RN

and by Routledge
52 Vanderbilt Avenue, New York, NY 10017

Routledge is an imprint of the Taylor & Francis Group, an informa business

British Library Cataloguing-in-Publication Data
A catalogue record for this book is available from the British Library

Library of Congress Cataloging-in-Publication Data
Names: Karandinou, Anastasia, editor.
Title: Data, architecture and the experience of place / edited by Anastasia Karandinou.
Description: New York : Routledge, 2019. | Includes bibliographical references and index.
Identifiers: LCCN 2018031351 | ISBN 9780815352464 (hb : alk. paper) | ISBN 9780815352488 (pb : alk. paper) | ISBN 9781351139328 (ebook)
Subjects: LCSH: Architecture—Human factors—Data processing. | Design—Human factors—Data processing. | Architecture and science.
Classification: LCC NA2542.4 .D35 2019 | DDC 720.1/08—dc23
LC record available at https://lccn.loc.gov/2018031351

ISBN: 978-0-8153-5246-4 (hbk)
ISBN: 978-0-8153-5248-8 (pbk)
ISBN: 978-1-351-13932-8 (ebk)

Typeset in Bembo
by Swales & Willis Ltd, Exeter, Devon, UK

CONTENTS

CONTRIBUTORS

Negar Ahmadpoor is a PhD candidate at the Department of Architecture and Built Environment, University of Nottingham, UK. Her PhD project focuses on studying the effects of using GPS-based systems on people's navigation within the built environment and the respective role of place design. Her research interests include studying environmental psychology, applied neuroscience in architecture, cognition of place and human environment interactions, in order to integrate them into design to make the built environment predictive and responsive to users' needs.

Alejandro Mieses Castellanos is an architect, programmer and urbanist, currently developing software that uses neural networks to trace variations in knowledge across massive sets of written theory, in order to understand how knowledge changes geographically and through time. He is the principal of a USDA/NRCS-funded Conservation Innovation Grant, dedicated to generating software for NRCS scientists to study and visualise environmental transformations due to climate change, and to convey these scenarios to the public. He is currently an adjunct professor and coordinator at the Pontifical Catholic University of Puerto Rico – School of Architecture, and has developed products for AT&T, Verizon Wireless and the Tourism Company of Puerto Rico.

Derek Clements-Croome is Emeritus Professor at the University of Reading and has worked extensively across academia and industry. Derek founded and now edits *Intelligent Buildings International Journal* published by Taylor and Francis and is a coordinator of CIB Commission W098 Intelligent and Responsive Buildings. Derek is also a commissioner for Hammersmith, Fulham and Haringey, BEE for the CABE arm of the Design Council, Fellow of the BRE Academy and Fellow of the Royal Society of Medicine. He has published over 200 papers across a broad range of building-related topics, particularly on intelligent buildings, health, wellbeing and productivity in buildings and holistic approaches to wellbeing and sustainability.

Richard Coyne is Dean of Postgraduate Research in the College of Humanities and Social Science at the University of Edinburgh where, until 2011, he was Head of the School of Arts, Culture and Environment. Coyne researches and teaches information technology in practice, computer-aided design in architecture, the philosophy of information technology, digital media and design theory. He is Academic Director of the MSc programme in Design and Digital Media and Programme Director of the MSc by Research in the Digital Media and Culture. He is author of several books on the implications of information technology and design with MIT Press and Routledge. His research has been supported by AHRC, EPSRC and SCRAN, and demonstrates the value of a broad, interdisciplinary framework for examining the relationship between computing, design and contemporary cultural theories. He is currently investigating the way we configure spaces through the use of pervasive mobile devices, such as smartphones, iPods and GPS.

Constantinos Daskalakis is a professor of Electrical Engineering and Computer Science at MIT. He holds a Diploma in Electrical and Computer Engineering from the National Technical University of Athens and a PhD in Computer Science from UC-Berkeley. His research interests lie in Theory of Computation and its interface with Economics, Probability Theory, Machine Learning and Statistics. He has been honoured with the 2007 Microsoft Graduate Research Fellowship, the 2008 ACM Doctoral Dissertation Award, the Game Theory and Computer Science (Kalai) Prize from the Game Theory Society, the 2010 Sloan Fellowship in Computer Science, the 2011 Outstanding Paper Prize from the Society for Industrial and Applied Mathematics (SIAM), the 2011 Ruth and Joel Spira Award for Distinguished Teaching, the 2012 Microsoft Research Faculty Fellowship, the 2015 Research and Development Award by the Vatican Giuseppe Sciacca Foundation and the 2018 Google Faculty Research Award. In 2018 he was also awarded the prestigious Rolf Nevanlinna Prize, for explicating core questions in game theory and machine learning.

Felecia Davis is an assistant professor at the Stuckeman Center for Design Computing in the School of Architecture and Landscape Architecture at Pennsylvania State University and is the director of SOFTLAB@PSU, with a PhD from MIT. Davis's work develops computational textiles (textiles that respond to commands through computer programming), electronics and sensors for use in architecture. Davis' work with SOFTLAB@PSU links art and science and has been featured in a PBS/NPR broadcast titled 'Women in Science'. She is currently working on a book *Softbuilt: Computational Textile Architectures*, forthcoming in 2018 from Actar D Press. Davis is principal in her design firm 'Felecia Davis Studio', which has received several awards in open and invited design competitions. Felecia has lectured, published and exhibited her work internationally, including at the Swedish School of Textiles, Microsoft Research and MIT's Media Lab.

Arlene Ducao is a creative engineer who makes technologies that examine the relationship between the natural landscape, our built environment and ourselves.

She is a principal at the DuKode Studio, a scientific and environmental design firm in Brooklyn, and CEO and cofounder of DuKode's affiliate company Multimer (DuKorp). At Multimer, she developed her invention, MindRider, a geospatial mind-mapping system profiled in *WIRED*, *New York Times*, *Discovery Channel*, *MSNBC*, *Fast Company*, *Science Channel* and many more. A recipient of the South by Southwest Winburne Community Service Award for her work on satellite mapping in Indonesia, she teaches at NYU and MIT, where she presents a range of topics, from multidimensional data visualisation to digital fabrication and its cultural underpinnings. She holds degrees from UMD, SVA and MIT.

Roua Ghosh is a Senior Architect at SETS, a Lebanese engineering firm, a PhD candidate, and a teaching assistant in the Faculty of Architecture, Design and Built Environment in Beirut Arab University. She has been awarded a scholarship to complete her Master's degree, through which, she focused on the multisensory approach in designing architectural spaces. To fulfil her passion in the field, she always tries to correlate her practical work and experience with her academic life. For her, travelling is the best way to learn, experience, feel and live architecture.

Tim Heath is Chair of Architecture & Urban Design at the University of Nottingham, UK. He is a registered architect, qualified town planner and experienced urban designer who is actively engaged in research, teaching and practice. He is also the course director for the MArch programme in Sustainable Urban Design in the Department of Architecture & Built Environment. Professor Heath's research interests are broad, spanning architecture and urban design. As an academic, he has published extensively, with many books, chapters and journal papers, and has delivered keynote presentations at major international conferences in the areas of urban design, heritage conservation, adaptive re-use of buildings and sustainable urbanism.

Phevos Kallitsis is an architect (National Technical University of Athens) and senior lecturer at the University of Portsmouth. His theoretical work focuses on Media, Architecture and Urban Space, working with Horror Films, as well as Gender and Sexuality. He teaches Architecture and Interior Design, and contributes to modules about Gender and Queer Theory Cultural Approaches on Urban Space. He has worked as a freelance architect on projects of different scales in various countries. He has also worked as a cinema editor and set designer for theatre and TV productions, and has curated events exploring the interconnections between architecture, urban design and cinema.

Dorothea Kalogianni is a PhD candidate and tutor at the School of Architecture and Landscape Architecture of the University of Edinburgh. She examines the notion of threshold in space and architecture through a series of projects and art installations that employ digital media and sound. For her investigation, she maps the EEG and emotional responses of occupants to digitally mediated offline and virtual environments. Part of her exploration includes understanding the potential applications of EEG in informing architectural design. She received her graduate diploma in architecture from the Aristotle University of Thessaloniki in Greece and has completed the MSc in Adaptive Architecture and Computation at the Bartlett School of Architecture, University College London. She has been an AHRC-funded student. She is a registered Greek architect.

Anastasia Karandinou is an architect and senior lecturer at the University of East London in the area of Architecture and Design. She has taught at the University of Portsmouth and at the University of Edinburgh and conducted research in the areas of architectural design, urbanism, digital media, interactive design, architecture and neuroscience. She represented Greece in the 11th Venice Biennale of Architecture as the main curator/architect of the 'Athens by Sound' project, exploring the non-visual aspects of architecture. She recently co-led the 'Cities in Transition' project, funded by a British Council Newton grant, examining the political and social role of public space in cities of rapidly changing demographics.

Trevor Keeling has carried out extensive research on developing methods for holistically evaluating and monitoring indoor-environmental quality of buildings. He is now leading the Sustainability & Building Physics Group in Asia for BuroHappold Engineering, working out of the Hong Kong office. At BuroHappold, he continues to integrate research into design practice. Keeling completed an EngD, sponsored by BuroHappold, at the University of Reading, with supervisors Professor Derek Clements-Croome, Dr Etienne Roesch and Andy Keelin. His research looked into how indoor-environmental quality affects people's wellbeing and performance and led to a number of journal and conference papers. He was honoured with the TSBE Researcher of the Year Award 2015.

Pablo Lorenzo-Eiroa is an architect, artist and scholar, focusing on the emerging architecture of information. He is an Associate Professor at the New York Institute of Technology, and has previously been an Assistant Professor at The Cooper Union. Lorenzo-Eiroa is a Fulbright and National Endowment for the Arts scholar. He holds an MArch II degree from Princeton University and a Diploma in Architecture from the University of Buenos Aires. He has edited and authored many books and articles, and among others, he co-edited *Architecture in Formation* (Routledge, 2013). Pablo Lorenzo-Eiroa is also the design principal of e-Architects – Eiroa-Architects NY-BA (www.e-architects.net).

Sven Mündner is a partner in Leitsystem, an urban practitioner and place maker engaged with many urban-regeneration and design initiatives across London. His expertise and recent practice include consultation on the development of suitable places for creative industries, community engagement, co-creation processes, commercial strategies for new developments and areas of change. Sven Mündner is also a visiting academic at the Central Saint Martins MArch Architecture programme.

Etienne Roesch is Associate Professor of Cognitive Science at the University of Reading, UK, affiliated to the Centre for Integrative Neuroscience and Neurodynamics, and to the School of Psychology and Clinical Language Sciences. He conducts and supervises research, combining empirical work and mathematical modelling, at both cellular and systemic levels. His team uses psychophysics, electrophysiology and neuroimaging methods, as well as mathematical modelling.

Samer El Sayary is a researcher, award-winning architect and an assistant professor of architecture. He has led and attended workshops in several countries, and through his research and design work focuses on the relationship between the past and the future. He attempts to redefine this relationship through examining, theorising and testing the use of contemporary technologies. Professor Samer El Sayary examines local heritage through methods involving the use of cutting-edge tools and technologies.

Bridget Snaith CMLI is a partner in Shape Landscape Architecture, London, programme leader for Landscape Architecture programmes at the University of East London and a built-environment expert with the Design Council CABE. She has been working with landscapes and communities in London since 2001. She was part of the Central London Partnership/GLA client group for London's walking strategy and led a pilot in Waterloo for TfL's 'Legible London' project. Alongside practice in the public realm and landscape design, her current research interests include issues of equality, ethnicity and spatial design for cultural inclusion. Dr Snaith has participated in a number of funded-research projects, most recently a British Council Newton funded workshop exploring place and migration issues, 'Cities in Transition', held in Ankara in 2017.

Matthew Wagner is an assistant professor in Virginia Tech's School of Architecture + Design. His research focuses on the development and utilisation of responsive interior surfaces that mitigate workplace distractions. The aim of his work is on optimising the built environment for occupant performance. Wagner received a Master of Architecture from Virginia Tech and a Bachelor of Fine Arts in Interior Design from the School of the Arts at Virginia Commonwealth University.

ACKNOWLEDGEMENTS

I would like to express my gratitude to the colleagues who contributed as members of the scientific committee of the conference 'Data and Senses', which led to this publication. The members of the scientific committee were: Professor Hassan Abdalla, Dr Aghlab Al-Attili, Alan Chandler, Professor Cherif Amor, Dr Satish Basavapatna Kumaraswamy, Barbara Bochnak, Dr Julien Castet, Nefeli Chatzimina, Profes Ruth Conroy Dalton, Dr Heba Elsharkawy, Professor Ozlem Erkarslan, Professor David Fortin, Ruairi Glynn, Dr Vangelis Lympouridis, Dr Kat Martindale, Rosa Mendoza-Robles, Professor Panos Parthenios, Dr Kerstin Sailer, Maria Segantini, Dr Sally Shahzad, Dr Bridget Snaith, Dr Renee Tobe, Professor Duncan Turner and Dr Louise Turner. I would particularly like to thank Professor Richard Coyne, Professor Constantinos Daskalakis, Professor Deborah Hauptmann and Professor Jan Wiener, keynote speakers of the 'Data and Senses' conference, and key contributors in steering engaging conversations and debates during the conference and beyond. Major sponsors of the 'Data and Senses' conference were RIBA, ARUP, UEL and the Museum of Architecture. Thanks to their support, a cross-disciplinary group of researchers and practitioners came together and shared their latest work. Special thanks are due to Dr Kat Martindale, RIBA Head of Research and Innovation, who actively supported this knowledge-exchange event and the dissemination of its outputs, as well as the follow-up discussions amongst the researchers involved. Special thanks are also due to Joseph Hargrave and Felicitas Zu Dohna from ARUP, who contributed significantly to the organisation of the conference. I would like also to express my gratitude to Will Jennings, who proofread sections of this book and helped with issues of language and clarity. Additionally, acknowledgements are due to UEL for the sabbatical scheme offered, and to Pete Cobb, Carl Callaghan, Alan Chandler and to Prof. Stephen Maddison, Chair of the Sabbatical Scheme Committee, for their support.

Many thanks to Shin Egashira for kindly offering us the possibility of using a photo of a model he had created with his students. Special thanks to all the authors of this book for the numerous, fruitful conversations and collaboration during the conference and beyond, as well as to all the conference participants and attendees. The model shown on the cover image was created by a team of UEL students, led by Shin Egashira.

1

DATA AND THE EXPERIENCE OF PLACE

The use of data in contemporary spatial and cultural studies

Anastasia Karandinou

Big Data and artificial intelligence (AI) have been increasingly discussed over the last few years and are significantly influencing a number of disciplines. In parallel to that, the notion of 'data' is being increasingly encountered in spatial, creative and cultural studies. Processes, methods and vocabularies from the sciences are borrowed, discussed and tweaked, and new cross-disciplinary fields emerge. Several recent projects attempt to use data to map, measure and quantify the intangible – aspects of the human experience that had previously been addressed only qualitatively. This often demonstrates a genuine desire to comprehend human behaviour and human experience of different environments, and to – possibly – inform design processes accordingly. At the same time, this opens up questions as to why this desire and curiosity are emerging now, how they relate to recent technological advances and how they converse with the cultural and methodological context of the disciplines with which they engage. Questions are also raised as to how the use of data and data-informed methods may serve, support, promote and/or challenge political agendas.

In this book, a range of projects on the theme of data, architecture and the experience of place are presented. The projects reveal a desire to break the conventional boundaries of disciplines and an inquiring tendency to explore new territories – territories for which new methods and processes are currently being invented and debated. In this chapter, we will look into the main themes that each project presents and the major questions that recur or emerge through each discourse.

Data and the sensuous

The use of hard data, as well as the cross-over between the digital and the physical, is being increasingly addressed in design disciplines, architecture, arts and urban studies. Artists and designers increasingly make use of hard data to interpret the world and/or create meaningful and sensuous environments and design objects. Architects attempt to measure neurophysiological data to better understand the human experience in spaces. Designers script parametric processes to translate data into responsive, meaningful or aesthetically intriguing installations. Scientists and architects/artists/designers collaborate to visualise data in new and creative ways so as to trigger and reveal further connections, interpretations and readings.

Practices such as these attempt to break down the traditional dichotomy between 'data' and the 'sensuous' or 'experiential' – a discussion that relates to the earlier and affiliated dichotomy between the 'digital' and the 'physical'. Recent practices attempt to translate elusive, ephemeral and intangible aspects of a place into solid data. In other instances, the solid data are interpreted and represented so as to be perceived by the different senses and experienced immersively. In this context, methods and conceptual frameworks of different disciplines need to engage in a dialogue; through these cross-disciplinary practices, new strategies and processes emerge. This publication aims to present collaborative projects where methods from more than one discipline are involved. This publication also addresses how collaborators from different disciplines can work together to address current design, spatial and social issues – for example, the measurement of neurophysiological data – in an attempt to understand human experience, a recurring theme in this book. Could the mapping of the brain activity help designers gain a better understanding of human experience in different spaces? Could the use of electroencephalography (EEG), eye-tracking and other neurological or physiological data inform our understanding of human experience? And could that inform design? Could physiological data be used in parallel to other methods – such as observation and interviews – to assess navigation, human comfort or levels of stress in different environments? Can these processes lead to a deeper understanding of human nature? What is the potential of such processes, and what 'dangers' do they entail? Who commissions these studies, and how are the results interpreted and used? How can we avoid the results being transcribed into oversimplified design 'recipes', exploited by purely profit-driven developers or stakeholders?

One could read the data-driven mapping of emotions and human experience as a contemporary re-invention or re-interpretation of the Situationists' attempts to map ambiences – territories of different atmosphere or mood. These territories cannot be described through solid edges, but through other less tangible attributes (Constant et al., 2001; McDonough, 2002). Hence, what the psychogeographers called ambience or mood could be revisited or re-interpreted with the use of neurobiological data-driven or data-inspired methods. Contemporary EEG kits and applications record brain waves and translate them into mood-categories, such as engagement, stress, calmness, etc.; this could be interpreted as a different type of psychogeographic map. Data-driven processes open up new strategies for mapping the human experience and the ambience of places – and, as with every new tool and type of mapping, this can offer a different and enlightening understanding. Counterarguments need to be acknowledged, as the dominance of data-driven (on neurophysiological-data-driven) processes may displace the discourse on the aesthetic, cultural, social and political context and on dimension of place; how can we avoid neurophysiological data becoming the only or main driver for design, ignoring aesthetics, cultural and political context? (Wood, 2010; Moran, 2013; Karandinou and Turner, 2018)

Questions addressed through the projects presented in this book include: How can human emotions be categorised, grouped and mapped, and lead to either new types of mappings of urban environments or to inventive design processes and products? How can data, such as flows and movements in the city, demographic patterns (drawn from dating apps), environmental data, narratives, stories and articles, be organised and mapped in new meaningful ways, revealing hidden and unanticipated links? How do AI processes facilitate that? What *is* and what *is not* computed and represented, and how does the relationship between the two drive decision- and policy-making?

Inherent paradoxes: positivism and phenomenology

An emerging issue and challenge in cross-disciplinary projects, which is not often opened up, is the inherent contradiction, or paradox, between the methods used in different disciplines. In architecture, spatial and cultural studies, research is often driven by open-ended questions and by an open – often phenomenological – engagement with processes. In contrast, in other disciplines, such as natural sciences, the methods follow a positivist approach, which emerges from a Cartesian analytical way of seeing the world. There is often a specific and clear hypothesis in which the experiments prove right or wrong. The underpinning philosophical stance – although often not explicitly stated – drives a project's methods and processes, and places it within a discourse.

Architects and designers studying the experience of place, often follow methods emerging from a phenomenological approach; they attempt to gain better understanding of a place by exposing themselves to it, by observing it, by mapping various aspects of it, by performing different tasks within it and hence encountering it in a number of different ways. In this context, the immersion that such processes allow is what leads to the understanding and knowledge being sought.

For Husserl, who established phenomenology and influenced architectural research processes, understanding occurs through exposure and immersion in a situation (Husserl, 1999). According to Dermot Moran: 'Husserl wants to explore experience in a pure manner, unsullied by assumption' (Moran, 2002). As Jenson claims, drawing from Husserl's writings, phenomenology is more interested in seeing than analysing, and is associated to an open reading and describing of the world (Jenson, 2014). The discourse of mapping and understanding places, in the context of architecture and spatial studies, is influenced by this phenomenological context. James Corner, in 'The Agency of Mapping', argues for a kind of mapping that is generative, that reveals – through the processes it undertakes – what was previously unknown. He interprets and describes mapping as an open-ended process that allows for the unexpected to be revealed. As Corner (2002) claims, the mapping's 'agency lies in neither reproduction nor imposition but rather in uncovering realities previously unseen or unimagined, even across seemingly exhausted grounds'. He draws from Deleuze and Guattari's post-structuralist thinking and considers mapping as an open-ended process of questioning, mark-making, revealing, re-addressing and re-adjusting the question – as an engagement, an involvement in an exploratory journey (Corner, 2002; Perkins, 2003; Deleuze and Guattari, 2004).

Hence, we need to acknowledge some kind of paradox when projects draw from two seemingly contradictory worlds a positivist, scientific set of methods, and narrative-based, phenomenology-inspired processes. Methods emerging from different disciplines start developing a dialogue with one another, and new processes, methods and theoretical frameworks emerge. We need to acknowledge that within this transition, the processes seem at times in conflict with the established premises.

For example, at times, processes borrow tools from the sciences, but then develop a post-structuralist and phenomenology-inspired narrative without using the data as absolute, solid evidence for the validity of a hypothesis. (We will not elaborate on the relationship between phenomenology and post-structuralism here – we only acknowledge some affinity with regards to how these perspectives have informed architectural thinking (Stoller, 2009; Reynolds, 2010).) At times, processes involving data collection, data visualisation and data-driven discussion show an affinity with scientific methods, but also develop a narrative that does not follow the positivist conventions. The relationship between transcendental and naturalistic approaches has been broadly discussed in the context of philosophy, and less in the context of cross-disciplinary spatial studies (Petitot et al., 1999; Gallagher, 2015). Moran, in his essay '"Let's Look at It Objectively": Why Phenomenology Cannot Be Naturalized', discusses critically this issue, and claims that the two – phenomenology (and transcendental philosophies) and positivism – are in some sense incompatible. Referring to Husserl, he says: '[F]or Husserl, objectivism takes a stance that does not know it is a stance' (Moran, 2013). Positivism assumes that objectivity is possible, which is not the case for transcendental philosophies – whereby there is no such thing as the 'objective' or 'neutral' observer. The potential of some new data-driven tools can fascinate and allure one with their seemingly objective nature. Moran refers to the example of Google Street View to demonstrate that naturalists assume that the ever-increasing degree of detail offers objectivity, whereas, as he suggests, for phenomenologists each position is dependent on a specific point of view. Through the projects presented in this book, one of the aims is to reflect on the nuances of the cross-over of these different threads of thought, on the contradictions as well as on new potential paths, methods and conceptual frameworks.

Phenomenology, transcendental philosophies and AI

The recent advances in AI neural networks allow us to rethink phenomenology and post-structuralism theories in a new way. Like AI, neural networks use a huge number of data (or experiences, let's say) to learn from, without necessarily formulating solid visible/accessible 'rules'; similarly, a phenomenologist might argue that engaging with processes and activities in a non-necessarily 'scientific' way exposes one to new understanding (of places/human experience, etc.). There seems to be a parallelism between this kind of AI and the phenomenological approach. Both draw experience and understanding from exposure to large datasets or processes, and learn without necessarily formulating solid theories (as we know them) or pinning down a specific visible/comprehensive algorithm. The recent advancements in deep learning and AI neural networks reframe the theoretical discourse and relationship between positivism and phenomenological approaches. Daskalakis's chapter introduces some of the key notions of data science, statistics and AI, and discusses the potential and challenges of this emerging new field.

AI has been defined in a number of different ways and describes a number of different things – from Alan Turing's machine and attempts to imitate human intelligence, to recent neural networks whereby AI 'trains' AI to perform complex tasks. Deep neural networks are inspired by the way biological neural networks work; layers of artificial neurons process the input information and 'learn' by being exposed to large amounts of data/examples. During this self-learning, neural connections become strengthened or weakened depending on the correlations validated or not – similarly to what we understand as 'trial-and-error' (Müller, 2016; Ertel, 2017; Wolchover, 2017). Recent AI deep neural networks have been described as a 'black box', due to the fact that the 'learning' process – the way in which the neural network trains itself – is not fully understood and cannot be fully defined. As Bleicher describes them, 'the most capable technologies – namely, deep neural networks – are notoriously opaque, offering few clues as to how they arrive at their conclusions' (Bleicher, 2017). Natalie Wolchover describes it as follows:

> After a deep neural network has "learned" from thousands of sample dog photos, it can identify dogs in new photos as accurately as people can. The magic leap from special cases to general concepts during learning gives deep neural networks their power, just as it underlies human reasoning, creativity and the other faculties collectively termed "intelligence." Experts wonder what it is about deep learning that enables generalization – and to what extent brains apprehend reality in the same way.
>
> *(Wolchover, 2017)*

Both the initial algorithm, as well as the context – the numerous examples – formulate the 'intelligence'; and the fact that the numerous examples (inputs) are not fully controlled makes the output not fully controlled or predictable either. This seems equivalent to how humans learn – by exposure to numerous data/images/information, which are processed in a 'black-box'-like way. It also seems equivalent to phenomenological approaches, which argue for an understanding that emerges through exposure, immersion, engagement, experience and without a formulation of solid rules and algorithms.

With the above, I am not proposing a clear correlation between these theories – or worlds – that use quite different vocabularies and emerge from different traditions and philosophies; I am only opening the question as to how this parallelism could possibly offer new thinking tools.

New prototypes

The chapters of Ducao, Davis and Wagner present new prototypes, which translate environmental parameters or aspects of the human experience into data, to be used either for mapping and designing urban environments or for creating meaningful and useful aesthetic patterns and objects. Arlene Ducao examines new methods, devices and technologies for recording and mapping human neurophysiological signals for gaining a better understanding of human experience. She presents 'MindRider' and 'Multimer' – prototype systems that she initially designed and made as a researcher at the MIT Media Lab and later developed further through her own start-up. Ducao presents a series of uses that she tested through multiple experiments, and her critical thoughts on the potential value and use of these new digital systems. MindRider monitored – with the use of EEG embedded in the cyclists' helmets – the brain activity of cyclists in Manhattan, and categorised their experience in relationship to levels of concentration/relaxation. The maps produced were analysed in conjunction with other datasets for these areas of the city. Significant correlation was found – and possibly expected – between areas of high concentration and areas of bike collisions, showing that cyclists are more concentrated in areas that may be – or feel – of more complex traffic pattern, and hence at a higher risk of accident. Through their statistical analysis, Ducao and her collaborators observed that areas of high concentration and areas of high relaxation were consistent across users ($p = 0.03$). This shows that certain mental states are significantly associated with objective/pragmatic characteristics of a specific place. The Multimer system is evolving and is used by Ducao and her team for mapping and analysing human experience in various environments and in collaboration with different companies and industries. Multimer monitors data such as brainwave, heart rate, steps (pedometer) and acceleration, geo-locates them and correlates them with other datasets (depending on the nature of each experiment/application). It involves wearable kit and the mobile or cloud app, which processes the data, and in recent studies involves participants that move in the city on foot, by bicycle or car.

Her most recent study, funded by the US National Science Foundation (NSF), involves over 100 participants and attempts to correlate, through the use of Multimer, physical aspects of areas of Manhattan with the physiological and cognitive states of the users. Ducao critically discusses how these new systems can be used to respond to the requirements of different companies and sectors – such as advertising, real estate, etc. – while securing that the concern for the human remains a central priority. Ducao expresses her belief in the 'human scale' and presents her interpretation of this notion, associating it mainly with walkability.

She refers to design examples, such Le Corbusier's buildings and urban planning, or Robert Moses' masterplan of NY, which started from social and inclusive manifestoes but then subverted into less inclusive/socially aware/human-centred solutions in favour of efficiency or profit. Similarly, she refers to Robert Propst's 'Action Office' – designed with the human in mind to increase privacy, flexibility and movement for the office worker but was then transgressed into the conventional space-saving cubicle. With these concerns in mind, Ducao opens up the terribly crucial issue of inclusion, in the age of 'Big Data'. As research involving Big Data affects all aspects of human life and interaction, and informs critical political and social decision-making, Ducao stresses the importance of inclusion of all types of people, so that the outcomes of relevant research do not reflect only a mainstream majority – the most represented types of people – but all.

Felecia Davis looks into how emotion and/or information can be communicated and experienced through smart textiles. Davis presents her MIT-based research project 'FELT', a computational textile wall panel and a series of experiments conducted to explore the relevant human response. The smart panel is large-scale (150×180cm), white and its surface moves and transforms over time. The visual patterns – shapes of the fabric and the movement of the components of its surface – are inspired by behavioural patterns observed in nature. Davis examines how the notion of 'emotion' has been discussed in different theories and concludes that it has been generally described as the interpretation of a stimulus, which then results in either a bodily response or a feeling. Referring to Darwin, and reflecting on the issue of expression, Davis presents the categorisation of messages emitted (by humans or animals) as of two types: messages sent by inference; and messages sent for communication. A bird opening its feathers as an evolutionary response to danger is not an intentional communication of 'anger'; it helps its survival, and the emotion of 'anger' is only inferred. In contrast, other messages are expressed deliberately in order to communicate an emotional state and purposefully influence the response of the others. Through a series of experiments, Davis tested the response of participants to still and moving FELT designs, experienced – at different stages of the experiment – visually or by touch. She analysed the participants' responses in order to find correlations between shapes and patterns and the emotions inferred. She also analysed how the introduction of the tactile experience of the patterns (instead of only the visual) altered the participants' responses. Parts of the interview involved rating the inferred emotion on a number scale, and other parts involved open conversation, which brought up metaphors, memories and feelings associated with certain patterns, shapes, textures and movements. It is revealing how the patterns of computational textiles are interpreted and perceived by the users/participants and associated with personal references, homely memories and poetic metaphors. This demonstrates the design potential of such systems and the power of designing with both the tactile and visual in mind – increasingly facilitated in the context of computation.

Although computation is traditionally associated with the purely visual, over the last few decades it has increasingly facilitated designing that addresses different senses. Davis's exploration of the potential of different patterns, textures and movements of the FELT – addressing clearly both the visual and the tactile sense – is aiming at opening new directions for designing with computational textiles and introducing new uses and applications.

Matthew Wagner presents two prototypes that he is currently developing, the AuralSurface and the FlowerWall. The AuralSurface monitors the sound levels of an interior environment and responds in realtime in order to increase or decrease the acoustic dampening. Felt sheets are being designed to move and deploy to absorb sound, depending on the decibel volume in the equivalent area of the room. The FlowerWall is an interactive surface that responds in realtime to the levels of light; its panels contract to allow the right amount of light into the space depending on the weather and lighting conditions. Both prototypes aim to feed realtime data into a responsive design element. Its purpose is both practical and aesthetic; Wagner is researching how these responsive elements can be automated to address the practical need for adequate sound and light quality in an office environment, with an aesthetically unique and intriguing intelligent wall panel. In parallel to building and testing physical components of the prototypes, Wagner's team uses an immersive virtual environment to test different variations of the form of the prototype, its movement and the algorithms that control it.

Environmental, physiological and neurophysiological data

The studies presented in Chapters 6, 7 and 8 record and analyse physiological and neurophysiological data in order to gain a better understanding of human navigation, the effect of spatial thresholds and the correlations between pragmatic spatial parameters and the user experience.

Trevor Keeling, Etienne Roesch and Derek Clements-Croome measure physiological data with the use of wearable sensors to assess the human experience and comfort in an office environment. More specifically, they measure certain parameters of the physical environment – temperature, light levels (luminosity and light temperature), sound levels and CO_2 – in parallel to measuring the user's heart rate and skin conductivity. The experiment was conducted with 50 participants and involved both recorded data and a questionnaire. Keeling et al. aim at developing methods for managing and assessing complex data sets, in order to understand how specific changes within a physical environment affect the experience and physiological response of the user. They make an interesting distinction between stimuli that have a very low impact on human physiology and mainly affect how a user consciously perceives their environment (such as a disturbing light) and stimuli that have a significant impact upon the human physiology. Keeling et al. argue that findings from research that assess only one parameter (i.e. only sound levels) have limited value, and reflect on the need for more complex models that explore simultaneously the effect of different parameters, and attempt to correlate the nature and intensity of their impact.

One of their main observations was that higher sound levels are at times associated with higher heart rate. This observed pattern needs further testing to be validated, but already forms a significant hypothesis for further research. Also, the fact that this pattern does not apply to all participants make us think that some sounds are more disturbing than others, regardless of their loudness. Hence, one of the main remarks is that some parameters, such as sound, although initially treated as a one-dimensional parameter, in reality is not. So, some parameters need to be treated differently from others, as their degree of complexity varies. This may seem obvious in the case of sound and temperature, but it opens a very interesting discussion as to how we simplify certain stimuli in order to analyse them scientifically. Other stimuli may be more complex than temperature or sound, and harder to categorise as one-dimensional or not. Another interesting observation is that correlations observed are limited due to the overall comfort level of the environments tested. It seems that the conditions of all office spaces tested were fairly comfortable and ordinary – without huge fluctuations of temperature, noise or light, which would have mapped in much more obvious ways on the physiological recordings.

Examining the relationship between environmental parameters and human response is also valuable – besides raising the above-mentioned questions and issues – in creating general guidelines as to the required levels of temperature, light, sound, etc. for an environment of a specific function (e.g., office space), and in understanding how deviation from these conditions may lead to a less comfortable experience or reduced productivity, either for all users or for a significant majority.

In parallel, it makes one reflect on what *IS* comfort and productivity, and whether it should always be a priority. Are there compromises with other aspects of human experience made, in favour of comfort and productivity, as we conventionally perceive them? Mallinson (2004) in her article 'Metaphors of Experience: The Voice of Air' provocatively argues that buildings – and spaces in general – become increasingly controlled, and points out how exposure to a fluctuation of temperature, rain or wind may be an enlightening, immersive and desirable experience. This discussion is not aiming at suggesting that we should design offices exposed fully to the elements of nature. It only raises an open question with regards to some values (e.g., conventional measurable comfort) that may become panacea and addressed as absolute, universal and timeless desires, and not as culturally, socially, politically or historically loaded, and place- and time-specific – to a certain extent – conventions.

Bridget Snaith and Sven Mündner examine the potential of the use of EEG technology for recording and analysing navigation in an urban environment. Their attempt is to quantify – to measure and represent – how effectively people can navigate in a specific environment. They discuss the potential value of an objective, solid method for measuring this type of human experience. Their hypothesis and arguments make one reflect on the increasing need and desire to quantify and measure aspects of the human experience, and of the subsequent current debates on this issue. One would ask if there is a real need to quantify certain aspects of human experience and make the intangible measurable, or if it is a by-product of the increasing tendency for solid data and scientific (or scientific-looking) proofs. They reflect themselves on these issues, by discussing the complexities of the relationship between research and an actual live-design project, as well as the limitations of several methods and processes tested. Snaith and Mündner discuss how the use of solid data, which would help one map and better comprehend the human experience, could make a design proposal more persuasive. Objective evidence that a design proposal would lead to better navigation would be more convincing to a potential developer, client or funding body.

Their research discusses methods, processes and practices, as well as a specific case study – a navigation experiment in Thamesmead. Snaith and Mündner were commissioned by the current owner of Thamesmead, the social-housing provider Peabody, to propose how navigation could be redesigned more effectively for the pedestrians of the area. Thamesmead was designed as a 'new town' in the 1960s by the Greater London Council, with high-speed roads and separate paths for pedestrians, some of which – as the authors claim – include confusing intersections. Groups of volunteers were asked to navigate key parts of the pedestrian-path network. Throughout the different stages of the experiments, the team of researchers used combined methods involving – amongst others – semi-structured interviews, questionnaires, focus groups, workshops and observation of the way-finding process of the experiment participants. At a key-stage of the experiments, Snaith and Mündner observed that participants navigated more successfully to their desired destination when temporary signs (designed by the researchers) were installed along the paths, as opposed to participants who only used a map. The researchers acknowledge the limitations of their findings, which are mainly due to the small number of participants. Still, though, the small sample, analysed in conjunction with the interviews, focus groups and workshops with the local community, could lead to a research hypothesis, to be tested and validated further. It is worth mentioning that this research process led to interesting findings beyond the questions that were originally set. For example, the interviews revealed how aspects of the existing system of signage misled the participants' navigation (rather than helping them). Hence, for some participants it was not necessarily the researchers' signage (or lack of it) that allowed them to navigate successfully (or not), but other aspects of the environment. Some of the observations of the researchers make us reflect on the recurring theme of this book, of the relationship of quantitative and qualitative methods, and of the paradoxes and complexities of the processes of navigating through these methods and their variations.

Dorothea Kalogianni and Richard Coyne examine the experience of spatial thresholds in VR, with the use of EEG. In collaboration with their master's students, they designed a number of virtual environments, which included different types of thresholds – transitions between environments of different qualities and character. Users could experience and navigate in these environments with the use of a head-mount VR display (Oculus). This set-up was used for a series of pilot experiments. The participants navigated in the VR environment while their brain activity was monitored with a portable EEG device (Emotiv). Questionnaires and interviews with the participants followed. The researchers used the Emotiv application 'Affective Suite', which translates the EEG signals into four states; excitement, engagement, frustration and meditation. Although the algorithm is not released by Emotiv, hence works as a 'black box', the validation of this algorithm (published in several studies) shows that it can be used as an indication of broad categories of cognitive/emotional states. Kalogianni and Coyne analyse the individual EEG and interview responses of each participant to gain a better understanding of how people experience thresholds of different types. A few participants, for example, show through their EEG recordings an excitement peak before the crossing of the threshold, whereas their engagement remains high for much longer, after the crossing of the threshold and while exploring the new environment. This observation might be a starting point for understanding more deeply what happens in one's brain when exploring new places and in moving from one environment to another. How do we interpret this transition from excitement to engagement in a cultural context, and what does it mean in neurophysiological terms? This pilot study opens intriguing questions, which are being examined further in their upcoming experiments.

GIS data: navigation, emotions and gender issues

Negar Ahmadpoor and Tim Heath present their research on how people navigate in an urban environment with and without the use of a GPS. They argue that new information systems and technologies allow for new ways of inhabiting and experiencing places. Hence the old vocabulary and understanding of how people use space may no longer be valid or perfectly accurate. For example, with the use of smart phones – and embedded GPS apps – the way-finding process changes. One may be looking for different clues from before the emergence of these technologies. Additionally, the verbal narrative of how you can reach a place and the instructions that one may give another as to how to find a location change as well. In this context, one would ask, what are, hence, the implications for the designing of places, and more specifically for the designing of urban environments? Ahmadpoor and Heath start addressing this issue by exploring how the use of GPS changes how people navigate and, more specifically, how the recognition of landmarks affects their way-finding. Their experiment is conducted in Nottingham, with 76 participants. The participants were asked to navigate from a given point, to eight different specific destinations; half with the use of a GPS and half without. The first stage of their data analysis shows that non-GPS users did better in the task of recognising landmark buildings, shown to them in photos, after their way-finding activity. Ahmadpoor and Heath examined, then, the characteristics of the landmark buildings that were better remembered as opposed to those that were not. They present a very interesting graph, showing a series of buildings that are best remembered by both groups (GPS users and non-GPS users), and a series of buildings that are remembered by non-GPS users and not by the GPS users. These are the places in the graph where the biggest gap in level of remembering is observed between the two groups. The researchers observed that the historically and culturally significant buildings, buildings that were different from their context and 'buildings with unique architectural qualities' were more remembered by GPS users as well.

This raises an interesting question with regards to how one describes or interprets what makes a building memorable. What do we define as 'historically and culturally significant'? One could argue that this may be different for an architectural expert or historian, and different for other inhabitants of the city. For example, some monuments of modernism are hugely admired by architects, and form significant landmarks in their reading of the city, whereas the same buildings may be less noticeable for others. Another interesting discussion that the authors initiate has to do with how these findings may inform design practices. A 'reflex' response might be to create 'memorable' buildings, so that both GPS and non-GPS users notice some landmarks. However, we need to be critical with this kind of direction for various reasons. On the one hand, memorable buildings may also be the terribly badly designed ones. The density of 'different' buildings also needs to be considered; too many different buildings may be questionable. On the other hand, this argument could be totally flipped around and questioned altogether. Should design be directed by the kind of buildings people notice while navigating using a GPS, or not, to what extent, and why? Ahmadpoor and Heath's research opens all these exciting questions for further debate.

Roua Ghosh and Samer El Sayary attempt to create a map of emotions in order to gain a better understanding of human experience in an urban environment. Their aim is to correlate specific spatial attributes and sensual stimuli to the emotions invoked, and to assess any observed patterns. In this chapter, Ghosh and El Sayary present an overview of how the notion of 'emotion' has been defined by different theorists. They also present the different ways in which human emotions have been categorised and grouped in the context of different cultural and psychological studies. Ghosh and El Sayary attempt to record and represent in the form of a layered map the emotions experienced by a number of people in areas of Beirut's central district. They designed and conducted an experiment with 30 participants, who were asked to walk along a route in the centre of Beirut and then complete a questionnaire. The questionnaire focused on three senses – vision, sound and smell – and on three main categories of emotions – enjoyment, fear and anger. The questionnaire comprised a set of two tables, for each individual key-area of the journey: The first table was asking the participants to assess the intensity of the different visual-, sonic- and smell-related sensual stimuli and describe the elements of space that they associate with each. The second asked the participants to assess the level of each emotion (enjoyment, fear, anger) and describe the reasons – the spatial elements associated with that emotion. In this study, the participants are asked to both self-map the sensual stimuli they perceive, their emotions, and also to interpret them – to present what they think is the spatial element that leads to each. It seems that the researchers aimed to create a new variation of a psychogeographic map of Beirut city centre, based on the emotions and interpretations of the people who took part.

Phevos Kallitsis looks into how data retrieved from online dating apps reveal narratives about the use of public space, the evolution of different demographics in the city, the human interaction, and the changing culture within specific groups, such as the gay community. He uses these data as a starting point for a range of discussions, including the relationship between narratives of the virtual and the physical, the issue of sexuality, privacy, identity, communication and presence of the gay community in areas of the city. His work shows how through raw data, retrieved though apps that use geo-location, complex narratives and interpretations of the life in a city can emerge. Data, such as the number of users of a social-dating app at different parts of the city, in different moments in time (different times, or days of the week), can reveal the patterns of human behaviour and interaction. Kallitsis attempts to use data to gain a better understanding of the human experience. For example, he looks into how, when and where people intending to interact through an online dating platform are. Additionally, he attempts to correlate the human presence and interaction appearing on the digital app with the density and activities observed in the physical city. He uses the metaphor of the map and discusses place as seen through a set of two overlaying maps – the conventional map of the physical space and the map of the presence and interaction in the digital online platform.

Kallitsis' case study is carried out in the city of Portsmouth, UK, and the dating app he used for his experiment was Grindr – an online dating app, addressed mainly to gay men. Through his study, he observed that online dating apps do not reduce the face-to-face social and personal interaction; they rather offer an additional layer and possibilities in the human interaction. He examines how users at times use the online platforms to conceal their identity, location and enjoy privacy, and how – in other instances – they use them to actually increase their visibility in the physical real space, by presenting their exact location through their online profile. Kallitsis also reflects on the issue of physical proximity. This type of app shows profiles of users within a certain distance. Hence, physical location matters. Kallitsis discusses the issue of proximity – the relationship between the distance as shown through the app, and the actual distance, which may involve physical geographic obstacles (such as the sea, physical boundaries, etc.). Kallitsis's observations make one reflect on how notions such as proximity, distance, density, availability, privacy and time acquire new meanings and connotations in the context of meeting/dating apps and hybrid social interaction. The meeting place in a hybrid context can be either an online chat or an actual café; and the time to make oneself available and visible hence varies. Disappearing from the online grid may mean that one wants to be away from social interaction, or it may as well be that one is in an actual physical meeting place. such as a bar, with the app off. Through this chapter, we do not only observe the actual findings of the experiment, but we also find out about the author's general beliefs that reflect general social assumptions – such as the assumption that younger people use meeting apps more than older generations (contradicted by the findings), or that Saturday night is a busy time on meeting apps (again contradicted by the findings). It is also remarkable how seemingly simple data, such as where in the city someone walks, can reveal quite a lot about their life and profile. This, at the same time, raises questions of privacy and power, when it comes to who manages and has access to the data.

Narratives as data and data as narratives: the politics of what we map

Alejandro Mieses Castellanos presents his advanced programming practice, through which he maps the use of words, their frequency, locality and interconnections, with the use of neural networks. He explores how this type of advanced mapping can reveal enlightening dynamics, relationships, gaps and narratives of the contemporary discourses (in architecture and beyond) – not through reading of the actual texts, but through a kind of meta-reading: through feeding huge numbers of data-texts into the algorithm, which then reveals patterns, dynamics, relationships, between words and notions. The densities, relationships, gaps and other phenomena observed can be associated both to place – locations where the words were found – and to time – as this 'nebulous' transforms over time. At the moment, the software uses 2.25 billion words taken from architectural journals and databases to formulate this initial case study. Castellanos presents the critical discourse that drives this project. He raises the broader question – what is it that we are computing? And what about things that are not computed – or computable? Social and political issues that can only be handled and understood through narrative usually remain outside the – increasingly data-driven – discussions. Castellanos argues that most of human knowledge and experience is narrative-based, and not easily quantified and managed. He attempts then to examine whether and how through neural-network computation, huge narrative-based databases can be mapped and looked at in a new and meaningful way.

As Castellanos argues, each school of thought, each profession, each environment develops its own 'vocabulary' or use of language. In certain environments, or schools of thought, some words are used more, and words are interconnected and used in a certain proximity with other words. Additionally, the way in which words are used changes over time, as well as their relative proximity. As he mentions, the word 'sustainability', for example, brings instantly to our mind other terms, such as environments, emissions, etc.; its frequency and interconnections, though, change over time, and also change if seen in different contexts (i.e. construction-related industries as against social-sciences discourse). Castellanos describes words as 'neurons in brain tissue'. Words do not only carry the value that each user loads them with: they also carry the value-connotations created by how others have used them, how often they are used, and with what other words/notions they are associated – and this complex and constantly transforming 'nebulous' is what Castellanos aims to map, and draw meaning from.

Pablo Lorenzo Eiroa reflects on the political and ideological dimensions of the data collecting, managing, representing and sharing processes. He reflects on how decisions with regards to data collections, organisations and managements create 'content' and can potentially serve the interests of the body or organisation/government/corporation that leads those processes. Similarly, he points out how data collecting, management and representation processes can potentially reveal unpredictable narratives, generating new ideas and arguments. He points out that there are biases inherent in every such process. For example, the categories through which data are collected, cannot be neutral; they reveal pre-existing beliefs and biases. And as such, they project/construct a reality. As Lorenzo Eiroa argues, 'this apparently neutral process of measurement often projects categories to reality and may even determinate social behaviour, normalizing models for a society being progressively engineered through feedback processes of measurement and representation'. One could argue that in the context of cultural studies, this issue has been addressed through the post-structuralism discourse. In such a context, Lorenzo Eiroa's argument is not read as a call for objectivity. It is rather read as a call for opening up, revealing and discussing the inherent biases in indexing and data-collecting processes. Through the experimental examples of data collection, juxtaposition and mapping that he presents, his arguments are read as a call for inventive data-collecting and representation processes that deviate from pre-accepted categories and destabilise conventional correlations.

Measuring the intangible

A recurring theme in this book is the tendency to quantify, measure and visualise intangible or hard-to-quantify things. The reasons vary – from genuine playful curiosity to the need to be convincing. Data-based evidence can make something that is either common sense, or intangible, appear objective and undoubted.

Contemporary computation allows for Big Data to be analysed quickly and effectively. This evolution is not only being used in areas where this has a clear practical output, but has also influenced and informed research in other areas – areas in which the use of data is still very new, can be quite problematic and can lead to controversial processes and outcomes; when – for example – data are used to map/discuss/analyse the 'happiness' of different cities, or 'comfort' of different environments, several philosophical questions raise. What is 'happiness' – do we refer to the 'eudaimonic' or 'hedonic'? (Kashdan, T. *et al*, 2008) Or to other aspects of it? Can it be measured? And aren't the criteria used for measuring it dependent upon cultural, social and political contexts? Similarly, as discussed earlier, the assumed desirable condition of 'comfort', or of 'productivity' or easiness of way-finding can be debatable. One could argue that the issue objectivity–subjectivity has been already addressed through the post-structuralism discourse, by explicitly making the context an inherent part of the phenomenon observed. However, studies measuring things such as 'happiness', 'comfort' or equivalent debatable parameters, often leave out the potential discussion on the contextual nature of such terms.

One might also wonder whether at times things are discussed in terms of 'comfort', 'productivity', 'happiness', 'easiness' of navigation, etc. in order to meet the current needs of the market, the calls of the funding bodies or the agendas of relevant stakeholders. Williamson et al. discuss how knowledge has a different meaning for academics, researchers, policy makers, commercial industries, etc.; an issue that funding bodies and other institutions at times do not open up, assuming that knowledge has the same essence for all. In this context, Williamson et al. argue that, 'for the lobbyists knowledge is a means to an end. It is either successful in these terms or not. It has no further interest' (Williamson et al., 2011). With regards to the above, the projects presented in this book trigger two main threads of questions: how data and information are organised, processed and dealt with to allow discussions that we believe are meaningful and inclusive and, in parallel, how the issue of emerging data-orientated practices itself shifts the research methods, and challenges the theoretical and discipline-related context of thought. On the one hand, this book explores new territories and cross-disciplinary collaborations that use data in new and inventive ways and contexts, to understand and map the experience of place and creative, inventive design projects. On the other hand, it discusses how the handling of data, the meta-design of what we choose to measure and how, is not 'innocent' and 'neutral', but can potentially follow or drive meaningful, desirable, ethical – or not – political, cultural and social agendas.

References

Bleicher, A. (2017) 'Demystifying the black box that is AI', *Scientific American*, (Aug. 2017). Available at: www.scientificamerican.com/article/demystifying-the-black-box-that-is-ai/

Corner, J. (2002). The agency of mapping. In Cosgrove, D. (ed.) *Mappings*. London: Reaktion, pp. 213–252.

de Zegher, C. and Wigley, M. (eds) (2001) *The Activist Drawing: Retracing Situationist Architectures from Constant's New Babylon to Beyond*. Cambridge, MA: The MIT Press.

Deleuze, G. and Guattari, F. (2004) *A Thousand Plateaus: Capitalism and Schizophrenia*. London: Continuum.

Ertel, W. (2017) *Introduction to Artificial Intelligence*. Weingarten: Springer.

Gallagher, S. (2015) 'On the possibility of naturalizing phenomenology', in Zahavi, D. (ed.) *Oxford Handbook of Contemporary Phenomenology*. Oxford: Oxford University Press.

Husserl, E. O. P. (1999) *The Idea of Phenomenology*. Dordrecht: Kluwer Academic Publishers.

Jenson, M. (2014) *Mapping the Global Architect of Alterity: Practice, Representation and Education*. Abingdon: Routledge.

Karandinou, A. and Turner, L. (2018) 'Architecture and neuroscience: what can the EEG recording of brain activity reveal about a walk through everyday spaces?', *International Journal of Parallel, Emergent and Distributed Systems*, pp. 1–12. doi: 10.1080/17445760.2017.1390089

Kashdan, T. B., Biswas-Diener, R. and King, L. A. (2008) 'Reconsidering happiness: the costs of distinguishing between hedonics and eudaimonia', *The Journal of Positive Psychology*, *3*(4), pp. 219–233. Doi:10.1080/17439760802303044

Mallinson, H. (2004) 'Metaphors of experience: the voice of the air', *The Philosophical Forum*, *35*(2).

McDonough, T. (2002) *Guy Debord and the Situationist International: Texts and Documents*. Cambridge, MA; London: MIT Press.

Moran, D. (2002) *Introduction to Phenomenology*. Abingdon, New York: Routledge.
Moran, D. (2013) '"Let's look at it objectively": Why phenomenology cannot be naturalized', *Royal Institute of Philosophy Supplement, 04/03*, 72, pp. 89–115. doi: 10.1017/S1358246113000064.
Müller, V. C. (ed.) (2016) *Fundamental Issues of Artificial Intelligence*. Oxford: Springer.
Perkins, C. (2003) 'Cartography: mapping theory', *Progress in Human Geography*, *27*(3), pp. 341–351.
Petitot, J., Varela, J. F., Pachoud, B. and Roy, J.-M. (eds) (1999) *Naturalizing Phenomenology: Issues in Contemporary Phenomenology and Cognitive Science*. Stanford, CA: Stanford University Press.
Reynolds, J. (2010) 'Time out of joint: between phenomenology and post-structuralism', *Parrhesia*, *9*, pp. 55–64.
Stoller, S. (2009) 'Phenomenology and the poststructural critique of experience', *International Journal of Philosophical Studies*, *17*(5), pp. 707–737. doi: 10.1080/09672550903301762
Williamson, J. Cloonan, M. and Frith, S. (2011) 'Having an impact? Academics, the music industries and the problem of knowledge', *International Journal of Cultural Policy*, *17*(5), pp. 459–474.
Wolchover, N. (2017) 'New theory cracks open the black box of deep learning', *Quanta Magazine*. Available at: https://www.quantamagazine.org/new-theory-cracks-open-the-black-box-of-deep-learning-20170921/
Wood, D. (2010) 'Lynch Debord: about two psychogeographies', *Cartographica*, *45*(3), pp. 185–200.

2

DATA SCIENCE IN THE AGE OF BIG DATA

Opportunities and challenges

Constantinos Daskalakis

Recent decades have witnessed an explosive increase in data collection, driven by dramatic improvements in the size, capacity, reliability, and cost-effectiveness of data collection and storage technology, as well as a ubiquitous deployment of digital devices, and a broad transfer of human activity to the Internet. These days, online social networks and online markets provide fine-grained data on social and economic behavior; online media provide detailed data on the spread of information; and wearable devices provide personalized data on the state of humans as they navigate the physical world.

Our increased capabilities in data collection have also brought an increased penetration of data science into many fields of research and practice, including those that have traditionally been light in the collection and usage of data. Data analytics has entered virtually all aspects of business and government, while statistics and machine learning are now in the vocabulary of the vast majority of academic disciplines.

Increased data collection capabilities have also improved our ability to study complex phenomena. Where previously we might have compromised, with the development of simple models of simple phenomena, or simple models approximating more complex phenomena, the abundance of data has made us more ambitious, seeking to build complex models of complex phenomena. Attesting to how more data can be exploited to develop more accurate models are the impressive recent advances of machine learning in image and speech recognition, and the commercial applications that these advances have enabled, e.g. Amazon Alexa, self-driving cars, etc. Ultimately, developing models from data and verifying the accuracy of these models is a question of statistical power. More complex phenomena typically require more complex models to explain accurately, and these require in turn more observations to fine-tune.

The abundance of data is, however, a double-edged sword. The larger the amount of data becomes, the more likely it also becomes to find interesting and unexpected, yet statistically insignificant, patterns in the data. This is just the nature of stochastic phenomena – the more samples that are collected, the more likely it becomes that low-probability events are realized. In browsing your samples to mine interesting patterns increases the probability of discovering spurious ones, making it a treacherous path to knowledge discovery. For an amusing collection of interesting yet coincidental correlations, such as that shown in Figure 2.1, see Vigen (2015). On the broader topic of how misuse of statistics and bad publication norms can lead to a preponderance of spurious statistical research findings, see Ioannidis (2005). For an account of a recent large-scale reproducibility project with research findings, in top psychology journals, that are more likely be non-reproducible than reproducible, see Open Science Collaboration (2015).

Of course, the field of statistics is very aware of the risks underlying careless use of data. The danger of *p*-value hacking is well-understood, the lessons from Simpson's paradox (Wagner, 1982) and other statistical paradoxes are recognized, and it is fully understood that correlation does not imply causation. Statistical research is striving to develop theoretical techniques and practical protocols for the good use of data. As data analytics is entering virtually every aspect of human endeavor, it is important that these protocols and techniques are vigorously implemented to protect humanity from the perils of spurious statistical conclusions.

While we should all work toward becoming more rigorous as data scientists and more astute consumers of data analyses, we also need to pay increased attention to a central challenge underlying data science in the Big Data era. The root of the challenge is that Big Data and the recent success of machine learning in speech and image recognition have made data scientists more ambitious in terms of the complexity of the models they seek to explain complex phenomena. The motivation is simple. A statistical model has free parameters that are fine-tuned so that the predictions of the model conform to the observations available from the phenomenon being modeled. The more parameters a model has, the more expressive it is,

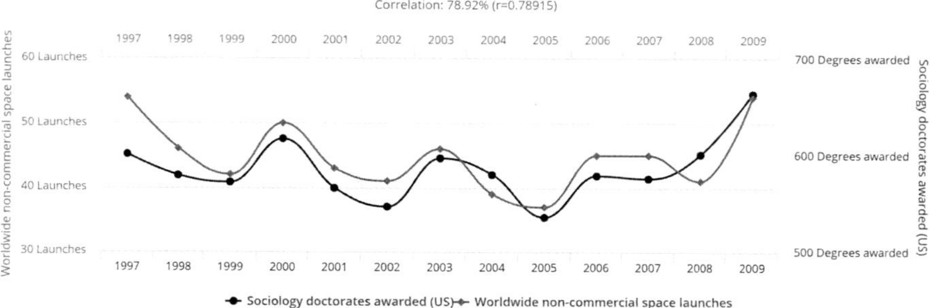

FIGURE 2.1 A spurious correlation between sociology doctorates awarded in the United States and worldwide non-commercial space launches. Chart from http://www.tylervigen.com/.

hence the more accurately it can match these observations with appropriate tuning of the parameters.

Increased model flexibility is, however, both a blessing and a curse. The more flexible and expressive a model is, the easier it becomes for it to *overfit* – that is, for it to express ridiculously complex explanations of why the observations have come about, basing its explanations on coincidence and not on the real mechanics underlying these observations. An everyday example of overfitting is when a friend exclaims: "If I wear this outfit, my team will win." Of course, the outfit has nothing to do with whether the team will win. What the friend has done in his head is to look at previous games his team has played and identify a model for predicting under what circumstances his team wins or does not win. He endows his model with the flexibility to use in its prediction a rich set of variables, including his outfit on the day of the game, what food he had ordered to watch the game, which chair he was sitting on while watching the game, and combinations thereof. The more variables your friend uses, the easier it becomes for him to create an irrational model based on these variables, which appear to have perfect predictive capability against *past* games (yet, of course, poor prediction for future games). The remedy for this kind of overfitting is to avoid arbitrarily complex models and to collect more data, as more data can prune spurious models and promote healthy ones.

There are, of course, well-studied tradeoffs in statistics and machine learning between how expressive a model is and how many observations are needed to tune it in a statistically accurate way. The more expressive a model is, the more data are needed to tune it so that overfitting does not take place. Conversely, the larger the available data becomes, the more complex become the models that can be tuned using these data. This is why Big Data increases the appetite of data scientists for models with ever-growing complexity.

However, the appetite of current practice has considerably exceeded what is theoretically understood to be statistically safe. The impressive performance of deep neural networks in speech and image recognition has shifted machine-learning practice toward deep-neural-network-based models. People are now training deep neural networks with many thousands, even millions, of parameters; however, they are training these networks using sample sizes that are comparable to the number of parameters. In this regime, it has been shown that overfitting is possible in principle (Zhang et al., 2017), and despite intense research effort it has been difficult to characterize theoretically how overfitting can be avoided. For this reason, training deep neural networks to avoid overfitting is presently in many ways more an art form than engineering. Even in application domains, where deep neural networks have undeniably beaten the competition out of the water, there is still considerable debate on whether real learning or overfitting is taking place. See e.g. Athalye et al., (2018) and its references for critiques of state-of-the-art, deep-neural-network-based, image-recognition algorithms, and Ilyas et al., (2018) and its references for defenses of these algorithms. For the important debate on overfitting to settle and for research on training deep neural networks to arrive at theoretical guarantees and best practices against overfitting, it is important that this "guerilla war" between attacks on and defenses of deep neural networks should continue to take place.

Parallel to the debate on overfitting, there is another way in which deep neural networks pose threats to data-science research and practice. With their complex architecture and the large number of parameters that influence their behavior, it becomes difficult to discern what leads these models to make a prediction one way or the other in any given situation; in other words, it becomes difficult to *interpret* why the model predictions came about and, in particular, difficult to identify the input variables or combinations thereof that are most influential for the prediction of the model to go one way or the other. In turn, the lack of interpretability raises a slew of ethical issues on the use of this technology. To illustrate, consider a deep neural network that takes, as input, information about a loan requester and predicts the probability that they will default on their loan (which, in turn, is used by a bank to determine whether to give or deny a loan). If it is not possible to interpret what is driving the predictions of the model, how can you demonstrate that race or gender information is not being misused to discriminate against groups of people? How do you know that sensitive information about the loan requester is not being misused? How can you know that the model is not using private data that it is not supposed to be using? For both ethical and legal reasons, we need to be able to interpret how our models make predictions.

As machine learning is penetrating all aspects of human endeavor and is progressively being employed in more important, often life-critical, applications, it becomes extremely important to have a rigorous understanding of machine-learning technology, to develop best practices to avoid overfitting, and to improve the interpretability of our models. Otherwise, all bets are off . . .

References

Athalye, A., Engstrom, L., Ilyas, L., and Kwok, K. (2018). 'Synthesizing robust adversarial examples', in *Proceedings of International Conference on Machine Learning*. Available at: https://arxiv.org/pdf/1707.07397.pdf (accessed May 2018).

Ilyas, A., Jalal, A., Asteri, E., Daskalakis, C., and Dimakis, A. G. (2018). 'The robust manifold defense: adversarial training using generative models'. arXiv:1712.09196.

Ioannidis, J. P. A. (2005). 'Why most published research findings are false'. *PLoS Medicine*, *2*(8): e124.

Open Science Collaboration (2015). 'Estimating the reproducibility of psychological science'. *Science*, 349.6251:aac4716.

Vigen, T. (2015). *Spurious Correlations*. New York: Hachette Books.

Wagner, C. H. (1982). 'Simpson's paradox in real life'. *The American Statistician*, *36*(1): 46–48.

Zhang, C., Bengio, S., Hardt, M., Recht, B., and Vinyals, O. (2017). 'Understanding deep learning requires rethinking generalization', in *Proceedings of International Conference on Machine Learning*. Available at: https://arxiv.org/abs/1611.03530 (accessed May 2018)

3

DATA + MULTIMER

Mapping human signals for improved spatial design

Arlene Ducao

Introduction

Sensor technology, particularly biosensor technology, has become widely, cheaply available and portable (GE, 2016). In 2018, more than a third of the world's population is expected to own a geolocatable smartphone (Statista, 2014), devices that can pair with biosensors so that, for better or worse, we can track ourselves in all kinds of ways, in all kinds of settings, and learn new things about ourselves and our environments. Call it the Era of the Spatially Quantified Self.

This chapter discusses the antecedents, initial studies, system components, and larger considerations regarding Multimer, a technology I codeveloped based on prototypes I initially built as a researcher at the Massachusetts Institute of Technology (MIT) Media Lab. Multimer is among the first to examine crowdsourced, quantified biometric data in a spatial, temporal, social, and environmental context. It also provides experiential data about populations at large spatial scales, with the aim of improving spatial design through quantified, uniformly and passively collected human signals. Multimer data, which include brainwave, heart rate, pedometer, and geographic positioning system (GPS) information, have been collected and analyzed for a range of applications, from measuring perceptions of danger and safety in Manhattan traffic (Ducao, 2014) to quantifying what "immersion" is for users of virtual reality (AP Insights, 2017). Multimer data have also been collected in other places, including London, Glasgow, Nairobi, Manilla, Milwaukee, and San Francisco.

This technology, which was originally featured in the United Nations ITU's 2015 "Measuring the Information Society Report" (Measuring, 2015), can contribute high-resolution, highly detailed data about where and when city residents and transport users perceive danger and safety. By using human signals to better understand what people experience as they move around the city, Multimer offers a unique way to quantitatively measure information that was previously only qualitative (Figure 3.1).

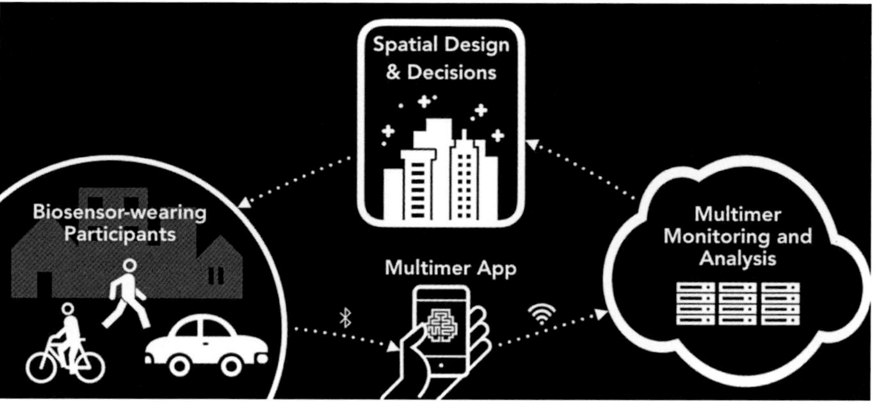

FIGURE 3.1 Schematic for the Multimer system.

Some (subjective) issues that led to Multimer

Human scale. As a creative engineer, I dearly value this concept. For instance, consider a building. If the building wasn't erected at human scale – that is, if a human without physical disability cannot use the building's stairs to walk to the roof in a reasonably short period of time – I generally won't find the building attractive or inviting. The same goes for neighborhoods. I'm not drawn to most business districts, or to most suburbs for that matter – most business districts are full of buildings that are vertically beyond the scope of human scale – at least my own sense of it – and many suburbs are planned so that horizontal distance between buildings doesn't allow for a non-physically disabled human to walk from their house to various destinations in a reasonable amount of time. I suppose, in this case, the notion of "human scale" is tied to the notion of "walkability," and for both my work and life, I prefer buildings that are both vertically and horizontally walkable. Perhaps this is why I've always lived in old buildings, the kinds that were built before the advent of enormous construction machines, like those huge cranes that can soar several hundred feet into the sky.

Of course, this is just my opinion. And it has all kinds of caveats – as a set of buildings becomes a neighborhood, and as a set of neighborhoods becomes a town or city, the relationships between human scale, walkability, and even livability change. But in the effort to understand how these relationships change, and how they affect the built environment, I strongly believe that it's imperative to factor as many humans as possible, and as many kinds of humans as possible, into the process of designing an environment. Failure to do so can lead to a built environment where no one wants to live, work, play, or even briefly traverse.

For instance, the architect Le Corbusier envisioned cities in which "not all citizens could become leaders. The technocratic elite, the industrialists, financiers, engineers, and artists would be located in the city centre, while the workers would be removed to the fringes of the city" (Corbusier, 2011). Today, this kind of thinking sounds dangerously exclusionary. I agree with architectural historian Witold Rybczynski, who wrote of Le Corbusier that:

> [. . .] He called it the Ville Radieuse, the Radiant City. Despite the poetic title, his urban vision was authoritarian, inflexible and simplistic. Wherever it was tried – in Chandirgarh by Le Corbusier himself or in Brasilia by his followers – it failed. Standardization proved inhuman and disorienting. The open spaces were inhospitable; the bureaucratically imposed plan, socially destructive. In the US, the Radiant City took the form of vast urban-renewal schemes and regimented public housing projects that damaged the urban fabric beyond repair.
>
> *(Rybczynski, 1998)*

In the mid-twentieth century, New York City "master builder" Robert Moses came under the influence of Le Corbusier, with effects widely considered to be unsuccessful:

> Most of Mr. Moses' public housing was designed in the bland style of such architecture in the 40's and 50's, when monotonous, sterile towers in open space were the rule for low-income residences. The care Mr. Moses lavished on the design of Jones Beach and his early parkways tended not to show itself in the architectural plans for his public housing; as with many builders of public housing, he was concerned more with order and with numbers of apartment units than with making buildings that would relate to their occupants' ways of living. The general model for such housing was the 1920's plan for the rebuilding of Paris by Le Corbusier, which called for a city of towers surrounded by parks and divided by highways instead of traditional streets. Mr. Moses, like so many American planners, came to the Le Corbusier approach not for reasons of esthetics but for reasons of efficiency.
>
> *(Goldberger, 1981)*

In the 1960s, another attempt at non-human-scale efficiency led Robert Propst, inventor of the office cubicle, to say of his own invention: "The cubiclizing of people in modern corporations is monolithic insanity." The cubicle was originally designed by a team led by Propst for furniture company Herman Miller Inc., as part of a suite of office components known as Action Office II. Propst, a researcher at Herman Miller Research Corporation, had conducted multiple studies of the open-plan office, the style that dominated most office layout through the 1950s. These studies determined that the open-plan office decreased worker productivity due to lack of privacy and personal autonomy, and it increased sedentariness due to long hours of sitting for most office workers. From these studies of actual office workers, Propst applied a kind of human-centered design in his development of Action Office II, which consisted of lightweight, movable desks, chairs, walls, and support structures that were meant to be modularly applied to changing office tasks while supporting increased physical activity. While Action Office I, the predecessor to Action Office II, was a financial failure for the company in that it was expensive and difficult to assemble, Action Office II was a success; sales over the next several decades reached $5 billion (Abercrombie, 2000). But Propst, who had hoped that Action Office would "give knowledge workers a more flexible, fluid environment than the rat-maze boxes of offices" (Lohr, 1997) was saddened to see how Action Office components – primarily the cubicle – came to be used by most corporate offices, where "spaces crammed with cubicles eventually became a symbol of faceless drudgery" (Sheu, 2017).

The story of the office cubicle is sobering. Even now, cities, buildings, and offices are built with cost savings and efficiency as the priority, sometimes even at the expense of human health and wellbeing. Propst might be encouraged that, with the reemergence of humanist urban thought, governments and businesses are increasingly focused on how spaces can directly impact human outcomes such as safety, creativity, and productivity. However, "there are few research and evaluation methods that effectively capture how spatial environments lead to these outcomes. Even as cities and companies such as WeWork and Google seek to create more human-friendly environments, professionals such as architects, urban planners, and investors struggle to create and evaluate spaces that positively affect human outcomes" (Sheu, 2017).

Multimer, and where it came from

By developing Multimer, a system that collects, visualizes, and analyzes continuous human experience data in the form of biosensor signals and other inputs, my team and I aim to add a human-centered layer of data to spatial design, supporting what we think is a worthwhile goal: that spatial design and placemaking, even for big, complex places, should always keep humans at the center of the process, using the spatiotemporal scale and resolution at which humans actually engage. We believe this goal can be achieved even as cost savings and efficiency remain a priority.

All built environments are designed, and it really is design that distinguishes human beings from all other species on earth. We've designed buildings, cities, infrastructure so significant that you can see them from space. Yet we don't have a robust, continuous way to understand how people experience place. By adding a data layer of spatial, biometric insights to the maps we already make, Multimer is built to support a more data-driven approach to human-centered design.

Multimer evolved from MindRider, a brain-reading bike helmet that I prototyped in 2011, while I was a graduate student at the MIT Media Lab. More specifically, MindRider was a bike helmet outfitted with a single-electrode electroencephalogram (EEG) sensor, a string of RGB LED lights, and a microcontroller that was programmed to take in EEG data, process it, and output commands for the LED lights to display a gradient of colors from red, which indicated when the helmet user was exhibiting the most concentration, to green, which indicated when the user was most relaxed.

At the time, MindRider was meant to be a quick project, even a toy, but it sparked a high level of interest from other researchers at MIT, as well as news and technology journalists. As a result, even though my particular focus at the time was the application of infrared satellite data to environmental crowd-mapping applications, MindRider stayed in my mind because of so many inquiries about the project. In 2013, researcher Sandra Richter used a more robust version of MindRider for her study on female novice cyclists and, while the results were inconclusive, they helped set the stage for more extensive studies when the MindRider project moved to New York later that year.

Since then, development on MindRider, and later Multimer, has been supported by the DuKode Studio, a scientific visualization studio I cofounded in 2010 with Ilias Koen who, like me, is a creative technologist with a background in engineering and art. When I moved back to Brooklyn after my "sabbatical" at MIT and brought the MindRider project with me, Ilias and I decided (with the support of MIT Media Lab's new incubator program, E14) to spin out a new small business that would focus on the development of MindRider and related IoT products such as Multimer. Our first major project was the development of MindRider from a couple of hacked-together prototypes into a fleet of durable "appcessories" – that is, the MindRider hardware was reengineered to include a Bluetooth radio that would send realtime signals to our custom-built iOS (iPhone) app. We then manually produced a dozen of these more robust prototypes. The affordances of this fleet were demonstrated in the first major data-collection project for MindRider, a crowdfunded book called *MindRider Maps Manhattan* (Ducao, 2014). This book marked the first of three feasibility pilot studies in Manhattan, which was an ideal site because not only is it near our Brooklyn headquarters, but its transportation landscape is also gridded, well-monitored, and the basis for a significant amount of open data from the City of New York. During these pilots, we developed and refined the fleet-deployment model and integrated it into our workflow. We recruited, trained, and deployed fleets of MindRider users, or Data Collectors, to wear the MindRider sensor while in transit through a city or region.

Initial pilot studies and findings

MindRider Maps Manhattan (Ducao, 2014) explained the process of using MindRider to make a basic "mental mood map" of Manhattan. This process was focused on the utility of MindRider data for the analysis and evaluation of the current cycling infrastructure. Ten cyclists, including myself, volunteered to be "Data Collectors" who would record their biometric data with the MindRider device as they rode on one or more major streets in Manhattan, within the timespan of several weeks in the autumn of 2014. By "major streets," I mean that we stuck to the north–south avenues that traverse Manhattan's large longitudinal length, rather than the east–west streets that traverse Manhattan's relatively small latitudinal width. Collecting data through cycling only, as opposed to walking or driving, supported the purpose of controlled wide-area coverage. Each route was covered only one time by one person, so this study was very much a proof-of-concept: there were not enough people participating or data collected to establish statistical significance at any spatial or temporal level. However, the 2014 study established data-collection norms for the larger studies to come. These norms include basic training for data collection, best practices (like not talking or listening to music while collecting data), and the collection of qualitative (textual and photo) data to help calibrate the quantitative biosensor data.

And even though the 2014 study does not have statistical significance, it produced a dataset large enough to compare against other Manhattan datasets, which was another major aim of this pilot. For *MindRider Maps Manhattan* my coanalysts, Ilias Koen and Jennifer Sta. Ines, and I produced more than two dozen maps that compared the MindRider 2014 dataset against government datasets like commercial zoning, public parks, traffic collisions, and bike routes. The pilot demonstrated promising results based on a simple proximity analysis, in which areas of urban infrastructure, traffic, and safety concerns were evaluated against the aggregate of EEG data points within 100 feet of those areas.

For the purposes of simplicity, analyst Jennifer Sta. Ines isolated EEG values indicating high concentration levels (a possible indicator for perception of danger), and then she separately isolated EEG values indicating high relaxation levels (a possible indicator for perception of safety). For the areas of traffic and safety concern:

- Bike collisions: counts of high concentration were 72% higher than counts of high relaxation within 100 feet of where a bike collision took place in 2014.
- Fatal collisions: counts of high concentration were 300% higher than counts of high relaxation within 100 feet of where a fatal collision took place in 2014.
- Truck/HGV (Heavy-Goods Vehicle) Routes: counts of high concentration were 27% higher than counts of high relaxation within 100 feet of an HGV route.
- Traffic complaints: counts of high concentration were 333% higher than counts of high relaxation within 100 feet of where a traffic complaint took place in 2014.

The 2014 pilot and book paved the way for the first statistically significant MindRider study in 2016 (Multimer 2014 Analysis, 2017), which was supported by a smart cities startup accelerator called Urban-X. For this study, we recruited 60 cyclists and pedestrians in New York City, with a range of occupations and backgrounds – bike commuters, professional couriers, and avid athletes – to collect MindRider data for four weeks in the spring of 2016. We constrained the study area to Manhattan south of Central Park so that we could conduct a more in-depth analysis for each city block in the study area: for each block, multiple people collected data over multiple days. The results helped to refine the preliminary insights from the 2014 study. During the 2016 study, we realized that the process of visualizing and analyzing data is as involved and important as that of collecting data, and that we wanted to apply our model to data beyond EEG sensors and cycling. This is how the MindRider wearable system grew into the Multimer analytics system. From this point onward, we used the term "Multimer" to refer to the larger system we were building, and "MindRider" to refer to the ergonomic EEG wearable we developed. The 2016 pilot tested the feasibility of the fleet-deployment model, which involved:

- A larger and less controlled sample size: Data Collectors were allowed to ride streets most convenient to them so as to collect more data.
- More structure in terms of community meetings, data management, safety training, compensation/incentivization and informed consent.
- Iterative user experience design to account for very long sessions/rides of data collection.

The analysis of the 2016 data, led by Jennifer Sta. Ines, involved conducting spatial regression and correlation tests with the Multimer data (set as dependent variables) against data from the City of New York (set as explanatory variables). As in our 2014 pilot, we isolated EEG values indicating high concentration levels (Figure 3.2) and high relaxation levels. The analysis showed that:

- Using the Spatial Autocorrelation (Global Moran's I) tool in ArcGIS, the z-score (standard score) for areas of high concentration was calculated as 8.16, indicating that there is less than a 1% chance (99% confidence level) that this clustered pattern is the result of random chance in our study area of Manhattan.
- Using the Spatial Autocorrelation (Global Moran's I) tool in ArcGIS, the z-score for areas of high relaxation was calculated as 2.18, with a p-value (probability value) of 0.03. This indicates that there is a less than 5% likelihood (95% confidence level) that this clustered pattern is the result of random chance in the same study area.
- Ordinary Least Square (OLS) regression analysis was run to help explain areas of high concentration and high relaxation in the study area. The explanatory variables used to model these phenomena included some of the same variables that were analyzed during the 2014 pilot: locations of collisions*, traffic complaints, 311 calls logged to NYPD, 311 calls logged to DOT*, truck/HGV routes*, and bike routes*. Variables marked with * were found to have statistically significant p-values, indicating that these variables might help the model.
- All of the statistically significant explanatory variables had a negative relationship to the dependent variable, with the exception of 311 calls logged to DOT (positive). This was the case for both high concentration and high relaxation. This is a topic for further analysis.
- The adjusted R-squared value was calculated as 0.209 when OLS regression was run to explain the areas of high concentration. When the model was run to explain areas of high relaxation, the adjusted R-squared value was calculated as 0.164. The Spatial Autocorrelation tool was run on both OLS regression residuals to confirm that the models are not biased, which was also indicated by the non-statistically significant Jarque-Bera value.

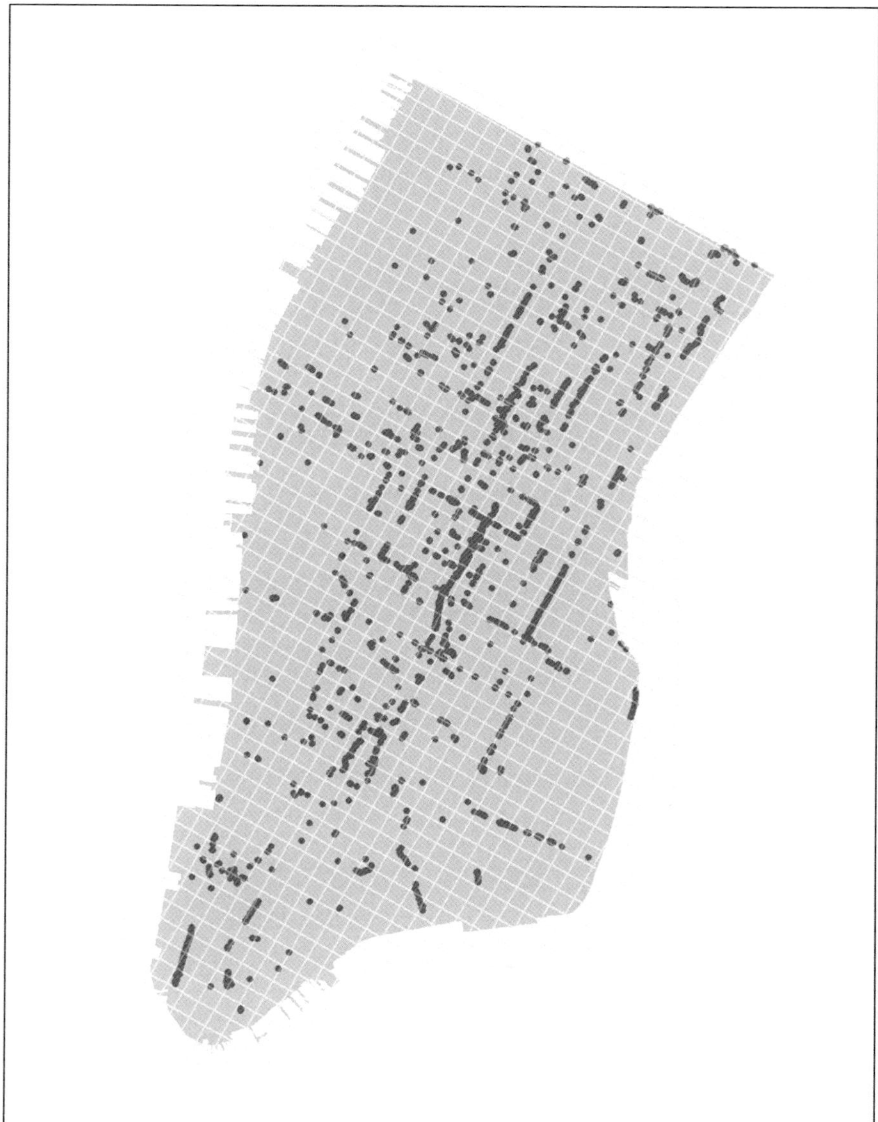

FIGURE 3.2 Areas of high concentration from the 2016 pilot.

- A few considerations could be taken into consideration to increase model performance:
  - Adding more explanatory variables, such as primary land use of adjacent properties.
  - Refining existing variables, such as filtering the complaint type of 311 calls to DOT to focus on street conditions, or traffic signal conditions.

- Fitting a new OLS regression into a smaller focus area within the study area, such as blocks with the highest building heights.

The 2016 pilot dataset was more than thirty times larger than the dataset from 2014. From the process of collecting and analyzing these data, and talking with potential customers and users of the data, we realized that Multimer was not enough as only an automated data-collection system. The population-level, spatial method of collecting this data was so novel that potential end-users of the data would need assistance in analyzing and interpreting. Some potential customers were only interested in the final outcomes of the analysis, not the tools for analysis. So, to make our collected data actionable for the location-oriented decisions of commercial partners in urban planning, transportation, retail, and real estate, we are in the experimental stages of developing a location analytics SaaS (Software as a Service) platform that integrates MindRider data and other data collected through our system, into an end-user's existing site-selection or spatial-design process. As originally conceived, this SaaS uses geographic information systems (GIS) and statistical algorithms to quantitatively reveal geographic areas associated with stress, relaxation, and other mental experiences. The SaaS can then combine these "mental maps" with external data (e.g. banking, zoning, transportation, amenities), as part of its Decision Engine algorithms, to recommend potentially undervalued locations for stores, homes, outdoor advertisements, and other features of the built environment (Figure 3.3). I will discuss this SaaS at more depth in the "Multimer System Components" section.

In October 2017, we finished the largest New York City Multimer pilot to date, in which more than 100 participants were trained to collect brainwave, heart rate, pedometer, accelerometer, and GPS data while walking, running, cycling, or driving. The 2017 study is funded by the US government's National Science Foundation (NSF) Small Business Innovation and Research (SBIR) program, and the aim of this study is to produce a more complete picture of how all people experience place; namely, the place of downtown and midtown Manhattan. Because this study is federally funded and involves "human subjects," it has been

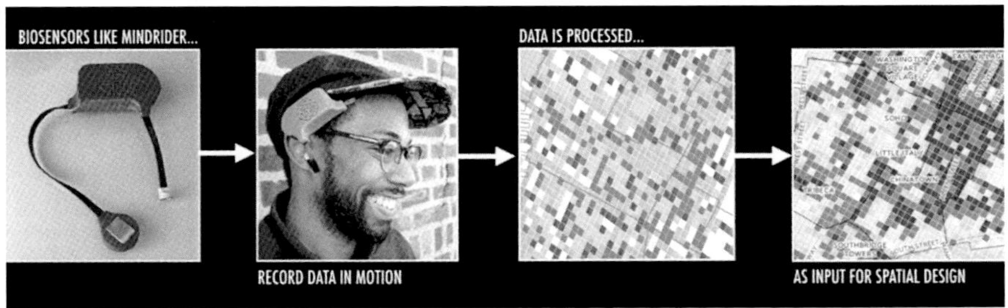

FIGURE 3.3 Data flow from MindRider sensor, to human Data Collector, to Multimer Process/Analysis.

required to undergo a privacy and ethics review by an institutional review board (IRB) that oversees clinical trials in the United States. For this, we have built out a more robust mobile app and reporting system to help our team monitor the entire data-collection process and to help individual Data Collectors monitor their own progress. This is useful for a number of individual applications: for some, it adds a layer of fitness data to their daily activity; for others, it helps them to better understand how the built environment affects them; and for others, this reporting system helps them manage their incentives and payment. I will discuss the challenges of data collection from human subjects, including IRB and incentivization, in the "Challenges" section. At the time of writing, we are in the process of analyzing the collected data with geospatial, neural, and spectral techniques.

While we continue to refine the feasibility of collecting these data and the utility of applying them to exterior spatial design such as urban planning and transportation analysis, we have also been conducting business research to better understand how our technology can be viable over the long term. This has led us to conduct data-collection tests in non-outdoor spaces, like workspaces and virtual spaces, both of which change and evolve more rapidly than those of the built outdoor environment. In particular, the fast growth of co-working spaces and tech offices shows promise as a sector for which this kind of data may be most useful, and because of the collaborative requirements in these kinds of spaces, the highly quantitative analysis of people in these places may ultimately prove essential. We have rebuilt our existing data-collection and analysis system to accept additional data that may be relevant to workplace strategists. I will discuss this system at more length in the next section.

In addition to the aforementioned Manhattan studies from 2014, 2016, and 2017, we have also collected data and/or conducted spatial biosensor analyses for a number of organizations, including Harley-Davidson (Milwaukee), Sustrans UK (London and Glasgow), Nairobi Bikeshare (Nairobi), Matter (indoor office space), and the Associated Press (in virtual reality). While most of the resulting reports are private, the study conducted for the Associated Press was part of a larger report on current practice and recommendations for the use of virtual and mixed reality technology in journalism (AP Insights, 2017).

Multimer system components

The previous section gives an overview of the pilots conducted in Manhattan, our primary study area. It also discusses the general findings from these pilots so far, and shows how, in the urban context, there are significant correlations between areas of high mental concentration and areas of complex traffic patterns.

This section discusses the components of the Multimer system that my team and I have built. There are four major parts: hardware, mobile apps, data monitoring software, and data analysis SaaS. We have also put significant effort into a recruitment and training model, which I will discuss as part of the Challenges section.

Technology Background: In recent years, engineers developed inexpensive, consumer-grade apparatuses and methods for sensing biological processes. This includes electroencephalography, the monitoring of the brain's electrical activity. Medical-grade EEG apparatuses use multiple electrodes to provide high neural resolution, but they are costly and cumbersome to wear, which makes them difficult to deploy outside the clinic or lab. Recently developed consumer modules, such as the Emotiv EPOC headset and NeuroSky TGAM signal-processing chips, are simple, portable, and can be used outside of the research laboratory.

Smartphones, many of which contain GPS modules and embedded sensors, are used for a wide array of consumer applications. Smartphone sensor data, along with other kinds of geolocated data, such as demographic and social network data, provide valuable insights on user location and behavior. Some notable examples of such data come from smartphone software applications such as Strava, Uber, and Twitter. The widespread interest in the data from these applications, and the growth of the location analytics market in recent years (Location Analytics Market, 2016), demonstrates that these datasets have multiple uses at the individual, social, and municipal scales.

Innovation Overview: Multimer's unique datasets, algorithms, and its data-collection system, which pairs custom ergonomic headsets with GPS-enabled smartphones to record EEG and location data, can provide key insights for data-driven decision making. With Multimer, we are developing products from geolocated biosensor data, which has implications not only for individual users, but for many kinds of spatial design and site-selection projects, which incorporate new kinds of sensor data into location analytics and planning. Multimer may be the first system to systematically, quantitatively show in high spatiotemporal resolution and continuous coverage how a large demographic of people has mental experiences of different locations.

General System Overview: The flow of data in the MindRider and Multimer systems (Figures 3.1 and 3.3) starts in the MindRider hardware. As the user wears the headset, it digitizes a stream of EEG signal data. Data are transmitted from the MindRider hardware to a smartphone via the MindRider mobile app, then transmitted to DuKorp's Cloud servers. The aggregated data are visualized using Cloud services, then analyzed offline using Multimer's algorithms. Currently, much of the data processing and analysis is handled manually and adjusted to the needs of the pilot. At the same time, we have outlined workflows for automating processes based on client needs. In the future, the Multimer platform, which is still under development, will enable analysis to take place in the Cloud, at the customer's convenience and configuration. Each of the components in this flow of data is described below.

MindRider Hardware: MindRider, now an ergonomically designed EEG wearable, utilizes a wearable commercial grade EEG headset paired with a Bluetooth smartphone and custom software that collects and geolocates the user brain waves as the user moves in the environment. The MindRider headset (Figures 3.3, 3.4 and 3.5) touches the body at two points: a forehead sensor transmits electrical signals from the brain, while a sensor on or near the ear transmits non-brain electrical signals (and thus is a grounding electrode that is used to remove noise from the

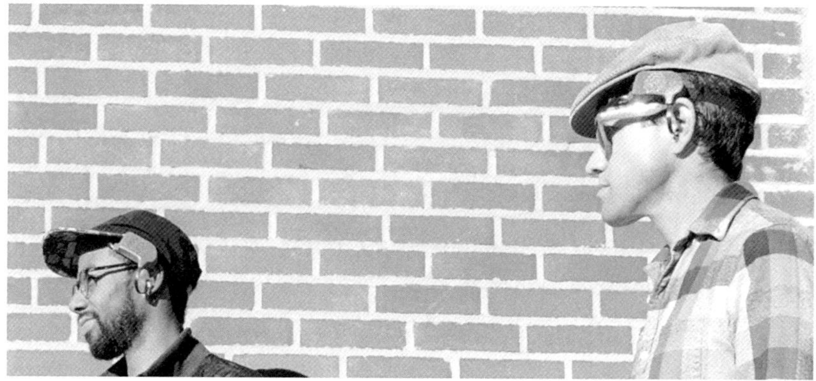

FIGURE 3.4 Data Collectors wearing MindRider headsets. Photo by Ben Tudhope.

final signal). This configuration, which only uses one (forehead) sensor near the brain, is significantly simpler than medical-grade EEG devices, which use upwards of 19 sensors. However, the reduction of neural resolution allows for an increase in population and spatiotemporal resolution, in that the MindRider can be easily purchased or rented at lower cost than other EEG headsets, and it can be worn for longer in many places outside of the clinic or laboratory. For our purposes, the single forehead electrode, which measures electrical activity predominantly from the brain's frontal lobe, is useful for measuring attention, motivation, higher-level emotion, and conscious choice (NeuroSky, 2017).

MindRider's forehead and ear electrodes are connected to a battery-powered microcontroller unit that records and processes the brain's electrical signals, then sends this processed data via Bluetooth to the Multimer app installed on the user's iOS or Android device. Since MindRider's microcontroller unit is currently the NeuroSky TGAM, the processed data are amplitudes (powers) of activity in certain frequency ranges (bands). The temporal resolution of each EEG band is typically at 1 second intervals, plus raw electrical signal values at 512 samples per second (NeuroSky, 2014). MindRider's electrical components are contained in a small case that attaches to a headband or helmet.

Mobile App: The Multimer app, available in closed beta for iOS and Android, performs several functions: it identifies unique users and takes in initial demographic information, it records the kind of activity the user takes while collecting

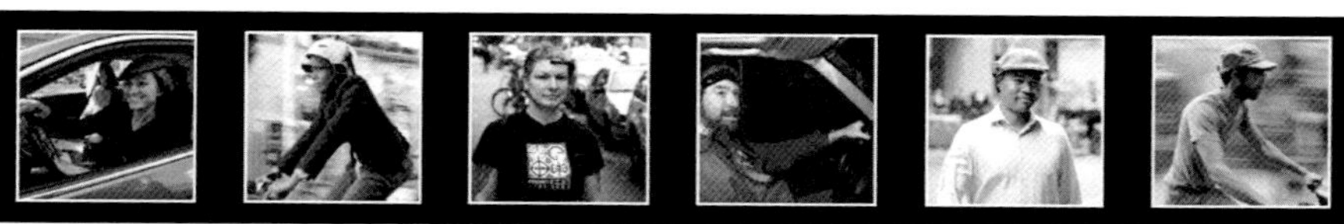

FIGURE 3.5 Various MindRider form factors, Data Collectors, and transportation modalities. Photos by Ben Tudhope.

data (e.g. walking or cycling), it establishes wireless connection to the user's wearable biosensors (including MindRider, Bluetooth heart rate straps, Apple Watch, and other devices) via Bluetooth, it starts and stops biosensor data collection, it records location- and phone-based sensor data, it takes in microsurvey data and written notes of the user's opinions, it displays a near-realtime page of the user's data map and relevant statistics, and finally it uploads the collected data to our server (Figure 3.6). A demonstration of the current data-collection system is available through an online video (Multimer Demo, 2017).

The user interface for the current Multimer app evolved to a simple design with only two main screens: *Record*, in which the user can contribute their data and configure the contribution methodology, and *Data*, in which the user can check and upload the data they have contributed. The stark design was the result of an iterative design strategy implemented during our large-scale data collection in 2016. During that time, we scheduled regular UI and UX interviews with our Data Collectors. The results of these interviews were implemented as revisions to the MindRider iOS app during the course of the data collection. Based on the interviews, major considerations for app revisions were battery conservation, interface transparency, proper sensor functionality, ergonomics, and user habits and preferences.

Collection Server and Monitoring Software: For each geographic area in which large-scale, structured data collection is planned, we recruit Data Collectors based on the area's demographics and its most commonly used transport modes (Figure 3.5). Participant Data Collectors use their apps to transmit data to the Multimer server. These data are stored in a relational database. To date, the database stores millions of data points from hundreds of Data Collectors. The Multimer dataset may be the first that can quantitatively, systematically demonstrate how people have mental experiences of different locations.

To help our team and individual participants monitor the progress of a data-collection project, geolocated biosensor data are visualized on a near-realtime web

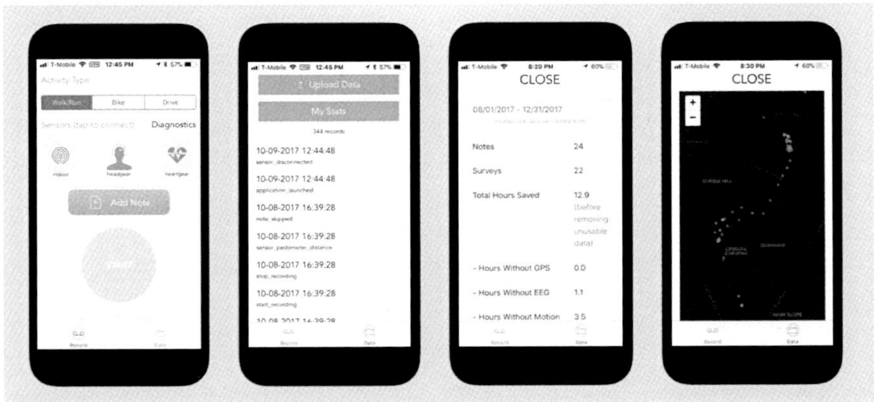

FIGURE 3.6 Screenshots from the Multimer App: the Record screen, the Data Screen, and the user's "stats" and map of data.

map as they are collected. For presentation purposes we have implemented a geographic server (GeoServer, 2017), which allows for rapid visualization of our pilots based on user groups. A sample map of our pilot in 2016 is located at http://collected.multimerdata.com (Figure 3.7) and shows the location of each data point, roughly colored based on EEG data to show areas of particularly high concentration and low relaxation (red; black in this publication) and particularly high relaxation and low concentration (green; light gray in this publication). The map, updated every ten minutes, is useful in that it shows Data Collectors where they have successfully collected data; it shows our team where data still need to be collected, and it shows everyone a rough picture of the aggregated mental experiences.

To support individual Data Collectors even further, especially Data Collectors who are paid as part of a research study (such as our 2017 Manhattan pilot), our team has developed personal "My Stats" pages (displayed on the last two screens of Figure 3.6) that show how many surveys, notes, and eligible biosensor data points have been contributed. For the Multimer Manhattan studies, "eligible" is defined as a data point that has non-zero EEG values and GPS values within Manhattan south of 59th Street.

Analytics Software: To make the biosensor data we collect more actionable and usable, we are currently developing a web-based, interactive SaaS tool that analyzes biosensor data like that of MindRider to make them usable for commercial sectors. This software performs two primary functions: it processes biosensor and other human signal data by normalizing and categorizing them, and then it integrates those categorized data into a standard urban analysis using external GIS data. All the analysis algorithms have been developed and prototyped using standard GIS software. Existing MindRider data have been processed with these algorithms, and the results are being evaluated with partner organizations, as we explain below. We are currently using the evaluations to adjust the algorithms, make them applicable for all spatial applications (not just outdoor projects), and fully automate them.

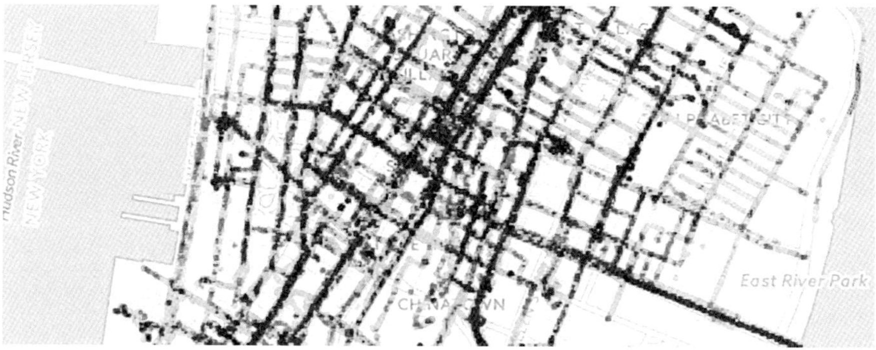

FIGURE 3.7 A map of MindRider data from the 2016 pilot, http://collected.multimerdata.com.

Multimer's Categorization functionality begins with a survey of relevant vocabulary for the market segments in which Multimer's Decision Engine will be used. In keeping with our original goal of supporting outdoor applications, our team conducted a qualitative survey of current retail, outdoor advertising, automotive, real estate, hospitality, and accommodations web sites to develop a vocabulary of how the mental atmosphere of physical sites and spaces tend to be described. We have also conducted surveys with different kinds of professionals to gage the relevance of this vocabulary. The vocabulary was then grouped by types of places and synonyms. Finally, frequently occurring words were chosen from each group and assigned to a particular combination of independent variables in the MindRider data. Since there were four combinations, there are four resulting categories (Figure 3.8).

- Restorative, where people are the most open-minded, is relevant for outdoor advertising
- Stimulating, where people are the most excited, is relevant for accommodation and hospitality services
- Fascinating, where people are the most interested in their surroundings, is relevant for the real estate sector
- Powerful, where people are paying the most attention to their surroundings, is relevant for retail, automotive, and transportation sectors

(Please visit the webpage shown under the figure to see the color-coded areas of the above mentioned four states)

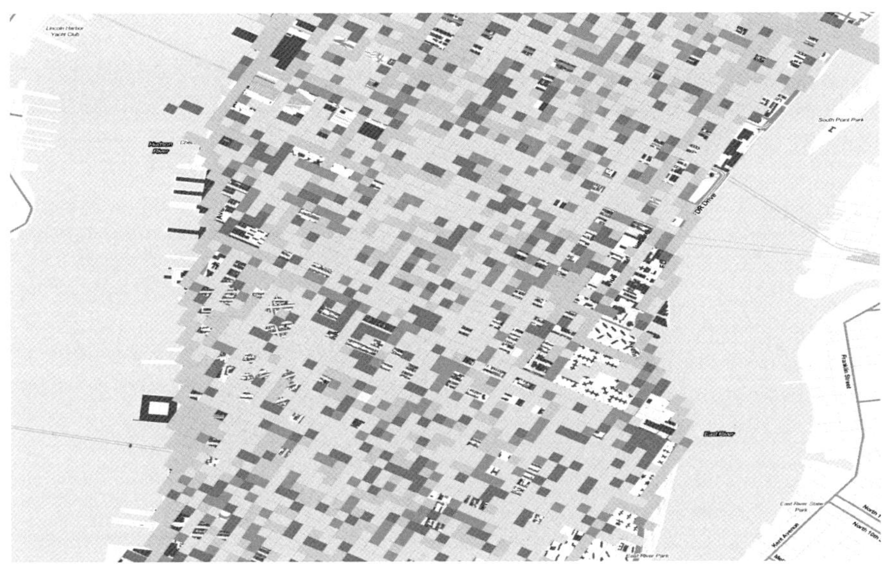

FIGURE 3.8 Multimer's Categorized blocks, based on the MindRider data in Figure 3.7. *http://categorized.multimerdata.com/*.

Multimer's Analysis functionality is divided into several algorithms, or Decision Engines, each tailored to a different commercial sector. These algorithms, which can be configured by the user, will deliver actionable output including *Places for Retail Stores, Places for an Outdoor Advertisement, Recommended Neighborhoods*, and *Healthy Places*. Each of these Decision Engines is based on criteria from such groups as the American Planning Association, the Center for Disease Control, and state Real Estate Boards. These Decision Engines will be available through a web interface and through Application Programming Interfaces (APIs) for third-party integration.

For Multimer's *Places for Retail Stores* Decision Engine proof-of-concept, which is being evaluated by marketing and communications companies, we geospatially processed MindRider data in the context of external data including bank deposits, zoning, and income data, and output recommended places to find new customers that are open-minded and curious. As there is no standard site-rating system for retail, outdoor advertising, and commercial real estate companies, our team developed a rating system based on information from the Real Estate Board of New York, which was then modified based on consultations with retail and real estate professionals.

For Multimer's *Recommended Neighborhoods* Decision Engine proof-of-concept, which is being evaluated by real estate and hospitality companies, we geospatially processed MindRider data in the context of external data including zoning, income, amenities, trees, proximity to transit, and pedestrian and bike lanes, to output a configurable "Recommended Neighborhoods" rating (see Figure 3.9).

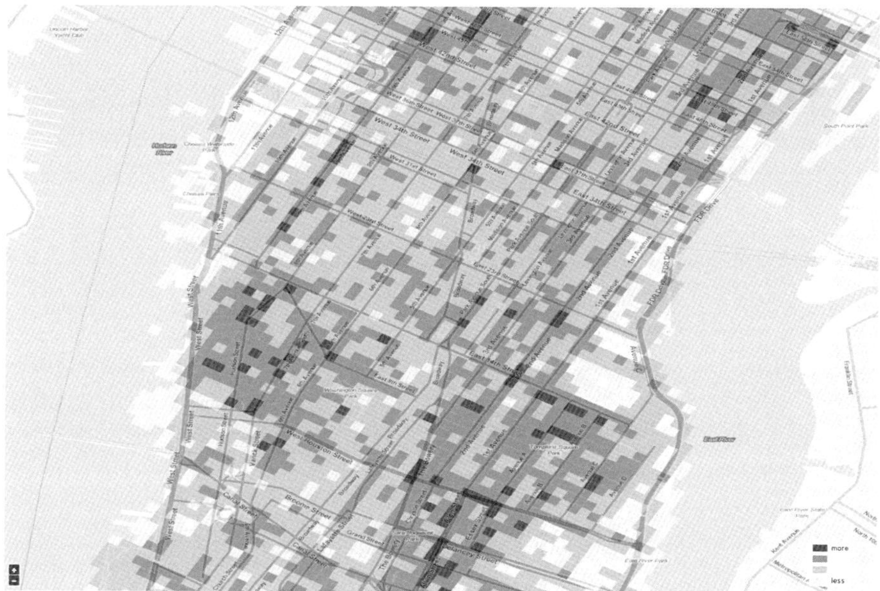

FIGURE 3.9 Multimer's Recommended Neighborhoods proof-of-concept, http://bestneighborhoods.multimerdata.com/.

The ratings system we developed is based on a set of qualitative criteria by the American Planning Association (Characteristics and Guidelines, 2017) to evaluate cities throughout the United States.

Challenges

Multimer is considered to be an innovative project, in that its work presents a considerably "high technical risk" by government reviewers: "It is a good sign if the R&D has never been attempted and/or successfully done before or is attempting to overcome significant technical hurdles" (NSF, 2017) Understandably, Multimer's development has surfaced many technical challenges. Some of these challenges arise with outdoor studies, some with indoor studies, some with both.

Challenges with outdoor studies: With outdoor studies, one persistent challenge is the recruitment of samples that represent a given city or town's population. For example, in our New York City studies, we strive to recruit a participant group that reflects the city's demographic makeup as laid out by the most recent census. In practice, our team has encountered two sorts of primary issues in recruiting a representative sample: regulatory and cultural. The regulatory issue primarily applies to professional drivers (e.g. those who work for the City of New York's Taxi and Limousine Commission), who by law are not permitted to wear any electronic devices on their head (Michael, 2009). This likely affected the number of drivers in the study, which at less than 10%, was very low. Broader cultural issues, particularly in relation to technology familiarity and ease of use, also had an effect on the study. Even though our internal core team is 50% female or higher (depending on the stage of the study), the composition of data collection participant group was skewed toward young males. We are still investigating why this may be the case, but one theory is that since Multimer data collection requires extended interaction with intricate electronic devices, younger people and males are more likely to adapt quickly to this methodology because of the existing cultural messaging about technology, which tends to target youths, young adults, and males.

As Multimer's outdoor studies have grown progressively larger, the process of compensation for data-collection participants has also raised challenges. These challenges reflect some of the larger questions that companies and governments face in regard to recent debates about the "gig economy." One primary issue is the legal distinction between an "employee" and a "contractor." App-based ride companies like Uber and Lyft have faced widespread protest, from governments and unionized drivers in cities across the world, because the companies classify their drivers–users as "contractors." This classification means that these companies do not have to pay benefits (like health insurance and unemployment pay) to their drivers, and they can then offer cheaper ride rates, thus undercutting the rate that has been established by city governments in negotiation with unionized drivers. Other app-based "gig economy" companies, like Airbnb, have attempted to avoid similar regulatory issues.

Many of these government regulations are put in place to protect individual workers and consumers; nevertheless, after consulting with several legal experts and studying well-established groups that conduct research studies on a regular basis (e.g. research universities), it seems that the common practice is to classify a research study participant as a "contractor" if they are to be financially compensated. Multimer's studies follow the broad outlines of most research studies in that they are short-term (temporary) and are not meant to interfere with a participant's ability to earn a living wage; at the same time, the study compensation is not a wage in itself. And more broadly, like other contract engagements, Multimer studies do not dictate a specific location or time that work must be performed. A large study area (e.g. Manhattan below Central Park South) and a long study period (e.g. 12 weeks from August to October) are laid out as constraints, but participants have a lot of flexibility as to when and where they collect data within those constraints.

Even so, because Multimer has previously paid outdoor participants based on valid data minutes, and time-based payment is also the method that is used to pay professional taxi drivers, we are aware of potential ambiguities when it comes to study compensation. If Multimer continues to be used for outdoor studies, we will continue to pay close attention to legal and research practices around participant compensation, so that we do not just follow common practice, but create best ethical practices for all stakeholders.

Challenges with indoor (workplace) studies: While our team has not yet conducted many studies in indoor spaces, we have run a short indoor beta test with the technology developed for the 2017 Manhattan study (Figure 3.10). Currently, several indoor workplace studies are in the planning stages, and it's already clear that the challenges associated with indoor studies will be quite different from those

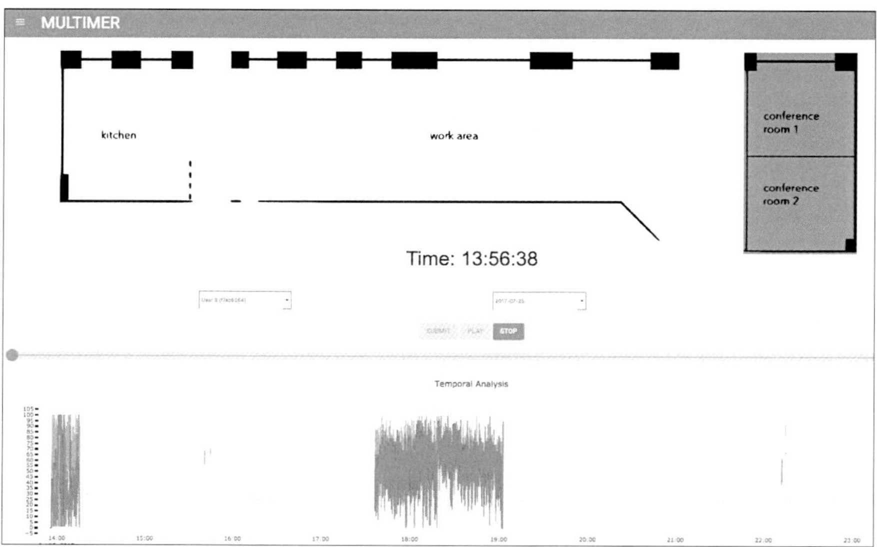

FIGURE 3.10 Screenshot from visualization of indoor data collected during a Multimer beta test in 2017. Prototype by Aaron D'Souza.

of outdoor studies. These workplace studies are generally to be funded by large, multi-site companies that contract architects and spatial strategists to improve worker wellbeing and productivity, which nullifies the recruitment/representation and compensation issues that Multimer faces in its outdoor studies. A workplace, which brings together similarly trained practitioners, is generally more homogeneous than a city, so that, plus the fact that there is company buy-in, makes it much easier for Multimer to recruit a representative sample. This sample set of workers is also already compensated in an established way, so, especially with the participant's company playing a managing role in a Multimer workplace study, we do not expect to compensate financially participants in the workplace for their participation in a Multimer study.

However, compensation is a powerful motivator, and that lack of motivation leads to a first set of new challenges: incentivizing workplace participants to consistently collect data. Unlike pedestrians, runners, cyclists, and even drivers, who are often already predisposed to integrate some kind of wearable communication or fitness technology into their transportation activities, many indoor workers may not have this predisposition. For one thing, it's unusual for indoor office workers to wear something on their head, and this is a current requirement for Multimer studies – using the MindRider head-gear to measure brainwave data. Even workers that are interested to wear MindRider will likely take it off during intense computer work or meetings, and in our early indoor workplace tests, we found that this led to significant data gaps.

As Multimer's technology has evolved, we have iteratively worked within our internal team and externally with data-collection participants to improve the ergonomics of the MindRider for different applications. The current MindRider model is a mix of off-the-shelf and custom components and, with a few exceptions, this model seems to provide enough customization options for users consistently to wear it comfortably for several continuous hours, while still being rugged and durable enough to not break over several weeks. However, we realize that a much smaller, less ruggedized, model is required for workplace participants, especially if we aim for those participants to collect data continuously. We are working to produce a smaller model now, and we are integrating other kinds of popular wearables, including Apple Watch and Fitbit, so that participants can continue to contribute data even when they are not wearing the MindRider.

Location metrics and analysis integration are another challenge with indoor studies, though we foresee this challenge to be easily surmountable after a few studies. Unlike with outdoor studies, which take place at geographic scale, can easily integrate GPS data as a location metric, and can easily be integrated with GIS systems for the purpose of analytics, there is no standard indoor equivalent to GPS. Nevertheless, there are few enough choices for location metrics (e.g. Bluetooth beacons, other wireless surveying) that we expect to determine a system for indoor metrics fairly quickly, and there are few indoor analytics systems (e.g. building information management (BIM)), that we expect to quickly determine an integration workflow as well. While we foresee these challenges for our next indoor studies, all of which are planned for "white-collar" office workplaces, we foresee some of these challenges persisting to other indoor spaces, including "blue-collar" workplaces such as factories, as well as retail, restaurant, and other service spaces.

Challenges with all spaces: Some challenges persist, no matter the kind of space under study. For instance, there is the challenge of managing and analyzing a large volume of data. With MindRider and Multimer, we have built the basic system to collect and analyze geolocated biosensor data, and we have proven the technical feasibility of collecting these data from a pilot sample population for an extended period of time. Our primary objective now is to improve our data modeling and analysis so as to offer a fully robust product that our customers will confidently use. To do this, we will finetune our system to interpret human signal data more accurately at the individual and aggregate levels. We are focusing on these questions:

1. Affective Interpretation: Once data are collected and cleaned, is there a significant correlation of certain brainwave patterns to individual opinions of positive affect, negative affect, and affective intensity?
2. Biosensor Comparison: Is there a significant relationship between brainwave patterns to other biosensor (e.g. pulse, sweat) patterns?
3. Geospatial Comparison: Is there a significant relationship of certain aggregated brainwave patterns in proximity to geographic features in the urban environment or infrastructure, such as areas of complex traffic, parks and green spaces, and commercial areas?
4. Temporal Comparison: Is there a significant relationship of certain aggregated brainwave patterns to times of day and/or days of the week?
5. Reproducibility: Can this research be reliably, robustly reproduced in New York City? Can the research be documented and prepared for reproduction in other locations, beyond the scope of our few pilots?

Ultimately, the analytics challenges are really challenges of resources and capacity – at present, the Multimer team is less than ten people – so, in my opinion, this challenge can be addressed if we manage our resources well.

There is one last challenge that is less certain, and really underlies the bedrock of Multimer as a small business: are there enough people who need Multimer to exist in order to support their own work? Human signal data, unlike food and water, are not a basic human need. Unlike communication and transportation, they are not yet a societal requirement. Human signal data are still a relatively abstract topic, and its best uses are still not yet fully determined. Based on dozens of interviews with different kinds of professionals, we have developed a working theory that this kind of data will be most useful for architects and spatial strategists, but only as our data and analytics systems develop, and the only prediction I can confidently make about the viability of Multimer is that it may ultimately be used in ways – both positive and negative – that none of us can predict.

Concluding comments: Multimer, diversity, and social inclusion

To conclude this chapter, I'd like to emphasize a concept that I have valued well before it became such an important part of the public conversation, that of diversity and inclusion (Ducao, 2016). Multimer is a research project, but it is also a small technology business, and neither technology nor business are sectors known for diversity or inclusion. As a woman of color, I have witnessed, experienced, and been deeply affected by the aggressive, repressive culture that results from a lack of diversity and inclusion. But perhaps even more importantly in regard to the scope of this book, I have seen the sheer inaccuracies resulting from work that fails at every level, from staffing to user testing, to include the people that it purports to represent. I have been infuriated to see gatekeepers to important resources – funding, recognition, space, personal connections – reward groups that don't even try to include the people they purport to represent. This not only perpetuates toxic culture, it perpetuates an all-too-human bias, even bigotry, into the technology under development.

At the opening of this chapter, I wrote that human scale is a concept that I value dearly. I believe that in order to design, develop, or build something for humans, at human scale, the designer (or developer, or builder) must include not just as many people as possible, but as many kinds of people as possible, in the entire process, from staffing of the internal team, to codesigning with the user population, to iterative user testing, to roll-out and scale-up. For Multimer, which is based in New York City, one of the most diverse cities in the world, that initial population is by nature diverse, and we have done our best to reflect that diversity in both our core team and our initial participants. I was initially concerned with the gender and ethnic diversity of our core team and participants, but as our core team and user base have expanded, they have, through both conscious effort and a lot of luck, come to reflect additional kinds of demographic range: income, age, and ability. Of course, these progressions are not without complications – in the previous section, I discussed challenges ranging from recruitment bias to incentives. Nevertheless, I have been heartened to learn, through repeated user studies, that even with all the bugs, issues, and kinks that are bound to arise from a complex, rapidly evolving system, that Multimer participants have evaluated interaction with my team to be one of the best parts of their experience, and that they have rated a curiosity about the possibilities of their collective data as a higher incentive to participate than even financial payment!

And this comes back to why we – or at least I – make Multimer. Developing a new technology, especially outside of an institutional research lab, is a high-risk endeavor. Combine this with the statistic that most startup businesses fail, and it becomes clear that I haven't worked on this project for years because of the easy rewards. Multimer grew from a funny, experimental prototype called MindRider, and much of its progress continues to be fueled by a spirit of playful curiosity. But beyond that, I have an ironclad conviction that as the world of "Big Data" grows to encompass data about social interactions, personal health, individual choices, population behavior – in short, data about how we exist as a people – and as that information is implemented to affect all kinds of serious institutional, infrastructural, and economic decisions – it is of the utmost importance that as many kinds of people steward the data as possible. I don't want data to be another tool to push underrepresented groups to the margins, in the way that Le Corbusier suggested (Le Corbusier, 2011). And if, in this age where intolerance and polarization have been unwittingly supported by homogeneously designed technologies, I can help steward diversity in the planning, design, and development around the collection of human data, I will.

Acknowledgments

I would like to thank the entire Multimer team, both past and present, for their contributions. I especially thank my co-founder Ilias Koen, as well as Scott Sheu and Jennifer Sta. Ines for their writing, edits, and revisions over the course of several MindRider/Multimer reports, studies, and proposals. I'd also like to thank Chris Willard for his help with brainstorming the structure of this chapter.

References

Abercrombie, Stanley, and George Nelson (2000). *George Nelson: The Design of Modern Design*. Cambridge, MA: MIT Press.

AP Insights (2017). 'How Virtual Reality Will Impact Journalism.' *Associated Press Insights Blog*. Available at: www.insights.ap.org/industry-trends/report-how-virtual-reality-will-impact-journalism

Characteristics and Guidelines of Great Neighborhoods (2017). *American Planning Association*. Available at: www.planning.org/greatplaces/neighborhoods/characteristics.htm

Ducao, Arlene (2014). *MindRider Maps Manhattan*. New York: DuKorp.

Ducao, Arlene (2016). 'Bike helmet with lights displays rider's mood.' *WGBH News*, 9 Jan. 2016. Available at: www.news.wgbh.org/post/bike-helmet-lights-displays-riders-mood

GE (2016). 'The average cost of IoT sensors is falling.' *Atlas, Quartz*, 27 Apr. 2016. Available at: www.theatlas.com/charts/BJsmCFAl

GeoServer (2017). 'GeoServer is an open source server for sharing geospatial data'. *GeoServer*. Available at www.geoserver.org/

Goldberger, Paul (1981). 'Robert Moses, master builder, is dead at 92.' *New York Times*, 30 July 1981.

Le Corbusier (2011). *Urbanisme*. Paris: Flammarion.

Location Analytics Market (2016). 'Forecast and analysis to 2020 – Research and markets.' *Location Analytics Market by Tools & amp; Services – Forecast and Analysis to 2020 – Research and Markets | Business Wire*, 5 Apr. 2016. Available at: www.businesswire.com/news/home/20160405006189/en/Location-Analytics-Market-Tools-Services---Forecast.

Lohr, Steve (1997). 'Rethinking privacy vs. teamwork in today's workplace.' *New York Times*, 11 August, 1997.

Measuring (2015). 'Measuring the information society.' *ITU*. Available at: www.itu.int/pub/D-IND-ICTOI-2015

Michael (2009). 'New rule for cabbies: no devices in the ear.' *The New York Times*. Available at: www.nytimes.com/2009/12/18/nyregion/18taxi.html

Multimer 2014 Analysis (2017). 'MindRider maps Manhattan'. *Multimer 2014 Analysis: MindRider Maps Manhattan*. Available at www.book.multimerdata.com/

Multimer Demo (2017): 'How We Do It' (Prototype Demo), November 2017. *Vimeo*, 15 Dec. 2017. Available at: www.vimeo.com/243964003

NeuroSky (2017). EEG algorithms. Available at: www.neurosky.com/biosensors/eeg-sensor/algorithms.

NeuroSky (2014). 'What's New', *developer_tools_2.5_development_guide [NeuroSky Developer – Docs]*, 1 July 2014. Available at: www.developer.neurosky.com/docs/doku.php?id=developer_tools_2.5_development_guide.

NSF (2017). 'National Science Foundation – where discoveries begin'. *Frequently Asked Questions (FAQs) for SBIR/STTR Program (nsf15125) | NSF – National Science Foundation*. Available at: www.nsf.gov/pubs/2015/nsf15125/nsf15125.jsp

Rybczynski, Witold (1998). 'The architect LE CORBUSIER'. *Time*, 8 June 1998. Available at: www.content.time.com/time/magazine/article/0,9171,988492,00.html

Sheu, Scott (2017). *SBIR Phase 2 Commercialization Plan*. December 2017. Unpublished typescript. New York.

Statista (2014). Statistics portal. Available at: https://www.statista.com/statistics/203734/global-smartphone-penetration-per-capita-since-2005/ (accessed Jan 2018 and Aug 2018).

4

DATA, EMOTION, SPACE

FELT communication through computational textile texture

Felecia Davis

Introduction

Privileging touch and experiences with senses other than vision in architecture only expands architecture's capacity to connect and communicate with people. In fact, in his book *The Eyes of the Skin: The Senses and Architecture* (2013), architect Juhani Pallasmaa argues against the systematic incorporation of architectural design and spaces into the realm of the purely visual as produced by CAD and 3D computer programs. For Pallasmaa, the sensuousness of architecture is disappearing along with any consideration in the design process of how people come to experience architecture; if we look to the image of Lina Loos's fur-lined bedroom in Figure 4.2, "there is a strong identity between naked skin and the sensation of home. The experience of home is essentially an experience of intimate warmth" (Pallasmaa, 2013: 58). Home, for Pallasmaa, is about the expansion of sheltering walls by merging with the naked skin of a body. He writes: "My body is truly the navel of my world, not in the sense of the viewing point of the central perspective, but as the very locus of reference, memory, imagination and integration" (2013, p. 12). The body, therefore, is intelligence itself. Perhaps, we might understand Pallasmaa's use of his body to think and, indeed, of other bodies in this way as another form of ubiquitous computing through the senses.

If architects, artists, designers, engineers and scientists, and others could begin to understand the nature of what various textile expressions communicated through vision and touch, and what computational textiles communicated in transformation, then it would be possible to more clearly understand the role texture plays in communicating emotion through an object. A textile that changes its shape could be used on a robot as robot skin, for example for people who may live alone and benefit from some communication through touch. A computational textile may be used on a wall, a pillow, curtain, furnishings, toys, and many other designed

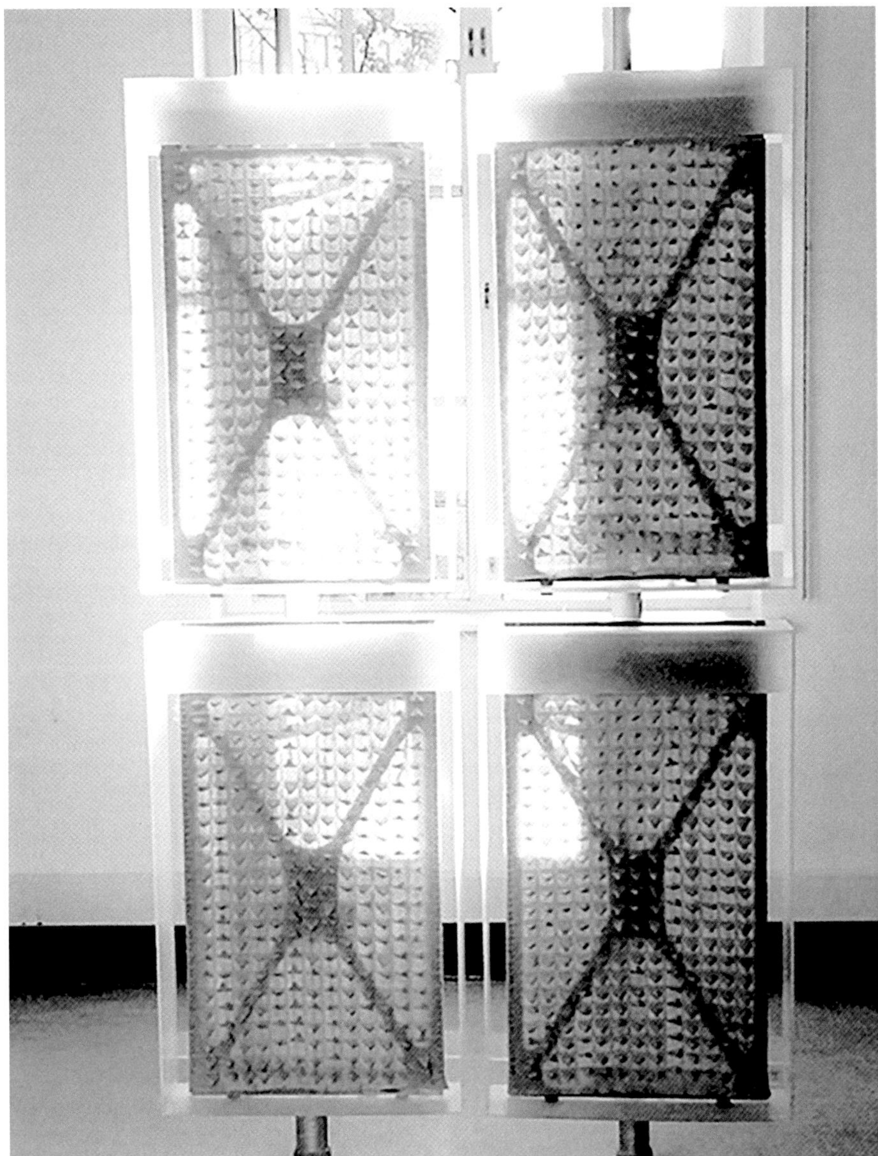

FIGURE 4.1 The FELT wall panel.

objects to communicate emotion to people and children who do not have access to their emotions. These may be people such as children with autism, or adults with Alzheimer's disease. These textiles may be used to connect with someone not in touch with what they are feeling, unable to communicate what they are feeling or elicit communication from people who otherwise would not have been able to.

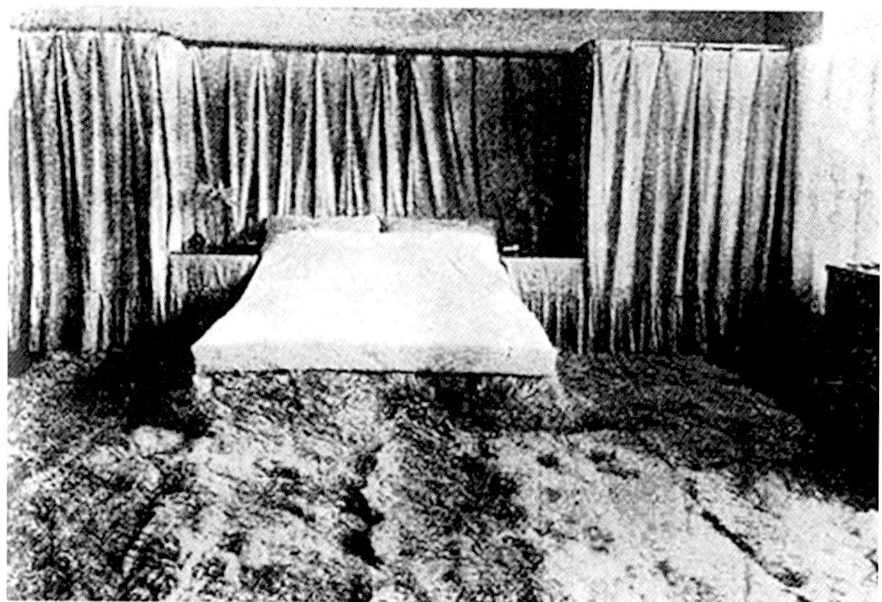

FIGURE 4.2 Lina Loos's Bedroom, Vienna, Austria, (1903). This figure was reprinted courtesy of The MIT Press from *Privacy and Publicity: Modern Architecture as Mass Media*, by Beatriz Colomina.

A textile can be used as a form of non-verbal communication with people through vision and touch.

Emotion and communication

Let us look into emotion as a concept for a moment. Psychologists, neuroscientists, philosophers, and others each have their disciplinary ways to define or discuss emotion. It really all comes down to relating a body to an environment or, some would say, situation. Figure 4.3 shows a list of some of the differing theories of emotion and what an emotion is. Most theories describe emotion as a process whereby the body, animal or human, receives some stimulus in an environment, interprets that stimulus and then produces either bodily responses or emotions. The critical part of these theories is interpretation, otherwise there is just a stimulus and no judgment is given on that stimulus by the body, which is the emotion (Russell, 1980:1176)

Emotion expressed through bodily responses communicates or allows others to infer a situation. It is the expression that carries the communication.

In *The Expression of the Emotions in Man and Animals* of 1872, Darwin examines the issue of expression (Darwin, 2009b). In this follow-up to *The Origin of the Species* (2009a), he describes hundreds of animal and human body expressions in minute detail and maps them to different emotions and functions. In Darwin's account, many expressions of emotion, such as the hair rising on the back of

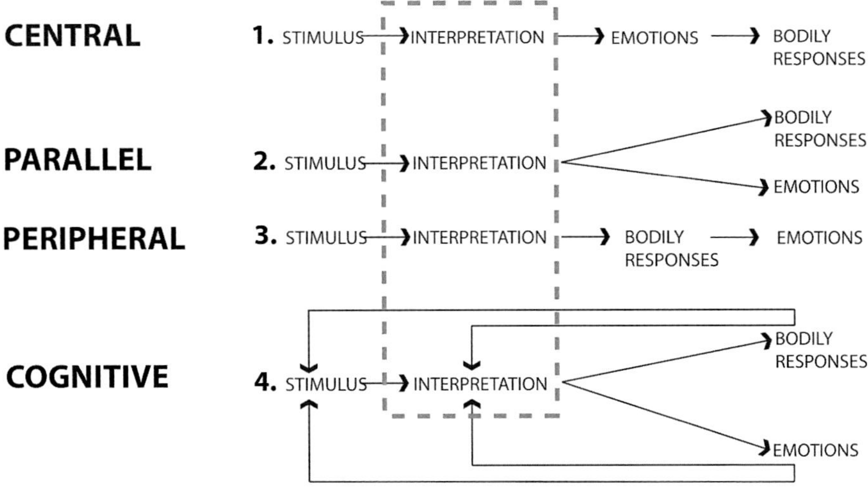

FIGURE 4.3 Four theories of emotion – redrawn from Panksepp (1998, p. 33).

a person's neck when afraid, are leftover responses related to an evolutionary function designed to maximize chances of survival in some prehistoric time. For example, writing about the behavior of a hen trying to chase a dog from away its brood, Darwin notes what he considers to be the principle cause of erect feathers, as follows:

> Birds when frightened, as a general rule, closely adpress all their feathers, and their consequently diminished size is often astonishing. Though with birds, anger may be the chief and commonest cause of the erection of feathers.
>
> *(Darwin, 2009b, p. 97)*

Darwin was trying to understand the function of emotional expression in the context of evolution. Expression in this sense is about changing the body in relation to the environment. In the case of the birds, by closing their feathers, they withdraw from the environment and by opening their feathers in anger they make an approach to it. Witnesses to this bird behavior may *infer* that the bird is angry or afraid through its body expression in context. A message was sent by the behavior – however, it was a byproduct of evolutionary function and not sent intentionally.

The psychologists Nico Frijda, Carroll Izard, Silvan Tomkins and Bertram Karon agree with Darwin and propose that these kinds of expressions are functional adjustments; they are part of the emotion process that adjusts the body's relation to the environment (Izard, 1971; Frijda, 1986: 60; Tomkins & Karon, 1992). Frijda's description also follows Darwin's concept of function. Bodily responses do not change the environment. Instead, a bodily response furthers the chances for survival (Frijda, 1986: 60).

Other emotional expressions are interactional and communicate intentionally in a more restrictive sense. These expressions are produced *in order to* influence the behavior of others. This expressive behavior is not an evolutionary byproduct. It is intended and relational. For Frijda, this interactional behavior is more akin to bluffing with the intention of changing a situation that an animal or person does not like. These are communicating expressions. Designers care whether or not their designs are loved or repulsed and they care about the message that goes to a person from the thing or spaces they are designing. Sometimes these messages are communication, and sometimes messages are sent by inference.

Computing through the senses

Let's return to Pallasmaa's declaration that his body is intelligence itself. James Gibson, a psychologist, argues that there is no separation between the body and the environment. In Gibson's account, therefore, energy flows into bodies from the environment and flows out from bodies into the environment, such that it is impossible to understand the body without considering the environment (Gibson, 1966, p. 5). He writes about the environment as a place of flow and forces. The haptic system, unlike any other perceptual system, encompasses most of the body and literally puts us in touch with our world; it 'lets us grab a hold of things' (Gibson, 1966, p. 97).

A specific quality of our haptic system is that, unlike our visual system, it enables us to explore and alter our environment. Further, this ability means that we can also change what we perceive with our haptic system, which is not possible with our visual system. Gibson gives a good example of this: "When we reach out to feel the edge of a table, we feel the edge, but simultaneously the table makes a dent in us." He argues that there are poles of experience that place the concepts of subject and object in a continuum. If you wish, you "can focus on the dent made in your hand or you can focus on the edge of the table." (Gibson, 1983, p. 99) The equipment we use to explore, feel, and alter our environment is the same equipment we use to feel and produce emotional experiences (Gibson, 1983, p. 99).

Related projects and background

There are a few projects and experiments that examine communicating emotion using vision and touch on textiles. None of the studies or projects mentioned here are in the field of architecture or examine how designers might use the haptic sense to communicate in architecture. However, the results of these experiments might serve as a guide architects and designers could consider. A relevant study by Akshita et al. looks at the interrelationship between vision and touch in affective communication using photos from the International Affective Picture System (IAPS) and a ViviTouch haptic actuator. This actuator can vary the "intensity, frequency, waveform, duration, rhythm and spatial location" of vibration on an actuator pad to achieve different textures that are felt by the hand (Akshita et al.,

2015, p. 2045). Akshita et al. found, using a two-dimensional grid where the x-axis is ranged between happy and sad and the y-axis is ranged from excited to calm, that vision dominated how happy or sad a texture rated. In other words, vision dominated response on the x-axis. Felt texture determined how calming or excited that texture rated on the y-axis. The higher the degree of vibration or roughness of the texture, the more exciting a texture was rated on the y-axis. Another relevant study by Kim et al. includes emotion-based indexing of textiles using photographic images by color, texture, and pattern. The point for Kim and colleagues is to create a neural network that works with a set of fuzzy rules to simulate how humans rate emotion communicated by the textile images (Kim et al., 2006). However, the results by Davis in the dissertation *Softbuilt: Computational Textiles and Augmenting Space Through Emotion* show that emotional ratings or evaluations of photographs of textures are very different when the same textures can be both seen and touched by people (Davis, 2017, p. 191).

A second group of related projects concerns those which develop actuated panels or walls. Unlike the study with the FELT panel, these projects used the transforming expression of the wall to make the viewer of the wall or panel aware of something about themselves. Davis et al. proposed the Textile Mirror, a Nitinol-actuated wall panel linked to expressing human emotion through feedback from a smart phone (Davis, Cherry, Roseway, & Czerwinski, 2012). Yu et al. prepared a series of small samples that were exhibited on the wall as well as one large wall panel to communicate feedback from biosensors located on a participant's body (Yu et al., 2016).

Design of FELT

FELT is a large (150cm x 180cm) modular panel, seen in Figures 4.1 and 4.4. FELT provides an opportunity to explore how changing the scale of a textile could change the emotions communicated to people from the textile expression through vision and touch. Four key steps were followed to make FELT. The first was making the fabric, the second was designing the framework to hold the textile, the third was connecting the electric motors to the frame and textile, and the fourth was mounting the frames with textiles onto a Plexiglas box, which allowed it to be used as a screen or a divider in space. For this project, two methods of actuation were considered, Nitinol and servo-motors. Nitinol was initially preferred because it does not make any noise when activated. However, I did not use Nitinol for two reasons: Nitinol becomes too hot to touch, such that wires made from it must be covered; in addition, Nitinol requires a lot of power. Using servo-motors, a simpler power system running with a lower current could be used.

The Study with Five Textures

The purpose of the Study with Five Textures was to obtain feedback from participants regarding emotions communicated to them from several textiles through

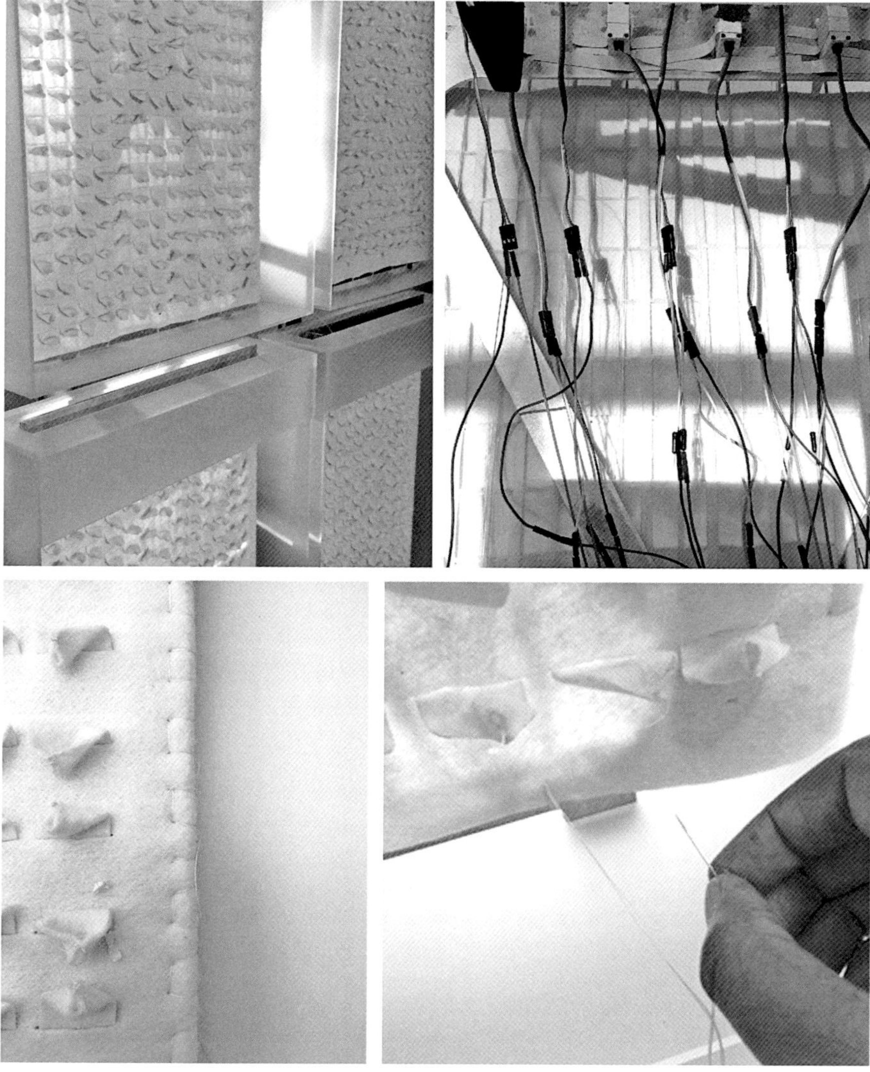

FIGURE 4.4 Top photo left: close-up of four panels; photo right: motors and wiring. Bottom photo left: close-up of edge detail; photo right: attaching felt to aluminum panel.

vision alone in a still state and also in a moving state. The study was also designed to obtain feedback on emotions communicated to participants from several textiles in a still state and in a moving state using both vision and touch together.

The Study with Five Textures took place at the MIT School of Architecture and Planning January 2014. There were 19 participants, 15 women and 4 men. The age range was 18–55. Each session took an hour to complete four rounds of questions. The participants interacted with the five textures one-on-one with me in the room. Participants were primarily faculty and students from the MIT School of Architecture and Planning.

The Study with Five Textures used exactly the same format, methods, and Hypotheses 1–4 that will be presented in the FELT study. All textures were inspired from animal reactions (see Figure 4.5(a)). It was expected that the movement of each animal's skin, fur or feathers would communicate or permit a person to infer a different emotion(s). There was much experimentation with the 15–20 different textures, which could be simply transformed by pulling threads or wire to change the texture. Motors were programmed to pull threads that changed the textures.

In the end, five textures were settled on for the Study with Five Textures. During this study, five 23cm × 23cm textures were mounted on top of foam-core boxes, with motors and wires inside. The foam-core boxes were mounted on the wall at eye height, so that participants could see and touch them easily (see Figure 4.5(b)). The motors were programmed to move the textiles slowly, at the pace of a calmly breathing creature. Small slats of wood weighted the textures so that they were pulled back down into their original position. Here is a link to a video that shows the five textures and the textures' range of motion and speed: http://vimeo.com/85620116.

Texture 3 was selected as the base pattern for FELT because it had the highest variance between responses in comparison to the other four textures (see Figure 4.5(c)). In other words, the study participants either loved it or hated it – there were few in-between responses. This made it one of the most interesting textures. A thorough explanation of the results of the Study with Five Textures may be seen in Davis' paper "The Textility of Emotion," and dissertation *Softbuilt: Computational Textiles and Augmenting Space Through Emotion* (Davis, 2015, 2017). Compared to the Study with Five Textures, the results for the experiment with FELT showed calmer and happier reactions to the different presentations of the textile. The results of both the Study with Five Textures and the experiment with FELT show some principal ways that people connect with the textile expressions including: analogy and memory; understanding potential for aggression or harm; and consideration of vitality or lack of vitality.

The FELT study

The purpose of the FELT study was to obtain feedback from participants regarding emotions communicated to them from the wall panel or large screen through *vision* alone, in a still state and in a moving state. The study was also designed to obtain feedback about emotions communicated to participants from the wall panel, in a still state and in a moving state, using vision and touch together. In addition, the purpose of this study was to understand if communication changed by changing the scale of the texture.

The *FELT* study took place at the Pennsylvania State University School of Architecture and Landscape Architecture in August 2016. There were 17 participants, 13 of whom were women and 4 were men. The age range was 20–65, with

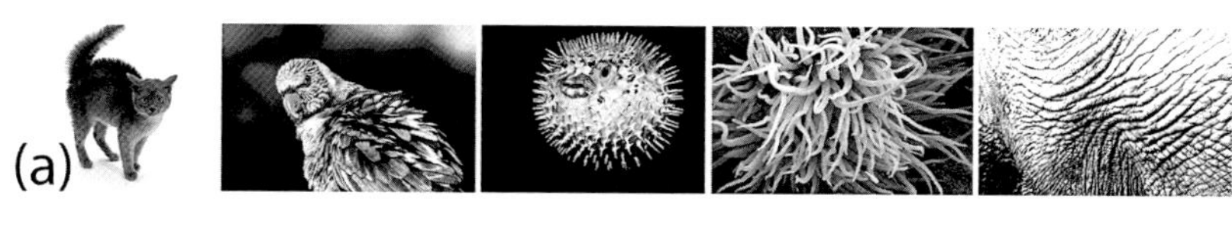

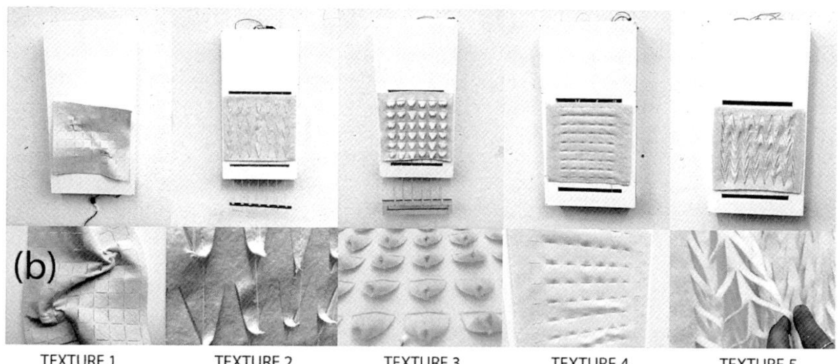

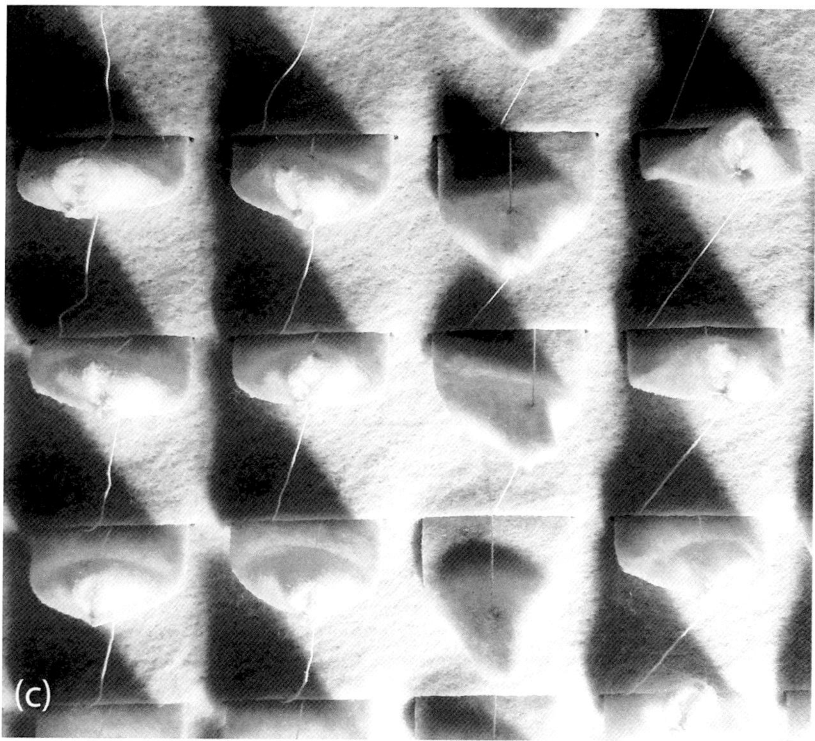

FIGURE 4.5 (a) Animal reactions used as inspiration for the Study with Five Textures; (b) Five textile samples mounted on foam-core boxes, photos above. Textile samples up close, photos below; (c) Texture 3 base texture for FELT – Texture 3 used cotton thread instead of nylon monofilament to lift "petals."

the men's average age at 36 and the women's average age at 35. Each session took half an hour to complete four rounds of questions. The participants interacted with the *FELT* panel one-on-one with me in the room.

An outline of the study format is as follows:

1. FELT panel is Still
   a. Looking (ROUND 1)
   b. Looking and Touching (ROUND 2)
2. FELT panel is Moving
   a. Looking (ROUND 3)
   b. Looking and Touching (ROUND 4)

Study methods

There were four rounds in the study, each of which comprised four questions seen in Table 4.1. The participants had the opportunity to see the FELT wall panel by standing or sitting in front of it. The participants were asked to free associate for the first question.

TABLE 4.1 Hypotheses used for the FELT study.

Hypothesis Number	*Hypothesis Description*
SCALE & CONTEXT HYPOTHESIS	*It was expected that participant responses would change if the textile was designed as a large architectural panel or space divider rather than small textile sample.*
HYPOTHESIS 1 ROUND 1	*It was expected that using vision alone, people would consistently associate specific emotional states with specific characteristics of the textures of textiles in a state of stillness. Crisp, curvilinear shapes associated with positive, excited, and happy feelings; smooth curvilinear shapes associated with positive and calm feelings; triangulated shapes associated with negative and angry feelings; smooth triangulated shapes and superimposed systems or a poorly defined combination associated with negative, depressed, and calm feelings.*
HYPOTHESIS 2 ROUND 2	*It was expected that when people used vision and the haptic senses together, the emotional associations would change. It was expected that when people could see and touch a still texture, a negative emotional association using vision alone would change when using both vision and the haptic senses to a positive emotional association.*
HYPOTHESIS 3 ROUND 3	*It was expected that when the textures were in a state of motion this characteristic would raise or lower the participants' rating of what was communicated on a Circumplex grid based on what was associated with that texture motion.*
HYPOTHESIS 4 ROUND 4	*It was expected that the act of touching the moving textures would again change the ratings and what the textiles communicated.*

1. For the free association I proposed three kinds of questions to encourage the participants to respond. For example: "What are some words that describe some of the emotions that you could attribute to this textile?"; "What are some adjectives that you could use to describe the mood of this textile?" I told the participants that the free association should focus on what the textile communicated to them in terms of emotional attributes. The participants were also told that it was fine to talk about things that the textile reminded them of and to talk about any particular associations or memories that they attached to the textile. Their responses to this question were recorded in my notes.

After this first question, the participants answered the next three questions presented on stapled 8.5" × 11" (A4) sheets of paper. These are as follows:

2. What does the texture communicate to you?

   (Negative Mood) 1 2 3 4 5 (Positive Mood)

   The participants were asked to circle a number between 1 and 5.

3. What does the texture communicate to you?

   (Relaxed) 1 2 3 4 5 (Stimulated)

   The participants were asked to circle a number between 1 and 5.

Last, the participants were given a sheet of faces that projected emotions and asked to pick a face in order to answer Question 4.

4. Face: What mood would you associate with this texture? Happy, Cross, Scared, Sad, O.K., Horrible, Worried, Excited.

Then they circled the words that they thought described one of the faces on the sheet. Figure 4.6(a) shows the sheet of face/emotion choices presented to participants. The participants could circle as many of faces/words as they wished and were told they could add emotion words and faces as needed. (See Figure 4.6(a)).

What Emotions are Communicated by FELT?

In this section I will discuss the responses to the four questions. I have used the letter P for participant and identified the different participants by number.

Comments on FELT as a wall panel

Compared to the Study with Five Textures, participants in the FELT study changed their positions often to view the panel. This was as I had expected and enabled participants to see the large- and small-scale features of FELT. Two people (P8 and P12) immediately and instinctively went to touch the large panel in spite of the verbal instructions I had issued not to touch it until requested. Before responding to my free-association question, four participants (P6, P8, P12 and P17) moved

8–10 feet away from the panel to have a look and then came back closer; in addition, two participants (P13 and P17) sat down on a chair that was near the panels or squatted to see what was going on in the lower panels.

In addition, several participants remarked on the light coming through the panels and that they were like windows when asked "what comes to mind?" One participant responded: "A window, a curtain for a window, not a modern house, one like mom's or grandmother's house; this is like a cross and there is an extra band on one. It is a safe protected area. There was a war where I was growing up; windows were strengthened with tape to prevent glass from shattering" (P9). Also, the large panel reminded people of walls, as in this example; "What comes to mind is a pattern in a continuous wall; I am concerned with not knowing this material, which is just a physical aspect. It looks aggressive; like the thrown concrete on property walls in my country (Brazil). If you hit these walls and they are very sharp, you can be cut. But because the material is soft, that will not happen here. But the pattern is not positive because it is like that concrete and because it is pointed and regular" (P6). Other participants connected it architecturally with descriptions like "high design corporate chic; an interpretation of 1960s modernism" (P3). In addition to connecting it visually with things associated with architecture, people talked about the frames holding the textile, unlike the Study with Five Textures where no one mentioned the boxes hung on the wall. Participant 17 for example saw "duplicity, in the fact that there is more than one panel, which means each panel is not unique. I did not notice before but the backbone is different; the whole series of four is mirrored about a vertical axis, probably unintentional. It is the idea of a hung textile in a frame with a sub-frame. I feel a lot of tension in backbone. It looks like it is pulling it apart and the fabric is trying to escape the frame more on the right side than left; it is like a person being stretched" (P17). This participant, an architect was reacting to the fact that the piece was made in four identical panels or frames, but the aluminum "backbones" could be seen through the translucent felt showing different shadows, making the appearance duplicitous. Participants asked about the lighting, and often tried to determine what was and was not a part of the study. For example, Participant 8 asked if the shadow behind the panels was part of the project.

The comments I have selected above show some of what was said about the scale and architectural quality of the FELT panel. During the free-association question there emerged several themes that connected the comments. I have listed these themes or categories below. While these are categories I saw as emergent, these are surely not the only ones, and indeed many of the comments that could be put into one category would be just as valid in a second category. Here is a list of the most prevalent categories that emerged in all four rounds:

1. Analogy and Memory. This category shows participants connecting to the FELT texture by using their memories of previous experiences and noting similarities to other things.
2. Vitality and Lack of Vitality. Participants described how lively or living the texture was, or how lifeless and dead it was in behavior.

3. Aggression or Harm. Participants described their fear of the texture, that it could hurt them or that they could harm the texture.
4. Comparison. Participants compared their experiences with FELT to the previous round.
5. Feels to Skin. Participants described what their skin felt.
6. Color. Participants mentioned or discussed color.
7. Noise. Participants mentioned noise, but in Rounds 3 and 4 only).

In Round 1 the remaining comments fell into the same categories that were seen in the Study with Five Textures. I speculate that these categories were the same as those in the Study with Five Textures because during the free-association question, when it came to really capturing their thoughts and words, participants stood close or about two feet away from the panels to look at the texture. This is the same physical position participants took in the Study with Five Textures. Thus, most of the responses were primarily about the texture up close.

Free-association results

The use of memory and analogy was the most prevalent category and often the first mentioned during the free association response. In addition, no participants had the same responses from round to round. A sampling of the free association responses is provided below. As you can see, not all categories appeared in every round.

Round 1

- Participants use vision only
- Textile in still state

Memory/Analogy: Two responses related to analogies about boobs and nipples was also mentioned for Texture 3 in the Study with Five Textures. For example, "my gut reaction is motherhood, nipple of motherhood, sucking teat of a pig; sustained comfort, flesh. Reminds me of Missouri farm where there is livestock" (P5) and "udders and nipples" (P11). Two responses were related to previous analogies about alligators and crocodiles, or animals' skins for Texture 3 in the Study with Five Textures. For example: "A bit spiky; a back of a scaly animal, like an alligator or crocodile skin animal association" (P13). "It is like an alligator makes me want to touch but also telling me to stay away" (P17) and "looks like the skin of an animal" (P15).

Vitality/Lack of Vitality: "It is like a frozen moment of something that has been in motion before. The surface captures every point at a certain moment like a taxidermy creature. It can be like a natural plant to me more than an animal. It is like a plant that you have stored or dried; it looks sad; seeing little things which are in need of sun or [I] did not nurture them and now they are dead" (P10).

Aggression or Harm: "I am thinking of keeping things safe, baby blankets, safety and security" (P1) and its opposite: "I can see a tight angle, which reminds me of a weapon with sharp angles, but they are actually fabrics; the shape is not soft but the material is soft" (P14).

Color: Several participants mentioned color: "If it were colored it would make a difference – if it was green or yellow or red it would change it' (P6); "It is conceptual because it has no color and many parts. In a quilt you can see colorful parts. Here it is just a feeling of quilting" (P7); "It is happy because of the color and light coming in and texture" (P15); "It is like flower petals or scales, in neutral colors so it is pacifying. It is like a banner in church" (P16).

Round 2

- Participants use vision and touch
- Textile in still state

Many of the responses for Round 2 depended on the kinds of touch people used to explore the texture. Some participants did a quick series of touch explorations and then stopped to give their responses. Some people spread-eagled and touched the panels with both hands, or one hand and arm, trying to fully immerse themselves in the fabric. Others gave their responses during their exploratory touch and look. If Round 1 was spent trying to understand what the panel was, while Round 2 seemed to call forth many more processes of thinking. The processes of seeing and touching changed the nature of the responses, which reflect the duration of their description and the time of touching. Many responses show a transformation from one idea to another. I have included some examples below:

Memory/Analogy: "Feels like touching foliage or a tree, if I look at it, it is like an animal but softer than a crocodile because it is soft and pleasant. It is positive. There is not a disgusting texture; it is like naturally coarse and at the same time soft. The texture is relaxed because I like to keep touching it. It is soft like petting a dog or a cat. I am happy" (P7). Participant 11 said the texture in the panel "reminds me of cat tongues with little hooks all over them. It feels different than I thought it would feel, because of the plastic thread, but it is engaging because of this contrast. There is a micro macro thing happening where we could be way zoomed in looking at this super close or way zoomed out. Touching it if you get closer, looking at it is really different than looking at it far away; I feel uncertainty, touching it does not placate me; I was more placated by vision and more stimulated" (P11).

Vitality/Lack of Vitality: Participant 10 said (gingerly moving hand, touching points): "If I put my hand like this they touch different areas, up to down it feels smooth and relaxing; but bottom to top it feels like scales of a fish and it rough. It is like touching the surface of a live creature, but it is not responding, but it is also soothing; like petting a kitten; satisfied with petting it, but I am not satisfied with no response. It is still sad because it is not responding. It is dead but not that the panel is sad" (P10).

Feels to Skin: "It is resistant to being touched. Does not feel responsive, the texture is annoyed as if it is saying 'I'm just going to go back to what I am doing'. I'm less invited to touch" (P1). Also "it is soft if I move my hand from top to bottom, bottom up, it is not as soft. It can be soft but may not be depending on position, could be soft if it was moving down, but not if moving up. The texture toggles; happy with the soft position; cross with the negative and sharp position" (P6).

Aggression or Harm: "Like touching an animal you have never touched but seen like a rhino. It seems at rest; but I did not know if it will change on a dime; I am cautious and curious" (P17). "It feels like animal's hard skin [gently strokes with open palm + pinching some too and feeling with both hands]. It is scary. Why? Because it is something unknown and has a high degree of randomness." (P8).

Comparison: Many participants were surprised by how the textiles felt in comparison to their visual experiences in Round 1. For example, there were responses like: "Oh my gosh a lot more stiff that I thought it would be to touch! There is fishing line that can pull it up and down. I feel exceptions though like borders of the finish stitching reminds me of a kids' project and I like that the most. Visually not surprising my and now my eyes not working as much. The fishing line is now felt and I am surprised by the stiffness. I am more curious and have more questions now" (P3).

Color: There was no discussion of color in Round 2.

Round 3

- Participants use vision
- Textile in moving state

During this Round the textile panels were in motion using servo-motors, which made a noise. I have included a new category for the noise, which influenced the responses people gave. I think that mention of the noise was much more prevalent in FELT compared to the Study with Five Textures because FELT used many more motors, which were all turned on at once. In the previous study only 2–6 motors were on at any one time to move the textiles. Below are some of the responses from Round 3:

Analogy/Memory: "It has chaotic movement. It is not all moving at the same time. It is like being at a picnic and there are bugs like ants crawling all over the table, a trail of ants coming to get food and then you try to shoo them away and then chaos ensues. It is many of the same entity moving faster and slower not a flowing motion like a sea anemone. This has turmoil because the elements are moving independently, every now and then they get a wave" (P2). "It is a hive mind, colony of bees or ants without immediate purpose. There is some life but not an agenda or purpose for what is going on. I'm giving this a perplexed face because as it moves it is harder to understand. It does not jib with 'milk of mother' idea I had" (P5).

Vitality/Lack of Vitality: "It is hard for the eyes to see it is moving, breathing and stretching, it is purposeful and there is a release of energy waiting to happen, it is busy. I do not feel invited, I am not a voyeur and it is not inviting me to come closer but it is not annoyed. It is just doing its breathing. Looks like it is filling its purpose and it does not matter we are here, it's independent" (P1). "It is so cute, it communicates cute. It needs nothing. It looks like tiny birds, who need food and are shouting out to us to feed them. This motivates me to touch them. I want to go forward and see what they have to say and not to step back. I am excited because I want to touch them and feel happy because they are not dead anymore. I think they see me and are giving me responses and reactions" (P10).

Aggression or Harm: "It gives me goose-bumps, not eerie but excited-like. I have anxiety touching it because of the strings. Touching it will I wreck it?" (P3). "My gut reaction is negative; makes me think of creepy crawly things, so I am picking a 2 on the negative positive scale. I am more stimulated, not passive and so focused on seeing all four panels that I'm more engaged with trying to see everything at once and my aversion to creepy things!" (P16).

Comparison: "It is waves, or an inhaling and exhaling, like a respirator. The noise is definitely impacting my reaction. It is like snoring, a person snoring. This is more positive to me because there is an incorporation of moving and rhythm. I have more a sense of calm because there is some purpose other than all points going in one direction – the chaos makes more sense than it did before" (P4).

The Noise: "I can look at it and close my eyes and listen to it; sounds like a rain storm on metal; close my eyes and I can imagine a metal roof; reminds me of ants that have a purpose, but do not know what they are doing" (P17). "The sound is distracting" (P7). "I like the white noise, but in addition to the nipple-like things; could you get anything done with this panel next to you at work?" (P3).

Color: "It reminds me of insects, slippery, gloppy and slimy, it does not have a color does not say what it is and that is scary the neutrality of it" (P14), "like when you touch velvet you can see different colors and textures; excited and happy" (P15).

Round 4

- Participants use vision and touch
- Textile in moving state

Many Round 4 responses showed participants' attempts to validate memories, analogies and ideas from previous rounds; therefore, the comparison category had the most responses in this Round:

Analogy/Memory: Participant 4 (touching gingerly): "It is pulsating and that makes me think of a heartbeat and breathing. There is more of softness to it now. The stiff thread is there but it is not as bothersome" (P4). "Reminds me of the side of an animal, inhaling/exhaling. It reminds me of plants moving autonomously and growing. It is cool to feel it change under your hands, pressing in and then pushing off. I have a positive association when I touch it. There is a different level of connection, as compared to just watching more" (P11).

Vitality/Lack of Vitality: "I don't think it was meant to be an interface. I expected it to be but it is not there. I'm reacting to it. I do not want to impede its movement. It is like a diaphragm where people are breathing. I could feel like it is enlarged in scale from something at the level of skin. As I walked away the texture has the quality of ostrich skin. When you touch the middle, it feels like breathing. If I pull one of these it feels like you can infect it, you feel the resistance. It sounds like they are arguing and has the quality of a beehive and honeycomb. It has an organic feel. There is a contrast of the hardness of the grid, which are an a priori and softness and curvilinear quality of the tongues. As long as you do not think of them as severed tongues! Unfortunate metaphors!" (P17).

Feels to Skin: "I am drawn to parts working as a team, as a system makes it seem more complex, does not feel like I am supposed to touch it. It is not granting permission to touch it, when I do touch it I feel like I am interrupting it. Tickling and it is not relating to what I'm doing" (P1).

Aggression or Harm: "These are not just going up and down, these are breathing. I do not want to pet them, I want to lay a hand on them so that the fabric does the soothing now rather than me petting and soothing the fabric. I have a relaxing feeling when I put my hand on it. I would feel different if it moved faster or slower. It is relaxed not stimulated; why is it relaxed? It is like a cat's paw on you. It reminds me of mom who tries to relax you; not sexual; do not see that; not parts of the body; reminds me of birds' beaks" (P10). "This is scary. I cannot stand the movement. I hate it. I feel like I am in a position where I cannot control it. I worry about this. I am worried about it hurting me. Maybe if I sit on it or lay down on it I am worried that it will be hurt, but I am more worried about me. It's like a sea-water creature because of its soft movement and color. This is irritating because of the movement and rough texture of string and the weakness of that. It is less negative when I can touch and I can be sure it does not hurt me. When I could only see it, I was not sure. Now it is less ambiguous. I am sad because it is about pity again. It is weak and this makes me unhappy" (P14).

Comparison: (*P2 gingerly touching*) "Panel one feels like there should be more tension. I can see where cords are pulling, but some are not pulling. It is not like swatting the bugs off the table because it has a lot of resistance and as things move I can feel the potential to move but some are stuck. Others you can see moving but there is not as much tension. What I see and feel is different; I am not disrupting the movement. I am curious and it reminds me of an episode of Dr. Who" (P2). "I am disappointed as a different force of my hand prevents mechanism from moving. This answers my question. This is what I was curious about. I am not learning that much more after seeing it. The visual has more information and the tactile is preventing me from obtaining more information. It does not feel like what I thought it would feel like. I thought it was more inviting like nipples, tactile" (P3). "It is alien and foreign in a weird way. The movement gives it life in itself, but when I touch it, it stops. I am not interacting with it and I feel like I can interact with it in a different way than anticipated. O.K., I am not sure how to interact with it. I wanted to feel its tips versus in between because I wanted to feel cause and effect. I'm still not comprehending what it is doing. Like do we live in the same world? – Yes, when I felt it pulling between the nubs. My vision gives a different expectation than my haptic. The haptic changed it trying to connect the change with my touch" (P5). "I cannot feel as much as I can see. Now I am holding my hand still to feel movement but they stop. I try to search by being still but they stop when my hand is held over them. This is exactly like someone sleeping and breathing and I can put my hand to feel breath and body movement; positive because it feels active and relaxed – the breathing feeling; when you touch someone you love it feels relaxed" (P7). "I think it is what I expected, it is not surprising because I had already felt it statically. When touching it there is a level of anticipation and I wish it did a little more. If we knew it was alive it would be really scary, but since I know it is fabric it is O.K. Why is it a 4 for stimulated? This choice is related to physical touch. Now having that memory is actually switching roles. In Round 2 I stimulated it, now it is stimulating me." (P12). On the other hand, P16 had responses that transformed or rather toggled between positive and negative during the time of interaction. For example: "It is weird! It is kind of like touching a living thing but I know it is not. It is still subtle and if I hang out it feels like it is breathing. This is more negative to me because 'it is not supposed to do that!' This is opposite of my initial reaction in Round 1. I did not know what to expect. The motion seems regular makes me thing of breathing or life like function; on the one hand cool on the other hand I associate it with creepy, crawly things" (P16) [standing up, using back of hand on noses, bending to lower panel, feeling with both hands].

The Noise: Not one participant mentioned the noise in Round 4.

Color: "The color is also calming if it were black maybe not so; the fabric is not transparent so it adds to the calmness and protected feeling" (P9). "It is like a sea-water creature because of its soft movement and color" (P14).

Free-association results: General discussion

All but one of the 17 participants in the FELT study had general comments to offer at the end of the four Rounds. Some of the most salient are included below:

Concerning the environment of the study, P3 raised the issue of the environment in which the FELT study was taking place. She stated: "The environment is antiseptic; feels like a design crit; clean but welcoming environment; feeling like a hospital; ethos of cleanliness; curious how these response would have been in different context." P12 also had his expectations framed by the location of the FELT study, and stated: "We are in an iconic building on campus and so I anticipated something different from walking in the front door."

Some participants were not sure what was and was not part of the FELT study. Some found the light shining through the felt panels, which made dark shadows on the panels, distracting; for example, P13 stated: "The X shadows at the back were a distraction, interrupts the way we are looking at it." In addition, P2 stated: "The light coming through pulls one's eyes to the darker areas until it starts moving; then one starts to notice the lighter areas."

Also, in terms of the noises participants heard, one remarked: "The panels were not moving as much as it sounded like they were moving." And: "It is difficult to classify in terms of sound and difficult to classify in general because of the noise. It is less obtrusive" (P2).

The narrowness of the face emoticons was another large topic for comment not just in the general comments section but also throughout the four study rounds. 10/17 participants (P4, P5, P7, P8, P9, P11, P12, P13, P15, P17) drew in their own faces, wrote in additional emotions or mentioned that the faces did not offer enough variety in emotion to be adequate to describe what they thought was being communicated by the texture.

Some mentioned that if this panel were a breathing wall, that would be scary. This was somewhat a confusing statement made by participants because the panel was quite large.

Color emerged again as an important topic in the general comments section. Six out of seventeen participants had something to say about color at the end of the study: "It's not colored" (P2); "Color changes how you think about this or a print would change my reaction" (P4); "I like that there is no color and it is pure white – the sound works for it, adds to the liveliness of it" (P10); "I thought the change was going to be color, color is important and affects emotion and situation" (P13); "If the material could be smart then movement and color could change according to touch and mark the kind of touch, i.e. aggressive touch versus soft touch" (P15).

Circumplex analysis

The most useful analytical tool was James Russell's two-dimensional Circumplex Model of Affect. James Russell is a psychologist and professor of psychology at Boston University and designed a two-dimensional model of emotional affect in which people are asked to place words along an x-axis where positive is happy (on the far right of the axis) and negative is sad (on the far left of the x-axis). On the y-axis the highest point is excited or pumped. The lowest point on the y-axis is calm (Russell, 1980). Figure 4.6(b) shows words Russell mapped to a circumplex grid as an example. Note the position of words that express emotion on the grid. Happy excited words, like "astonished" and "delighted," are in the upper right quadrant. Calm and sad words, like "depressed" and "gloomy," are in the lower left quadrant. To create the circumplex plot for this study I took the numbers circled in Questions 2 and 3 on my survey that provided x-coordinates and y-coordinates for each participant. I then averaged the x-coordinates and the y-coordinates for each round, to make the circumplex plots in Figure 4.6(c).

The Circumplex Model of Affect in Figure 4.6(c) shows results that are consistent with the free-association analysis. Participants were very excited in Round 1; however, when they touched the panels in Round 2 they were disappointed, because the soft and pliable visual appearance of the textile panels was not as soft and as pliable to their touch. Participants were further excited when the texture in the panels started to move or show motility in Round 3; however, in Round 4 when participants were permitted to touch the panels in full motion, most but not all participants reported a happy, excited state as the emotion communicated back from the textile.

In terms of standard deviation, the highest negative/positive, or x-axis, data deviation was in Round 2, when participants could touch the textile texture. For the

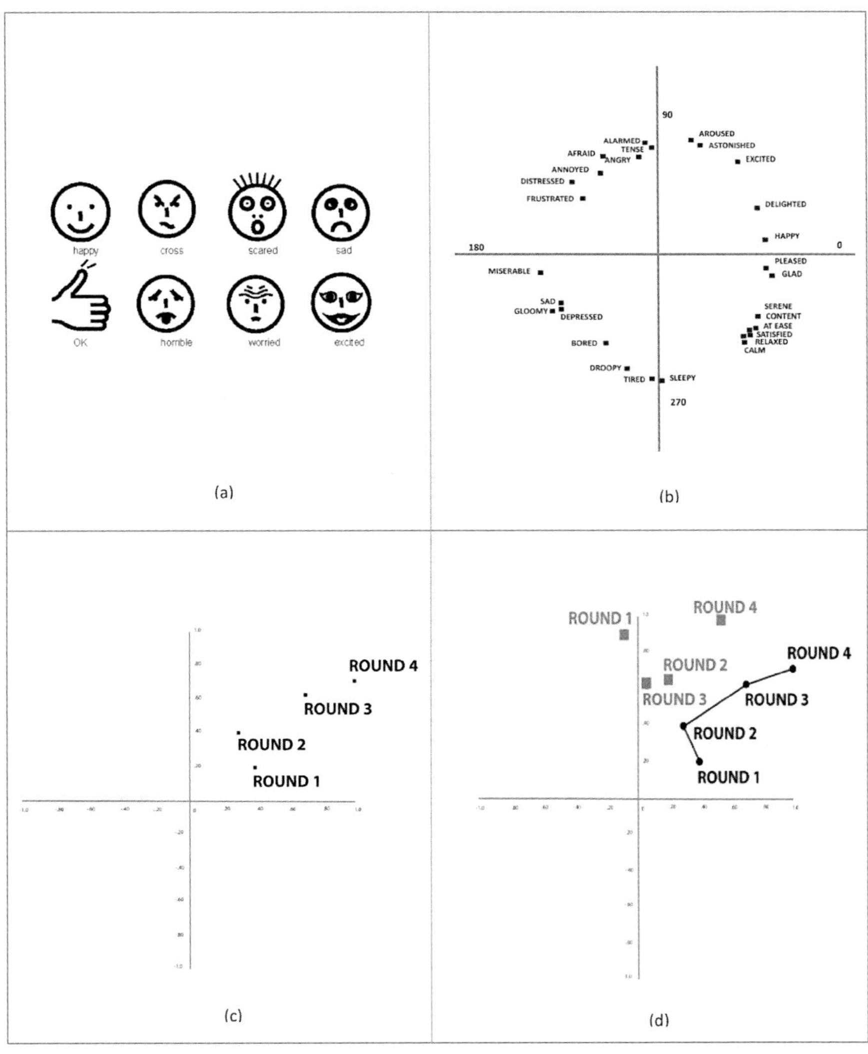

FIGURE 4.6 (a) Face Word graphics (The Makaton Charity: accessed 2-12-17); (b) Circumplex Model of Emotional Affect for Words, redrawn from Russell's Circumplex (James A. Russell, 1980: 1167); (c) Circumplex model of affect for the FELT panel with the averages for all four rounds plotted; (d) Circumplex model of affect Rounds 1–4 for the FELT panel (circle marks). Plots for the original 9' x 9' Texture 3 (square marks).

calm/excited, or y-axis, the highest deviation was in Round 3 when participants could see the textile panels moving but not touch the panels.

Figure 4.6(d) compares the plot averages for Texture 3 (square marks), which was a 23cm x 23cm sample. Texture 3 was the exact texture pattern used to make the large textile panel FELT. The results of the plot averages for FELT are in black in Figure 4.6(d). The FELT panel received more positive ratings than those for Texture 3 and the FELT panel received calmer ratings than those for Texture 3.

Face Word Graphic analysis

The Face Word Graphic analysis for all four rounds for FELT is above in Figure 4.7. All graphs are at the same scale and are based on word counts from the responses given to Question 4. As you can see in Figure 4.7 when looking at all the graphs together across all four rounds, "O.K.", "excited" and "happy" are words that stand out consistently. "O.K." starts off as the primary reading in Rounds 1 and 2, but "excited" and "happy" emerge in almost equal numbers to "O.K." in Round 2, and take over as equal in Round 3, with "excited" being the highest counted word in Round 4. This response is understandable, as it is the first time the textile motors were turned on. "Excited" in Round 4 never becomes as strong as "O.K." in Round 1. In addition to "O.K." fading from Round 1 to 4, the emergence of "worried" and "curiosity" and "curious" exist at the beginning in Rounds 1 and 2 but gradually fade in Round 3 and almost entirely gone in Round 4. This was to be expected, as participants became more familiar with the textile panel. In Round 2 "cross" appears as a second level of counts after "O.K.," "Happy," and "Excited". This is the only instance of the word "cross" rising to this secondary level in the four rounds. One speculation on the appearance of the word "cross" is that people were surprised by how rough the points and monofilament plastic strings felt when touched compared to the soft appearance. Fourteen out of seventeen participants indicated surprise, annoyance, or some negativity in their free-association responses in Round 2.

In addition to the observations mentioned in the above paragraph, there are fewer words generated in Round 4, 14 words as compared with Round 1 that has 17 different words. The density of words trails off as you look from left to right in Figure 4.7. This decreasing density seen in the word graph is the result of fewer counts for the smaller words in Round 3, and a coalescing of counts for fewer words.

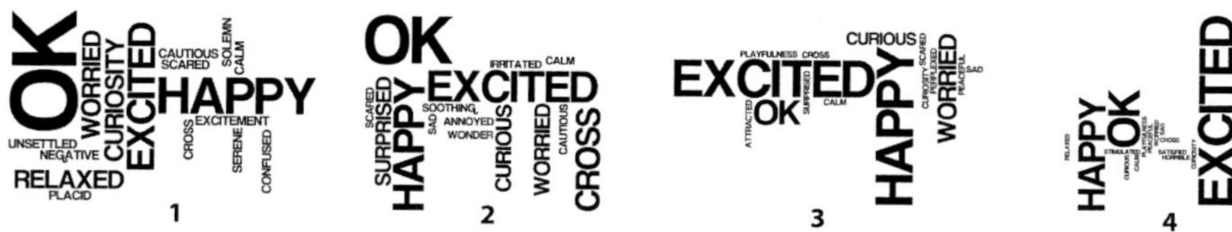

FIGURE 4.7 Face Word graph for the FELT panel in Rounds 1–4. Word graph generated using Feinberg's Wordle (2008).

Thus, the scale of all the words in Rounds 1 and 2 is closer together than the scale of the words appearing in Round 4, for example. In Rounds 1 and 2 the word graph is made up of a blend of large-, medium-, and small-scale words. In Round 4 there are primarily large-scale words juxtaposed with tiny-scale words with no intermediate scaled words.

Discussion of results to the five hypotheses for the FELT wall panel

The scale/context hypothesis and the four study hypotheses are summarized in Table 4.2. Each of these hypotheses were best answered by different methods. For example, the scale and context hypothesis was best answered by the free-association responses. Participants did address the scale and context of the textile panel, either in words or body movement, as I have mentioned in the section "Comments on FELT as a wall panel." The scale and context hypothesis is true, as expected.

TABLE 4.2 Summary of the results to the five hypotheses

Hypothesis Number	*Hypothesis Description*	*Result*
SCALE & CONTEXT HYPOTHESIS	*It was expected that participant responses would change if the textile was designed as a large architectural panel or space divider rather than small textile sample.*	True
HYPOTHESIS 1 ROUND 1	*It was expected that using vision alone, people would consistently associate specific emotional states with specific characteristics of the textures of textiles in a state of stillness. Crisp, curvilinear shapes associated with positive, excited, and happy feelings; smooth curvilinear shapes associated with positive and calm feelings; triangulated shapes associated with negative and angry feelings; smooth triangulated shapes and superimposed systems or a poorly defined combination associated with negative, depressed, and calm feelings.*	Not True
HYPOTHESIS 2 ROUND 2	*It was expected that when people use vision and the haptic senses together the emotional associations would change (as seen in Study 3). It was expected that when people could see and touch a still texture, a negative emotional association using vision alone would change when using both vision and the haptic senses to a positive emotional association.*	True
HYPOTHESIS 3 ROUND 3	*It was expected that when the textures were in a state of motion this characteristic would raise or lower the participants' rating of what was communicated on a Circumplex grid based on what was associated with that texture motion.*	True
HYPOTHESIS 4 ROUND 4	*It was expected that the act of touching the moving textures would again change the ratings and what the textiles communicated.*	True

The Circumplex Model of Affect most easily frames the remaining four hypotheses. However, the free association adds a level of explanation as to why people selected the choices they did for Questions 2 and 3, which provide the x, and y points for the model.

Hypothesis 1 is based on a belief that all humans are in some way hardwired, or can understand certain shapes and textures in a very basic way through emotion. The results with FELT did not prove this to be true. FELT designed as a triangulated shape did not plot as negative and excited, or as angry. On the contrary, it plotted as positive with modest excitement or happy in the Circumplex Model of Affect, and the Face Word graph. In addition, this was supported in the free-association question where there were responses that related to body parts like nipples and udders, skins of animals, but no expressions of things that indicated anger or scariness.

Hypothesis 2 is based on the belief that once a person touches something, that thing becomes known and thus is rated more positively. In addition, this hypothesis is based on the belief that, if something was rated negatively using only vision, a negative visual rating could be overturned and rated positively using touch. Once FELT was touched, it did change its rating; however, the change was not always positive. In fact, in Round 2 the positive rating on the circumplex model for the FELT was less. According to the free-association question, this can be explained by the roughness perceived in the edges of the felt and the monofilament thread used.

Hypothesis 3 was proven true. Indeed, positive/negative and stimulated/calm responses were raised or lowered when the textile changed shape or moved. The FELT study did affirm that when something in an environment changes, human reaction will typically, but not always, change as well. The FELT study did affirm that motion or shape change did increase the excitement rating of the FELT, as shown in the experiments done by Akshita et al. (2015).

Hypothesis 4 is true. This hypothesis is relevant for studies where participants interacted with live textile textures that could be touched and textiles, and could move. Yes, the ratings for positive/negative and stimulated/calm changed in every instance in the FELT study.

Contributions to this work

In closing, there are a few points of generalizable knowledge that can be demonstrated in the FELT study. I have made a list of these points below.

1. Using vision, or vision and touch, the emotion(s) communicated to people change(s) during the process of exchange.
2. Emotions communicated through vision by a textile are different from those communicated using vision and touch.
3. Introducing motion or motility to a textile expression increases the stimulation and excitement of the emotion communicated by that textile. (The one exception to this statement is seen in Round 3 of the FELT study).

4. Analogy and memory are primary methods people use to understand what emotion is communicated by a textile.
5. The scale of the textile changed what emotion(s) were communicated from the textile, because people must change their bodies to engage with the larger scale.

Much communication that we take from expression is context-based and is perhaps inference rather than direct communication. There is much more work to be done if we are to fully understand the relationship between aesthetic expression and communication. In the end, I have shown through my experiment that emotion communicated from computational objects is woven between that object or space and an individual body. In my experiment with FELT, we have seen each individual form his/her own analogy or memory map searching for and connecting experience to something else he/she has learned or experienced before about that material and emotion. In my experiment, I have witnessed people in the moment of seeing, or seeing and touching, making new analogies and memories to keep with them about the material and emotion. There is more work to be done, too, in the field of neuroscience to further our understanding of how these analogy maps are created, their location in the brain, and how, whether, and to what extent specific aspects of artistic expression, such as texture and certain kinds of experiences with textures, construct similar emotional maps in the brains of most people.

I would like to thank my four graduate Research Assistants in SOFTLAB@PSU, at Penn State University. They are Niloufar Kioumarsi, Arman Esfahani, Niloofar Nikookar, and Nasim Motalebi who with great patience and care helped bring the FELT wall panel to fruition.

References

About Makaton. (n.d.). Available at https://www.makaton.org/aboutMakaton/. Retrieved December 2, 2017.

Akshita, Alagarai, Sampath, H., Indurkhya, B., Lee, E., & Bae, Y. (2015). 'Towards multimodal affective feedback: Interaction between visual and haptic modalities', in *Proceedings of the 33rd Annual ACM Conference on Human Factors in Computing Systems* (pp. 2043–2052). New York, NY: ACM. Available at https://doi.org/10.1145/2702123.2702288

Darwin, C. (2009a). *The Origin of Species: 150th Anniversary Edition* (Rep Anv edition). New York: Bantam Dell.

Darwin, C. (2009b). *The Expression of the Emotions in Man and Animals*. 2nd Edition. London: Penguin Books Ltd.

Davis, F. (2015). 'The textility of emotion: A study relating computational textile textural expression to emotion', in *Proceedings of the 2015 ACM SIGCHI Conference on Creativity and Cognition* (pp. 23–32). New York, NY: ACM. Available at: https://doi.org/10.1145/2757226.2757231

Davis, F. (2017). 'Softbuilt: computational textiles and augmenting space through emotion' (PhD). Cambridge, MA: MIT.

Davis, F., Cherry, E., Roseway, A., & Czerwinski, M. (2012). *Actuating Mood with the Textile Mirror: An Architectural Wall Prototype*. Unpublished Paper.

Frijda, N. H. (1982). 'The meanings of emotional expression', in Mary Ritchie (Ed.), *Nonverbal Communication Today: Current Research*, Berlin: Mouton, 1982, pp. xiv, 319 (103–119).

Frijda, N. H. (1986). *Studies in Emotion and Social Interaction. The Emotions*. New York: Cambridge University Press; Paris: Editions de la Maison des Sciences de l'Homme.

Gibson, J. (1966). *The Senses Considered as Perceptual Systems*. Oxford: Houghton Mifflin.

Gibson, J. (1983). *The Senses Considered as Perceptual Systems* (1st ed.). Santa Barbara, CA: Praeger.

Izard, Carroll E. (1971). *The Face of Emotion*. New York: Appleton-Century-Crofts.

Kim, S., Kim, E. Y., Jeong, K., & Kim, J. (2006). 'Emotion-based textile indexing using colors, texture and patterns', in *Proceedings of the Second International Conference on Advances in Visual Computing – Volume Part II* (pp. 9–18). Berlin, Heidelberg: Springer-Verlag. Available at: https://doi.org/10.1007/11919629_2

Pallasmaa, J. (2013). *The Eyes of the Skin: Architecture and the Senses* (3rd Edition). New York: John Wiley & Sons.

Panksepp, J. (1998). *Affective Neuroscience: The Foundations of Human and Animal Emotions*. Oxford: Oxford University Press.

Russell, J. A. (1980). 'A circumplex model of affect'. *Journal of Personality and Social Psychology*, *39*(6), 1161–78. Available at: https://doi.org/http://dx.doi.org.libproxy.mit.edu/10.1037/h0077714

Tomkins, S. S., & Karon, B. P. (1992). *Affect, Imagery, Consciousness: Cognition: Duplication and Transformation of Information* (Vol. 1). Berlin: Springer.

Yu, B., Bongers, N., van Asseldonk, A., Hu, J., Funk, M., & Feijs, L. (2016). 'LivingSurface: Biofeedback through shape-changing display' in *Proceedings of the TEI '16: Tenth International Conference on Tangible, Embedded, and Embodied Interaction* (pp. 168–175). New York, NY, USA: ACM. Available at: https://doi.org/10.1145/2839462.2839469

5

RESPONSIVE-SURFACE DESIGN INFORMED BY IMMERSIVE DATA VISUALIZATION

Matthew Wagner

Introduction

Our responsive-surface research begins with the question of whether or not interior spaces can contextually and autonomously respond to the occupants. Artificial intelligence (AI) is changing the way many industries function and perform, from information gathering to self-driving cars. Algorithmic approaches to informed and autonomous decision making are becoming the new normal, and what we should expect for the future (Stanford University, 2016). We want to understand how these principles can lead to better scenarios in buildings and spatial typologies. While AI does not have much of a presence in architecture and interior design, the fundamental ideas of smart building systems are perhaps the building industry's equivalent. Mainstream interests in energy efficiency, renewable energy, and environmental design have been brought to the forefront of architecture. As a result, building control systems leverage the use of environmental data, informing new architectural approaches and outcomes. By responding to environmental factors, this form of autonomous architecture has established a new baseline for energy performance (International Energy Agency, 2011).

The aim of our work is not to focus on how to further optimize buildings for energy performance, but how to optimize buildings for occupant performance. We take a creative-design approach to contextualizing interior elements that can become autonomous systems. By responding to their immediate interior environment, self-regulating surfaces have the ability to increase occupant performance and overall wellbeing (The WELL Building Standard v1, 2015). With this framework in mind, our research began with responsive surfaces designed to mitigate workplace distractions. As office cultures trend toward collaborative working environments with mobile workstations, office space designs are becoming increasingly open. There is a growing need to mitigate distractions such as solar glare and interrupting noise. Our research demonstrates efforts to generate examples of potential solutions to these distractions through the use of responsive design elements.

Naturally for us, we are just as much problem-makers as we are problem-solvers. Our means to conceptualize autonomous methods to optimize occupant performance has reinformed our overall design process. As a parallel research effort, we have reasoned with the idea that a data-driven design process will result in a more informed, and overall more effective, approach to realizing prototypes.

Our early prototypes used computational design to assist in visualizing our digital assumptions of what distractions might occur, and how to represent our response through design. With the emergence of well-developed virtual reality and augmented-reality tools, we are taking our visualization techniques from parametric assumptions to mixed-reality realizations. This method streamlines the prototyping process by evaluating the effectiveness of a digital prototype through multisensory experiences and realtime data visualization. By evaluating the specific design parameters needed to visualize responsive data on changing surfaces, a more informed prototype design can be digitally optimized and approved for empirical testing. These research findings describe the process we have designed to yield efficient and more accurate results. Physical prototypes of both design projects have been manufactured, and are currently being tested and refined further.

Noise mitigation: AuralSurface prototype

AuralSurface (Figure 5.1) is inspired by the need to control ambient noise created from everyday life in the office, while also serving as an adjustable separator that maintains a sense of open space. For workplace performance and comfort, the responsive interior surface optimizes interior environments by adapting to the changing reverberation rhythms of voices and footsteps. AuralSurface can also be parametrically calibrated to a desired acoustic setting, which would allow for increasing or decreasing acoustic damping depending on the needs of the interior space and its occupants.

The WELL Building Institute writes in The WELL Building Standard v.1: "Built environments can harbor sounds that are distracting and disruptive to work or relaxation. Employee surveys show that acoustic problems are a leading source of dissatisfaction within the environmental conditions of an office" (The WELL Building Standard, 2015, p. 119). There is a growing need to mitigate distracting and interrupting noise. Studies show that exposure to noise generated within the building can lead to reduced concentration and mental-arithmetic performance, and increased distraction due to reduced speech privacy (The WELL Building Standard, 2015, p. 124).

AuralSurface seeks to reduce fatigue and stress in the workplace by controlling ambient-noise disturbance. Employee fatigue affects wellbeing, productivity, and the propensity to commit errors; in addition, one study shows that a three-hour exposure to low-intensity office noise induces a small increase in adrenaline level (Jahncke 2012). AuralSurface's design allows it to autonomously deploy an acoustic material at specific locations when the perceived decibel levels are higher than normal. In addition to a physical response, the acoustic material may be seen as a visual cue once deployed. Those holding conversations may recognize this as a subtle sign to speak more softly or to take their conversation to another area. AuralSurface, a panelized surface, is otherwise a seemingly typical modular system.

Daylight mitigation: FlowerWall prototype

FlowerWall (Figure 5.1) is a responsive surface that optimizes interior environments by adapting to changing outdoor environments. While exploring the physical space that exists between building and nature, the design for this responsive surface was informed by the natural response of phototropic flowers.

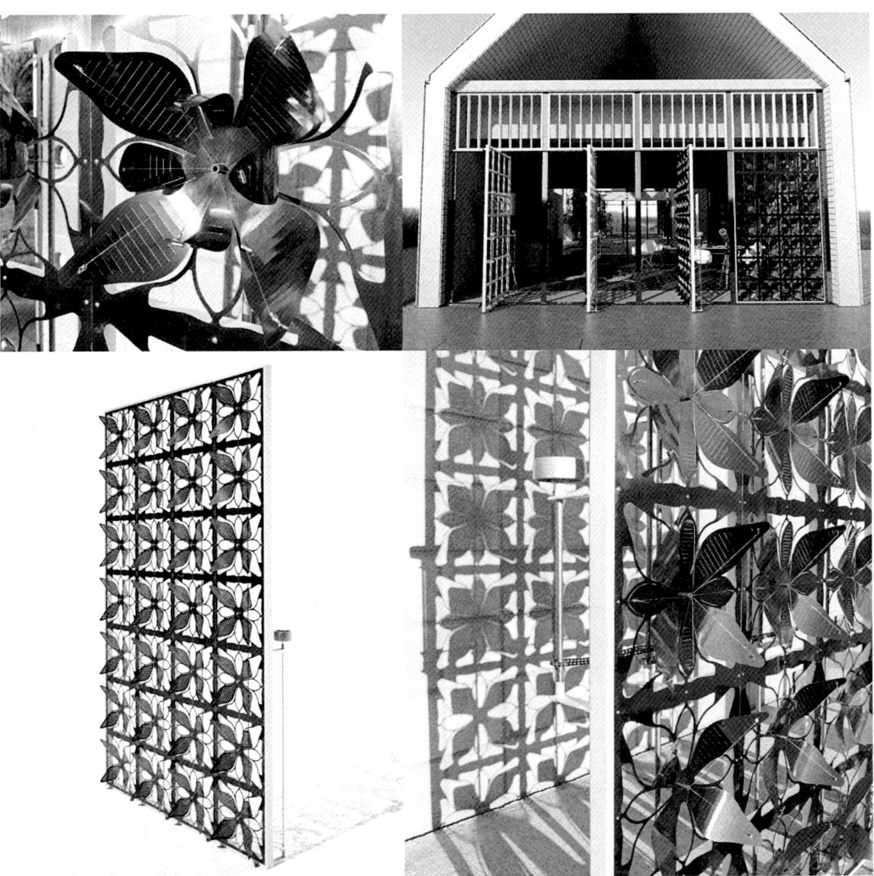

FIGURE 5.1 AuralSurface: design visualization (top). FlowerWall: three mechanical variations (bottom). Source: (Wagner 2018).

FlowerWall's array responds autonomously to both outdoor weather conditions, and interior lighting levels. For interior performance and comfort, the responsive surface optimizes interior lighting levels by constant actuation through performative weather data and realtime lighting metrics.

In addition to its originally intended use of strategic solar-shading to mitigate glare, FlowerWall arrays can be arranged to control view and privacy. To this effect, subsequent observations in our own research encourage the use of programmed arrays for interactive response to human proximity. Through a one-to-one scale interface of human and system interaction, FlowerWall has the ability to be manually tuned through a digital user interface.

As a result of our observations and testing, the FlowerWall has been developed into three distinct mechanical-design variations. The first variation is a manually tuned dynamic-shading module, referred to as the "array variation," whereby all the 28 flowers on the module respond together. The second variation is a digitally tuned dynamic-shading module, referred to as the "column variation," where the four vertical columns, each comprising seven flowers, respond individually. The third variation is a digitally tuned proximity and privacy module, referred to as the "single variation," whereby each flower responds individually.

Design methodology

Parametric analysis

Parametric software was used in the early design stages to inform decisions based on assumptions for both conceptual ideas and material tolerances. For FlowerWall, we relied on this method of visualization to understand the curl ratio of spring steel (Figure 5.2), a material that can maintain its original form without deformation. For AuralSurface, we simulated wavelengths that represented sound waves to visualize how the surface would respond. With the visual outcome being much of an assumption, we recognized the importance of moving forward with the new process of using data visualization in immersive environments.

Material characteristics

Through performance and evaluation, material characteristics shaped each iteration by revealing tolerances and limitations. As a result, design criteria had to evolve with each prototype. The FlowerWall design adapted to a unique mechanical movement by curling an array of flowers, CNC laser cut from spring steel (Figure 5.2).

Spring steel was ultimately chosen for its shape memory. Material testing revealed that stainless steel would crease, and polystyrene as well as other acrylics would fail. Since the mechanism to curl the flowers was fairly intricate, a second mechanism to uncurl the flowers was not desirable. With spring steel, when the tension on the flowers is eased, they uncurl without mechanical assistance.

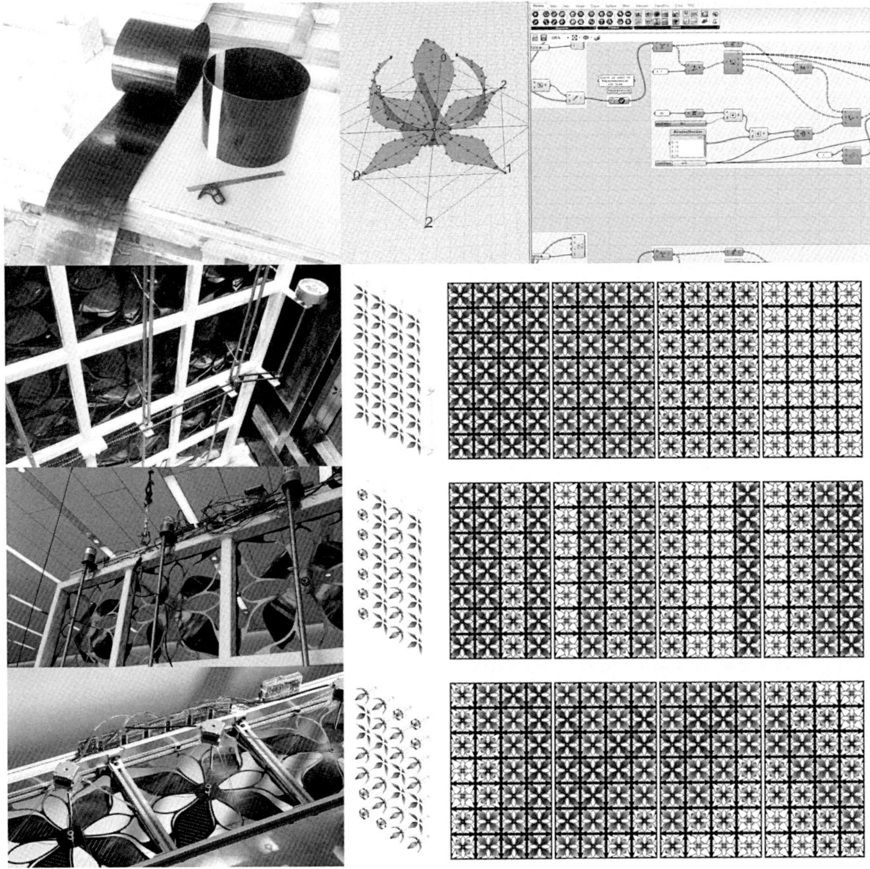

FIGURE 5.2 FlowerWall: parametric analysis (top), built prototype (bottom). Source: (Wagner 2018).

Spring steel has good wear resistance due to its high carbon content, and is commonly used to make parts that are repeatedly stressed.

Immersive data visualization

Reinforming the design process

The emergence of our parallel research, the use of immersive data visualization along with the development of a responsive surface, gained traction through the idea that we would end up with a more informed design to take into the prototyping phase. Early design iterations were hit-or-miss, with built prototypes, particularly with FlowerWall. Our assumptions about the effectiveness of the surface design, as well as the materials, mechanisms, and sensors used, were not evaluated until we had a completed prototype. While each new prototype was fully functional and served a purpose as another proof of concept iteration, our process was not efficient and lacked preevaluation assessment.

The use of immersive environments will be critical to visualize the effectiveness of AuralSurface as a responsive surface. While the process is still work-in-progress, the method provides promise for the future of AuralSurface's development. By involving people in realtime behavior, we are able to see our digital model respond to their actions (Figure 5.3).

Realtime data visualization + immersive environments

We are implementing an augmented-reality design tool for realtime immersive data visualization experiences within existing spaces. Through the immersive environment, we are able to view a digital prototype in a space at full scale. The data visualized and collected contribute to the evaluation of our design, which we see as a step toward refinement with our digital prototype that did not previously exist. This approach should streamline the prototyping process by evaluating the effectiveness of a digital prototype through multisensory experiences, leading us to a more informed prototype design.

Responsive sensors, programmed within the digital model, can respond to both human proximity and any sound generated from human interactions. The 16:9 aspect ratio of our headset can be somewhat limiting, but we expect to visualize our results without issue. The immersive environment provides a better understanding of how the responsive surface responds to multisensory input (proximity and sound), as well as how it performs in various spaces.

Multisensory data channels

Through immersive data visualization, we are able to evaluate the effectiveness of several design parameters through multisensory environmental channels prior to prototyping. For AuralSurface, these parameters include material effectiveness, acoustic properties, surface module design and form optimization, structural framework design, mechanical response time, and scale. Each of these parameters is a factor that influences the outcome of the next one.

One of our design options is evaluating the acoustic absorption impact of felt. The felt sheet will deploy by unrolling when digital sensors respond to realtime people and voices in the space and trigger environmental acoustic decibel sensors. The responsive function of the modular surface will pinpoint the origin point of sound through proximity sensors, and each adjacent panel will have a gradient association: the loudest location will have fully deployed panels, with each adjacent panel slightly less deployed, etc.

These multisensory data channels are both viewed and heard through the augmented-reality headset. By adding a graphic layer of data visualization seen through the augmented-reality headset, we are able not only to hear acoustic differences, but also to verify the material effectiveness visually with acoustic data (Figure 5.3).

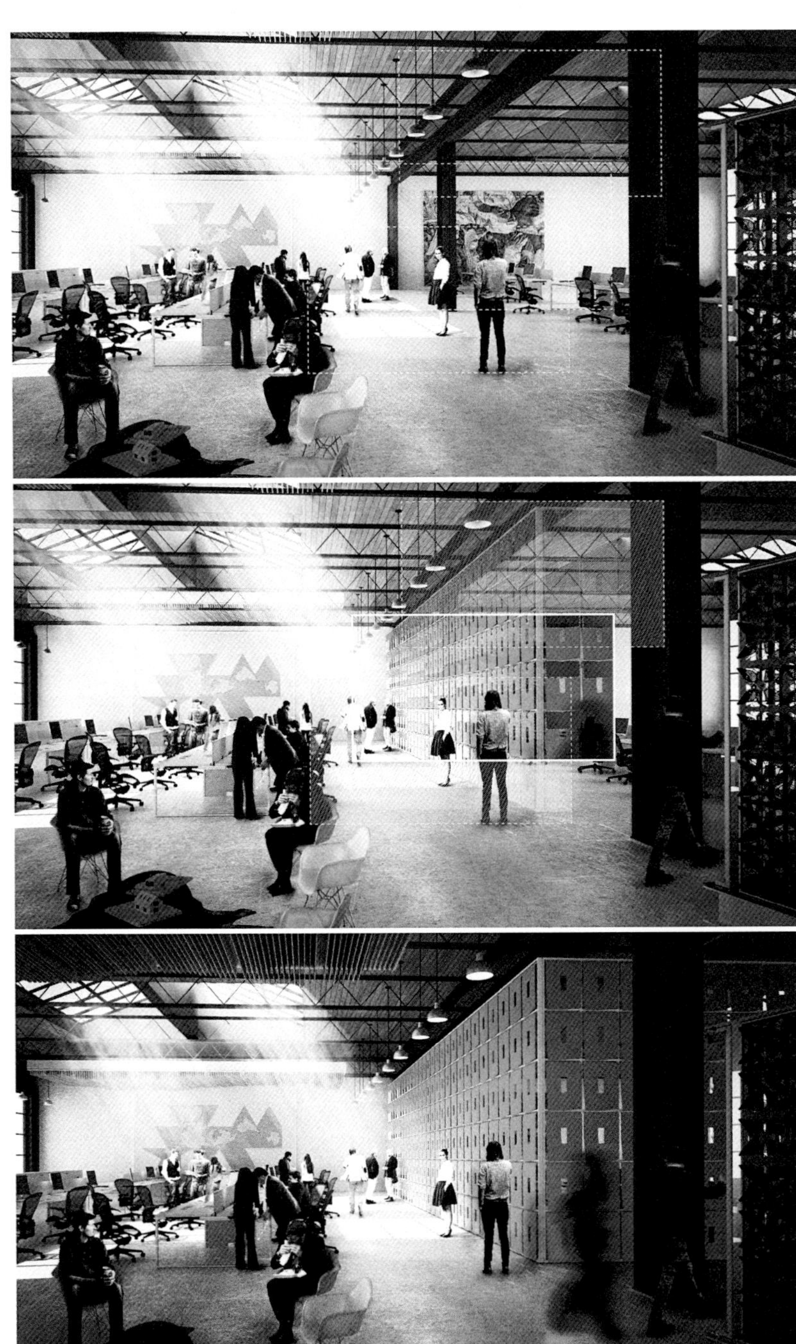

FIGURE 5.3 AuralSurface: sequential representation of realtime data visualization in an immersive environment // existing space (top) // view through alternative reality headset (middle) // implemented responsive surface (bottom). Source: (Wagner 2018).

For material effectiveness, we have the ability to test multiple thicknesses of the felt. We can virtually evaluate 1/8" felt to visualize and experience its effectiveness, and then we can immediately swap the virtual material data asset to evaluate 1/4" felt.

The study of the responsive surface through an augmented-reality headset is only valid for our research when it is calibrated and synchronized with realtime environmental sensors in the space being evaluated.

Acknowledgments

The author would like to thank Joe Wheeler, Robert Dunay, Chip Clark, Denis Gracanin, and Daniel Senning for their contributions to the development of FlowerWall, as well as Ivica Ico Bukvic and Dane Webster for their contributions to the development of AuralSurface

References

International Energy Agency (2011). 'Technology roadmap: energy-efficient buildings: heating and cooling equipment'. Available at: https://webstore.iea.org/technology-roadmap-energy-efficient-buildings-heating-and-cooling-equipment.

International WELL Building Standard (2015). *The WELL Building Standard v1*. Available at: https://www.wellcertified.com/en/resources/well-building-standard-1.

Jahncke, H. (2012). *Cognitive Performance and Restoration in Open-Plan Office Noise* (doctoral thesis). Lulea University of Technology. p. 9–10. Available at: https://www.diva-portal.org/smash/get/diva2:991382/FULLTEXT01.pdf.

Stanford University (2016). 'One hundred year study on artificial intelligence (AI100)'. Available at: https://www.ai100.stanford.edu. Accessed 20 Feb 2017.

6

DATA AND COMFORT ASSESSMENT

Examining the suitability of physiological sensors for assessing comfort in an everyday environment

Trevor Keeling, Etienne Roesch and Derek Clements-Croome

Introduction

This research measures and correlates certain spatial qualities and certain physiological recordings of the users of a space. Participants' heart rates and skin conductance are measured while they work in their natural office environment. This is combined with measurement of background light levels, temperature, CO_2 and sound levels. The analysis of these is split into two parts. The first suggests there are key differences between the senses: for component factors that are more energy-based (i.e. thermal comfort), sensors are more useful; while for component factors that are more information-processing-based (i.e. sound), sensors are less useful. The second analysis demonstrates that heart rate can be used to monitor the effect of sound levels on some but not all people. The technique could be used to monitor the environment in realtime and reveal differences in people's sensitivity to noise. However, these analyses suggest that recordings from multiple sensors are needed to capture the complexity of user experience. Since this work, the BCO Report on the use of wearables in the workplace (Clements-Croome, 2018; Taub & Clements-Croome, 2016) concludes that many kinds of physiological measures can be used to increase awareness of how environmental settings affect the body and mind, health and wellbeing.

A simple way to study some of the ambient conditions is by measuring lux, dBA and air temperature (ISO 28802, 2012), which provide a one-dimensional account of four environmental variables. This study explores how these, along with a number of other measures, can be used in combination with wearable sensors, to understand user experience. These one-dimensional measures of the physical environment are often used to predict one-dimensional scales of acceptable human experience (i.e. from discomfort to comfort). In design practice, background levels of the physical environment are used to specify health limits above and below which it is not safe or feasible to work (ASHRAE, 2010; Hygge, 2007; SLL, 2012). Comfort is the state of the environment without environmental stressors. The presence of stressors, i.e. being outside the comfort zone, leads to arousal. This has been observed in a number of experiments: the colour temperature of light has been shown to both the positive (PA) and negative affect (NA) scales (Knez, 1995; Viola et al., 2008) and prolonged elevated noise levels raise blood pressure (Aydin & Kaltenbach, 2007). This suggests that the levels of an environmental stimulus result in a physiological response from the participant, which may make them feel comfortable or not.

However, it is difficult to describe complexity using one-dimensional scales. One-dimensional scales of comfort and satisfaction inadequately describe multisensory experience, visual scene and soundscapes (Clements-Croome, 2014; Ong, 2013). One-dimensional scales have no room for complex experiences that are neither good nor bad but instead have their own quality. Hence, assessing several one-dimensional parameters within a study can give a good understanding of the experience of that place.

Information processing of environmental stimuli can happen unconsciously. The cocktail-party effect suggests that people are continually screening unattended stimuli to see if conscious attention should be paid to them (Cherry, 1953). More complex speech-shadowing tasks are used to understand the perception of attended and unattended sounds. They require that a listener repeats words that are being played into a single-headphone ear, while a separate audio channel is played in the other ear. This set-up neatly divides attention into attended and unattended sound stimuli (Spence & Santangelo, 2010). These experiments find that some (but not very much) semantic content of the unattended recording is recalled. Often subjects would not realise if the language was changed halfway through, but they would perceive changes in sex of the speaker. Based on recent studies, people with large working memories were better able to ignore their own name and would later not recall hearing their name. However, people would also show physiological responses to target words that they would later not recall. It is evident from these that some subconscious processing of the signal is occurring and that this is sometimes on a semantic basis (Spence & Santangelo, 2010). This suggests that sound can be distracting because of its semantic content and not just because of its loudness. The degree to which it distracts depends upon the signal, the listener

TABLE 6.1 The differences between an energy and information interaction with the environment

Energy	*Information*
Background levels	Interpretative meaning
Quantity	Quality
One-dimensional	Multidimensional
Physical and biological	Psychological, cognitive and conceptual

and the complexity of the task they are doing. It also suggests that a person's subconscious reaction to environmental stimuli can be both cognitive and physical.

From this we deduce that physiological arousal occurs in response to both energetic stimuli (e.g. background noise levels raising blood pressure) and semantic stimuli (e.g. semantic content causing distraction, such as the cocktail-party effect). Given this, there will be three types of arousal response to background levels of temperature, lighting, air quality and sound levels. These three types are: responses caused by the level of the environmental stimuli, e.g. volume of noise and brightness of light; responses caused by environmental semantics, i.e. information exchange; and responses caused by no measured stimuli (false positives).

Hypothesis development

The essence of our approach is to test the limit of using background levels to evaluate the user's experience of an environment. On the one hand, background levels are useful because they can be measured by remote sensors; on the other hand, they do not provide a full and complete understanding of all aspects of the user experience. The same can be said of physiological sensors. Physiological responses can be used to differentiate markedly different psychological states but they are not capable of reading minds.

To test this, we use two different forms of analysis. First, session averages of all environmental factors are compared to session statistics of personal factors. Environmental factors are: air temperature, humidity, CO_2 levels, lux levels, colour temperature and sound levels. Personal factors are: skin conductance variability (SCV), heart rate variability (HRV), positive affect and satisfaction level. We hypothesise relationships between each of these factors (H1).

The second analysis tests the physiological response of individuals to different noises. This method breaks down an individual's session into approximately 30 to 70 events. It is hypothesised that the greater the relative loudness of the event, the larger and more likely will be the startle response, and therefore the larger the heart rate and SCV response (H2). However, before we develop the details of our hypotheses, it is necessary to explore how these methods have been used in the past.

To define multisensory environmental experience, singular environmental measures must be combined (Clements-Croome, 2013). Most multisensory studies aim to understand the interplay of the senses by assessing their effect on a common outcome (Cao et al., 2012; Huang et al., 2012). These approaches all account for multisensory experience by weighting the single senses and summing these into a single one-dimensional outcome – typically, through a multiple linear-regression type approach.

An alternative approach is to contrast the qualitative differences of the senses (Pallasmaa, 2005). Pallasmaa (2005) suggests that it is not possible to combine and sum different sensory experiences; rather, it is the balance and contrast of the different senses that makes an experience. He describes vision as detached, abstract and a snapshot in time, whereas sound is intimate, situated and can only be comprehended in terms of its unfolding in time. For him, understanding the contrasting and interweaving of effects is more important than using a single concept, such as satisfaction, to unify them. This chapter emulates this approach by aiming to understand the multiple and differing effects building environments have on their occupants.

We do this by taking a field-based (ambulatory) approach that combines environmental measurements, a comfort survey and data from wearable physiological sensors. This allows the integration of Pallasmaa's situated interpretative approach with the sort of physiological measurements that would most often require laboratory-based investigation. By collecting concurrent data about subjective experience, environment and physiology, it is possible to investigate the experience of real-world environments (Schnell et al., 2013; Tröndle et al., 2014).

This study uses the response of the autonomic nervous system (ANS) because it is linked to alertness, a key attribute for wellbeing and productivity (Cacioppo, Tassunary & Berntsson, 2007). Two components of the ANS response were measured: skin conductance level and electrocardiogram. These can be continuously measured by equipment that is relatively unobtrusive and accurate. When people pay attention to a stimulus, this causes a response of the ANS. This can cause a change in skin conductance and heart rate, as well as other physiological indicators (Thackray, 1972). Loud noises with sudden onset have been studied in some detail because of the sonic boom effect. Heart rate (HR) either increases, decreases or both depending upon stimulus type; louder, more sudden noises tend to result in HR acceleration. Peak acceleration in HR occurs approximately 3–5 seconds after stimulus onset, peak deceleration of HR occurs later, at about

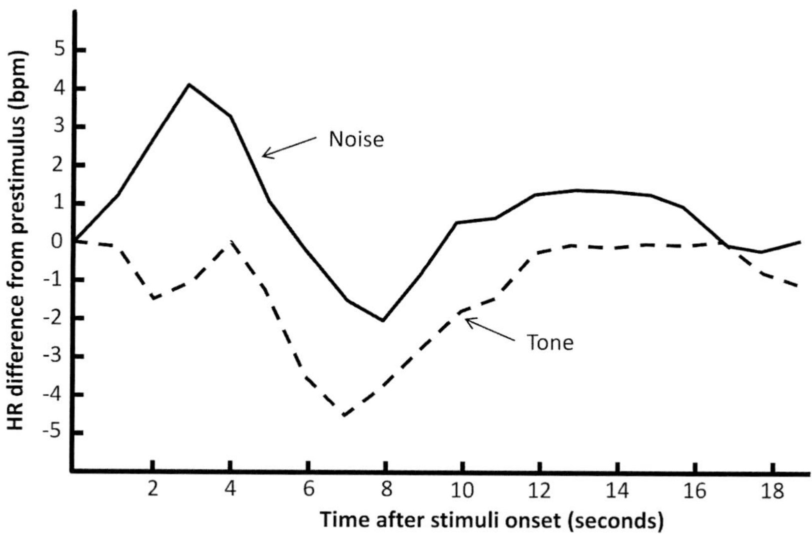

FIGURE 6.1 HR reaction to two different sound stimuli (Graham & Slaby, 1973).

5–8 seconds (Graham & Clifton, 1966; Graham & Slaby, 1973). Changes in HR between 2 and 6bpm have been detected (di Nisi, Muzet & Weber, 1987; Thackray, 1972), and people who self-reported as being more sensitive to noise had a greater increase in heart rate (di Nisi et al., 1987). These studies have all been carried out in laboratories with highly controlled stimuli and environments.

We supplemented the physiological data with a survey of participants' subjective experience. The positive and NA scale (PANAS) survey is a practical option to do this because it is well established, short and easily adaptable (Watson, Clark & Tellegen, 1988). This was combined with a satisfaction survey. The PANAS survey is a standard 20-question survey. PA and NA are not opposites but in fact comprise two orthogonal dimensions. High PA suggests enthusiasm, activity and alertness. High NA suggests sadness, lethargy and distress; low NA is a state of calmness and serenity (Watson et al., 1988). PA and NA are both related to the quality of one's work (Huppert, 2009) and contribute to productivity (Clements-Croome, 2018).

For this study, the H1 relates to analysis where session averages of all factors are compared between subjects. We compare environmental factors (air temperature, humidity, CO_2 levels, lux levels, colour temperature and sound levels) with personal factors (SCV and HRV, positive affect (PA), and satisfaction level). Our first hypothesis H1 is that a response in personal factors will be seen if environmental factors are outside the comfort zone for prolonged periods during the session and/or where extensive semantic stimulation occurs. The semantic stimuli will add unpredictability and therefore error to the measured personal factors. This semantic error will occur most strongly where there is greater potential for environmental stimuli to convey meaning, i.e. noise levels. Table 6.2 shows the hypothesised relationships (H1). Where no effect is predicted it is because we expect that background levels will not be sustained outside the comfort zone for prolonged periods during our observations (i.e. humidity and CO_2 levels) or because the effect of environmental stimuli will be conflated with the effect of semantic stimuli (i.e. noise levels). Further to this, a larger than normal increase in SCV is expected with elevated temperatures (Gagge, Stolwijk & Hardy, 1967).

TABLE 6.2 Hypothesised effects of the environment factors upon personal factors

Dependent variables	*Independent variables*					
	Lux level	*Colour temperature*	*Sound level*	*CO_2 level*	*Air temperature*	*Relative humidity*
HRV	Effect	Effect	No effect	No effect	Effect	Effect
SCV	Effect	Effect	No effect	No effect	Large effect	Effect
PA	Effect	Effect	No effect	No effect	Effect	Effect
Satisfaction	Effect	No effect	Effect	Effect	Effect	Effect

The second hypothesis H2 tests the physiological response of individuals to different sound stimuli. This was carried out using a within-subject design. To do this we broke down an individual's session into approximately 30 to 70 events and compared these events with each other. It is hypothesised that, for a given person, the greater the relative loudness of the event, the larger and more likely the physiological response (i.e. the larger the HR and SCV response) (H2).

Methods

We recruited participants (27 male, 23 female, age range 18 and above) by email and on an ad hoc basis while at their building. In certain instances, a full quota of data was not obtained because of the failure of one device or another. Further to this, full sound-level measurements were limited to ten individuals. Similar studies have used similar numbers of participants. Schnell et al. (2013) used 36 participants to explore the effect of the external environment on HRV. Tröndle et al. (2014) used 576 participants to map how each experienced different museum spaces. In contrast, Debener et al. (2012) tested an ambulatory EEG device on just 16 participants. Our number of participants is insufficient for making conclusions about the general population, but suitable for drawing some conclusions about the specific building populations studied and the potential of the methods used. Participants were selected from eight buildings (labelled A to H in Table 6.3). The range of settings provides a sharp contrast to more controlled laboratory tests; this is imperative for demonstrating wearable sensors as a useful building performance-evaluation tool.

Data were gathered at the participant's desk, for an hour, while the participant continued working (Figure 6.2). Participants were asked to choose a time when they would be predominately alone at their desk; however, they were also free to get up, move around and have conversations if needed. After each session, data were uploaded to a PC then combined and processed using specially written scripts for 'R software'.

TABLE 6.3 Overview of buildings

Building	*Occupier*	*Typology*	*Plan*	*HVAC*
A	Design	Open plan	Shallow	MM
B	Academic	Open / cell	Shallow	NV
C	Academic	Open / cell	Shallow	NV
D	Academic	Open / cell	Shallow	MM
E	Design	Open plan	Shallow	NV
F	Charity	Open plan	Deep	AC
G	Design	Open plan	Shallow	NV
H	Design	Open plan	Shallow	NV

NV = naturally ventilated, MM = Mixed mode, AC = fully air conditioned.

Sound level meter
CO_2, Humidity , Temperature
Light meter
Skin conductivity

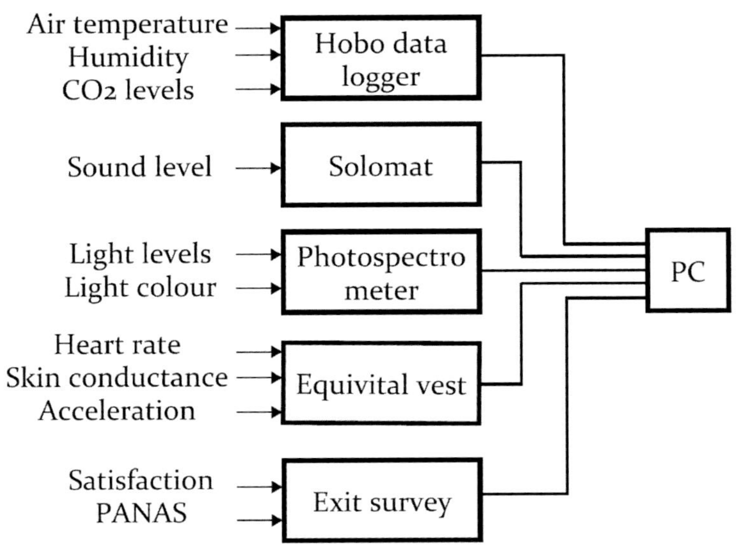

FIGURE 6.2 Study set-up, showing environmental and physiological sensor kit.

We used a number of different sensors to monitor the physical conditions. Air temperature, humidity and lux levels were logged every second using an Onset HOBO U12 data logger. Connected to this was a Telaire 7001 sensor to measure CO_2 levels. When available, a Solo sound-level meter was used to measure background sound level at a rate of 10 measurements per second. A Gigahertz-Optik BTS256 photospectrometer was used for measurements of the intensity and spectrum of light, and this device took readings every minute. These sensors were placed around the participant's desk. This was done so that they would obtain accurate readings and not obstruct the participants' work.

The physiological measurements were made using an Equivital vest (Liu et al., 2012). Electrocardiogram (ECG) signal was measured at 256Hz, skin conductance and the accelerometer at 25Hz. ECG data were converted by the Equivital software into an RR value (interbeat interval) and an associated confidence level for this conversion (0 to 100%). The software converted the output from the accelerometer into an estimation of one of three movement levels: stationary, moving slowly or moving fast. Skin conductance level (SCL) is used in its raw form.

At the end of the session the participants answered a short survey. This included the PANAS and their satisfaction with ambient conditions (five-point scale: Satisfied, A little satisfied, Neither, A little dissatisfied, Dissatisfied). They were asked to consider only their experience during the measurement session.

This set of measurements required the coordination of time series from several different devices. Each time series had a unique clock and frequency of measurement. Manual time stamps were inserted at the beginning and end of each session. This coordinated all of the time series to within ±1second. This temporal accuracy is sufficient because it is shorter than the response times of the physiological signals measured (Cacioppo et al., 2007) and shorter than the averaging periods used in our analysis. General convenience and coordination of time series would be improved by use of a wireless system that transmits to a common receiver in realtime. However, there is no single piece of proprietary kit that does this.

Another drawback is that the vest for physiological measurements was put on the torso and underneath clothing. Systems that improve handling times and decrease the intrusiveness of the device would have been preferred. There is also scope for altering the types of sensors used. Blood oxygenation may be good for monitoring the effect of indoor air quality. Electroencephalography (EEG) may be useful for studying combined effects of environment on stress and restoration. This study did not use these because they are more intrusive (they require attachment to hands or face).

Data handling

The environment was uncontrolled in these investigations, and there was great variation in measured values. Average CO_2 and sound levels were the only variables that remained within their design limits across all sessions. Looking at a single participant's data for the hour it is possible to note patterns in how the data change (Figure 6.3). Temperature, humidity and carbon dioxide stay relatively steady for the whole hour, and where they change it is generally a steady, slow shift in one direction. Light levels change at a slow, continuous shift, though there are times when changes of greater than 100lx happen within a couple of seconds. These time

TABLE 6.4 Summary of participants' session averages

Measure	*Min.*	*1st Qu.*	*Median*	*3rd Qu.*	*Max.*
Light levels (lx)	138	375	574	764	1,855
Colour temp. (K)	2,686	3,174	3,879	4,528	5,872
Sound level (dBA)	50	51	52	54	58
CO_2 level (ppm)	462	542	619	697	932
Temperature (°C)	21	24	25	26	29
Relative humidity (%)	33	43	47	50	60
Mean RR interval (ms)	262	752	822	979	1,226
HRV (ms^2)	2,183	9,400	16,920	33,600	157,100
Mean SCL	−1	165	362	707	2,258
SCV	0	3,491	12,870	50,910	156,100
Mean HR confidence (%)	37	89	96	98	99
Variance in HR confidence	1	1	17	121	499
Positive affect	11	22	25	30	37
Negative affect	10	11	12	16	31

series can be contrasted with sound levels that change much more rapidly, moving from 45dBA to 65dBA and back again within seconds.

In contrast to the environmental data, the physiological data fluctuate at high frequencies. HR has a base rate that varies, with some rapid changes in places and more settled in others. Skin conductance exhibited two trends, a steadily falling average and, in some participants, a number of extreme spikes.

The average values of data from each session were compared between participants. There were six people for whom physiological data did not record; these data were excluded from further analysis. NA scores had a highly skewed distribution, therefore they were not used for further analysis. Data for all sessions were clipped to reduce start and end effects.

HRV was obtained by taking the variance of the RR interval for the whole session (Berntson et al., 1997). A large HRV indicates arousal of a person's ANS (Cacioppo et al., 2007). SCV was obtained by taking the variance of SCL for the whole session. This indicates activation of the sweat glands, which can be part of the sympathetic response of the ANS or thermoregulatory response (Cacioppo et al., 2007).

Session statistics, for HRV, SCV and PA scores, were compared with demographic factors to check for correlation (Figure 6.4). The value of ***p*** displayed on each graph shows the probability that scores are the same using either the *f*-test or *t*-test statistic. Despite there being a range of organisations and locations, there was no significant difference between buildings. Gender had a significant effect on HRV and PA score, and age had a significant effect on PA score.

Development of analysis method for within-subject analysis

The within-subject analysis selects and compares a number of events from a single participant. This analysis provides insight into the unfolding of events in three

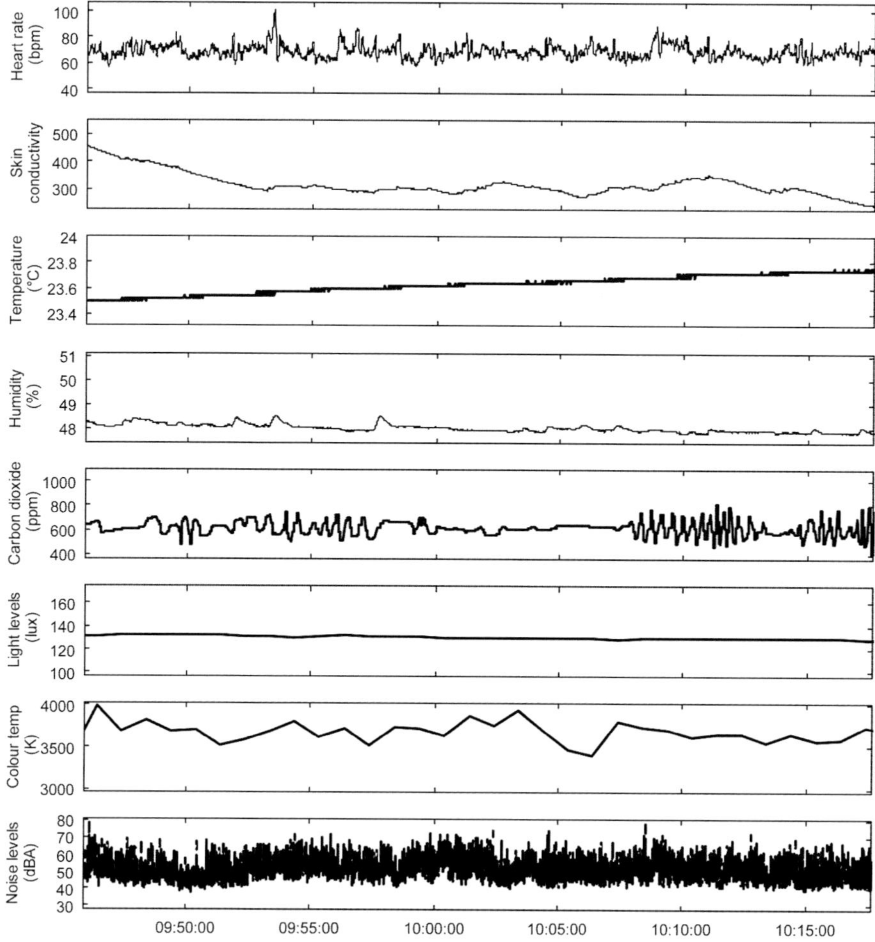

FIGURE 6.3 Whole session time series for a single participant.

time series: sound levels, HR and SCL. For the analysis we used R Software (R Development Core Team, 2016) because it allowed us to write a special algorithm to identify sound events. Events were defined as periods (10s long) when background sound levels were louder than they had been in the previous 30s. Events were identified by going through the entire time series and comparing the average sound level of a 10s section with the preceding 30s. This can also be described as comparing the relative loudness of P_3 (the event) to P_1 (the preceding 30s) (Figure 6.5). This results in the identification of many overlapping events. The number of events can be reduced by choosing the louder when two overlap. This identifies approximately 30 to 70 events per session. The timings of these events are then used to look at the corresponding physiological response (see Figure 6.6).

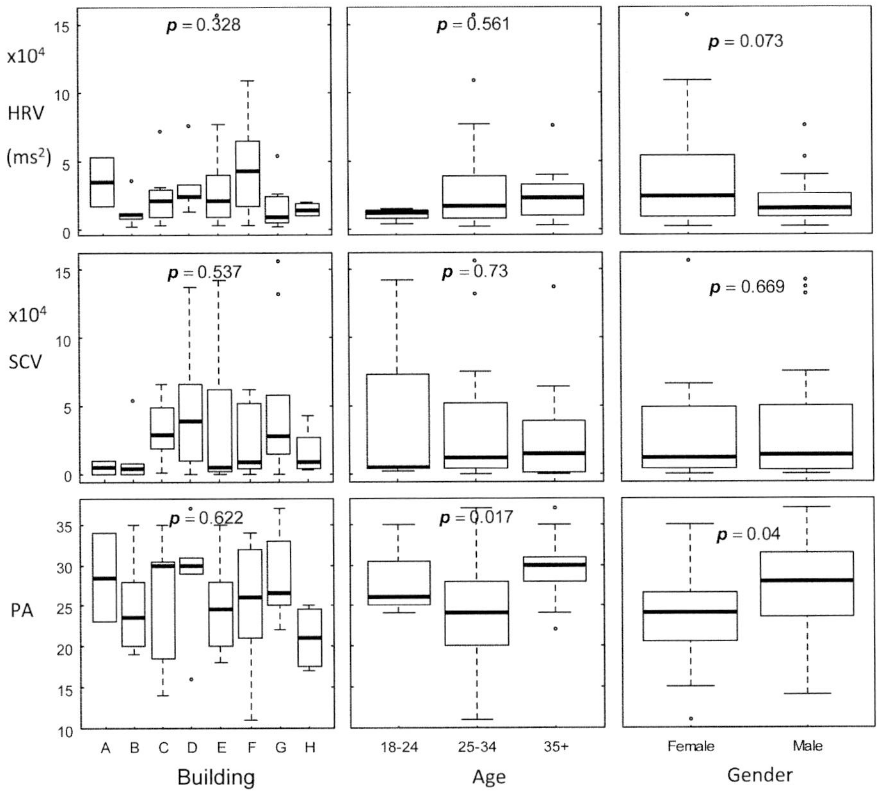

x10⁴ HRV (ms²)

p = 0.328 | p = 0.561 | p = 0.073

x10⁴ SCV

p = 0.537 | p = 0.73 | p = 0.669

PA

p = 0.622 | p = 0.017 | p = 0.04

A B C D E F G H | 18-24 25-34 35+ | Female Male

Building | Age | Gender

FIGURE 6.4 Between-participants comparison of physiology, positive affect and demographics.

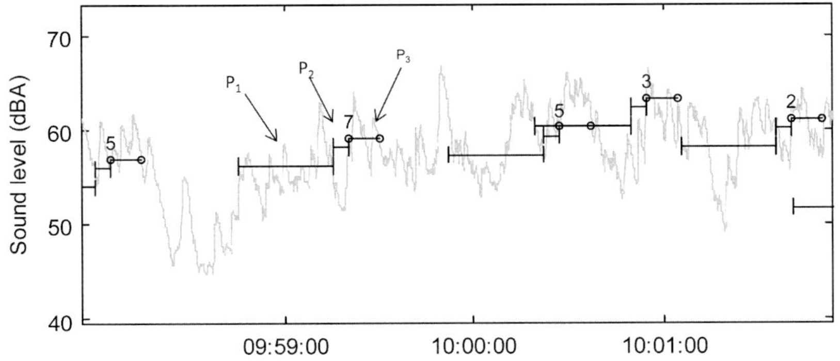

FIGURE 6.5 Example of time series analysis method. P_1 = reference background level, P_2 ensures segmentation, P_3 = foreground level for comparison.

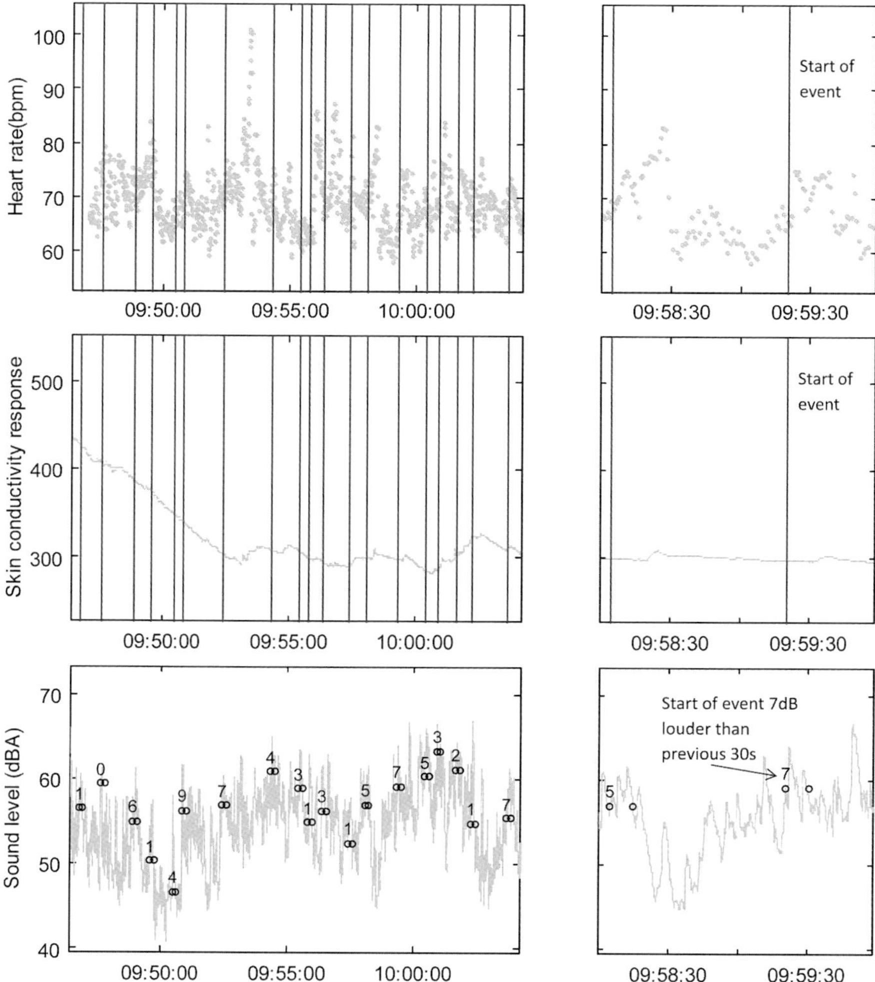

FIGURE 6.6 Time series for HR, skin conductance and sound level for a participant (half session and close-up on two events).

An alternative approach would have been to segment the time series into a number of arbitrary lengths and compare the data in these (Tiesler & Oberdoerster, 2008). That approach seeks to understand the effect of general background levels upon occupant stress (Tiesler & Oberdoerster, 2008). We prefer our approach because it observes specific events rather than environmental averages. It is similar to laboratory analysis of event related potentials (ERP) (Alain, Arnott & Picton, 2001; Boksem, Meijem & Lorist, 2005; Luck, 2005). ERP was developed to understand how environmental events were processed by occupants. In summary, our approach looks at whether background noise levels can be used to understand an occupant's reaction to single events rather than whether background levels are a general stressor.

Our method identifies many sound events in a single participant's data. Then it compares the loudness of these events with the physiological response. This technique has various strengths. First, it makes it possible to compare the same person's response to different noises, which removes the large interperson variation in physiological response. Second, the technique can be used to focus analysis on short-lived environmental events; this removes physiological noise when no environmental event is happening. Lastly, this technique allows detailed study (i.e. multiple data points) of single individuals; therefore, it could be used to identify people who are more sensitive to environmental change than others.

There are inherent differences between the time series of the physical conditions and the physiological measures. During this study, temperature, CO_2 levels and humidity have their progression characterised by slow shifts rather than sudden fluctuations. Light levels and colour temperature are generally similar but may undergo a small number of rapid shifts during a session. In contrast, sound levels fluctuate rapidly throughout the session, as does the physiological response. This makes sound levels and physiology well matched and therefore suited for within-subject analysis. To identify as many events (>30) for the other physical variables would require a much longer session or the introduction of artificial stimuli.

It is difficult to define a reliable protocol for identifying when environmental events occur and how big they are. This is because real-life events have neither a definite onset nor a definite size. Sometimes events are missed by our algorithm, and at other times the identification of an event seems spurious. Regarding event size, sometimes two events can appear similar when the times series is visually inspected yet have quite different sizes attributed to them. Despite this, there are times when our simple algorithm works well, many of the significant peaks in sound level are recorded as events and often the estimation of their size seems a reasonable approximation.

However, even if the algorithm for event identification were perfect, it would still rely on the use of dBA. Therefore, it would not identify those sound events that are salient for reasons other than their pressure level. To track and characterise these events, some other aspects of saliency must be coded into the analysis. This could be achieved by recording audio for the session and manually identifying events. Or we could introduce reference sound events for comparison. Such an approach of introducing events would suit the investigation of other sensory perceptions that did not change so rapidly.

Results for between-subject analysis

Each point on Figure 6.7 is a summary statistic for a single participant's session. Humidity measurements are compared with the satisfaction score for air quality, and for all other variables it is with their respective sensory perception. The inferential statistics on the graphs are obtained from applying linear models to the data: "p=. . ." is the probability that there is no link between the variables; "R^2=. . ." is

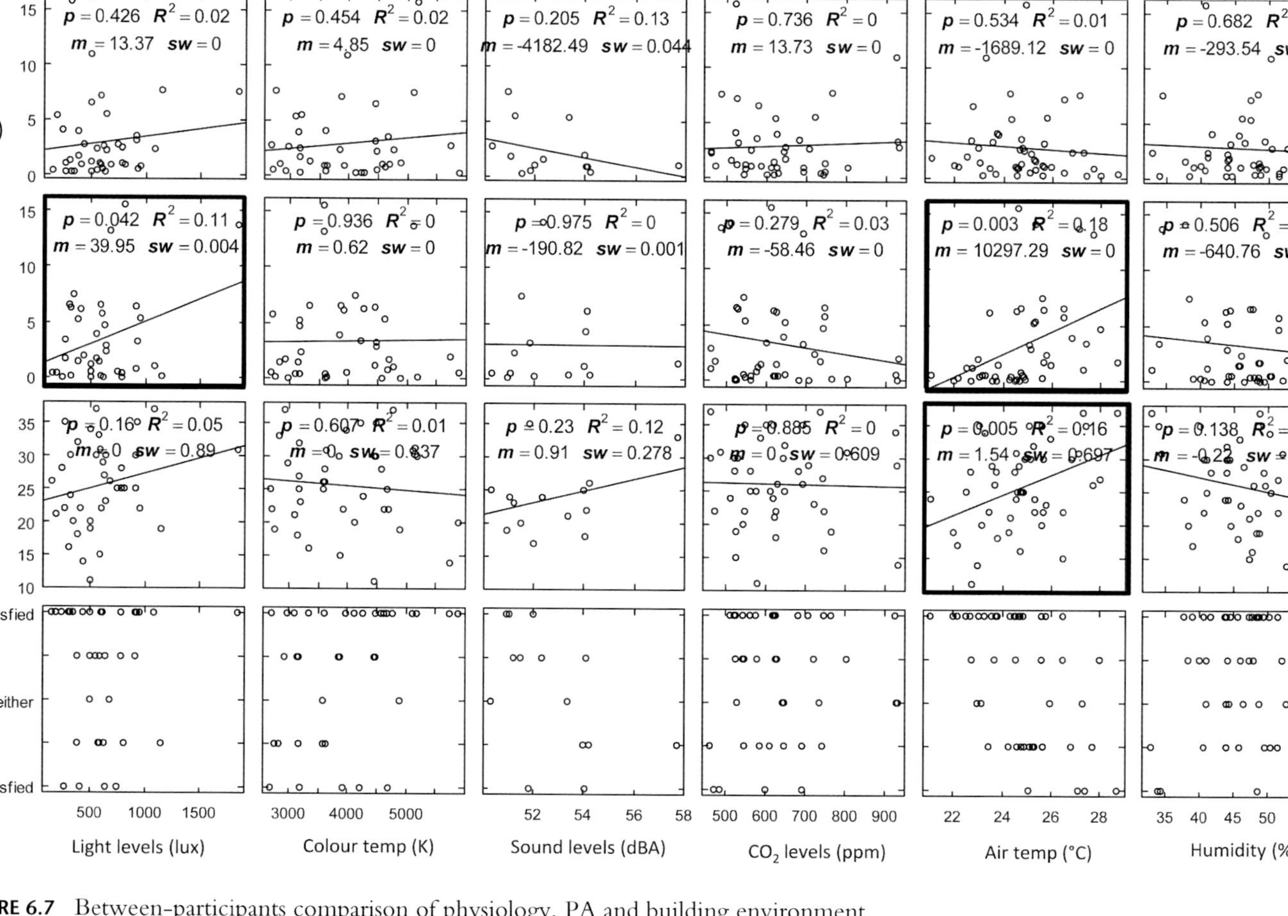

FIGURE 6.7 Between-participants comparison of physiology, PA and building environment.

the correlation coefficient, "*m*=" is the gradient (i.e. effect size) and "*sw*=" is the score for the Shapiro–Wilk test for normality of the residuals.

After running 18 tests of correlation between the different variables, there is a significant relationship between only three of them. Two of these are with the average temperature; skin conductance variation and PA are greater at higher temperatures. The third is between light levels and skin conductance variation; higher light levels are associated with increased skin conductance. The correlation between temperature and light levels was tested, and it was found to be not significant. These results mostly run counter to H1. The residuals pass the Shapiro–Wilk test (i.e. $sw<0.1$) for the PA scores but not the physiological scores.

Results for within-subject analysis

H2 predicted a correlation between the relative loudness of an event and the size of the physiological response. Figure 6.8 shows a selection of results, and each graph shows the data for one selected participant. The statistics displayed on the graphs are obtained from applying linear models to the HR data and the natural log of the SCV data i.e. $\ln(y)=x$. The labels on the graph are the same as the between-subjects analysis: "***p***=. . ." is the probability that the gradient of the regression line is zero (i.e. no correlation); "$\boldsymbol{R^2}$=. . ." is the R^2 correlation coefficient, "***m***=" is the gradient (i.e. effect size) and "***sw***=" is the score for the Shapiro–Wilk test for normality of the residuals.

Some participants show a clear correlation between the loudness of the event and the raising of HR. The probability of no significant relationship ranges between $p=0.006$ and $p=0.5$ for the ten participants where full data were available; three have $p<0.05$. R^2 coefficients vary between 0.02 and 0.17. Where $p<0.05$, the gradient is approximately 0.5 or greater, which indicates that a 10dB change in background noise level would raise the HR by 5bpm, which is a similar amount to the effect of sonic booms in controlled environments on the HR. These results suggest that H2 holds for some individuals but not all.

When comparing skin rate variability and relative loudness the relationships between events is not so clear (Figure 6.9). Each graph represents data for the same participants as Figure 6.8. Some quiet events have large skin conductance response while other louder events have very little response at all. Because of this, the natural log of the SCV was used for analysis. The R^2 correlation is generally lower for SCV (0 to 0.17) and the likelihood that there is no relationship between the factors is higher (0.01 to 0.98). The correlation is significant for only two participants out of the ten. This suggests that H2 does not hold as well with regards to SCV.

Discussion

The between-subject analysis showed some correlations between the environment and personal factors. However, these were generally different from

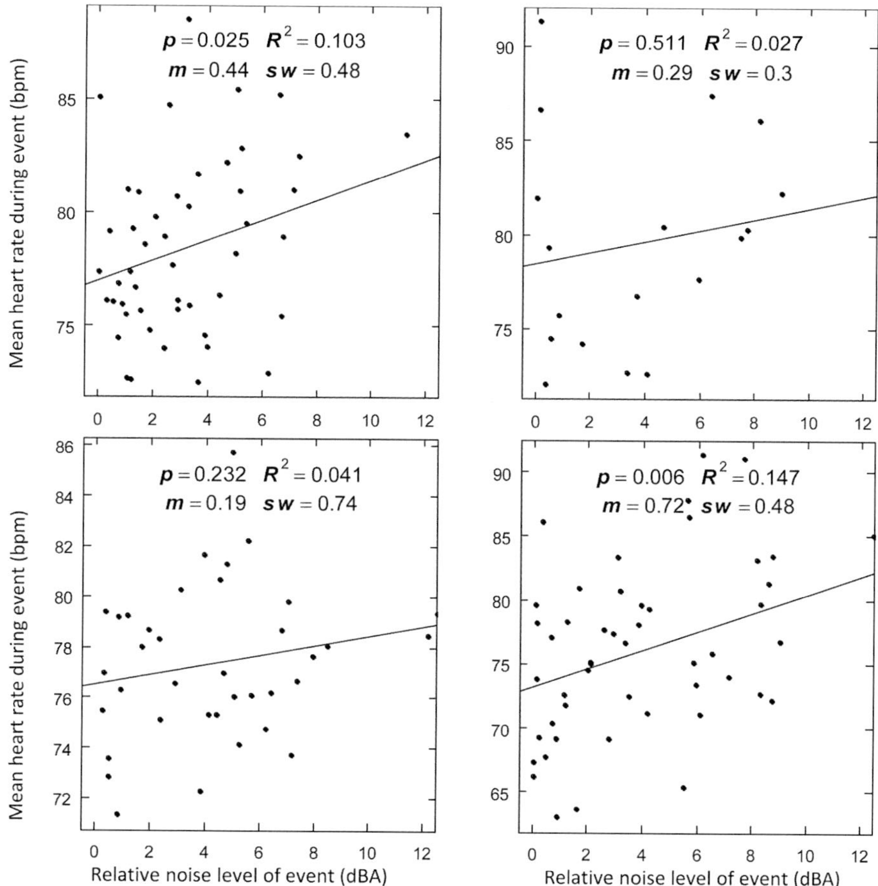

FIGURE 6.8 Correlation between HR and sound levels for selected individuals.

those hypothesised. Some of the missing correlation can be explained by the narrow range of environmental conditions encountered. For instance, changes within the range of CO_2 levels and humidity measured in this study (IQR = 155ppm, 7%rh) are barely perceptible.

Background light levels showed a small and weakly significant relationship with skin conductance variance. The significance is only just below 0.05 and there is no correlation between light and any other indicators. Nonetheless, this suggests that background light levels did impact user experience. This adds supports to work that shows high light levels can be alerting and stimulating (Cajochen et al., 2000).

Temperature showed the greatest pattern in the between-subject analysis, correlating with both SCV and PA. The increase in SCV was a particularly strong correlation. This reproduces results that show skin conductance increases at higher temperatures (Gagge et al., 1967). This suggests that the source of

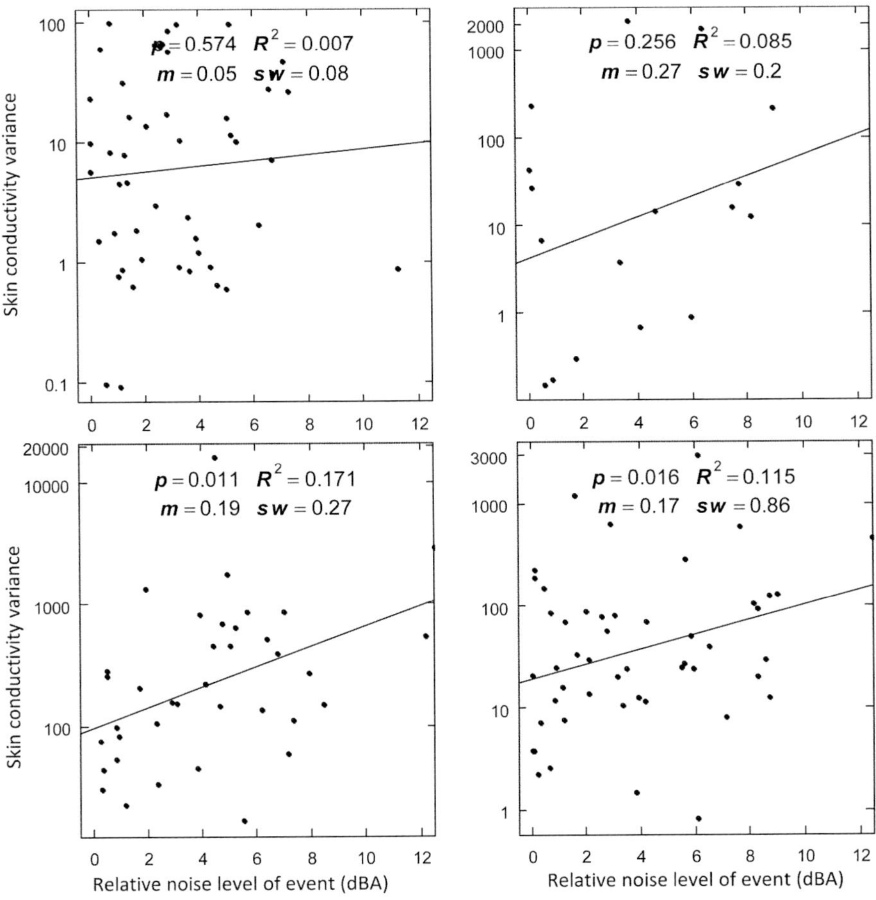

FIGURE 6.9 Plots of skin conductance variance and sound levels for selected individuals.

the SCV correlation is the direct effect of the temperature on the physiological response. The increase in PA is more remarkable. Most other studies suggest that alertness and performance reduce at higher temperatures (Griffiths & Boyce, 1971). Although more recent studies show warmth linked to positive outcomes such as increased interpersonal behaviour (Williams & Bargh, 2008) and high external temperature correlating with increased subjective wellbeing in the UK (MacKerron & Mourato, 2013).

The within-subject analysis showed that, for some individuals, HR is a useful method to track their response to different sounds and that this can be done in situ. This supports H2. This method was adapted from methods used in schools (Tiesler & Oberdoerster, 2008) and to study sonic booms in laboratory settings (Thackray, 1972). Our work suggests that this method can be used to study everyday environments in situ. However, most occupants did not show a clear physiological response to events, this could have been because of limitations of the method or because they were less affected by the noises. Furthermore, if Bonferroni correction had been applied then no results would have been significant. Hence, we consider these findings as provisional pending further testing and as indications that can help us formulate more specific hypotheses for further testing.

The data, especially the SCV, highlighted the non-linearity between the size of physical stimuli and the physiological response. This made it hard to fit a linear relationship between the two. The data also show that there is not a one-to-one mapping between the relative loudness of a sound and the physiological response. It is apparent that not every noise causes a response and not every response is caused by a noise. However, despite the simplicity of the models used, some of the variation in physiological response can be explained by relative loudness. This supports the idea that loudness (i.e. background sound level) is just one facet of what makes a sound salient (Spence & Santangelo, 2010). The use of physiological sensors to identify salient environmental experiences suggests a way of overcoming the problem of characterisation of complex environments (complex characterisations). Instead of characterising IEQ by its physical manifestation, it could also be characterised by the physiological response it produces in people. Such a system could be used to engage machine learning to determine the most suitable environments for different people and tasks (Eadie et al., 2016).

In contrast to temperature, background light levels and physiological response show only weak correlations in the between-subject analysis. This could be because background light levels are only one feature of the visual field. This suggests that using a single parameter, such as background level, to characterise experience is suitable for temperature but not so suitable for sound and vision. This suggests that everyday experience of the thermal environment is simple compared with the complexity of visual and acoustic experience. This is despite the complexities of temperature experience observed by Heschong (1979). This could be interpreted as evidence for the standardisation of thermal experience (Shove, 2003) as much as an innately simpler relationship.

This balance between complexity and simplicity of our sensory experience can be related back to the balance between information exchange and energy exchange. The range of the physical conditions measured in this study illustrates the qualitative difference between everyday experience of different senses. In the office environments studied, the range of sound levels can have only a limited effect on the occupants' experience. They can be distracting and annoying but they are unlikely to damage hearing. The range of light exposure measured here would also be mostly within the 'informatic' or cognitive range and generally not high enough to have an energetic (i.e. direct physical) impact. In contrast, across all the buildings visited, there is a wide range of temperatures, enough to stimulate an energetic exchange between occupant and their environment. Therefore, background levels (i.e. energy content) are an appropriate measure of ambient conditions for temperature but less so for sounds and light. This suggests that those that use background levels to characterise acoustic and visual experience (Cao et al., 2012; Huang et al., 2012) are not taking the right approach.

Pallasmaa (2005) describes temperature as encompassing and embracing, while vision is detached. Our results show that background levels are most useful for temperature, likely because it is the energetic exchange that is so important for thermal experience. This energetic experience goes on throughout an individual, so in some sense it is encompassing and embracing. In contrast the sensory experience of light is predominately an informatics or cognitive one that happens at just two point in our bodies, this could contribute to the feeling of detachment that Pallasmaa (2005) suggests for vision.

There are further differences, described by Pallasmaa (2005), that have been observed in this study. He describes the temporal nature of sound as differentiating it from vision. Our data show the physical variables evolve differently in time. These differences lead to different ways to summarise their physical manifestation and their effect on user experience. This suggests that sensor systems for the two could be quite different. Our work here suggests that temperature is suited to a simple background-level measurement, while something more complex, like light and sound, would require multiple sensors, combining physical and physiological measurements.

Conclusions

Overall, physiological response is correlated with sound, temperature and light levels. The usefulness of background levels and physiological response is limited because they are unable to characterise the complex information processes inherent in user experience. Background levels are a first order measurement of magnitude. To understand information content and meaning it is necessary to make second order measurements that delve into the complex relationship between people and their environment. We have shown that, for sound, combining environmental and physiological measurements gives us an indication of what is salient, and this may be useful for overcoming the problem of complex characterisation.

The first analysis (between subjects) of this chapter demonstrates important differences in the sensory experience of light, sound and temperature. For some component factors, such as temperature/thermal comfort, background levels are more useful, for environmental factors that are more information-processing-based (i.e. sound), sensors are less useful. For all environmental factors there are both single dimensional measurable components and information-carrying components. Sound, for example, can be measured in terms of volume, but needs also to be analysed as a complex information-carrying stimulus. Because information processing is more complex than energy exchange, sensor methods must be vastly improved if they are to be used for understanding complex and information-rich environmental experiences.

The second analysis (within subjects) demonstrates the effect of sound levels in offices on people's HRs. It can be used to monitor workers reaction to their sound environment in real time and reveal differences in people's sensitivity to sound.

It enables the continuous tracking of rapidly unfolding events. This allows the researcher to compare the effect of different events against each other. It is most useful when used alongside contextual information, in this case the sound levels. Here it helped to distinguish between environmental events that are salient and those that are less so. This combination of environmental and physiological data could overcome the problem of complex characterisation, because the physiological data can be used to categorise the nature of the user experience and the environmental data.

References

Alain, C., Arnott, S. R., & Picton, T. W. 2001. 'Bottom–up and top–down influences on auditory scene analysis: Evidence from event-related brain potentials'. *Journal of Experimental Psychology: Human Perception and Performance, 27*(5), 1072.

ASHRAE. 2010. Standard 55–2010. *Thermal Environmental Conditions for Human Occupancy*. Atlanta: ASHRAE.

Aydin, Y. & Kaltenbach, M. 2007. 'Noise perception, heart rate and blood pressure in relation to aircraft noise in the vicinity of the Frankfurt airport'. *Clinical Research in Cardiology, 96*(6), 347–58.

Berntson, G., Bigger, T., Eckberg, D., Grossman, P., Kaufmann, P., Malik, M., . . . Molen, M. V. D. 1997. 'Heart rate variability: Origins, methods, and interpretive caveats'. *Psychophysiology, 34*, 623–48.

Boksem, M. A., Meijman, T. F. & Lorist, M. M. 2005. 'Effects of mental fatigue on attention: an ERP study'. *Cognitive Brain Research, 25*(1), 107–116.

Cacioppo, J. T., Tassinary, L. G., & Berntson, G. G. 2007. *Handbook of Psychophysiology* (3 ed.). Cambridge: Cambridge University Press.

Cajochen, C., Zeitzer, J. M., Czeisler, C. A., & Dijk, D.-J. 2000. 'Dose-response relationship for light intensity and ocular and electroencephalographic correlates of human alertness'. *Behavioural Brain Research, 115*(1), 75–83.

Cao, B., Ouyang, Q., Zhu, Y., Huang, L., Hu, H., & Deng, G. 2012. 'Development of a multivariate regression model for overall satisfaction in public buildings based on field studies in Beijing and Shanghai'. *Building and Environment, 47*(0), 394–9.

Cherry, C. 1953. 'The cocktail party problem'. *Journal of the Acoustical Society of America, 25*, 975–9.

Clements-Croome, D. 2006. *Creating the Productive Workplace* (2nd ed.). London: Taylor & Francis.

Clements-Croome, D. 2013. *Intelligent Buildings: Design, Management and Operation* (2nd. ed.). London: Thomas Telford.

Clements-Croome, D. 2014. Sustainable Intelligent Buildings for Better Health, Comfort and Well-Being. Available at: http://www.researchgate.net/publication/266739139_Sustainable_Intelligent_Buildings_for_Better_Health__Comfort_and_Wellbeing

Clements-Croome, D. 2018. *Creating the Productive Workplace* (3rd ed.). London: Taylor & Francis.

Debener, S., Minow, F., Emkes, R., Gandras, K., & de Vos, M. 2012. 'How about taking a low-cost, small, and wireless EEG for a walk?' *Psychophysiology, 49*(11), 1617–21.

di Nisi, J., Muzet, A., & Weber, L. D. 1987. 'Cardiovascular responses to noise: Effects of self-estimated sensitivity to noise, sex, and time of the day'. *Journal of Sound and Vibration, 114*(2), 271–9.

Dutson, C. 2010. *Light Volumes, Dark Matters*. J. Myerson & R. Gheerawo (Eds). London: Helen Hamlyn Centre.

Eadie, J., Craddock, R., Becerra, V., & Nasuto, S. 2016. *Use of Human Captured Data to Assist in Automated Event Recognition*. TSBE Annual conference, Reading, UK.

Gagge, A. P., Stolwijk, J. A. J., & Hardy, J. D. 1967. 'Comfort and thermal sensations and associated physiological responses at various ambient temperatures'. *Environmental Research*, *1*(1), 1–20.

Graham, F. K., & Clifton, R. K. 1966. 'Heart-rate change as a component of the orienting response'. *Psychological Bulletin*, *65*(5), 305.

Graham, F. K., & Slaby, D. A. 1973. 'Differential heart rate changes to equally intense white noise and tone'. *Psychophysiology*, *10*(4), 347–62.

Griffiths, I. D., & Boyce, P. R. 1971. 'Performance and thermal comfort'. *Ergonomics*, *14*(4), 457–68.

Heschong, L. 1979. *Thermal Delight in Architecture*. Cambridge, Massachusetts: M.I.T. Press.

Huang, L., Zhu, Y., Ouyang, Q., & Cao, B. 2012. 'A study on the effects of thermal, luminous, and acoustic environments on indoor environmental comfort in offices'. *Building and Environment*, *49*(0), 304–9.

Huppert, F. A. 2009. 'Psychological well-being: Evidence regarding its causes and consequences. *Applied Psychology: Health and Well-Being*, *1*(2), 137–64.

Hygge, S. 2007. Noise: effects on health' in S. Ayers (Ed.), *Cambridge Handbook of Psychology, Health and Medicine* (2 ed.). Cambridge: Cambridge University Press.

ISO 28802. 2012. *Ergonomics of the Physical Environment* (Vol. BS EN ISO 28802). London: BSI Publications.

Knez, I. 1995. 'Effects of indoor lighting on mood and cognition'. *Journal of Environmental Psychology*, *15*(1), 39–51.

Liu, Y., Zhu, S. H., Wang, G. H., Ye, F., & Li, P. Z. 2012. 'Validity and reliability of multiparameter physiological measurements recorded by the equivital lifemonitor during activities of various intensities'. *Journal of Occupational and Environmental Hygiene*, *10*(2), 78–85.

Luck, S. J. 2005. *An Introduction to the Event-Related Potential Technique*. Cambridge MA: MIT Press.

MacKerron, G. and Mourato, S. 2013. 'Happiness is greater in natural environments'. *Global Environmental Change*, *23*(5), pp.992–1000. Available at: https://www.sciencedirect.com/science/article/pii/S0959378013000575

Ong, B. L. 2013. *Beyond Environmental Comfort*. Abingdon: Routledge.

Pallasmaa, J. 2005. *The Eyes of the Skin: Architecture and the Senses*. Chichester: Wiley-Academy.

R Development Core Team. 2016. 'A language and environment for statistical computing'. Available at: https://www.r-project.org/

Schnell, I., Potchter, O., Epstein, Y., Yaakov, Y., Hermesh, H., Brenner, S., & Tirosh, E. 2013. 'The effects of exposure to environmental factors on heart rate variability: An ecological perspective'. *Environmental Pollution*, *183*(0), 7–13.

Shove, E. 2003. 'Converging conventions of comfort, cleanliness and convenience'. *Journal of Consumer Policy*, *26*(4), 395–418.

SLL, 2012. *The Society of Light and Lighting Code for Lighting*. London: CIBSE.

Spence, C. & Santangelo, V. 2010. 'Auditory attention' in D. R. Moore, P. A. Fuchs, A. Rees, A. R. Palmer, & C. J. Plack (Eds.), *The Oxford Handbook of Auditory Science*. Oxford: Oxford University Press.

Taub, M. & Clements-Croome, D. 2016. *Wearables in the Workplace*. London BCO 2016 Report. Available at: www.bco.org.uk

Thackray, R. I. 1972. 'Sonic boom exposure effects II.3: startle responses'. *Journal of Sound and vibration*, *20*(4), 519–26.

Tiesler, G., & Oberdoerster, M. 2008. 'Noise-a stress factor? Acoustic ergonomics at schools'. *Journal of the Acoustical Society of America*, *123*(5), 3918.

Tröndle, M., Greenwood, S., Kirchberg, V., & Tschacher, W. 2014. 'An integrative and comprehensive methodology for studying aesthetic experience in the field: merging movement tracking, physiology, and psychological data'. *Environment and Behavior*, *46*(1), 102–35.

Viola, A. U., James, L. M., Schlangen, L. J., & Dijk, D.-J. 2008. 'Blue-enriched white light in the workplace improves self-reported alertness, performance and sleep quality'. *Scandinavian Journal of Work, Environment & Health*, *34*(4), 297–306.

Watson, D., Clark, L. A., & Tellegen, A. 1988. 'Development and validation of brief measures of positive and negative affect: The PANAS scales'. *Journal of Personality and Social Psychology*, *54*(6), 1063–70.

Williams, L. E., & Bargh, J. A. 2008. 'Experiencing physical warmth promotes interpersonal warmth'. *Science*, *322*(5901), 606–7.

7

DATA AND WAYFINDING AT THAMESMEAD

Applying geolocation and EEG recordings of brain activity for navigation design

Bridget Snaith and Sven Mündner

Introduction

'Wearable' electroencephalography (EEG) devices allow collection of brain-activity readings in the real world, linked to movement and to spatial location. They have potential to offer new and persuasive methods of quantitatively measuring and representing navigation in space, and responses to place, which may have practical application for urban-regeneration projects.

Within a positivist framework, such quantitative data offer objective evidence for decision making; however, in addition to challenges of data interpretation and experimental control, the time required to link data and spatial information, through subsequent synchronisation and analysis of video for example, may limit application in commercial spatial-design practice.

Geolocation apps, if synchronised with EEG, could remove the need for post hoc synchronisation and subsequent mapping, reducing the time required in analysis and potentially making a commercial application viable. This chapter describes fieldwork undertaken by a team of social researchers, and wayfinding and spatial-design experts, using commercially available technology and software, which is being promoted as accessible without neuroscience expertise. This chapter reviews their resulting empirical findings, and discusses the methodological and technological challenges faced by the team in trying to apply existing EEG and geolocation hardware and software in a live, spatial-design project in Thamesmead, South East London. The authors reflect on the potential of brain activity measurement and geolocation in spatial-design practice in 2016, and call for some development of simple software to facilitate greater use outside academic settings.

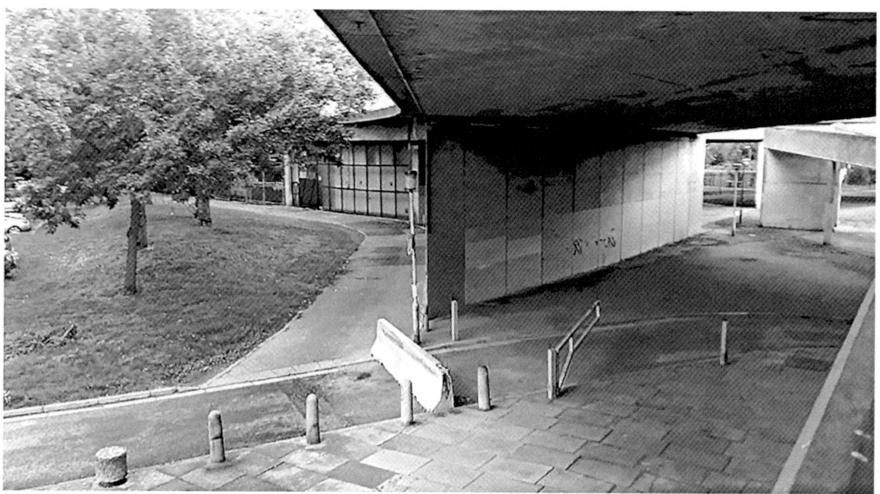

FIGURE 7.1 Approach to Corey Bridge, Thamesmead.

Thamesmead: setting the scene

Thamesmead was conceived as a 'new town' by the Greater London Council (GLC) in the 1960s to help solve post-war housing shortages. It had been planned and constructed in phases in a somewhat piecemeal fashion on reclaimed marshland in the Thames Estuary, almost 20 km east of London Bridge. From the 1960s to the 1980s Thamesmead was developed and managed by the GLC. In 1986 it became a 'trust company' holding and continued to grow. Now the entire estate is in the ownership of Peabody, a social-housing provider, with plans for up to 20,000 new homes. Its isolation from the rest of London is soon to change, with high-speed public-transport access via Crossrail and extension of the Docklands Light Railway (Peabody, 2017; Willey, 2016).

In keeping with the best practice thinking of the 1960–70s, Thamesmead has multilane, high-speed vehicle routes throughout, and a mainly separate off-road pedestrian-movement network, set in parkland. Parts of the pedestrian network are well used, but most routes are severed in places by confusing intersections with poor visibility (Figure 7.1). Urban block layout and architectural form vary with the different phases of development, from the precast concrete grid-based multilevel landscapes of the south, to the north where crescent shaped 'barrier blocks' meet complex cul-de-sacs, winding routes and circular streets of suburban houses from the later 1980s, interspersed with more recent gated developments and security 'improvements' that disrupt connectivity.

There are consequently many different challenges for navigation.

Navigation research findings in Thamesmead

The authors are part of a team commissioned by Peabody in 2015 to research existing practices of navigation and wayfinding in Thamesmead, identify areas for action and propose interventions to help existing and new residents navigate easily and access services. A mixed-methods study was undertaken in September 2015, with the participation of nearly 2,000 residents. The team used a wide-ranging mixed-methods approach. Techniques employed included: observation of movement patterns to/from key destinations; asking for directions to key sites at various locations; semi-structured interviews with residents and Thamesmead employees; face-to-face questionnaire survey; workshops drawing mental maps (Figure 7.2), focus groups identifying and naming places from photographs; web-based map making with students at a local secondary school; and codesign workshops with young people. All findings were used to support the team's recommendations regarding wayfinding interventions.

The findings of the study were revealing. The most popular phone-app-based navigation system with Thamesmead residents relies on vehicle access to locate addresses and propose routes. With much of Thamesmead accessed off-road, many routes and addresses are incorrectly mapped or even missing. Locations in Thamesmead have poorly defined 'edges' (Lynch, 1960). Neighbourhood boundaries are blurred, and parks just bleed into the public realm between buildings with no threshold. There is incongruence between names for routes and places given by 'officials', and the names used for wayfinding by residents. Some places have no known names at all. There are few direct routes or left–right junctions. The lack of agreed names, clear directions and distinct boundaries, and the incongruence of movement networks makes giving directions and mental mapping more difficult. Added to this, there has been an experimental approach to housing layout and numbering.

One recommendation was the design and promotion of a walking 'tube-map', with associated onsite waymarking and map-based signage, to provide legible strategic routes to follow and assist in building geographically based mental

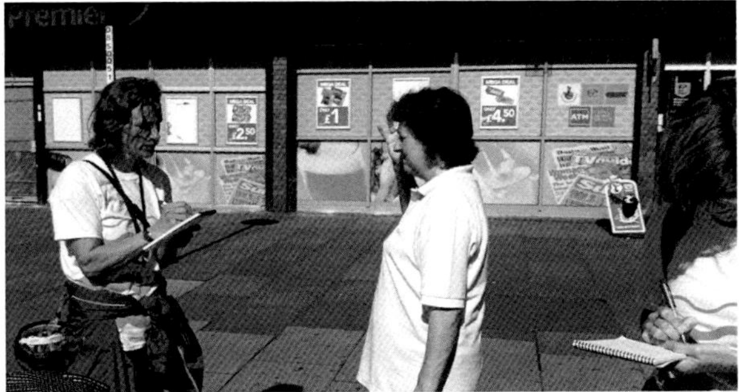

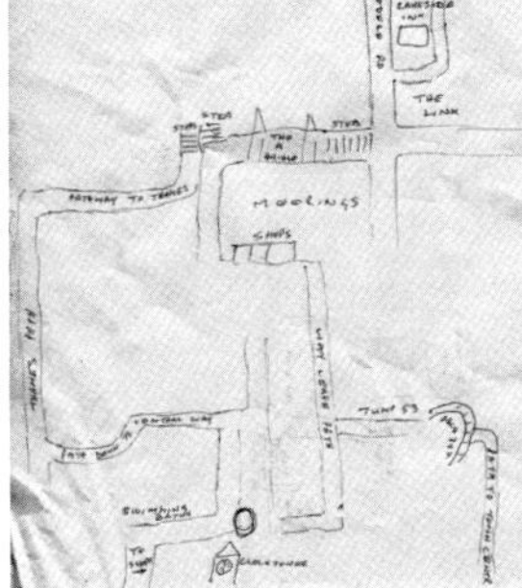

FIGURE 7.2 Surveys and mental mapping: navigation research in Thamesmead.

maps (Figure 7.3). As part of piloting the recommendations for signage and wayfinding, the authors proposed an experiment to investigate the potential efficacy of the walking tube-map and supporting signage through using wearable EEG.

While the experiment was undertaken in support of the overall Thamesmead Wayfinding commission, its main aim was to explore the emerging methodological and technological potential of brain-activity measurement and geolocation in commercial spatial-design practice.

Literature review

The study was inspired by findings that wearable EEG can detect brain activity, associated with decision-making points for people navigating in real-world environments, and studies investigating the potential for wearable EEG readings and geolocation/mapping in the urban realm.

Recent research by Karandinou and Turner (2017; 2018) involved wearable EEG in real-world environments and found peaks of 'Beta' brain activity to be characteristic of decision-making points along a route. Peaks were more extreme where participants were unfamiliar with environments they were navigating. The team were confident of their findings, but noted the challenges of identifying peaks in Beta activity allied with navigation, as other stimuli also prompted Beta peaks, hence the use of video to record what other stimuli were present in the participant's environment. Karandinou and Turner's findings supplement investigations

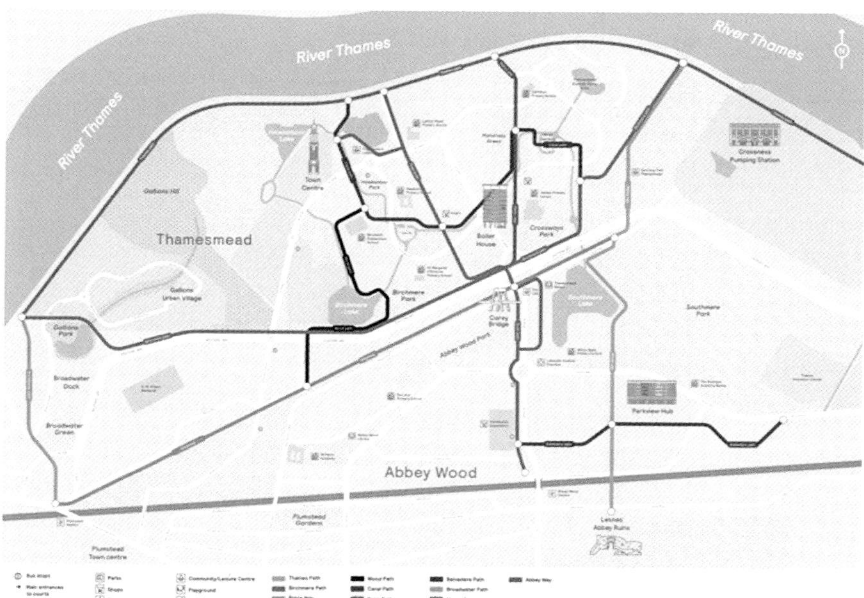

FIGURE 7.3 Proposed Shape/Leitsystem 'Walking Tube Map' for Thamesmead.

into navigation in virtual reality, using conventional EEG, that have also identified statistically significant and measurable peaks in brain activity allied with spatial decision making at specific points within virtual mazes across a number of participants (Bischof and Boulanger, 2003). In the 2003 study, however, 'Theta' activity peaks were found in relation to specific points within a wayfinding challenge, immediately after a corner had been turned, which authors associated with the onset of new spatial information requiring choice or recall. The association with high Theta activity supported other studies cited by the authors regarding Theta activity allied with navigation.

Karandinou and Turner synchronised video with EEG data generated by an Emotiv Epoc headset, collected wirelessly, via laptops in participants' backpacks. They then carried out post hoc analysis of the simultaneous visual displays to identify the relationship between navigation and brain activity, ultimately producing maps locating Beta peaks in place. Others have used the same headset and laptop arrangements to collect spatially located EEG data in 'real-world' settings, but not linked to navigation. Teams in Edinburgh and London have used Emotiv Epoc as the generator of static EEG displays claimed to represent emotional states along mapped routes, with location identified using geolocation apps (Skroumpelou, Mavros, and Hudson Smith, 2015; Mavros et al., 2012). The researchers had previously satisfied themselves of the validity of the emotional states identified in the commercial software, and accompanied participants to record location of stimuli outside those being tested that might result in brain activity, in annotated form.

Experiment design/methodology

Our empirical fieldwork aimed to investigate whether commercially available and wearable EEG and analysis software could offer new methods to complement 'traditional' observation or user survey, as a means of assessing the impact of wayfinding interventions. The assessment was for application in a typical commercial commission, rather than an academic setting. We aimed initially to use similar methods to those previously employed by Karandinou and Turner, and by Mavros et al. to investigate the potential for locating Beta peaks spatially. We hoped if possible to identify peaks as they occurred, and to subsequently cross-compare data post hoc, using static-map-based comparison, with location data generated using GPS systems rather than video recording.

Wearable EEG, specifically the commercially available Emotiv EPOC headset and its accompanying software, was envisaged as a tool that might readily provide objective data, illustrating the impact of spatial or graphic wayfinding interventions in specific locations. Emotiv promotes itself as an accessible interface for non-experts who are interested in detecting and visualising brain activity. It also includes independent spatial-research chapters on its website from credible academic sources (cited above), providing reassurance of its use in generating reliable, robust data.

All data collected using EEG/GIS technologies were to be complemented using the qualitative-research methods of participant and site observation during navigation, with subsequent interview. This would allow recording of any external stimuli, of participants' actions such as head movement/gaze direction, and allow the team to reflect on the potential for currently available EEG and geolocation technology as a complement to existing methodologies within commercial spatial practice. We were interested in the quality of the data generated, ease of use in the field, ease of analysis/representation of results and relative performance alongside 'traditional' methods. We hoped to be able to suggest further methodological and technological development based on our experience in the field.

Our empirical fieldwork began in autumn 2016 with trials to assess the feasibility of our proposed experiment. We were considering analysing data from approximately ten participants, each undertaking a 15-minute walk between two points. Our experimental design would include participants who both had and did not have place knowledge, and experiments would be run with and without signage in specific locations where we believed it could aid in navigation. The intention was to display a static version of geolocation information (map) in parallel with brain analytics (graph) as the team in Edinburgh had done, to seek common patterns, or differences, between participants. We intended, however, to use Beta and Theta activity to engage with previous studies in brain activity and navigation.

Trial 1

The first trial proved that this would be more difficult than anticipated. We carried out a 10-minute walk with a single participant, using a geolocation app, and simultaneously recorded EEG data from Emotiv Epoc. As the EEG had to be connected to software that in 2016 was only accessible via a live internet connection, we had to keep the laptop tethered to wireless networks throughout (earlier versions of the software had been available offline). If the internet connection were lost, we would potentially lose the software link and invalidate the test. We felt this might easily happen if the laptop was inside a backpack. We had in any case wanted to see if it was possible to identify peaks as they happened and so, to observe the data display during the trial, we proposed walking near the participant, carrying the laptop with the screen in view. Being tethered to the internet for one 10-minute walk was quite draining on the laptop battery, making a series of walks of 15 minutes with several participants seem challenging.

The trial established it was not possible to meaningfully assess the comparative size of Beta peaks 'live', but there was still a concern that internet connection might be lost so following participants while viewing the display at least periodically was still a requirement. In watching back EEG data as video recordings, we were able to see momentary variation in peaks of Beta activity, but when the data were downloaded by the team to make static graphs, all the labels identifying the various types of brain activity were lost and the data broke up into unrecognisable sections. We contacted the EEG manufacturer for support, but they could not resolve our issues, and provided no software to view or print the static data themselves. They did recommend reviewing the data using some open-source software, which we researched but were not familiar with. We sought assistance from academics working in neuroscience, without success. After several weeks with no further progress, we had two options to progress the trial. We could either play and replay the data as a video, but it would be difficult to compare the amplitude of peaks, or we would have to work with graphics taken as 'screen grabs'. Neither was ideal, nor robust, and either would only be possible for walks of very short duration. Combined with the issue of battery life, and concerns over continuous internet coverage, we decided to proceed but to revise our experimental plan.

Trial 2

The journey length had to be more restricted. We therefore decided to focus the experiment on a single intersection. This intersection is the primary connection between north and south Thamesmead, and one of the most confusing junctions in the entire pedestrian-movement network (Figure 7.1). There are few external cues to orientation, there are no clear direct paths, and there are multiple routes with no immediately visible destination. We felt this intersection would require perhaps the greatest amount of decision-making brain activity of any along the route originally envisaged for testing, and therefore might still yield some valid indication of how brain activity was influenced by place knowledge or wayfinding interventions.

We met again to trial how we might best record the brain activity within this far more geographically restricted environment. At the time of this second trial run, we also tested Emotiv's recently released app for mobile phone. The phone could easily be handheld and viewed at all times, and the app might offer fewer battery problems than the software used in the laptop. Walking with the laptop was possible, but less practical. The exposed laptop was more vulnerable to damage e.g. from rain, and its use more conspicuous, more likely to lead to questioning by passers-by during use, which could interrupt trials. A static display of the entire trial run was visible from the app, as well as moment-by-moment screenshots. With the full data download from the laptop not available to the team at the time of the trial, the app appeared to offer simplicity of use in the field, and less difficulty in post hoc analysis. From a practical perspective, it was a superior product.

There were, however, serious disadvantages. The app does not provide Beta or Theta as separate channels. Brain activity is only available via the app as pre-analysed 'emotional states' by Emotiv, namely 'stress', 'excitement', 'engagement', 'focus', 'interest' and 'relaxation'. Emotiv were unable to provide information to the team as to which frequency of brain activity was included within the different 'recipes', so it was not possible to assess whether any might act as proxies, indicative of Beta or Theta activity. However as preanalysed emotional states had been used in other spatial research, were argued to remove many extraneous anomalies (Mavros et al., 2012) and would arguably contain at least some indication of Beta and Theta activity within the various components, we felt we might still at least find some common patterns worthy of further investigation. Another serious disadvantage was that the app could not be recalibrated for many users. Again, as our primary intention was to investigate potential for commercially available products in commercial spatial-design practice, despite the clear problems we were facing, and the major limitations of the validity of any brain activity findings academically, we decided to proceed.

The second trial run showed little benefit in the use of geolocation software for such a short distance (less than 200m). For the experimental fieldwork, it was decided instead to use a simple timer with field annotations.

Fieldwork methodology

The final experiment worked with six participants on a single afternoon, undertaking a single 200m wayfinding challenge as described. With such a small sample size, any generalisation is inappropriate; however, if any patterns did emerge, these might be indicative, and suited to further testing at a later date. The journey of circa 2-minutes duration would be undertaken separately by six 'strangers' to Thamesmead, all briefed together and given the same map – the walking tube map – designed by the team to guide their journey. The first three participants would have only the map. The second three would have both the map and a small amount of supporting signage installed by the team on the day. All participants were equipped with a portable EEG device and the abovementioned equivalent mobile app.

The participants were all mature students in their first year of a spatial-studies-related postgraduate degree, three were from the UK and three were from outside the UK. Four of the six participants had significant experience in spatial design and map reading. Two spatial designers and one non-spatial designer were included in each of the two trial groups (one without supporting signs, one with supporting signs).

After their first navigation task, the participants would be told if they had followed the mapped route or not in their trial, and would be interviewed briefly about their thinking and any conscious wayfinding or navigation decisions they had taken. Then, if time allowed, each would be asked to walk the route again, this time as a knowledgeable navigator. This might allow the team to assess individual impacts of spatial familiarity, as well as attempting to compare across individuals.

Timings would be taken for each participant at a range of landmarks/marked points along the route (Figure 7.4) and notes made of any happenings such as loud noise, strong smells or other people encountered during the journey between the defined landmark points. Brain activity recordings could be compared within each journey, between different 'runs' for the same participant, and between participants. Both the laptop and mobile phone loaded with hand-held app were brought to Thamesmead, but as it was raining intermittently on the day of the experiment, the team decided to make use of the hand-held app only.

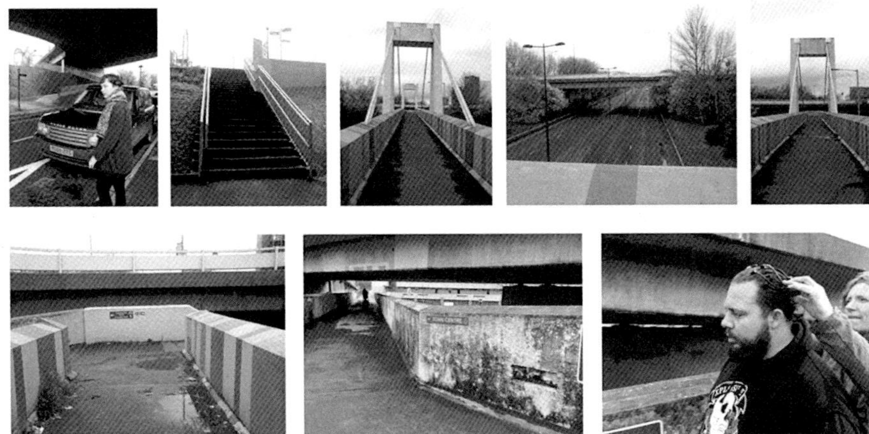

FIGURE 7.4 Participants and timing points on the route from 'The Link': buttress 1, central reservation, buttress 2, corner 1, corner 2.

Findings

Navigation accuracy

One participant from the 'map only' group, and all three from the group with the additional signage, were able to navigate the route as desired. This finding at face value would seem to indicate that the signage was effective in supporting accurate route choice.

This supposition, however, was not wholly supported by the post-trial interviews. Neither of those who failed to follow the route used the map, but followed alternate signage already in place. One followed signs of the same colour as the designated route on the map, but to a different destination. The other followed signs that would lead to the correct ultimate destination, but via an alternative route.

Two of those in the 'signage' group who made the correct route choice did not use the route-specific signage. One did not see it, the other did not recognise the wording as part of the desired route but instead navigated correctly using the map. All four people who made the correct route choice visibly paused to consult the map more than once during the journey.

One participant indicated that the issue of height of routes above ground was not anticipated from the map, and had been a source of some surprise. She indicated it made for additional difficulty in map reading.

Issues such as presence of conflicting signs, and different understandings of the task from the same spoken briefing, impacted on the participants' navigation through the junction.

From a small sample of people largely familiar with maps and plans, we have found that while the diagrammatic map alone provides some support for navigation, it is unlikely to be enough for many users wanting to navigate Thamesmead at such complex intersections. Signage, even if not entirely fitting to the task, is relied on in unfamiliar environments to support wayfinding decisions. Colour coding of routes can work, but unsurprisingly, in a confusing, visually cluttered, environment, choice of colour, location and coordination of other retained/ preexisting signage is critical.

Total journey time

The total journey time taken varied from 1 minute and 35 seconds to 2 minutes and 5 seconds. The second run was in all cases (four participants) quicker than the first. The reduction in time between 1st and 2nd run varied from 5 seconds to 21 seconds. The fastest participant was open about wanting the second run to be over quickly, while other participants described the second run as more enjoyable, providing an opportunity to enjoy the scent of spring blossom and to have more of a look around, rather than focus on the navigation task.

Brain activity and navigation

Brain activity, as displayed on the hand-held app, was reviewed throughout the whole journey then analysed post hoc for each participant, for each 'run' and for each 'group'. Post hoc analysis was achieved by plotting landmarks as timing points onto the plots generated by the app, to provide a spatially located graphic of brain activity. Drawing software (Adobe Illustrator) was used to connect peaks and troughs to generate a smoothed path, set between fluctuating peaks and troughs.

In general, there was little consistency in the graphs that could reasonably be allocated to any objective stimuli across the entire journey for any individual or across the group; however, closer investigation of the end point of the journey, where participants arguably had had a little time to become familiar both with the experimental conditions and the environment of the route, and at the point where the key wayfinding decision has to be made, did show some indicative consistency that might be worthy of further investigation (Figure 7.5).

In all cases recorded, the reading term 'Engagement' rose slightly between the final buttress and the first corner, dropped coming into and after turning the first corner, then started to rise again.

It might be that this brain-activity peak was associated with anticipation of the turn. The pattern was observed in both first and second runs. In most cases recorded, the reading termed 'Excitement' rises to a peak at or just after buttress 2, a point at which some participants looked to the left at the path from the bridge (or the sign in some cases). After this, the level of activity drops, perhaps as a decision is made, or the direction of future travel is identified.

Discussion

The validity and generalisability of findings from these trials were severely compromised, both by the type of EEG data available for analysis, and by the sample

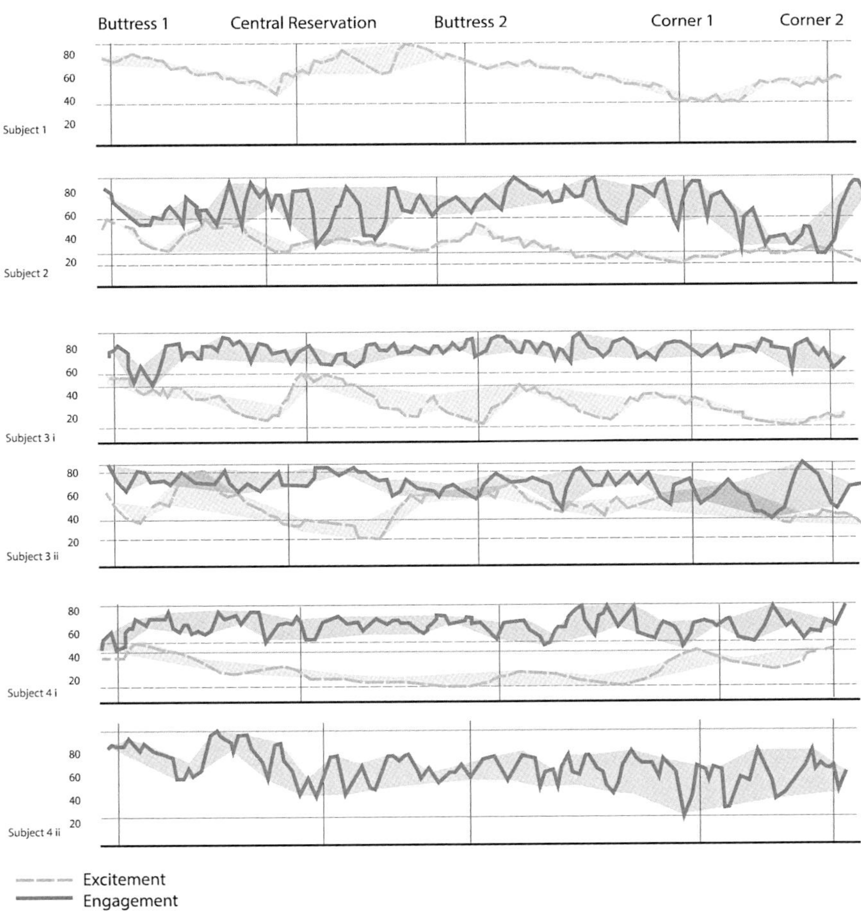

FIGURE 7.5 Brain activity graphic: interpreted plots for activity termed 'excitement' and 'engagement'.

size and composition. Nevertheless, the authors felt that in spite of the challenges faced there was an indication that useful insights might be able to be generated using similar methods, and portable EEG equipment, following further research to establish suitable products and software. There was interest from the client in investigating further.

The main challenges for the team related not to hardware for gathering data, nor to the time for analysis, nor to experimental control, as had originally been envisaged. The main challenge was in finding accessible software that could allow raw EEG data to be easily recorded and viewed as a static display or printout. Software changes that have occurred since the earlier experiments in wearable EEG cited in the literature for this chapter created significant problems for the team.

Where historically, recording could be carried out offline, now the data recording software is only available for new customers via subscription to a live internet connection. In the team's opinion, the specific hardware chosen for this trial is now of limited utility in a landscape setting, where internet connectivity may vary.

Second, we could find no simple method of printing the data collected to allow cross-comparison of data peaks. The advice we received from the EEG manufacturer was that data had to be downloaded and processed using separate software, which our team did not have to hand. While this may be readily overcome with more time, it presents a further barrier to use in a non-academic, non-specialist setting. The Emotiv mobile phone app showed significant potential for increased portability of data readout, and therefore ease of use for 'real-world' application, though in this case again, printable data were not readily available for subsequent analysis, and the data were restricted to pre-analysed emotions, rather than a full range of frequencies that the Epoc headset itself can generate.

Recommendations and opportunities for future development

This study finds potential for the development of wearable EEG in commercial spatial design, but did not find a suite of products that could easily be applied in the field. 'Wearable' EEG devices already allow brain activity readings to be linked to movement in the real world, but the accessibility of objective and robust data is surprisingly not guaranteed to accompany technological capacity. The product development focus at present seems to be on enhancing or augmenting experiences for users in the moment, rather than on use of the wearable and portable tools for subsequent analysis, which we believe is a missed opportunity. We believe there is a case for development of both handheld monitoring and remote monitoring of wearable EEG data, and a need for readily printable outputs that allow subsequent analysis. We also believe that data linked to Geolocation apps within a single software, generating spatially located brain-activity maps could have wider applicability in spatial-design practice, including landscape architecture. This study in Thamesmead shows there is a demand for software and hardware that support greater use of EEG outside academic settings.

References

Bischof, W. and Boulanger, P. (2003). 'Spatial navigation in virtual reality environments: An EEG analysis'. *CyberPsychology and Behaviour*, *6*(5), 487–95.

Karandinou, A. and Turner, L. (2017). 'Mind-mapping a way-finding process; the use of portable EEG brain mapping in the analysis of the experience of everyday spaces' in Alberto T. Estevez (ed.), *Biodigital Architecture*. Barcelona: UIC.

Karandinou, A. and Turner, L. (2018). 'Architecture and neuroscience; what can the EEG recording of brain activity reveal about a walk through everyday spaces?' *International Journal of Parallel, Emergent and Distributed Systems*. Taylor & Francis. ISSN: 1744–5760

(Print) 1744–5779 (Online) DOI:10.1080/17445760.2017.1390089 Available at: https://www.tandfonline.com/eprint/F4IGBYCammnIYydnVQbh/full

Lynch, K. (1960). *The Image of the City*. Cambridge Mass: MIT Press.

Mavros, P., Coyne, R., Roe, J. and Aspinall, P. (2012). 'Engaging the brain. Implications of mobile EEG for spatial representation'. *Emotiv Library*. Edinburgh, Scotland, UK. Available at: https://www.emotiv.com/category/independent-studies/ (Retrieved Oct 11, 2016)

Peabody (2017). 'London's growing new town'. *Thamesmead Now*. Available at: https://www.thamesmeadnow.org.uk/londons-new-town/homes/ (Retrieved 4 March 2017).

Skroumpelou, K., Mavros, P. and Hudson Smith, A. (2015). 'Are we there yet? Exploring distance perception in urban environments with mobile electroencephalography'. *Emotiv Library*. London, UK. Available at: https://www.emotiv.com/category/independent-studies/ (Retrieved 1 July, 2017).

Willey, R. (2016). *London Gazetteer Thamesmead*. 'Hidden London'. Available at: http://hidden-london.com/gazetteer/thamesmead/

8

VIRTUAL REALITY AND EEG DATA

Understanding spatial transitions

Dorothea Kalogianni and Richard Coyne

Introduction

Forbes Magazine heralded 2016 as the year that launched Virtual Reality (VR) for the everyday user (Ewalt, 2016). VR is an emerging technology that can potentially have multiple applications. We tested this claim for VR with two pilot experiments, using portable electroencephalography (EEG) technology and a head mounted display (HMD). Through these two sets of experiments we explored how participants emotionally perceive spatial transitions in a VR environment. We did so through analysis of the EEG recordings, interviews, and questionnaires. This study may also enhance our understanding of the way users experience spatial transitions in everyday offline spaces and transitions between places of different character of atmosphere. We present preliminary results that raise questions on the potential use of VR and portable EEG in investigating architecture and human perception.

With the use of EEG, we documented the neurophysiological responses of participants while they moved between VR spaces of contrasting character. We present two complementary case-studies: a simple VR environment, in which we investigated transitions from a confined to an open space; and a complex VR environment, where we examined more intricate transitions. We hypothesize that spatial transitions between spaces of contrasted character trigger intense emotional responses from the users, which are evident in the users' EEG readings.

We observed noticeable shifts in the participants' EEG measurements before and after crossing spatial thresholds. The shifts were in the form of peaks or gradual increases and decreases of the brain-data values. We noticed variation in the EEG readings among the experimentees and the different VR environments. We do not intend to perform data aggregation and statistical analysis with the brain data. Instead, we present individual cases of participants. Our observations are consistent with the subjects' accounts of their VR experience of spatial transitions.

The designing of the VR experience and space

In VR we can break the rules of space and time, pushing architecture to its limits. Architect Bernard Tschumi suggests (1996, p.91) that the defiance of limits is the starting point of architecture. With VR we can design complex transitions and unrealistic spaces of exaggerated and dramatic architecture, which are either impossible to find, very costly to construct, or they do not exist in the ordinary, everyday environment.

VR has been used together with wireless EEG technology (Torok et al., 2014) in psychology, in studies of human perception and cognition (Moussaoui, Pruski, and Cherki, 2007). VR and EEG have also been combined for investigating wayfinding behaviors in architectural contexts (Lelin Zhang et al., 2010; Edelstein et al., 2008). Researchers at the Academy of Neuroscience for Architecture (ANFA) at the University of California have used neuroscience as a tool for improving architectural design. They tested the brain responses of subjects to various architectural conditions in a CAVE VR environment. They moved on to suggest that neuroscience should be introduced as a tool in the architectural design process (Edelstein & Macagno, 2012; Edelstein et al., 2008) However, these studies focus on everyday, offline environments. We take a more exploratory approach based on the view that VR offers the opportunity for users to experience exciting, novel, and unfamiliar environments.

Experiments have shown that VR can engender emotional responses from users (Riva et al., 2007) that are comparable to responses to sensory stimuli in the everyday lifeworld (Slater et al., 1996). We developed three different VR environments to experiment with. The first was used for the first set of experiments, and the second and third for the second set of experiments. At both stages, our VR environments generated at times an uncanny, surreal feeling to the VR walker. Architect Antony Vidler (2003) states that the uncanny stands at the intersection of surrealism and architecture – and he describes surrealism as the discourse that shows "familiar objects" and scenes "in unlikely forms."

The first experiment focused on the design of one transition between two spaces of different character: walking from a very long, dark, and confined concrete corridor to a bright, open, and green space. Although this first VR setting resembles an ordinary environment, we intensified the experience of the transition by designing a very long corridor. At the end of the corridor there was light that hinted at an opening to a different space – the open, green space. The light poured through an opening on the side of the structure, so that one had to turn 90 degrees for the following space to be revealed. The first experiment was meant as a small-scale, preparatory study to help us understand how users respond to a single transition.

For the second experiment we designed, in collaboration with a team of digital-media designers, students of ours at the time, two complex VR environments, entitled "Concrete Jungle" and "Urban Escape." We created environments with fictional, surreal, unfamiliar, and exaggerated geometric and atmospheric qualities that employed multiple, intricate, and extreme spatial transitions. We anticipated

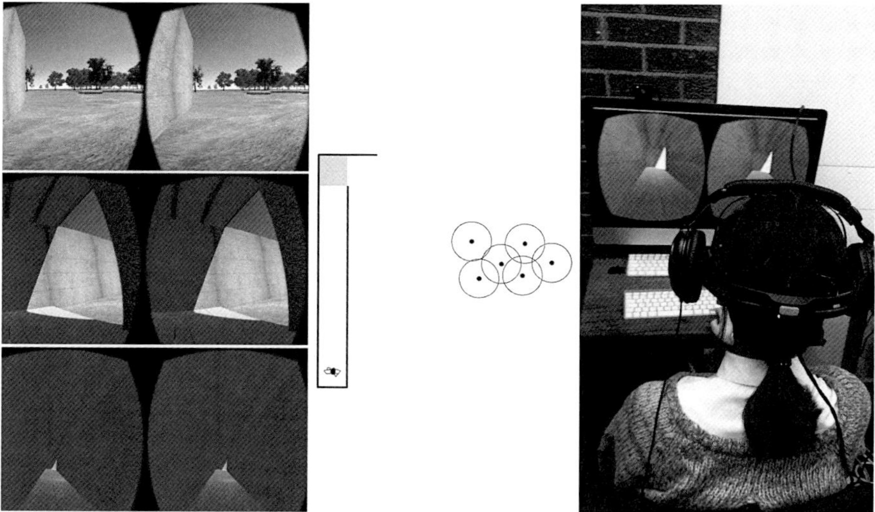

FIGURE 8.1 Left: Snapshots of the environment of the first VR experiment. Middle: Plan view of the design of the first VR experiment. Right: A participant mid-trial of the first VR experiment.

that the more extreme the spatial thresholds were, the more intense the emotional responses would be.

To attain more extreme transitions, we prompted the students to design a journey of fantasy that takes the VR stroller through a series of alternating familiar and unfamiliar spaces (DMSP Affective Immersion, 2016). The design of the scenes was inspired by dystopian science-fiction movies such as Terry Gilliam's Brazil (Gilliam, 2011; O'Neill, 2010), Star Wars (Lucas, 1983), and Inception (Robey, 2010). Literary theorist Brian G. McHale (2013) identifies fiction as the transition through highly contrasted spaces that we would normally not encounter in succession in real-life scenarios. We were also inspired by games with dystopian themes such as the *Portal*, where the player teleports through imaginary portals in an abandoned and empty factory (Valve Corporation, 2007) and the *BioShock Infinite* video game with surreal environments, and science-fiction elements ('BioShock® Infinite,' 2002). Surrealist artists freespace from any links with familiarity as they challenge architectural and spatial conventions (Mical, 2005, p. 61). We also infer from the literary theorist Northrop Frye's take on utopia that dystopia is a world of fiction and fantasy that goes beyond limits and existing rules (Frye, 1982–1990, p. 229 in Rampton, 2009), conveying fear and disruption (Rampton, 2009, p. 198).

The first VR experience was designed entirely in Unity 3D, a gaming engine, while for the second VR experience the students designed the environments in Blender and Sketch-up and then imported them into Unity 3D. We used C sharp and JavaScript to register the brain data and to design the elements of interaction and the sound implementation. The brain data were time stamped and marked.

The sounds added to the VR environment consisted of the navigator's footsteps and the ambience of the virtual spaces, and were spatialized and morphed in 3D.

The aim was to design a variety of spatial transitions to measure a person's EEG readings while they moved from one environment to another. We evaluate the qualities and characteristics of the spatial transitions we designed, and, in effect, of the two different environments, and investigate links to possible emotional shifts.

Recording brain data: EEG

We used the VR kit Oculus Rift DK 2 HMD and the Emotiv EPOC brain wearable. Emotiv EPOC is a lightweight, low-cost, consumer EEG headset, which records the electrical activity of the brain with 14 saline-based wet sensors and two reference points fixed and positioned along an individual's scalp (see Figure 8.2).

The Emotiv EPOC headset has been used primarily for gaming. One of the applications Emotiv offers is the Affective Suite. The Affective Suite detects four affective states recorded as instantaneous and long-term values: Excitement, Engagement, Frustration, and Meditation. These four detections output float values between 0 (minimum) and 1 (maximum). We excluded the Meditation label from our investigation, as our own empirical evidence has shown that it does not produce meaningful data.

Emotiv EPOC takes EEG out of the clinical lab and in the outdoor. Such advancements in neuroimaging technologies have allowed other disciplines to experiment with the use of EEG. The Emotiv EPOC headset has been validated against medical-grade brain caps for accurately recording brain activity (Badcock et al., 2013; Badcock et al., 2015; Taylor and Schmidt, 2012). The Emotiv EPOC Affective Suite has recently been successfully used to measure affective responses in real-life urban settings and environments of nature (Mavros et al., 2012; Aspinall et al., 2015; Neale et al., 2017; Debener et al., 2012). Some studies matched responses from a questionnaire to validate the Affective Suite readings of game players (Pröll, 2012; Cernea, Kerren, and Ebert, 2011; Cernea et al., 2011). According to Emotiv, the label Excitement has a high level of accuracy, followed by Frustration and Engagement, while the Meditation detections vary in accuracy (Emotiv Inc, n.d.).

Since Emotiv EPOC is a commercial device, the algorithms behind the Affective Suite have not been released to the public. Emotiv have stated that the Affective detection suite algorithms were trained with an artificial intelligence neural network (ANN). The ANN was fed examples of volunteers who were exposed to gaming environments. The volunteers were tested under various conditions that evoked different emotional responses. They wore the EPOC headset together with other biometric devices that measured the physiological responses (i.e. heart rate, breathing, galvanic skin response) of the participants. A psychologist analyzed the behavior and bodily responses of the subjects. "Frustration arises when the progress a user is making toward achieving a given goal is impeded" (Gilleade and Dix, 2004). Frustration is associated with stress and was measured when the default game

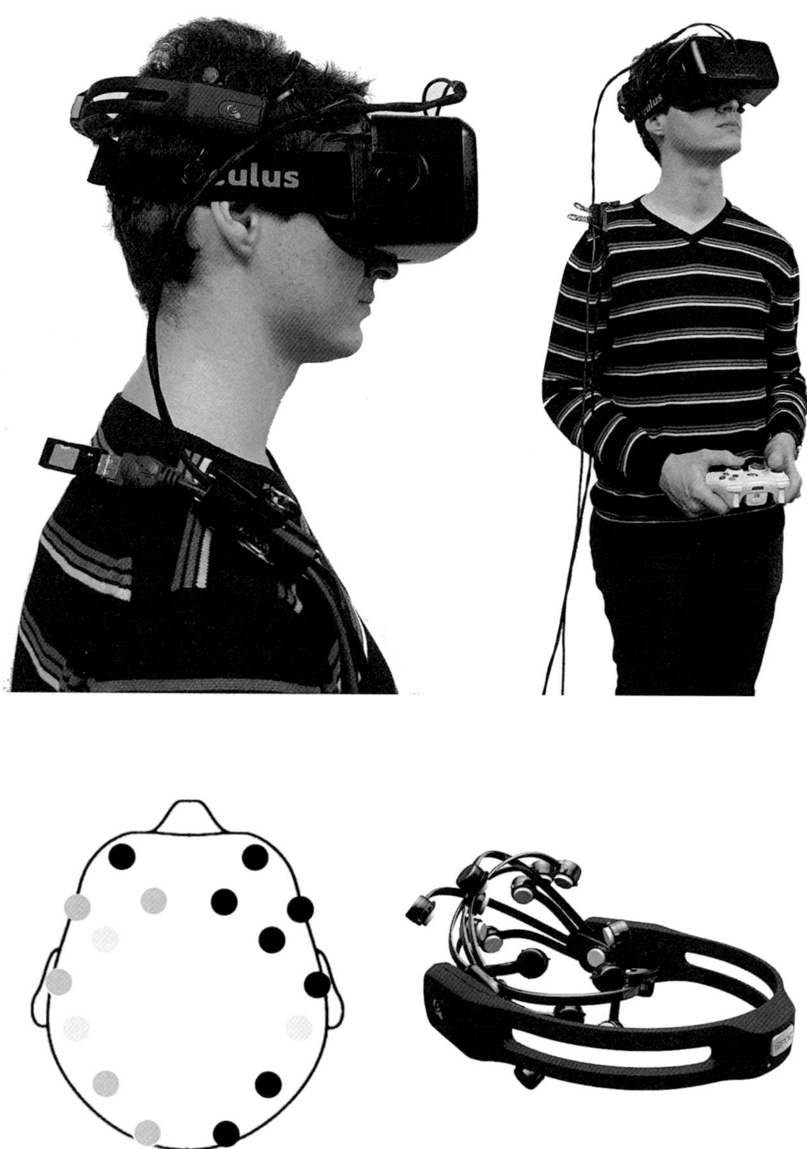

FIGURE 8.2 Top: Configuration of the experimental set-up (portable EEG combined with the Oculus Rift DK 2 Equipment). Bottom left: Screenshot of the EEG sensors on the Emotiv EPOC control panel app during calibration. The colors indicate the signal quality, ranging from red (no signal) to green (good signal) (here: from black to light gray). Bottom right: The Emotiv EPOC headset (EMOTIV Inc).

controls were disabled. This disrupted the process of the game and the gamer's goals. Engagement indicates focus and immersion at completing a task or being involved in an activity. It combines attention, interest, stimulation, and alertness toward the stimuli that relate to the activity or task. Engagement rises when a player concentrates on a difficult task, when they notice a new element in the game, or when they enter an area that is new. The EPOC registers Excitement when there is positive physiological arousal, such as when surprising events take place. Excitement also relates to feelings of nervousness and agitation (Emotiv Inc, n.d.).

The Affective Suite filters out electromyography (EMG) signals from muscle activation and the electrooculography (EOG) signals from eye movement. The Emotiv EPOC headset adapts to the emotional range of each individual user after 30 minutes of use (EMOTIV Inc, n.d.).

The two sets of experiments

A series of experiments was conducted involving 42 subjects. The participants were design students at the University of Edinburgh who volunteered to take part in our research. Their ages spanned from 18 to 25 years, except for two participants who were older. The research did not examine gender differences, and both male and female students were involved.

The experiments were carried out over a period of two academic semesters. As we progressed through the experiments we adjusted the format of the set-up, improving the designs and the techniques used. Participants followed a protocol throughout the experiments: we first described the procedure and technology used; we then sat the participants in front of a desktop computer where the VR system was set up. They were individually rigged up with an Oculus Rift VR HMD, a portable Emotiv EPOC EEG headset, earphones and, in some instances, a pair of noise-cancellation headphones. The subjects were exposed prior to the experiments to a commercial demo VR environment to familiarize them with the VR technology and the first-person navigation experience. At this stage, we also calibrated the technical settings of the Oculus. To navigate through the VR environments, our volunteers used a wireless keyboard and at a later stage a Super Nintendo controller.

For the first set of experiments (in the first VR environment), two rounds of tests were conducted. First, the experimentees were not given a specific goal. They were advised to roam freely in the space. Then they were given the task of finding an object. This VR environment was simple and somewhat monotonous, so having a goal helped the participants to avoid wandering in the space indefinitely, which also at times is responsible for VR sickness, in other words nausea.

For the second set of experiments (where the other two VR designed spaces were used) we invited the participants to walk through the architectural VR environments naturally, following the sequential narrative of the space. This time we did not provide them with specific instructions in terms of the navigation.

For both sets of experiments, the participants were stationary. Most experiments took place with the subjects standing up; however, a few trials took place with the volunteers sitting in a chair as well.

The experiments were not time-restricted. The amount of time spent in the environments depended on the volition of the user. On average the time spent was estimated between 8 and 15 minutes. Throughout the experiments the participants' brain data were recorded. We set spatial and temporal markers in the virtual environment that helped us locate the users as they navigated in the space and register their emotional responses at points of interest. At the end of their navigation the participants were either interviewed or they completed a questionnaire.

Spatial transitions in architecture

Without any contrast, the experience of strolling through a city becomes mundane. Architect and urban designer Gordon Cullen attests that contrast is essential for a lively experience of passing through a city. Walkers stroll through cities and notice contrast through "the drama of juxtaposition" (Cullen, 1961, p.9).

According to Canadian philosopher Brian Massumi's take on the 17th century Dutch philosopher Baruch Spinoza, affect closely relates to the experience of spatial transitions and intensity (Massumi, 2002, p.15). Transitions are also valuable in evoking atmospheres and setting the mood of architecture. Architect and theorist Juhani Pallasmaa asserts that atmosphere engenders emotions and tunes the occupants with their environment (Pallasmaa, 2016). Transitions presuppose serial vision. Geographer Jay Appleton suggested that when space encourages serial vision, it has a greater influence on the user. Appleton perceives serial vision as the traveler's movement through successive spaces of highly contrasting character – spaces of "strong prospect" followed by spaces of "strong refuge" (Appleton, 1975, p.102). Through serial vision the urban stroller experiences "a journey through

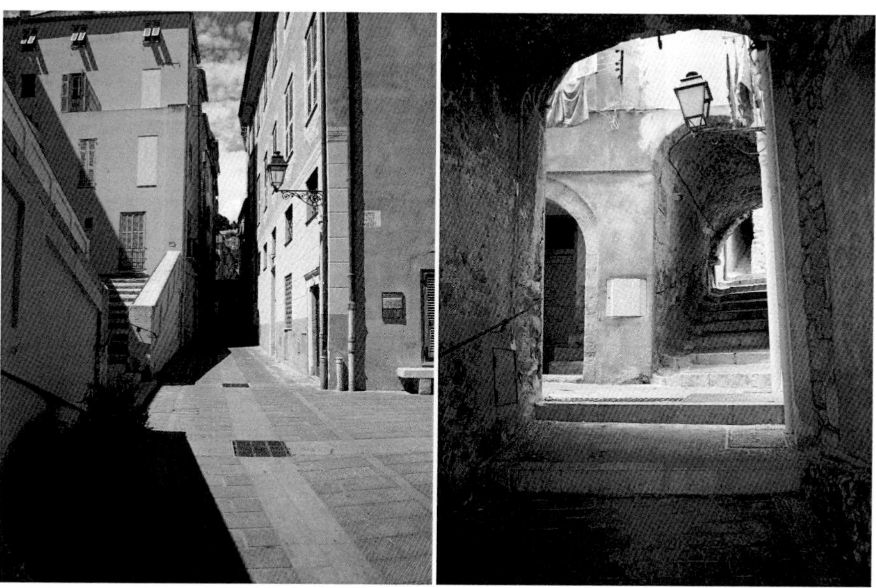

FIGURE 8.3 Experiencing contrast in the old town of Menton, France (Coyne, 2016).

pressures and vacuums, a sequence of exposures and enclosures, of constrain and relief' (Cullen, 1961, p.10).

Emotional transitions and observations

Based on the book *Essays on the Intersection of Music and Architecture* by Mikesch Muecke and Miriam Zach (p.78, 2007) we consider that spatial transitions have a fundamental role in forming the traveler's perception of space. In this paper we are concerned specifically with transitions between enclosed and open spaces.

The way space is designed, proportioned, and laid out is strongly linked to our sensory experience in the space. Professor of architecture Korydon Smith (2012) explains that differences in geometrical proportions in space can engender different responses to pedestrians. He gives the example of an elongated space with narrow width and low ceiling, and he compares this space with a cubic space of equal proportions.

Architect Paul D. Spreiregen (1965, p.75, in Hayward and Franklin, 1974) claims that we perceive a space as enclosed or open due to the combination of the dimension of height and the distance between the viewer and the physical boundaries of the space. Environmental psychologist Tommy Gärling suggests that the experience of openness and enclosure is possible when one is exposed to 2D colored pictures or perspective 3D drawings. VR takes this a step further in allowing immersive 3D representations of space (1969b: 1971, in Hayward and Franklin, 1974).

Here we analyze three transitions from an enclosed to an open space that were reported as the most intense by the participants. We present indicative brain data and accompanying accounts of some of the participants' affective experiences.

For the first environment, subjects transit from a narrow, elongated, concrete corridor to an open, green space. The brain data of most participants suggest a build-up of affective intensity leading to the threshold point. After the threshold, the intensity is released. We define as affective intensity the average of the summation of the readings from the Excitement, Frustration and Engagement labels (see Graph 2 of Figure 8.4). Deleuze (1994, p.190) outlines the notion of transition as a process of escalation and intensification that eventually reaches the right moment of the sublime.

We noticed that both Excitement and Frustration both rose or peaked either at the threshold or right before the threshold. Participants described the corridor as depressing, gray, claustrophobic, and stressful. Frustration increased probably due to the stress the space engendered (see Figure 8.4)

The Excitement levels rose when the users were exposed to strong hints such as sonic and light stimuli of a next, novel to them, environment. These stimuli entice the user and they generate mystery, curiosity, and anticipation about the space that follows. These emotions become stronger when the environment is fully revealed to them at the threshold. Hints of the new environment, or exiting the new environment, might also elicit feelings of surprise.

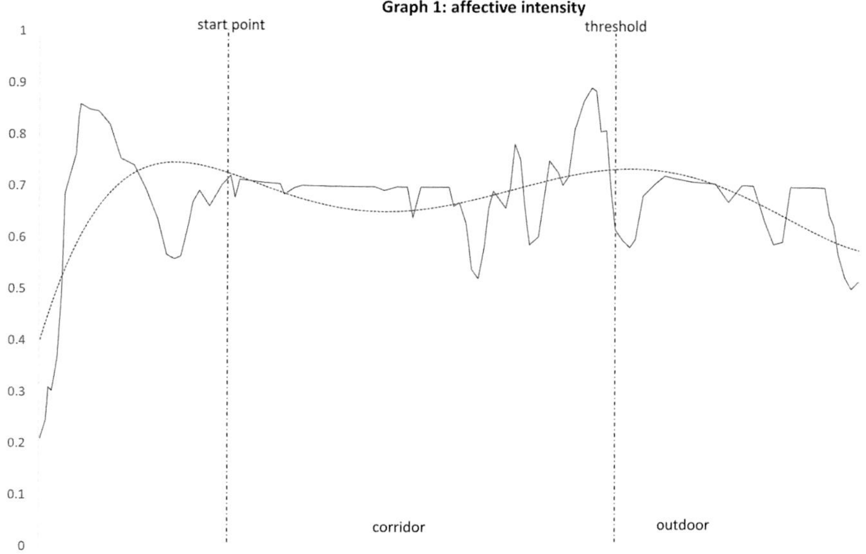

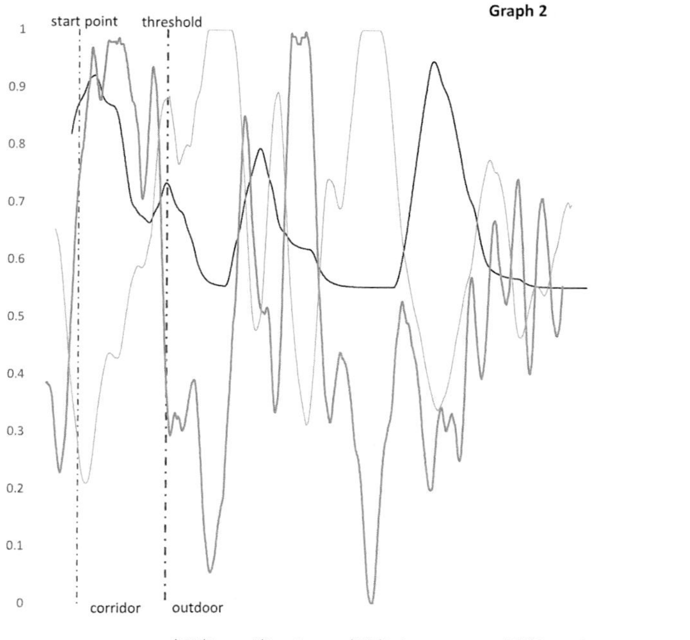

FIGURE 8.4 Top: Affective intensity in the first VR environment (Participant T). Bottom: Engagement, Excitement, Frustration in the first VR environment (Participant C).

> *"I felt curious when seeing the opening at the end of the corridor" (first VR experiment, Participant J)*
>
> *"I walked straight because I saw the light at the end of the corridor and wanted to see what is there . . . It gave me hope that there is a way out of the corridor" (first VR experiment, Participant S)*
>
> *"I was curious and really wanted to see what was behind the wall, so in that sense it was a very engaging moment. It also felt overwhelming but in a good sense. So, I guess turning around was the most important part of this sequence, and it truly felt that I was entering a different environment, and the actual surprise felt more intense than the anticipation." (first VR experiment, Participant C)*

When the participants reached the spatial threshold, and as they exited the confinement of the enclosed space and entered the contiguous, wide space, Anticipation ceased, and thus Excitement dropped. Frustration sloped downwards as participants found the succeeding space pleasant and relaxing.

It is worth mentioning that for some users it was more significant to see the light and opening as they approached the exit than to actually cross the threshold. They experienced an emotional transition, with high peaks in their affective data which preceded the spatial threshold point.

> *"It was quite exciting when I was walking closer and closer to the end of the corridor, the closer I went towards it the most excited I felt. It was more exciting than actually getting out." (first VR experiment, Participant T)*

During the second experiment, in the "Urban Escape" VR environment, one of the transitions we created formed a threshold between a narrow, dark tunnel modeled in the form of a sewer, and a vast, futuristic dome with a water tank that resembled a thermal spring.

Most subjects experienced the tunnel as unpleasant. Participant Y for example said: *"I felt pressure, the height is too low to cross."* ("Urban Escape," Participant Y). In contrast, the water tank was considered by many as pleasant. *"I felt excited, the steam is really amazing,"* Participant C mentioned.

Most of the times we observed a rise in Excitement at the threshold, right before or right after, followed by an immediate decline. We hypothesize that arousal rises together with the users' expectations and curiosity about the space to come as they approach the exit of the sewer. *"I feel curious. I wonder what is going on outside when I see the light at the end of the tunnel" ("Urban Escape," Participant Y).* As they were slowly freed from the constraining experience of the confined, dark tunnel, Frustration gradually declined.

Sometimes the confinement of the space overshadowed the participant's anticipation before the spatial threshold. In that case, Frustration increased and Excitement decreased as the participant reached the threshold. Excitement then went up at the entrance to the succeeding space. The latter triggers feelings of surprise. At the same time the vastness of the space replaced the cramped, stressful corridor and frustration reached a low (see second graph in Figure 8.7).

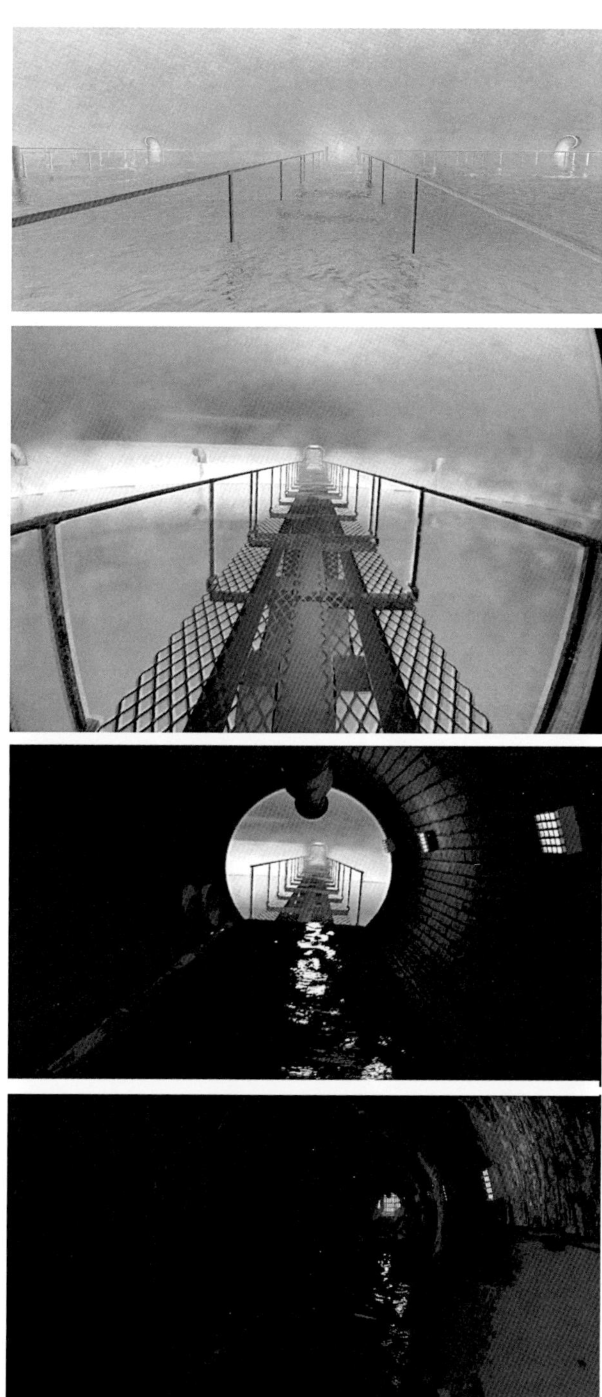

FIGURE 8.5 Transiting from the sewer to the water tank ("Urban Escape" VR environment).

In the "Concrete Jungle" VR we designed a transition that attempted to induce a sense of vertigo. French intellectual Roger Caillois describes vertigo as ". . . an attempt to momentarily destroy the stability of perception and inflict a kind of voluptuous panic upon an otherwise lucid mind" (Caillois, 1962, p. 23).

We designed a long corridor with several turnings. The corridor becomes gradually darker, narrower, and significantly low in height, abutting an opening toward a vertiginous space – this comprises a vast, cylidrical space that mimics the inside of a silo, and a high, narrow, suspension pedestrian bridge made of steel with perforated floor, which is followed by an elevator.

The disruption of perception triggered by the sensation of vertigo leads to experiencing intense emotions, such as fear and ecstasy, which in turn lead to feelings of excitement and pleasure (Caillois, 1962).

Participant Y characterized the vertiginous space as dazzling. Participant R explained: *"I was scared by the height and what was underneath the metal wired bridge"*

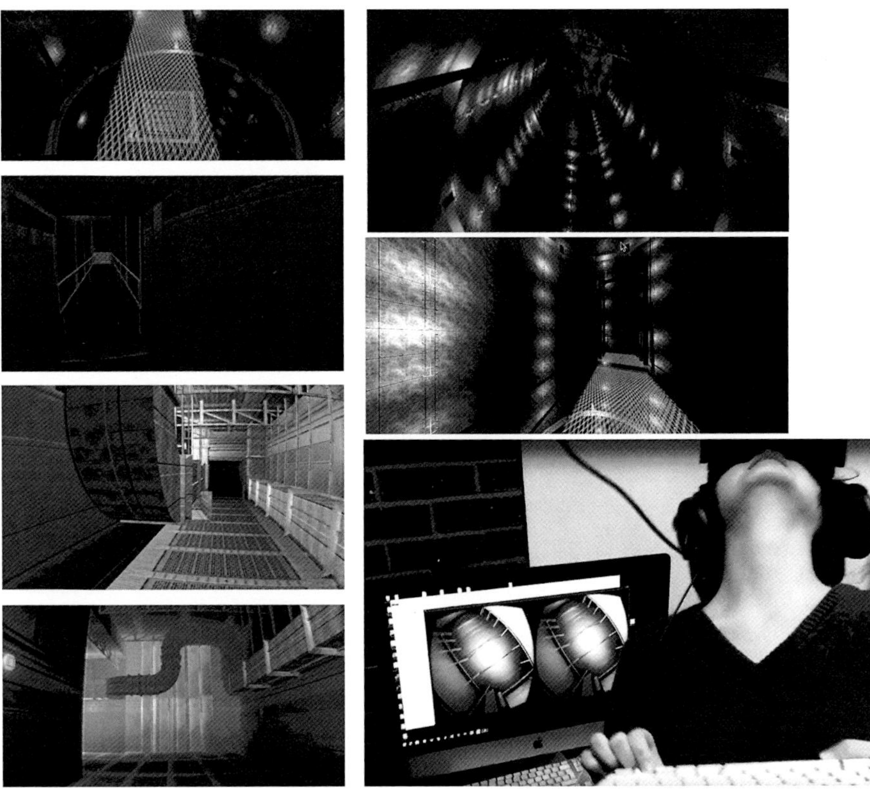

FIGURE 8.6 Snapshots from the transition to the vertiginous space ("Concrete Jungle" VR environment). Bottom right: A participant testing the vertiginous space ("Concrete Jungle" VR environment).

and *". . . fascinated by the high columns . . . The hanging bridge aroused my curiosity to the space as it's uncommon and unrealistic, reminds me of spy movies and futuristic designs."*

For some participants, navigating the cramped final part of the corridor invokes feelings of frustration as it limits their movement. Frustration then rises until the next environment is partially revealed. Here are some accounts of the experience of the corridor:

> *"The tunnel made me feel more curious and stressed . . . because it was a small space with little light." ("Concrete Jungle," Participant J)*
>
> *"I feel trapped at the corridor." ("Concrete Jungle," Participant C)*

As the new environment slowly unveils itself, Frustration drops and Excitement increases dramatically up to the threshold and upon the entrance to the vertiginous space.

In some instances when entering the final part of the corridor, the extreme reduction in the height and width, together with the decrease in brightness, generate a sudden increase in Frustration and Excitement. This may be due to both a sense of confinement and a rise in curiosity. Frustration and Excitement then follow a downward trajectory up to the threshold point. We can attribute this to the fact that one needs to turn around the final corner before seeing the exit (threshold), thus prior to that moment there are no spatial cues that trigger a change or suggest a transition to a different environment (see Graph 1, Figure 8.7)

In all three transitions presented here, for some participants Engagement rose at the threshold. This may signify that the participants were immersed and focused on the activity of moving through the enclosed space toward the opening. For most participants though, Engagement went up after crossing the threshold as they entered a novel environment.

In our VR scenes, one experiences what Geographer Jay Appleton (1975) calls the peephole vista. This type of view is restricted both in the horizontal and vertical direction and resembles the experience of looking through a keyhole. This experience is often exciting, stimulating, and suspenseful, arousing curiosity as one feels an urge to explore the secondary vista that awaits beyond the point of obstruction (Appleton, 1975). It also induces a sense of mystery as new information is implicit, hinted at, but not revealed directly (Kaplan, 1988).

Architect and architectural historian Grant Hilderbrand (1999) labels this process as "enticement." The view of the brighter space is not yet fully revealed. Once one reaches their destination this information might constitute a pleasant surprise or a dangerous threat (Hildebrand, 1999, p. 54). The expectation of what is about to come engages and captivates the walker (Kaplan, 1992).

Outcome and future work

It was observed that for most participants Excitement increased just before a threshold, whereas Engagement increased after the transition to the following space.

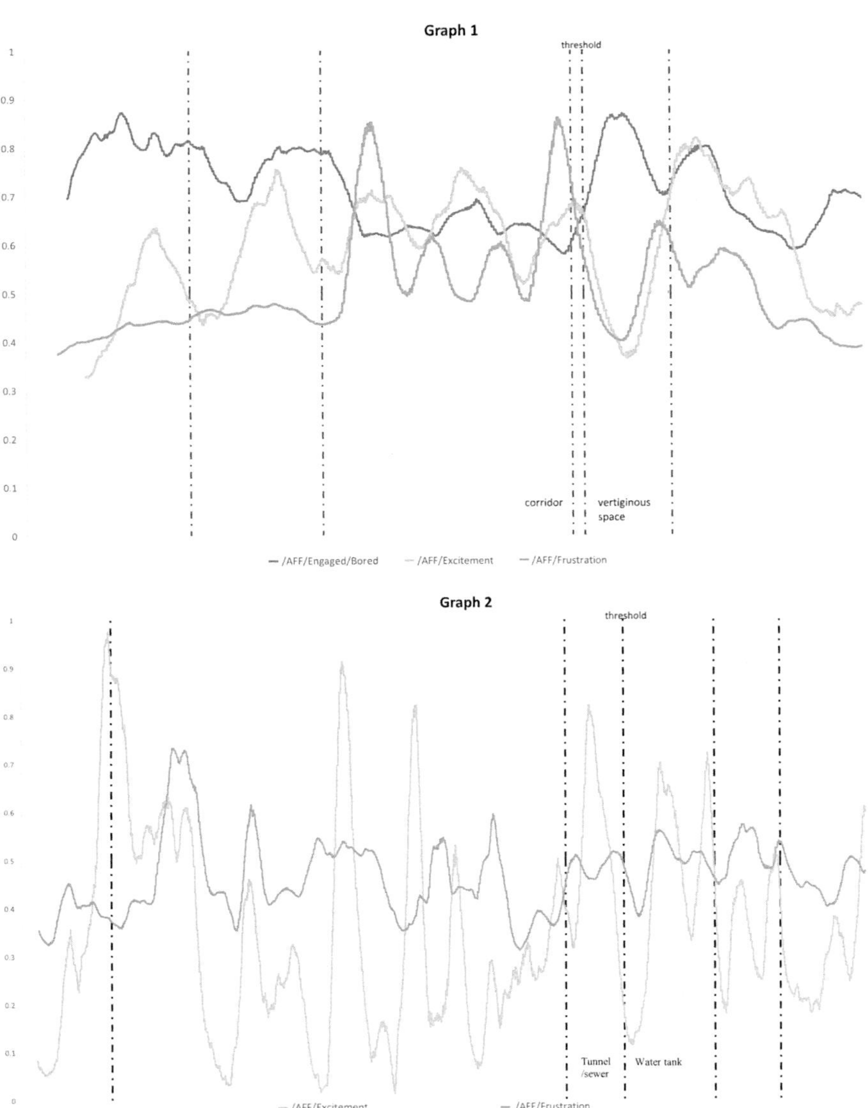

FIGURE 8.7 Top: Engagement, Excitement, Frustration in the "Concrete Jungle"' VR environment (Participant B). Bottom: Excitement, Frustration in the "Urban Escape" VR environment (Participant T).

This probably shows that the participant becomes more engaged as they enter the new environment. The new stimuli experienced may be the reason why Engagement peaks high. At the same time, the element of suspense and anticipated surprise is no longer there, reflecting on the decrease of Excitement. It is interesting to see what we usually discuss in an architectural context – the element of anticipated surprise before a change of environment – now mapped through the EEG.

It would be interesting to analyze, in future studies, how the actual brain activity and frequency bands (mainly the Beta, Alpha, and Theta) relate to such sequences of environments and spatial transitions. The use of the Emotiv algorithm translating the brain wave combination into categories of emotions and cognitive states (Excitement, Engagement, etc.) was a good start in the context of this series of pilot experiments, for testing certain methods, set-ups, and formulating some hypotheses.

References

Appleton, J. (1975). *The Experience of Landscape*. Chichester: Wiley. Available at: https://books.google.gr/books/about/The_experience_of_landscape.html?id=7LNPAAAAMAAJ&redir_esc=y.

Aspinall, P., Mavros, P., Coyne, R., and Roe, J. (2015). 'The urban brain: analysing outdoor physical activity with mobile EEG'. *British Journal of Sports Medicine*, *49*(4), 272–276. Available at: https://doi.org/10.1136/bjsports-2012-091877.

Badcock, N. A., Mousikou, P., Mahajan, Y., de Lissa, P., Thie, J., and McArthur, G. (2013). 'Validation of the Emotiv EPOC ® EEG gaming system for measuring research quality auditory ERPs'. *PeerJ*, *1*, e38. Available at: https://doi.org/10.7717/peerj.38.

Badcock, N. A., Preece, K. A., de Wit, B., Glenn, K., Fieder, N., Thie, J., and McArthur, G. (2015). 'Validation of the Emotiv EPOC EEG system for research quality auditory event-related potentials in children'. *PeerJ*, *3*, e907. Available at: https://doi.org/10.7717/peerj.907.

BioShock® Infinite. (2002). Available at: http://www.bioshockgame.com/.

Caillois, R. (1962). *Man, Play, and Games*. London: Thames and Hudson.

Cernea, D., Kerren, A., and Ebert, A. (2011). 'Detecting insight and emotion in visualization applications with a commercial EEG headset' in *SIGRAD 2011 Conference on Evaluations of Graphics and Visualization – Efficiency, Usefulness, Accessibility, Usability* (pp. 53–60). Stockholm, Sweden. Available at: http://www.ep.liu.se/ecp/065/008/ecp11065008.pdf

Cernea, D., Olech, P.-S., Ebert, A., and Kerren, A. (2011). *EEG-Based Measurement of Subjective Parameters in Evaluations* (pp. 279–283). Berlin: Springer. Available at: https://doi.org/10.1007/978-3-642-22095-1_57.

Cullen, G. (1961). *Townscape*. London: Architectural Press.

Debener, S., Minow, F., Emkes, R., Gandras, K., and de Vos, M. (2012). 'How about taking a low-cost, small, and wireless EEG for a walk?' *Psychophysiology*, *49*(11), 1617–1621. https://doi.org/10.1111/j.1469-8986.2012.01471.x

Deleuze, G. (1994). *Difference and Repetition*. (P. Patton, Ed.). London: Continuum.

DMSP (2016). *Affective Immersion*. Available at: https://dmsp.digital.eca.ed.ac.uk/blog/affectiveimmersion2016/submission-2/ (Accessed 9 April 2017).

Edelstein, E. A., and Macagno, E. (2012). *Form Follows Function: Bridging Neuroscience and Architecture* (pp. 27–41). New York: Springer. Available at: https://doi.org/10.1007/978-1-4419-0745-5_3.

Edelstein, E. A., Gramann, K., Schulze, J., Bigdely Shamlo, N., van Erp, E., Vankov, A., . . . Macagno, E. (2008). 'Neural responses during navigation in the virtual aided design laboratory: brain dynamics of orientation in architecturally ambiguous space'. In S. Haq, S., Hölscher, C., Torgrude (Ed.), SFB/TR 8 Report No. Report Series of the Transregional Collaborative Research Center SFB/TR 8 Spatial Cognition (pp. 35–41). Retrieved from http://web.eng.ucsd.edu/~jschulze/publications/Edelstein2008.pdf

EMOTIV Inc. (n.d.). EMOTIV Knowledge Base. Retrieved March 14, 2018, fromhttps://emotiv.zendesk.com/hc/en-us

EMOTIV Inc. (n.d.). Emotiv. Retrieved March 14, 2018, from https://www.emotiv.com/

Ewalt, D. M. (2016). *Oculus Rift Review: The Beginning of the Age of VR*. Available at: https://www.forbes.com/sites/davidewalt/2016/03/28/oculus-rift-review-the-beginning-of-the-age-of-vr/#1af8214a5aff (Accessed 1 April 2017).

Gilleade, K. M., and Dix, A. (2004). 'Using frustration in the design of adaptive video-games' in *Proceedings of the 2004 ACM SIGCHI International Conference on Advances in computer entertainment technology – ACE '04* (pp. 228–232). New York, New York, USA: ACM Press. Available at: https://doi.org/10.1145/1067343.1067372.

Gilliam, T. (2011). Director's Cut: Terry Gilliam on Brazil – Film 2011 with Claudia Winkleman – BBC One – YouTube. Available at: https://www.youtube.com/watch?v=BF2g5FGZMOU.

Hayward, S., and Franklin, S. (1974). 'Perceived openness-enclosure of architectural space'. *Environment and Behavior, 6*(1), 37.

Hildebrand, G. (1999). *Origins of Architectural Pleasure*. Berkeley, CA: Berkeley.

Kaplan, S. (1988). 'Perception and landscape: conceptions and misconceptions' in J. L. Nasar (Ed.), *Environmental Aesthetics* (pp. 45–55). Cambridge: Cambridge University Press. Available at: https://doi.org/10.1017/CBO9780511571213.006.

Lucas, G. (1983). *Star Wars: Episode VI Return of the Jedi*. United States of America. Available at: http://www.starwars.com/films/star-wars-episode-vi-return-of-the-jedi/.

Massumi, B. (2002). *Parables for the Virtual: Movement, Affect, Sensation*. Durham, NC: Duke University Press.

Mavros, P., Coyne, R., Roe, J., and Aspinall, P. (2012). 'Engaging the brain: Implications of mobile EEG for spatial representation'. *Molab*. Available at: https://www.research.ed.ac.uk/portal/en/publications/engaging-the-brain(742af2c4-e5d2-4307-8300-7e814aeee409).html.

McHale, B. (2013). 'Postmodernist fiction'. *Journal of Chemical Information and Modeling, 53*(9), 1689–1699. Available at: https://doi.org/10.1017/CBO9781107415324.004.

Mical, T. (2005). *Surrealism and Architecture*. Abingdon: Routledge. Available at: https://books.google.co.uk/books/about/Surrealism_and_Architecture.html?id=AR6bNi55BgUC&redir_esc=y.

Moussaoui, A., Pruski, A., and Cherki, B. (2007). 'Emotion regulation for social phobia treatment using virtual reality' in *HuMaN 07 Proceedings* (pp. 1–5). Timimoun. Retrieved from http://dspace.univ-tlemcen.dz/handle/112/891.

Muecke, M. W., and Zach, M. S. (2007). *Essays on the Intersection of Music and Architecture*. Ames, IA: Culicidae Architectural Press.

Neale, C., Aspinall, P., Roe, J., Tilley, S., Mavros, P., Cinderby, S., . . . Thompson, C. W. (2017). 'The aging urban brain: Analyzing outdoor physical activity using the Emotiv Affectiv Suite in older people'. *Journal of Urban Health, 94*(6), 869–80. https://doi.org/10.1007/s11524-017-0191-9.

O'Neill, P. (2010). *Brazil: No 17 best sci-fi and fantasy film of all time | Film | The Guardian*. Available at: https://www.theguardian.com/film/2010/oct/21/brazil-gilliam-fantasy (Accessed 6 April 2017).

Pallasmaa, J. (2016). 'The sixth sense: The meaning of atmosphere and mood'. *Architectural Design, 86*(6), 126–133. Available at: https://doi.org/10.1002/ad.2121.

Pröll, M. (2012). *Using a low-cost Gyro and EEG-based Input Device in Interactive Game Design*. Graz University of Technology, Institute for Knowledge Discover. Available at: https://diglib.tugraz.at/using-a-low-cost-gyro-and-eeg-based-input-device-in-interactive-game-design-2012.

Rampton, D. (2009). *Northrop Frye: New Directions from Old*. University of Ottawa Press.

Riva, G., Mantovani, F., Capideville, C. S., Preziosa, A., Morganti, F., Villani, D., . . . Alcañiz, M. (2007). 'Affective interactions using virtual reality: The link between presence and emotions'. *CyberPsychology and Behavior, 10*(1), 45–56. https://doi.org/10.1089/cpb.2006.9993.

Robey, T. (2010). Inception, review – Telegraph. Available at: http://www.telegraph.co.uk/culture/film/filmreviews/7892057/Inception-review.html (Accessed on 6 April 2017).

Slater, M., Slater, M., Linakis, V., Usoh, M., Kooper, R., and Street, G. (1996). 'Immersion, presence, and performance in virtual environments: An experiment with tri-dimensional chess'. *ACM VIRTUAL REALITY SOFTWARE AND TECHNOLOGY* (VRST, 163–172. Available at: http://citeseerx.ist.psu.edu/viewdoc/summary?doi=10.1.1.34.6594.

Smith, K. H. (2012). *Introducing Architectural Theory: Debating a Discipline*. Abingdon: Routledge.

Taylor, G. S., and Schmidt, C. (2012). 'Empirical evaluation of the Emotiv EPOC BCI headset for the detection of mental actions. *Proceedings of the Human Factors and Ergonomics Society Annual Meeting, 56*(1), 193–7. Available at: https://doi.org/10.1177/1071181312561017.

Torok, A., Sulykos, I., Kecskes-Kovacs, K., Persa, G., Galambos, P., Kobor, A., . . . Honbolygo, F. (2014). 'Comparison between wireless and wired EEG recordings in a virtual reality lab: Case report' in *2014 5th IEEE Conference on Cognitive Infocommunications (CogInfoCom)* (pp. 599–603). IEEE. https://doi.org/10.1109/CogInfoCom.2014.7020414

Tschumi, B. (1996). *Architecture and Disjunction*. London and Cambridge, MA: MIT Press.

Valve Corporation. (2007). PORTAL. Irrational Games, *BioShock, BioShock Infinite, Irrational Games, 2K Games*. Available at: http://www.valvesoftware.com/games/portal.html.

Vidler, A. (2003). *Fantasy, the Uncanny and Surrealist Theories of Architecture*. Available at: http://www.surrealismcentre.ac.uk/papersofsurrealism/journal1/acrobat_files/Vidler.pdf.

9

DATA AND GPS SYSTEMS

Comparing navigation and landmark knowledge between GPS users and non-GPS users

Negar Ahmadpoor and Tim Heath

Introduction

The experiments implemented in this research compare how people navigate in an urban environment with vs without the help of a GPS, and demonstrate that people who navigate an urban environment using GPS have poorer landmark knowledge than those who do not use GPS. Furthermore, discriminant analysis reveals certain attributes of urban landmarks that GPS users rely on for memory of urban place. The research also examines the reasons for poor landmark knowledge amongst GPS users and this is discussed from the perspectives of different disciplines. Finally, the chapter analyses how the findings of this study can inform urban design and enable greater cognitive engagement of GPS users with urban environments.

The physical environment is being increasingly considered in mobile human–computer interaction. (Cheverst et al., 2000; Li, 2006; Willis et al., 2009; Oulasvirta et al., 2003; Evans et al.; 1982, Evans et al., 1984). As Willis et al. (2009) identify, these studies tend to focus on merging the aspects of actual situations in the real world into the information delivered by mobile devices. As such, these studies have helped to develop computer-based technologies that take into account human factors by adopting the principles of the physical environment. There is now a large body of research presenting how urban-planning principles are applied to the design of virtual environments (Ingram et al., 1996; Darken and Sibert, 1996; Slone et al., 2015; Glander and Döllner, 2009; Evans et al., 1982). For instance, Kevin Lynch's theories from *Good City Form* (1984) and *The Image of the City* (1960) have been widely implemented in designing virtual cities and particularly navigation systems (Al-Kodmany, 2001; Rakkolainen and Vainio, 2001; Omer, Goldblatt & Orr., 2005; Pouke et al, 2016; Omer et al., 2006; Cubukcu and Nasar, 2005). Indeed, navigation systems use the design fundamentals initiated and developed by urban planners and environmental psychologists (Janzen et al., 2001;

Jansen-Osmann and Wiedenbauer, 2004; Oulasvirta et al., 2009; Burigat and Chittaro, 2007). To date, however, there has been limited research in the opposite direction, analysing the effects of digital technologies and digital mobile devices on the use and design of urban places.

Significantly, the recent emergence of the fluid, responsive, kinetic, data-driven worlds of information and communication technology (ICT) and their impact upon the way that people use and navigate urban environments suggests that urban designers may need realign some of their underpinning design principles. It has become increasingly important, therefore, for urban professionals to fully understand the effects of ICT and digital mobile devices on traditional urban principals (city imaging, wayfinding, context, comprehensibility, space, neighbourhood boundaries, etc.). Also, as a necessity for mediating our cities, urban designers can learn how to create a new discipline from a merger of urban design and urban planning with urban informatics. This would lead to the opportunity for creating fully networked public spaces that retain the values of the traditional physical qualities of cities whilst embracing the digital aspects of the developing ubiquitous world. As such, this research focuses upon 'navigation' as a key urban principal and attempts to understand the effects of using GPS-based systems on people's understanding of an urban environment and the respective role of urban design.

People's tendency to use GPS-based navigation systems is increasing (Speake, 2015), and Kalin and Frith (2016) note that people's movement through a city, in many cases, cannot be separated from their engagement with their smartphone screen. It has been argued that this constant use of mobile phones is turning people into 'phone zombies' who do not pay attention to their surroundings (Farman, 2013). As such, it could be claimed that people are losing their mental connection to physical place. Indeed, New Yorker architecture critic, Goldberger (2009) claims that such devices keep people isolated in an 'individualistic bubble' thereby releasing them from the physical place itself. Similarly, de Souza e Silva & Frith (2012) believe that, through using maps on mobile phones for navigation, people's engagement with the physical place is clearly decreasing. Baker (2004, p. 2) suggests that this is leading to 'the dissolution of place' and a consequently decreasing importance of physical place and physical objects as part of the wayfinding process. Increasing use of GPS-based navigation systems in urban environments is therefore increasingly raising questions over the role of physical places in navigation. These include: how to maintain a connection between people and the physical places they inhabit; and how to retain the value of legibility related to physical objects within our towns and cities?

Indeed, if we could predict how well components and structure of the city are known to GPS users, the designers of place (architects, urban designers and planners) would then gain a powerful design tool with which they could have more control over the design of the built environment in a way that GPS users could be more cognitively engaged with. To do this, we cannot only rely on identification of Lynchean elements (Lynch, 1960); however, we should find reasons why these elements are known to GPS users, which means finding the physical features that capture GPS users' attentions more and better contribute to their mental image of the place better.

This chapter therefore examines people's understanding of the urban environment and their spatial knowledge through using GPS-based maps on mobile phones to investigate people's awareness and knowledge of urban landmarks. The objectives of this paper are: first, to analyse the different level of landmark knowledge between people who use GPS-based navigators compared to those who experience the same environment without GPS support; second, to investigate which physical structural features of the landmarks make the landmarks more memorable to GPS users and that they are more cognitively engaged with; and finally, to discuss the implications and implementation of this study in relation to the professional discipline of urban design.

Learning about place through GPS

In the process of navigating within a city, individuals acquire spatial knowledge by moving through the environment, and in a new environment this spatial knowledge develops over time. Theoretically and empirically, it has been shown that the process of spatial knowledge development involves three stages: from the initial stage of landmark knowledge; to the stage of route knowledge; and the final stage of survey knowledge (Siegel and White, 1975; Gale et al., 1990; Golledge, 1997; Thorndyke and Hayes-Roth, 1982; Ishikawa and Montello, 2006; Spiers and Maguire, 2008). Landmark knowledge refers to knowledge of and about the objects that are salient and recognisable in the physical environment. Route knowledge relates to understanding how to move between two localities via sequences of landmarks and related decisions. Meanwhile, the final stage of survey knowledge refers to the layout of an environment together with the interrelationship between the salient elements within that layout.

Until recently, when people travelled within a novel environment they commonly used human guides, physical maps, city guides, etc. to experience these new places. However, nowadays people are increasingly reliant upon GPS-based navigation systems in their many guises for both automobile and pedestrian journeys (Baus et al., 2001; Wasinger et al., 2003; Krüger et al., 2004; Baus et al., 2005; Münzer et al., 2006). Significantly, as people are increasingly using GPS systems for navigation (Kitchin and Dodge, 2007; Laurier and Brown, 2008; Axon, Speake & Crawford, 2012; Speake, 2015), much empirical research has shown that GPS users function worse in wayfinding compared to those using physical maps and self-experience to navigate an environment (Krüger et al., 2004; Münzer et al., 2006; Ishikawa and Montello, 2006; Ishikawa et al., 2008; Willis et al., 2009; Ishikawa, 2016).

Spatial knowledge, survey knowledge and mental maps

Münzer et al. (2006) compared navigation in individuals who used physical maps for navigation to individuals who used GPS for navigation in a real environment (a zoo).

In their study, GPS users presented good route knowledge but poor survey knowledge. In contrast, 'traditional' map users presented better survey knowledge and nearly perfect route knowledge. Similarly, Krüger (2004) noted similar results in the same setting and showed that the people who used mobile-based navigation had difficulties in building up survey knowledge of the environment. In another study in an urban neighbourhood, comparison of sketch maps produced by GPS-based navigation systems, physical map users and self-experience users showed that GPS users had poorer topological accuracy (Ishikawa et al., 2008, Ishikawa, 2016). Unlike GPS navigation systems, research on map learning has shown that physical maps can help people to build up a coherent mental model of an environment (Denis and Zimmere, 1992; Rossano and Moak, 1998; Thorndyke and Hayes-Roth, 1982; Zimmer, 2004; Münzer et al., 2006). Willis et al. (2009) further studied the relative effectiveness of GPS-based navigation systems and physical maps and their findings demonstrated that people navigating with mobile phones were less accurate in producing sketch maps and also had poor configurational knowledge in urban environments. Additionally, this study showed that GPS users were poor in estimating route distance in comparison with people who had used physical maps

Wayfinding behaviour

Behaviour is the 'external' dimension of the navigation model that can be observed (such as people turning, stopping, looking around, etc.) by other people in the environment. The environment knowledge and survey knowledge are the 'internal' dimension of the navigation model, which is not observable but does control navigational behaviour. The effectiveness of GPS-based navigation systems has been examined in different studies by analysing the behaviour of GPS users in an urban environment. Indeed, different research projects have analysed aspects of navigation behaviour such as the travel distance, travel time, number of stops, and number of successes in achieving the desired destinations, direction errors, and so on (Reilly et al., 2006; Ishikawa et al., 2008; Field, O'Brien & Beale, 2011; Jung and Bell, 2014; Ishikawa, 2016; Hergan and Umek, 2016).

Landmark knowledge and GPS

Previous research that investigated the effects of using GPS on spatial knowledge mainly focused on route knowledge, survey knowledge and wayfinding behaviour within the city and the impact of using GPS on landmark knowledge has received little attention. By having landmark knowledge, people should be able to declare confidently if an object exists and they should be able to recognise it when it comes into their perceptual field (Gale et al., 1990; Westerbeek and Maes, 2013). Landmark knowledge has not only been neglected in the GPS studies, but even historically there has been limited study of the importance of landmarks as components of spatial knowledge (Allen, 1981; Kuipers, 1982; Stern and Leiser, 1988; Gale et al., 1990; Westerbeek and Maes, 2013).

Landmarks are subgoals that connect people to the environment and enable them to form their image of a place. Landmarks in terms of their contribution to navigation can be referred to as points (e.g. buildings) and paths (e.g. streets) (Allen, 2000; Tom and Denis, 2003; Klippel and Winter, 2005; Tom and Tversky, 2012). American urban planner Kevin Lynch (1960), in his research examining the way in which people observe and understand the city, introduced five fundamental elements: landmarks; nodes; paths; edges; and districts. In a similar vein, Gale et al. (1990) refer to them as spatial information that subsequently develops into spatial knowledge in the form of a structured reference system. Empirical studies have shown that the more people memorise and recognise landmarks, the clearer and more detailed image of the place they develop. In this process, individual differences and the level of familiarity with an environment can also affect an individual's landmark knowledge (Lynch, 1960; Appleyard, 1970; Siegel and White, 1975; Evans et al., 1984; Gale et al., 1990; Montello and Pick, 1993; Ishikawa and Montello, 2006; Stankiewicz and Kalia, 2007). When it comes to using GPS for navigating the cities, people appear to have poorer landmark knowledge as they gain less spatial information from the environment and consequently they are less able to remember the spatial components of the place. Therefore, as one of the objectives of this study, this paper compares the level of landmark knowledge between individuals who use GPS for navigation to those who navigate the same environment non-aided GPS. Also, through focussing on buildings as landmarks, it identifies whether there are certain features of landmarks that are more recognisable to people who use of GPS.

Physical features contributing to the memorability of landmarks

A key issue in learning landmarks concerns the features of the objects that cause them to be distinguished by people as landmarks and reference points. Appleyard (1969; 1976) developed a taxonomy on building form and provided evidence that the buildings that are most highly recognisable and easy to recall are those that are highly used and have important symbolic functions. In addition, he included those with physical features that have sharp contours, bright surfaces and noticeable size contrasts with their context, and he also emphasised the importance of location with buildings located near to an intersection being more recognisable. These characteristics have been further tested in subsequent research (Evans et al., 1982; Herman and Siegel, 1978; Pezdek and Evans, 1979; Evans et al., 1984; Caduff and Timpf, 2008). Moreover, Evans et al. (1982) extended Appleyard's work by empirically examining the relationship between building features and mental recall. They concluded that memorability relates to a building's function, its sociocultural significance, and surrounding traffic patterns. The characteristics of buildings adapted from (Appleyard, 1969; Appleyard, 1976) and (Evans et al., 1984) affecting their memorability are listed in Table 9.1.

A key objective of this research is to understand what physical features influence building recall differently for GPS users and non-GPS users. A major fear since

TABLE 9.1 The building characteristics affecting the memorability of buildings

Features		*Definition*	*References*
Form	Size	Vertical height of the building	(Appleyard, 1969) and (Evans et al., 1982)
	Shape/complexity	Complexity of shape ranging from simple block shape to more complexity with multiple shapes	
	Contour	The clarity of building contour ranging from blurred, partially obscured to free standing	
	Colour/texture	Uniqueness of colour and texture	
	Movement around the building	The amount of people and other objects moving in and around the building	
	Maintenance quality,	The amount of physical maintenance as reflected by the upkeep of the structure	
	Signage	Visibility and clarity of the building's signs	
	Style	Similarity to the majority of buildings on the street/unique from other buildings/context	
	Naturalness	The extent of landscaping and greenery immediately surrounding the structure	(Evans et al., 1982)
	Ease of pedestrian access/sitting	The way the building opens onto the street: directly/separated by porch, walkway/off-axis, separation by garden, plaza, etc.	
Visibility	Movement by the most prominent viewpoint	The number of people likely to daily pass the most prominent viewpoint of the building	
	Proximity to a major decision point	The proximity of the building to a major orientation decision point (e.g. street intersection)	
	Centrality to the circulation system	The proximity and centrality of the building to the city's circulation system	
Building use and building significance	Uniqueness of function	Uniqueness of building function: ranging from only one of its functions to many buildings with shared functions	(Appleyard, 1969) and (Evans et al., 1982)
	Use intensity	Extent of building use ranging from limited use by a small proportion of the population to daily use by large numbers of people	
	Building significance	The extent of the cultural, political, aesthetic or historical importance of the building	

the 2000s has been that the use of mobile phones distracts people from engaging actively with their physical environments (de Souza e Silva & Frith, 2012; Kalin and Frith, 2016). It is important, therefore, to know which physical features of a place more strongly affect a GPS user's navigation within urban environments. In turn, this can help urban designers to increase a GPS user's engagement with their physical environment when considering physical features in the design of towns and cities. This research therefore focuses in more detail upon the physical features of buildings that were remembered strongly by GPS users.

Methodology

This research employs an experimental approach in which quantitative methods are used to investigate the effects of using GPS for navigation in an unfamiliar urban environment on people's memory of urban landmarks. To do this, the participants of the study, in two groups (GPS group and non-GPS group) were exposed to an unfamiliar urban environment and required to do a series of tasks.

Participants

In this study, in order to minimise the effects of potential confounding variables (i.e. participant demographic features) and interparticipant variation and increase the observed differences across the independent groups (i.e., GPS vs No GPS), membership to the sampled was tightly controlled. We managed this in two steps: first by selecting the participants; and second by forming the groups. In selecting the participants, we used a 'purposefully-randomly strategy' (Sandelowski, 2000). The participants were randomly selected first-year students attending The University of Nottingham (September 2016) who met the following criteria: (a) they were British, born and bred in the UK; this increased the likelihood that they were familiar with the general culture of the neighbourhood; (b) they were unfamiliar with the study site; (c) they should have previously used GPS self-sufficiently in an urban area; (d) they were all right-handed. In total, 76 participants were selected for this study, 38 females and 38 males, aged between 18 and 28, the mean age of the group being 22.86 years and the standard deviation (SD) 3.36 years. In order to group the participants, they were assigned to one of two groups (GPS or non-GPS), ensuring an even spread in demographic features across the independent variable. Table 9.2 presents a summary of the two groups, their demographic features and the descriptive information with statistical testing to ensure there were no significant differences across the independent groups.

The study was approved by The University of Nottingham Research Ethics Committee for Human-based Research and all of the participants gave written informed consent. Participants were given Amazon vouchers in return for their participation.

The GPS users at the start point of the experiment were introduced to a mobile mapping software application (Google map) and its basic features on an

TABLE 9.2 Summary of demographic features across the independent groups

Group	*(N) Female*	*(N) Male*	*Mean age (SD)*	*t-test (age)*		
				t	*df*	*p -value*
GPS	19	19	22.87 (3.37) years	0.034	74	0.925 n.s.
non-GPS	19	19	22.84 (3.40) years			
ΔGroups	0 n.s.	0 n.s.	0.03			

$^{***}p \leq 0.001$; $^{**}p \leq 0.01$; $^{*}p \leq 0.05$; n.s.=not significant (p >.05).

iPhone 6 mobile. They were then given the mobile phone and asked to practice using the GPS-based navigation system on the phone (i.e. learned how to operate the system and walked a short distance using it). They began the task once they had demonstrated that they are proficient using the system.

Research setting

A 14-hectare area in the city centre of Nottingham, UK was selected as the case study area for this research. Nottingham is a medium-sized city in the centre of England with a greater urban population of around 730,000. The study site is a busy part of the city centre, with many shops, businesses, bars and restaurants. The site includes a mix of historic and modern architecture, with over 350 buildings, and it retains a historic mediaeval street pattern including 18 streets and 25 key street junctions. For the purpose of the experiment, the researchers identified 8 landmarks within the site, as destinations for the participants, with each landmark being a building that was located on a single street.

Experiment design

The research experiment was structured in two phases. In the first phase, participants from both groups, GPS group and non-GPS group, were exposed individually to the study area. Following a briefing, participants from both groups were asked to find the 8 destinations within the site, starting from the same start point. GPS users were asked to find the destinations using the GPS app, and non-GPS users were asked to find the same destinations by relying on physical features in the site and directional signs. The protocol for non-GPS users was designed to mirror their natural behaviour when they are exposed to an unfamiliar environment without access to their mobile phones.

The location of the destinations within the site and the order that participants were asked to find them were structured in a way that meant that both GPS users and non-GPS users were likely to walk through the same routes in the same sequence. This was tested many times in the pilot study by manipulating the order of landmarks to make sure that both groups for moving from one destination to the next one would go through the same route (Figure 9.1 & 9.2). GPS users were told to choose the shortest route that GPS offers and in the case of non-GPS users, the efficiency of directional signs was examined; there were guiding signs located at each main decision point of the study area indicating the way to the landmarks chosen for the test. The challenge of the experiment was to design a protocol for participants in a way that both non-GPS users and GPS users would walk through the same routes. The configuration of routes and syntax of the 8 chosen landmarks in relation to the routes as well as the placement of the directional signs at the main decision points of the study site (in the case of non-GPS users) could bring an advantage to the design of the test. As a result, participants for both groups chose the same routes for approaching the destinations and passed by the same sequences as predicted.

In the entire journey, participants were followed by two experimenters, keeping a distance of about 50 metres. Consistent with the navigational experiment designed by Ishikawa et al. (2008), in some cases the participants were going away from the boundaries of the study area or were heading to a road that was not part of the study and, after 10 minutes had passed, they were guided by the experimenter to the routes that were part of the study. In the second phase of the study, after finishing the first phase, the participants were asked to undertake a 'photo recognition task' in order to explore the level of their landmark knowledge by measuring the number of the buildings that they could remember better from the site. All the

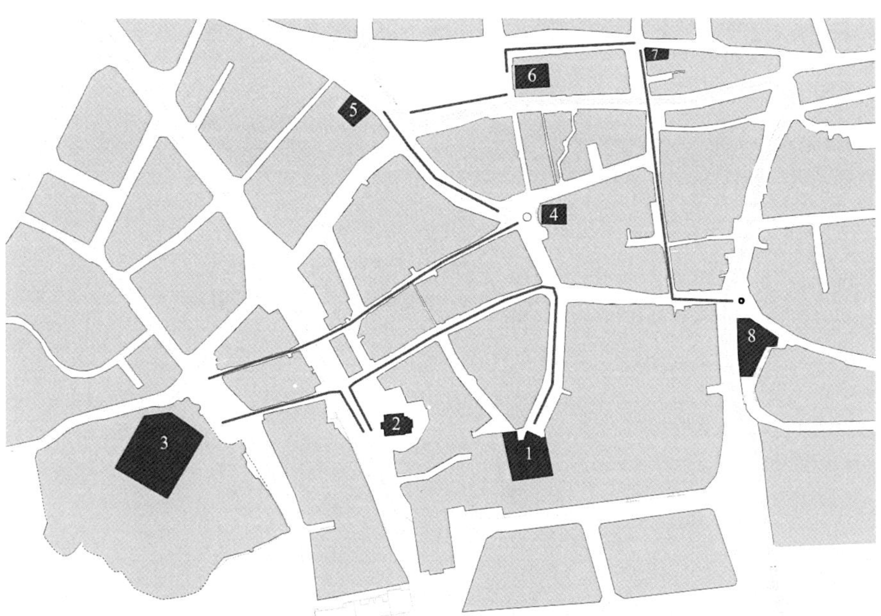

FIGURE 9.1 This map demonstrates landmarks (the order of finding landmarks is marked) and study routes in the site.

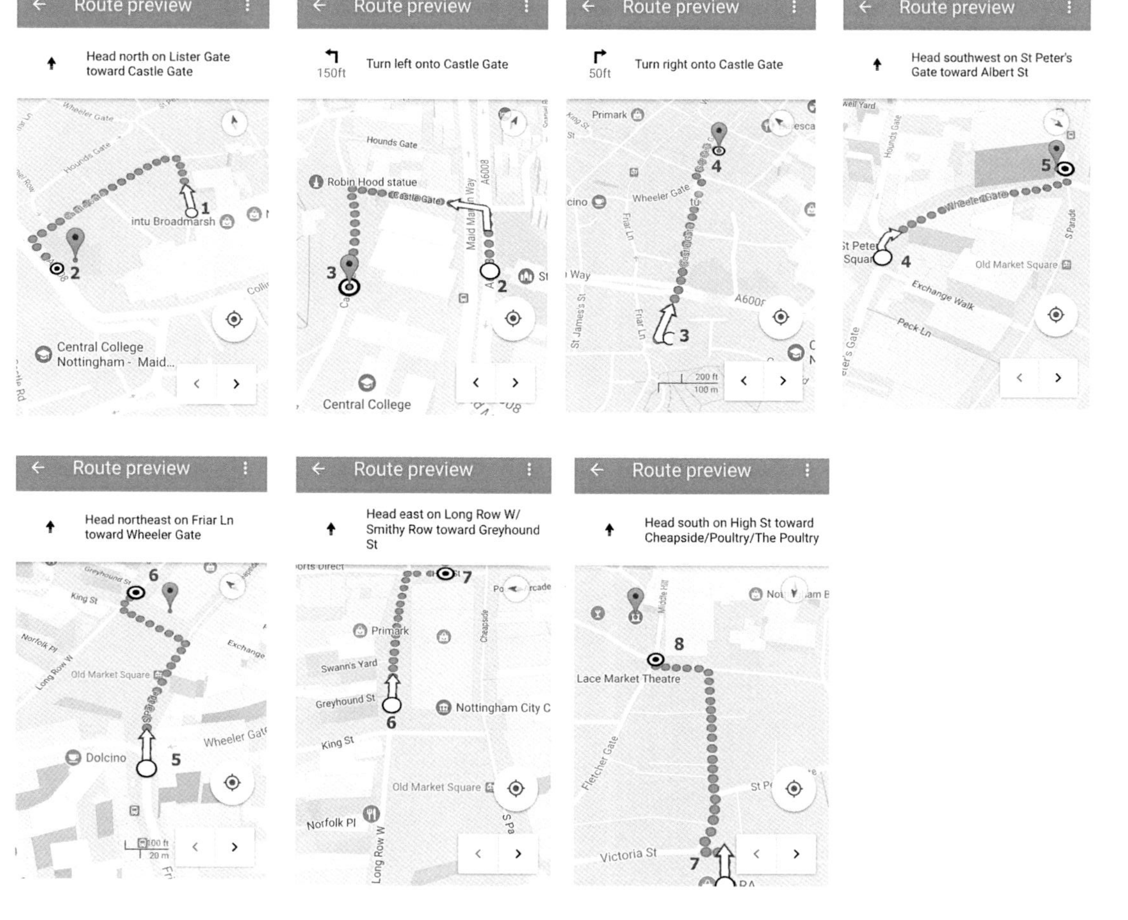

FIGURE 9.2 GPS map displayed for moving between destinations.

buildings for this task were chosen from the study routes and were buildings that participants passed by during their walk.

The experiments all took place between the 27th September and the 18th October 2016. We limited the time of the study to weekday mornings in order to avoid busy times in the study area during afternoons and weekends. Also, participants' exposure to the site in terms of time needed to be similar, as the time of the day (e.g. the number of pedestrians in the street, etc.), could affect their navigation and perception of place.

Photograph-recall task

In order to examine landmark knowledge amongst GPS users and non-GPS users, the photograph-recall test was designed to assess the level of their recall and recognition of different buildings. In this test, photographs depicting 68 highly imageable buildings within the case study site were presented to both groups of participants and they were required to indicate to what extent they could recall each building. For this question, they were asked to use a five-point Likert scale from 1 (definitely remember) to 5 (don't remember at all). The photographs were sized 210mm x 300mm and they were taken from a similar angle to that which each participant would see the building from in his/her journey through the site. Also, in this test, there was no time limit and participants were self-paced.

Similar photographic tests to assess people's recognition of a place have been previously used in several research projects (Milgram, 1972; Weber, Brown and Weldon, 1978; Hepner et al., 2007; Wen, Ishikawa and Sato, 2011; Campbell, Hepner and Miller, 2014). Indeed, Milgram (1972) and Weber et al. (1978) presented photographs taken from their study location to participants in order to determine whether they could recognise the scene depicted. Significantly, Weber et al. (1978) mention that although this method has a potential response bias, it is still strong method to analyse peoples' recognition of place. Campbell et al. (2014) use photographs as one method of measuring people's landmark recognition in Sydney as part of their project 'The Sydney City Test of Topographical Memory', where the test was designed to measure the level of building recognition within a defined case study area. In a navigation study, very similar to our experiment, Wen et al. (2011) designed a 'scene recognition test' in order to assess their participants' landmark knowledge. In their study, 24 photos were shown to the participants and they were asked to indicate if the photos had been taken from the routes that participants learned from videos with verbal, visual and spatial interference tasks and without any interference.

Procedure

The participants in this study were informed that the purpose of the research study was to help to inform urban designers in the pursuit of designing better places.

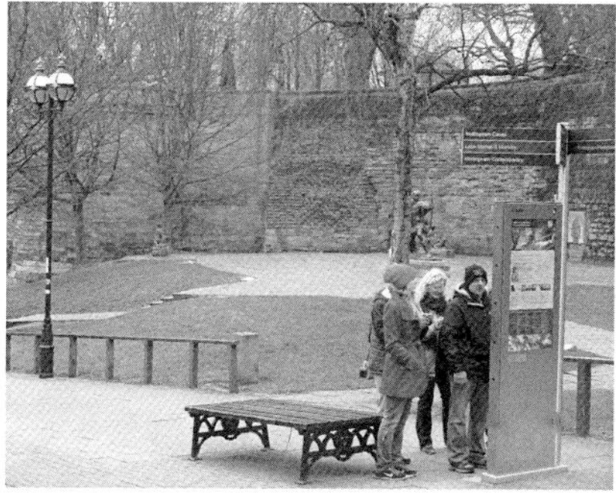

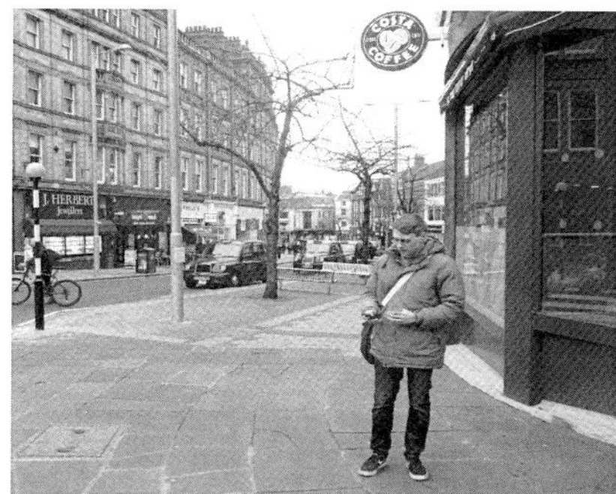

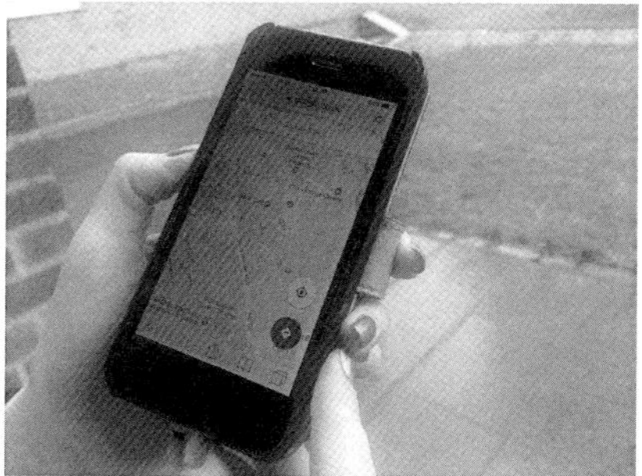

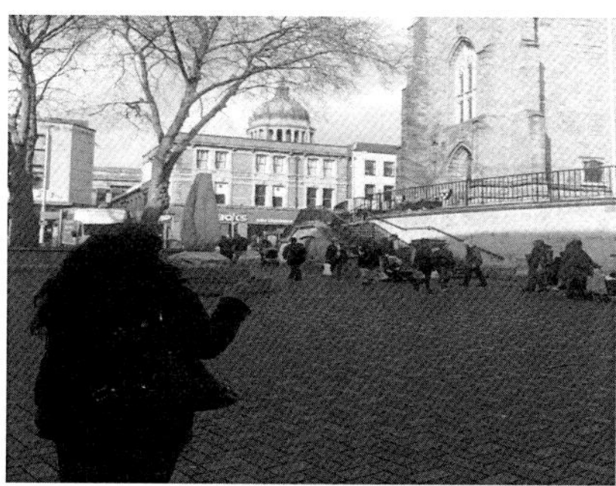

FIGURE 9.3 Illustrating the experiment procedure. Top images: a non-GPS participant is using the directional signs to find the destinations and a non-GPS user arriving at one of the destinations by paying close attention to landmarks. Bottom images: GPS participants using the GPS app to find the destinations.

At the start of the experiment, participants filled in the sense-of-direction questionnaire (SOD) and responded to the questions featuring their experience of using GPS-based systems and their self-evaluation of using GPS-based systems for navigation. All of the participants indicated that when they go to an unfamiliar urban environment, they use GPS apps and mainly Google maps. The participants were then taken individually to the start point of the experiment and were given the briefing representing the names and order of the landmarks that they should find within the site. Figure 9.3 illustrates some of the photos taken during the experiment.

Results

Level of building recall

To compare the differences in recalling the photographs of buildings within the site, Mann–Whitney tests were conducted. This test is appropriate when variables fall under two experimental conditions and when participants have been separated into independent groups (Field, 2013). A Mann–Whitney U test is also suitable when the dependent variable (i.e., photograph-recall task) is measured at discrete level of measurement (i.e., Likert scale). In addition, graphical (e.g. Q–Q plot) and statistical inspection (e.g. Shapiro–Wilk and Kolmogorov–Smirnov tests) of the data exposed that the sampling distribution around the mean was not normally distributed, thus one of the assumptions for a parametric test failed (Heiman, 2011).

In consideration of the family-wise error rate caused by the significance levels required to reject the null hypothesis (i.e., 0.05, 0.01, 0.001) from inflating across the 68 paired comparisons with the same hypothesis (Cabin and Mitchell, 2000), Bonferroni corrections were used. However, it is important to mention that, although Bonferroni corrections protect statistical significance (p-values) against Type I (family-wise) errors, they may introduce Type II errors (i.e., reduced statistical power) due to their over-conservative calculations (Cabin and Mitchell, 2000; Reiner, Yekutieli and Benjamini, 2003). Therefore, the emphasis of inferential tests was mainly placed on 'effect sizes' (i.e. a standardised measure of the magnitude of the observed difference between sample groups) and not only on its statistical significance (which, particularly for uneven sample groups, could confound effect size and sample size) (Kent et al., 2015). Effect sizes are independent from the sample size and show whether the predictor variable has any real significance (Cohen, 1965). In this research, calculation of effect size was completed by analysing the equivalence between the standardised measure of the observed difference and the Pearson's coefficient r based on the following formula (equation). In this formula, N is the number of observations, and the test statistic (Z-score) was extracted from the Mann–Whitney U.

$$\textbf{Effect Size} = \frac{\mathbf{Z}_{\text{scores}}}{\sqrt{\mathbf{N}}}$$ *Equation 1 : Effect Size*

The results of effect-size calculation were interpreted according to Ferguson's table (Ferguson, 2009). Benchmark values are given for 'small', 'moderate' and 'large' effect sizes ($r \geq 0.20$, 0.50 and 0.80, respectively). Values below 0.20 were considered as not substantive (i.e. 'negligible') and, thus do not present a practically relevant effect. Table 9.3 presents the differences between the two study groups, providing the mean (M) and the SD, the difference between the mean (ΔM), *p*-value, the result of U test statistic and effect size (r).

The statistical analysis of the photo recall test showed that in 41 building photos, non-GPS users had significantly 'a better performance' ($p \leq 0.00001$); the differences detected for these 41 buildings have a generally substantive effect size, mostly 'moderate' ($0.50 \leq r < 0.80$ in 33 cases out of 41) and some 'small' cases ($0.20 \leq r < 0.50$ in 8 cases out of 41) (Table 9.3); in 20 building photos, both GPS and non-GPS users had equivalently 'a good performance' ($1 \leq M \leq 2.5$), ($p > 0.00074$); and in 7 building photos, both groups had 'a poor performance' ($2.5 > M \geq 5$), ($p > 0.00074$).

TABLE 9.3 Mann–Whitney U test for comparing the level of landmark knowledge between GPS Users and non-GPS users

Building	*GPS M (SD)*	*non-GPS M(SD)*	*Δ M*	*U test*	*p-value*	*Effect size (r)*
Building1	1.00 (0.00)	1.00 (0.00)	0.00	756.00	1.00 n.s.	0.00
Building2	1.00 (0.00)	1.00 (0.00)	0.00	756.00	1.00 n.s.	0.00
Building3	1.39 (0.50)	1.29 (0.46)	0.10	678.00	0.34 n.s.	−0.11
Building4	1.67 (0.95)	1.48 (0.86)	0.19	666.50	0.29 n.s.	−0.12
Building5	3.75 (1.70)	2.33 (1.90)	1.42	504.00	0.01 n.s.	−0.32
Building6	4.50 (0.88)	4.33 (0.75)	0.17	630.00	0.15 n.s.	−0.16
Building7	4.75 (0.44)	2.50 (1.4)	2.25	157.500	0.00***	−0.72
Building8	5.00 (0.00)	2.50 (1.8)	2.50	252.000	0.00***	−0.67
Building9	4.75 (0.44)	4.17 (1.4)	0.58	661.500	0.20 n.s.	−0.14
Building10	4.14 (0.87)	2.10 (1.16)	2.04	157.000	0.00***	−0.70
Building11	4.33 (1.75)	2.33 (1.18)	2.00	150.000	0.00***	−0.71
Building12	4.25 (0.70)	2.38 (1.18)	1.87	150.000	0.00***	−0.68
Building13	2.33 (1.25)	2.31 (1.30)	0.02	740.500	0.87 n.s.	−0.01
Building14	4.42 (0.85)	2.62 (1.41)	1.80	247.500	0.00***	−0.60
Building15	4.50 (0.60)	2.55 (1.40)	1.95	208.000	0.00***	−0.64
Building16	4.44 (0.88)	3.36 (1.52)	1.08	446.000	0.001***	−0.38
Building17	2.67 (0.86)	1.81(1.08)	0.86	385.500	0.00***	−0.44
Building18	1.86 (1.1)	1.38 (0.73)	0.48	563.500	0.025**	−0.25
Building19	1.03 (0.16)	1.00 (0.00)	0.03	735.000	0.28 n.s.	−0.12
Building20	4.75 (0.43)	2.50 (1.40)	2.25	157.500	0.00***	−0.71
Building21	4.25 (0.84)	2.10 (1.16)	2.15	135.000	0.00***	−0.72
Building22	2.42 (1.02)	2.10 (1.16)	0.32	604.000	0.11 n.s.	−0.18
Building23	1.92 (1.05)	1.50 (0.74)	0.40	594.000	0.07 n.s.	−0.20
Building24	4.31 (.71)	2.32 (1.05)	1.99	572.500	0.00***	−0.52
Building25	4.33 (1.75)	2.38 (1.18)	1.95	150.000	0.00***	−0.70
Building26	4.00 (.71)	2.44 (1.75)	1.58	400.500	0.00***	−0.52
Building27	2.22 (1.36)	1.95 (1.10)	0.27	685.000	0.45 n.s.	−0.09
Building28	4.00 (0.72)	2.50 (1.8)	1.50	441.000	0.00***	−0.37
Building29	4.75 (0.44)	2.62 (1.41)	2.13	247.500	0.00***	−0.74
Building30	4.52 (0.70)	2.52(1.41)	2.00	202.500	0.00***	−0.68
Building31	4.31 (0.82)	3.98 (1.13)	0.33	649.500	0.25 n.s.	−0.13
Building32	4.25 (0.84)	2.50 (1.01)	1.75	166.500	0.00***	−0.69
Building33	1.78 (0.95)	1.52 (0.77)	0.26	651.000	0.24 n.s.	−0.13
Building34	4.72 (0.45)	2.79 (1.09)	1.93	361.000	0.00***	−0.60
Building35	4.00 (0.71)	2.43 (1.75)	1.57	400.500	0.00***	−0.42
Building36	4.75 (0.43)	2.55 (1.40)	2.20	157.500	0.00***	−0.71
Building37	4.39 (0.8)	2.38 (1.35)	2.01	199.000	0.00***	−0.65
Building38	4.36(0.52)	3.74(1.14)	0.62	530.500	0.01**	−0.27
Building39	4.75(0.43)	2.50 (1.4)	2.25	157.500	0.00***	−0.71
Building40	1.94(1.14)	1.43(.83)	0.51	548.500	0.02*	−0.27
Building41	4.33(0.71)	2.79 (1.09)	1.54	361.000	0.00***	−0.62
Building42	4.75(0.43)	2.55 (1.40)	2.20	208.000	0.00***	−0.74

(continued)

TABLE 9.3 *(continued)*

Building	*GPS M (SD)*	*non-GPS M(SD)*	*Δ M*	*U test*	*p-value*	*Effect size (r)*
Building43	1.69(0.95)	1.48(0.85)	0.21	647.500	0.21 n.s.	−0.14
Building44	4.72(0.51)	2.50(1.40)	2.22	164.500	0.00***	−0.70
Building45	1.83(0.97)	1.52(0.77)	0.31	625.000	0.14 n.s.	−0.16
Building46	1.81(1.00)	1.38(0.73)	0.43	570.500	0.03*	−0.23
Building47	4.97(0.16)	2.50(1.82)	2.47	259.000	0.00***	−0.66
Building48	1.03 (0.16)	1.00 (0.00)	0.03	735.000	0.28 n.s.	−0.12
Building49	4.53(0.62)	2.52(1.41)	2.01	202.500	0.00***	−0.64
Building50	4.25(0.84)	2.07(1.15)	2.18	130.500	0.00***	−0.73
Building51	2.28(1.20)	2.26(1.25)	0.02	747.500	0.93 n.s.	−0.01
Building52	4.19(0.92)	2.50(1.00)	1.69	190.000	0.00***	−0.66
Building53	4.31(0.82)	2.38 (1.35)	1.93	199.000	0.00***	−0.65
Building54	4.11(0.70)	3.86(1.00)	0.25	680.500	0.42 n.s.	−0.09
Building55	3.75(1.67)	2.33(1.90)	1.42	504.000	0.00***	−0.32
Building56	4.75(0.43)	2.55(1.40)	2.20	157.500	0.00***	−0.71
Building57	4.44(0.70)	2.36(1.35)	2.08	180.000	0.00***	−0.67
Building58	4.08(0.70)	2.36(1.70)	1.72	361.000	0.00***	−0.46
Building59	4.06(0.71)	2.36(1.50)	1.70	362.000	0.00***	−0.46
Building60	4.75(0.42)	2.45(1.40)	2.30	157.500	0.00***	−0.71
Building61	1.94(1.14)	1.43(0.83)	0.51	548.500	0.01**	−0.26
Building62	2.00 (1.1)	1.45(0.80)	0.55	554.500	0.02*	−0.26
Building63	4.75(0.43)	2.55 (1.40)	2.20	157.500	0.00***	−0.71
Building64	4.44(0.84)	2.62(2.62)	1.82	241.000	0.00***	−0.61
Building65	4.28(0.70)	3.57(1.51)	0.71	606.000	0.11 n.s.	−0.18
Building66	1.92 (1.16)	1.55 (0.80)	0.37	627.500	0.14 n.s.	−0.16
Building67	4.11(0.70)	2.50(1.82)	1.61	427.000	0.00***	−0.39
Building68	4.72(0.51)	2.45(1.41)	2.27	164.000	0.00***	−0.71

Bonferroni corrections:***$p \leq 0.00001$; **$p \leq 0.00015$; *$p \leq 0.00074$; n.s.=not significant ($p > 0.00074$).
r <.20=negligible; 0.20 ≤ r <.50=small; 0.50 ≤ r <.80=moderate; r ≥ 0.80=large

Figure 9.4 boxplots the major differences in remembering the buildings between GPS users and non-GPS users for four selected buildings out of 41 buildings, as an example.

Based on the aforementioned analysis, we assume each photograph yields randomly either 'a better performance by non-GPS users' or 'an equivalent good performance by both groups' or 'an equivalent poor performance by both groups'. In order to test if remembering 41 photos out of 68 photos significantly 'better by non-GPS users' could really support the argument that non-GPS users have better landmark knowledge, we used the Chi-Squared One-Variable Test. According to this test, we could demonstrate that there is sufficient evidence to reject the null hypothesis and conclude that the proportion of 'better performance by non-GPS users' is significantly different from the other two situations; $\chi^2(2) = 25.971$, p= 0.000002 (Table 9.4 shows the Frequencies table of

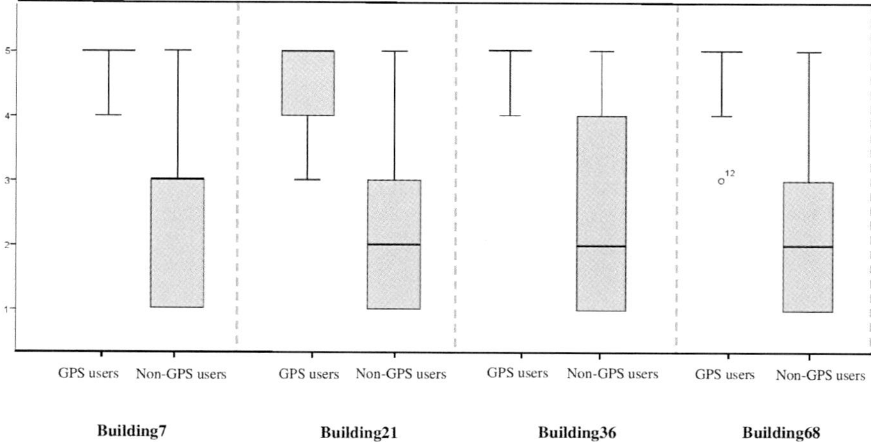

FIGURE 9.4 Boxplots demonstrating the major differences in remembering the buildings between GPS users and non-GPS users for four selected buildings out of 41 buildings as an example.

TABLE 9.4 Frequencies table of Chi-Squared One-Variable Test

Status			
	Observed N	*Expected N*	*Residual*
better performance by non-GPS users	41	22.7	18.3
an equivalent good performance by both groups	20	22.7	−2.7
an equivalent poor performance by both groups	7	22.7	−15.7
Total	68		

Chi-Squared One-Variable Test). Therefore, these analyses suggest that non-GPS users primarily had a better performance than GPS users in the photo recall test and had consequently better landmark knowledge of the site.

Factors contributing to the memorability of buildings (Discriminant analysis)

The results of the photo recall test showed that non-GPS users had better landmark knowledge of the site. Subsequently, discriminant analysis was conducted to identify the physical characteristics of the buildings differentiating the recall of buildings for 'GPS users' and 'non-GPS users'.

Discriminant analysis is a method of extracting features that preserve class separability and has been used to determine which variables discriminate between two or more naturally occurring groups (Cai et al., 2007; Sarabia-Sánchez et al., 2014). As a first step to apply discriminant analysis, two groups were formed based on the results of the photograph-recall task: 'the buildings recalled significantly stronger by non-GPS users' ($p \leq 0.00001$) with 41 observations and 'the buildings recalled at the same rate by GPS users and non-GPS users' ($p > 0.00074$, $1 \leq M \leq 2.5$) with 20 observations. Then, discriminant function analysis was applied to predict group membership from a set of predictors. The buildings were tested against a number of predictors (physical features): size, shape, signage, maintenance quality, texture, style, contour, colour/texture, visibility from roads, symbolic significance, use intensity, naturalness, siting characteristics, uniqueness of function, and type of nearby road. The building features were then scored based on a three-point rating scale determined by two independent observers unaware of the purposes of the study. Inter-rater reliability exceeded 0.90 for each building characteristic score.

Data testing

Discriminant analysis is robust regarding normality and multicollinearity when the size of the sample is large and degrees of freedom are equal to or more than 20; however, it is extremely sensitive to the outliers in the data set (Klecka, 1980; McLachlan, 2004; Lane, 2008). The number of observations for any of the two groups must exceed the number of predictor variables tested as one of the assumptions of this test; in our data set, the smallest group – the buildings recalled at the same rate by GPS users and non-GPS users – has 20 observations, which is more than the number of predictors employed in this study. The data set in this study (in terms of sample size, number of predictors, etc.) is very similar to the popular study by Evans et al. (1984). They used discriminant analysis to find the characteristics of the building, differentiating the recall of buildings between young and elderly adults. Moreover, as the main goals of discriminant analysis are classification and inference, homogeneity of variance–covariance matrices must be examined (Tabachnick et al., 2001). Therefore, tests for multicollinearity, normality, and variance–covariance matrices homogeneity were run on the 15 independent variables of this study to verify data quality.

The pooled within-groups correlation matrix was used to detect multicollinearity. This test showed that the correlation coefficients for all the variables are not larger than 0.8 (the largest one was 0.61 between sitting and naturalness) and therefore there is no significant correlation amongst the variables in both groups and multicollinearity of the variables is low. Furthermore, Box's M test for homogeneity of variances/covariances was run and determined no significant difference ($p = 0.1$) between the two matrices.

Another assumption for the discriminant model is that data values should be from a normal distribution. However, normal assumptions are usually not 'fatal' and the resultant significance tests may still be reliable (Poulsen and French, 2008). For this research, graphical (e.g. Q–Q plot) and statistical inspection (e.g. Shapiro–Wilk and Kolmogorov–Smirnov tests) of data showed that the independent variables are all normally distributed.

Discriminant analysis outputs

The linear discriminant test was run and determined that the discriminant function significantly discriminates the groups, Wilks' $\lambda = 0.27$, Chi-square = 51.40, $p \leq 0.001$. Also, the differences between the two groups account for 92% of the variance in the predicting variables, since the percentage of explained variance is calculated as [1− (Wilks' λ)] 100. Moreover, the discriminant function analysis yielded a composite of building features that significantly distinguished between two groups of buildings. The building characteristics that contributed significantly to the function discriminating between the two groups of buildings found to be 'style', 'contour' and 'significance of building'. They have large Canonical Coefficients, .78, .65 and .50 respectively and large correlation in Canonical Structure Matrix, .84, .43 and .44 respectively (the outputs of the discriminant analysis are illustrated in Table 9.5). The standardised canonical discriminant coefficients can be used to rank the importance of each variable and it is likely that if the groups differ a lot on a variable that it has a high standardised canonical discriminant coefficient. The Canonical Structure Matrix, which shows the correlations

TABLE 9.5 Outputs of discriminant analysis

	Group1: Buildings remembered at the same rate by GPS users and non-GPS users	*Group2: Buildings remembered significantly stronger by non- GPS users*	*Standardised Canonical Coefficients (weight)*	*Canonical Structure Matrix*
	M (SD)	*M(SD)*		
Size	1.74 (0.73)	1.83 (0.60)	−0.02	−0.05
Shape	1.58(0.50)	1.10(0.30)	0.17	0.265
Contour	2.11(0.81)	1.40(0.56)	0.651	0.338
Material	1.42(0.70)	1.23(0.51)	0.015	0.097
Movement	2.11(0.66)	2.17(0.70)	−0.077	−0.027
Maintenance	1.42(0.51)	1.73(0.70)	−0.346	−0.150
Signage	1.37(0.60)	1.53(0.68)	0.103	−0.076
Style	2.63(0.50)	1.23(.51)	0.778	0.840
Naturalness	1.37(0.60)	1.33(0.61)	−0.238	0.018
Siting	1.47(0.77)	1.37(0.56)	0.100	0.050
Viewpoint	1.68(0.75)	1.93(0.78)	0.327	−0.097
Intersection	1.95(0.705)	2.23(0.86)	0.305	−0.107
Circulation	1.95(0.70)	2.37(0.76)	−0.395	−0.170
Singularity	1.85(0.78)	1.37(0.61)	−0.068	0.102
Use	1.95(0.70)	1.80(0.71)	−0.070	0.062
Significance	2.26(0.93)	1.23(0.50)	0.505	0.442

The results for the canonical discriminant function were: Eigenvalue= 2.73; Wilks' $\lambda = .268$; χ^2=51.4; $p < 0.001$

between each variable in the model and the discriminant functions, should be used to assign meaningful labels to the discriminant functions. Mostly, any variable with a correlation of 0.3 or more is considered to be important.

The discriminant analysis also revealed that for both groups a high percentage of the cases were correctly classified: 93.3 for buildings remembered stronger by non-GPS users, and 89.5 for buildings remembered at the same rate by both groups. Overall, 91.8% of the original cases were correctly classified (Table 9.6).

From this discriminant analysis, it can be concluded that building characteristics particularly salient to GPS users include: major symbolic significance; unique style; and contrast to background/context. Indeed, buildings with these physical characteristics were recalled strongly by both GPS users and non-GPS users. Buildings lacking these features were recalled better by non-GPS users. Figure 9.5 illustrates the mean recall of each building for both groups and shows that non-GPS users recalled most of the buildings better than GPS users, and photographs of some of the buildings that were recalled equally strongly by both GPS and non-GPS users and buildings that were recalled better by non-GPS users, are also shown.

Discussion

Poor landmark knowledge for GPS users

According to the results of this research, GPS users were less able to remember buildings strongly in comparison with non-GPS users. The findings also suggest that GPS users have poorer landmark knowledge than people who experience the environment without the aid of GPS. This is likely to be because GPS users receive

TABLE 9.6 Classification summary

Classification Results[a]					
Groups			*Predicted Group Membership*		*Total*
			buildings recalled at the same rate by both groups	*buildings remembered stronger by non-GPS users*	
Original	Count	buildings recalled at the same rate by both groups	17	2	19
		buildings remembered stronger by non-GPS users	2	28	30
	%	buildings recalled at the same rate by both groups	89.5	10.5	100.0
		buildings remembered stronger by non-GPS users	6.7	93.3	100.0

91.8% of original grouped cases correctly classified.

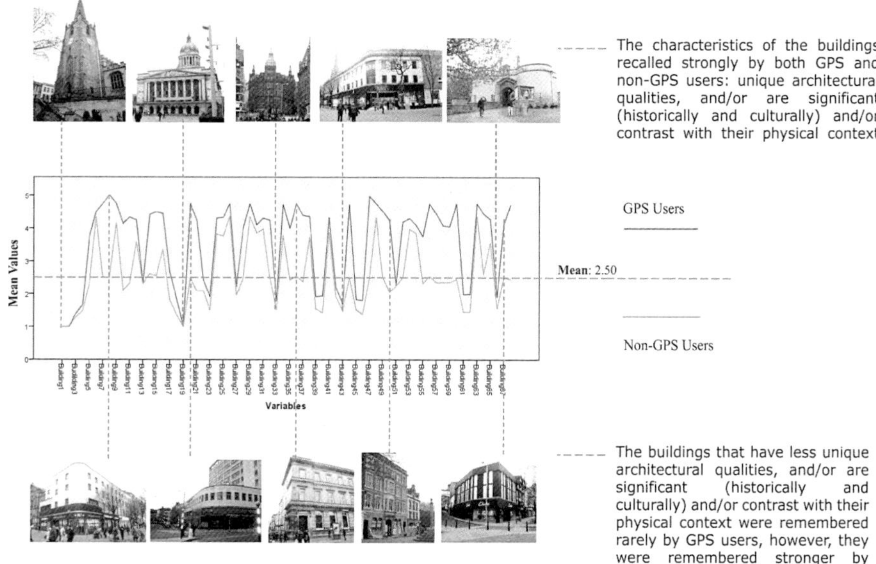

FIGURE 9.5 Demonstrating the level of recall of 68 buildings (mean) for GPS users and non-GPS users.

less information from the surrounding environment whilst using GPS. Many issues in GPS-based navigation systems could also cause this; indeed, GPS-based navigators, by design, focus on assisting people to reach their destination (from A to B) and do not encode information and landmarks. Their use, therefore, does not require users to recognise and memorise elements of the urban environment (Münzer et al., 2006). As such, people relying on these systems externalise the process of learning to these devices and therefore learn less about the environment themselves. Moreover, discovering a new environment brings many challenges in itself, and using GPS also requires people to multitask within a new environment. So, in addition to reliance on the GPS-based information, they will also naturally miss information about the place itself.

Much previous research has illustrated that GPS users have poor landmark knowledge (Krüger et al., 2004; Münzer et al., 2006; Ishikawa and Montello, 2006; Reilly et al., 2006; Ishikawa et al., 2008; Willis et al., 2009; Field et al., 2011; Frankenstein, 2012; Neyfakh and So, 2013; Jung and Bell, 2014; Ishikawa, 2016; Hergan and Umek, 2016). Significantly, neuroscientists have also discovered that contemporary use of GPS for navigation may affect how well people's brains function as they age. Indeed, Veronique Bohbot (Neyfakh and So, 2013) found that those who use a GPS system have an excessively higher chance of damaging a region of the brain, known as the hippocampus, involved with memory and navigation. As such, becoming dependent on GPS systems can lead to atrophy of the hippocampus as people age, which puts the person at risk for cognitive problems such as Alzheimer's disease later in life (Iaria et al., 2003). This potential impact of GPS use results from people relieving their brain from all navigational tasks (memorising landmarks, conducting route knowledge and cognitive mapping). Indeed, Maguire et al. (2000: 2) identify that: 'the brain is plastic' and that when people do more mental mapping they develop better cognitive navigation skills resulting in the part of the brain that encodes navigation tasks becoming stronger. Relying upon GPS for navigation can therefore result in the shrinking and weakening of the hippocampus leading to a further degrading of people's spatial abilities.

Physical features contributing to building memory for GPS users

Another aim of this research was to discover what physical features of buildings better contribute to the recall of those buildings amongst GPS users and non-GPS users. The analysis of the findings highlighted that the key building features influencing the recall of buildings between GPS users and non-GPS users are: 'style'; 'significance of the building'; and 'contour/contrast'. Indeed, the style of a building is an important factor in a GPS user's awareness and knowledge of an urban setting. Also, buildings that are historically and culturally significant are better recalled by GPS users, although it could be argued that many significant historic or cultural buildings also tend to have a unique architectural style and differ from their neighbours. Buildings that are similar to the majority of the buildings in a street are far less likely to be recalled less by GPS users and will be remembered better by non-GPS users, whereas buildings that stand out or contrast with their context are also likely to be better recalled by GPS users. These buildings do not necessarily have to be of any great aesthetic quality, for instance one of the better remembered buildings by GPS users in this research was under construction and surrounded by scaffolding. This helps to demonstrate that GPS users can strongly remember only the buildings that are very bold and outstanding and therefore difficult to miss on a journey even whilst following step-by-step GPS instructions.

Significantly, some particular features of buildings appearing to be important in differentiating the ability of recall between the two groups did not show a strong effect in the discriminant analysis. These included factors such as centrality to the circulation system and proximity to a major decision point. Indeed, this research discovered that location and the geographical position of buildings did not help GPS users to better remember buildings. The reasons for this may include, as previously mentioned, that when people use GPS maps, they normally tend to follow the route suggested by GPS system without paying significant attention to their surroundings, and therefore all the given features on the map have the same level of priority. Also, GPS users will be guided from A to B through the shortest route and they will not pass necessarily by the main junctions and streets. However, when people do not use GPS and find a route based on their own spatial knowledge, they are more likely to pass through main routes and main junctions and stop at decision points (junctions) to analyse their surroundings, in order to make decisions on the next stage of their journey. Hence, they are more directly involved with the task and will consequently better remember buildings at the main decision points. Indeed, looking at the data for non-GPS users in this research, the buildings that are closer to the main decision points are remembered far better than they are by GPS users.

Conclusions

This empirical research study has confirmed that people who use GPS for discovering an unfamiliar urban environment will have poor landmark knowledge of that place. Discriminant analysis has also identified the physical features of buildings that can be strongly remembered by GPS users. It was found that buildings that have unique architectural qualities, and/or are significant (historically and culturally) and/or contrast with their physical context are more likely to be well remembered by GPS users. Within this process, a number of issues arising due to the use of GPS systems were discussed from the point of views of different disciplines such as neuroscience, psychology and urban design. The findings identify that people who use GPS for navigation tend to get less involved cognitively with physical place and therefore have poorer spatial and landmark knowledge of that place. Having developed an empirical understanding of GPS users' relationship with and knowledge of their surrounding physical environments, a key question is: what can urban design do to increase GPS users' cognitive awareness of physical place? Significantly, this research suggests that at a primary level there are a number of physical features in an urban setting with which GPS users have stronger cognitive engagement. These physical features could, therefore, be further enhanced within the design of physical places to keep GPS users more cognitively engaged with their surroundings.

Based on the findings of this research, there are many design interventions that could enhance the relationship of GPS to users to urban environments and these can be reflected in the design of towns and cities. First, increasing the symbolic significance of a building or specific location can increase a GPS user's engagement with the environment by increasing their chances of remembering a particular place. This could include, for example, the conservation of important historical buildings and significant buildings, which, as this research has shown, can improve all people's navigation function including GPS users. In addition, uniqueness in terms of architectural style together with contrast to the surrounding context are also features that keep GPS users cognitively engaged. Significantly, therefore, whilst architects and urban designers are quite appropriately encouraged to design contextually sensitive buildings and urban developments, they should also be guided to produce creative and distinctive designs for specific buildings. Not only will this bring diversity to a place – it will also, importantly, enable people, including GPS users, to better remember and therefore engage with a particular place. Importantly, further research needs to be undertaken to understand the optimum type, number and relationship of such 'landmarks' (in terms of form, scale, distance, intervisibility, etc.) to maximise the memorability of these places for both

GPS users and non-GPS users. To do this successfully, further tests are needed in different urban environments, which will help us to further understand how to maximise the potential for achieving more detailed cognitive images of place for all users. This research study therefore encourages architects, urban designers and urban planners to develop a better understanding of how the use of technology is both changing and challenging the way that people relate to their built environment. Indeed, studying peoples' engagement with physical place and how this is affected by technology can lead to the design of physical places and environments that are more responsive to society's contemporary needs and preferences.

References

Al-Kodmany, K. 2001. 'Supporting imageability on the World Wide Web: Lynch's five elements of the city in community planning'. *Environment and Planning B: Planning and Design*, 28, 805–832.

Allen, G. L. 1981. 'A developmental perspective on the effects of "subdividing" macrospatial experience'. *Journal of Experimental Psychology: Human Learning and Memory*, 7, 120.

Allen, G. L. 2000. 'Principles and practices for communicating route knowledge'. *Applied Cognitive Psychology*, 14, 333–59.

Appleyard, D. 1969. 'Why buildings are known: a predictive tool for architects and planners'. *Environment and Behavior*, 1, 131.

Appleyard, D. 1970. 'Styles and methods of structuring a city'. *Environment and Behavior.*

Appleyard, D. 1976. *Planning a Pluralist City: Conflicting Realities in Ciudad Guayana.* Cambridge, MA: MIT Press.

Axon, S., Speake, J. & Crawford, K. 2012. '"At the next junction, turn left"': attitudes towards Sat Nav use'. *Area*, 44, 170–7.

Baker, L. 2004. 'Urban renewal, the wireless way'. *Salon.com*, 29.

Baus, J., Cheverst, K. & Kray, C. 2005. 'A survey of map-based mobile guides' in L. Meng, A. Zipf, T. Reichenbacher (Eds.) *Map-based Mobile Services*. Berlin: Springer.

Baus, J., Kray, C. & Krüger, A. 2001. 'Visualization of route descriptions in a resource-adaptive navigation aid'. *Cognitive Processing*, 2, 323–45.

Burigat, S. & Chittaro, L. 2007. 'Navigation in 3D virtual environments: effects of user experience and location-pointing navigation aids'. *International Journal of Human-Computer Studies*, 65, 945–58.

Cabin, R. J. & Mitchell, R. J. 2000. 'To Bonferroni or not to Bonferroni: when and how are the questions'. *Bulletin of the Ecological Society of America*, 81, 246–248.

Caduff, D. & Timpf, S. 2008. 'On the assessment of landmark salience for human navigation'. *Cognitive Processing*, 9, 249–67.

Cai, D., He, X. & Han, J. 2007. 'Semi-supervised discriminant analysis'. *Computer Vision, 2007. ICCV 2007. IEEE 11th International Conference on, 2007. IEEE*, 1–7.

Campbell, J. I., Hepner, I. J. & Miller, L. A. 2014. 'The influence of age and sex on memory for a familiar environment'. *Journal of Environmental Psychology*, 40, 1–8.

Cheverst, K., Davies, N., Mitchell, K., Friday, A. & Efstratiou, C. 2000. 'Developing a context-aware electronic tourist guide: some issues and experiences' in *Proceedings of the SIGCHI conference on Human Factors in Computing Systems*, 2000. ACM, 17–24.

Cohen, J. 1965. 'Some statistical issues in psychological research'. in *Handbook of Clinical Psychology*, 95–121.

Cubukcu, E. & Nasar, J. L. 2005. 'Relation of physical form to spatial knowledge in largescale virtual environments'. *Environment and Behavior*, 37, 397–417.

Darken, R. P. & Sibert, J. L. 'Wayfinding strategies and behaviors in large virtual worlds'. *Proceedings of the SIGCHI conference on Human factors in computing systems*, 1996. ACM, 142–9.

Denis, M. & Zimmere, M. 1992. 'Analog properties of cognitive maps constructed from verbal descriptions'. *Psychological Research*, 54, 286–98.

de Souza e Silva, A. & Frith, J. (2012). *Mobile Interfaces in Public Spaces: Locational Privacy, Control, and Urban Sociability*. London, New York: Routledge.

Evans, G. W., Brennan, P. L., Skorpanich, M. A. & Held, D. 1984. 'Cognitive mapping and elderly adults: Verbal and location memory for urban landmarks'. *Journal of Gerontology, 39*, 452–7.

Evans, G. W., Smith, C. & Pezdek, K. 1982. 'Cognitive maps and urban form'. *Journal of the American Planning Association*, 48, 232–44.

Farman, J. 2013. *Mobile Interface Theory: Embodied Space and Locative Media*. Abingdon: Routledge.

Ferguson, C. J. 2009. 'An effect size primer: A guide for clinicians and researchers'. *Professional Psychology: Research and Practice*, 40, 532.

Field, A. 2013. *Discovering Statistics Using IBM SPSS Statistic*. Sage.

Field, K., O'Brien, J. & Beale, L. 'Paper maps or GPS? Exploring differences in wayfinding behaviour and spatial knowledge acquisition'. *International Cartographic Conference, Paris*, Jul, 2011. 3–8.

Frankenstein, J. 2012. 'Is GPS all in our heads?' *New York Times*. Available at: https://www.nytimes.com/2012/02/05/opinion/sunday/is-gps-all-in-our-head.html

Gale, N., Golledge, R. G., Pellegrino, J. W. & Doherty, S. 1990. 'The acquisition and integration of route knowledge in an unfamiliar neighborhood'. *Journal of Environmental Psychology*, 10, 3–25.

Glander, T. & Döllner, J. 2009. 'Abstract representations for interactive visualization of virtual 3D city models'. *Computers, Environment and Urban Systems*, 33, 375–87.

Goldberger, P. 2009. *Building Up and Tearing Down: Reflections on the Age of Architecture*. Random House Digital, Inc.

Golledge, R. G. 1997. *Spatial Behavior: A Geographic Perspective*. Guilford Press.

Hepner, I. J., Mohamed, A., Fulham, M. J. & Miller, L. A. 2007. 'Topographical, autobiographical and semantic memory in a patient with bilateral mesial temporal and retrosplenial infarction'. *Neurocase*, 13, 97–114.

Hergan, I. & Umek, M. 2016. 'Comparison of children's wayfinding, using paper map and mobile navigation' *International Research in Geographical and Environmental Education*, 1–16.

Herman, J. F. & Siegel, A. W. 1978. 'The development of cognitive mapping of the large-scale environment'. *Journal of Experimental Child Psychology*, 26, 389–406.

Iaria, G., Petrides, M., Dagher, A., Pike, B. & Bohbot, V. D. 2003. 'Cognitive strategies dependent on the hippocampus and caudate nucleus in human navigation: variability and change with practice'. *Journal of Neuroscience*, 23, 5945–52.

Ingram, R., Benford, S. & Bowers, J. 1996. 'Building virtual cities: applying urban planning principles' in *Proceedings of the ACM Symposium on Virtual Reality Software and Technology* (VRST96), 1996. Citeseer.

Ishikawa, T. 2016. 'Maps in the head and tools in the hand: wayfinding and navigation in a spatially enabled society' in Hunter, H. R., Anderson, A. L. & Belza, L. B. (eds.) *Community Wayfinding: Pathways to Understanding*. Champaign, IL: Springer International Publishing.

Ishikawa, T., Fujiwara, H., Imai, O. & Okabe, A. 2008. 'Wayfinding with a GPS-based mobile navigation system: A comparison with maps and direct experience'. *Journal of Environmental Psychology*, 28, 74–82.

Ishikawa, T. & Montello, D. R. 2006. 'Spatial knowledge acquisition from direct experience in the environment: Individual differences in the development of metric knowledge and the integration of separately learned places'. *Cognitive Psychology*, 52, 93–129.

Jansen-Osmann, P. & Wiedenbauer, G. 2004. 'The representation of landmarks and routes in children and adults: A study in a virtual environment'. *Journal of Environmental Psychology*, 24, 347–57.

Janzen, G., Schade, M., Katz, S. & Herrmann, T. 2001. 'Strategies for detour finding in a virtual maze: The role of the visual perspective'. *Journal of Environmental Psychology*, 21, 149–63.

Jung, W. R. & Bell, S. 2014. 'Reforms in human wayfinding behavior based on the availability of GPS-based navigation systems'. *Spatial Knowledge and Information* (Conference). Available at: http://rose.geog.mcgill.ca/ski/system/files/fm/2014/jung.pdf

Kalin, J. & Frith, J. 2016. 'Wearing the city: memory P (a) laces, smartphones, and the rhetorical invention of embodied space'. *Rhetoric Society Quarterly*, 46, 222–35.

Kent, M., Altomonte, S., Tregenza, P. & Wilson, R. 2015. 'Temporal variables and personal factors in glare sensation'. *Lighting Research and Technology*, doi: 1477153515578310. Available at: http://eprints.nottingham.ac.uk/35431/1/Kent%20et%20al_LRT_2015.pdf

Kitchin, R. & Dodge, M. 2007. 'Rethinking maps'. *Progress in Human Geography*, 31, 331–44.

Klecka, W. R. 1980. *Discriminant Analysis*, Sage.

Klippel, A. & Winter, S. 2005. 'Structural salience of landmarks for route directions'. *International Conference on Spatial Information Theory*, 2005. Berlin: Springer, 347–62.

Krüger, A., Aslan, I. & Zimmer, H. 2004. 'The effects of mobile pedestrian navigation systems on the concurrent acquisition of route and survey knowledge'. *International Conference on Mobile Human-Computer Interaction*. Berlin: Springer, 446–50.

Kuipers, B. 1982. 'The "map in the head" metapho'r. *Environment and Behavior*, 14, 202–20.

Lane, B. W. 2008. 'Significant characteristics of the urban rail renaissance in the United States: A discriminant analysis'. *Transportation Research Part A: Policy and Practice*, 42, 279–95.

Laurier, E. & Brown, B. 2008. 'Rotating maps and readers: praxiological aspects of alignment and orientation'. *Transactions of the Institute of British Geographers*, 33, 201–16.

Li, C. 2006. 'User preferences, information transactions and location-based services: A study of urban pedestrian wayfinding'. *Computers, Environment and Urban Systems*, 30, 726–40.

Lynch, K. 1960. *The Image of the City*. Cambridge, MA: MIT.

Lynch, K. 1984. *Good City Form*. Camridge, MA: MIT Press.

Maguire, E. A., Gadian, D. G., Johnsrude, I. S., Good, C. D., Ashburner, J., Frackowiak, R. S. & Frith, C. D. 2000. 'Navigation-related structural change in the hippocampi of taxi drivers'. *Proceedings of the National Academy of Sciences*, 97, 4398–403.

Mclachlan, G. 2004. *Discriminant Analysis and Statistical Pattern Recognition*. Hoboken, NJ: John Wiley & Sons.

Milgram, S. 1972. 'A psychological map of New York City'. *American Scientist*, 60, 194–200.

Montello, D. R. & Pick, H. L. 1993. 'Integrating knowledge of vertically aligned large-scale spaces'. *Environment and Behavior*, 25, 457–84.

Münzer, S., Zimmer, H. D., Schwalm, M., Baus, J. & Aslan, I. 2006. 'Computer-assisted navigation and the acquisition of route and survey knowledge'. *Journal of Environmental Psychology*, 26, 300–8.

Neyfakh, L. & So, I. 2013. 'Do our brains pay a price for GPS?' *Boston Globe*. Available at: https://www.bostonglobe.com/ideas/2013/08/17/our-brains-pay-price-for-gps/d2Tnvo4hiWjuybid5UhQVO/story.html

Omer, I., Goldblatt, R. & Or, U. 2005. 'Virtual city design based on urban image theory'. *The Cartographic Journal*, 42, 15–26.

Omer, I., Goldblatt, R., Talmor, K. & Roz, A. 2006. 'Enhancing the legibility of virtual cities by means of residents' urban image: a wayfinding support system' in Juval Portugali (ed) *Complex Artificial Environments*. Verlag Berlin Heidelberg: Springer. Available at: https://www.springer.com/gp/book/9783540259176#

Oulasvirta, A., Estlander, S. & Nurminen, A. 2009. 'Embodied interaction with a 3D versus 2D mobile map'. *Personal and Ubiquitous Computing*, 13, 303–20.

Oulasvirta, A., Kurvinen, E. & Kankainen, T. 2003. 'Understanding contexts by being there: case studies in bodystorming' *Personal and Ubiquitous Computing*, 7, 125–34.

Pezdek, K. & Evans, G. W. 1979. 'Visual and verbal memory for objects and their spatial locations'. *Journal of Experimental Psychology: Human Learning and Memory*, 5, 360.

Pouke, M., Goncalves, J., Ferreira, D. & Kostakos, V. 2016. 'Practical simulation of virtual crowds using points of interest'. *Computers, Environment and Urban Systems*, 57, 118–29.

Poulsen, J. & French, A. 2008. 'Discriminant function analysis'. Available at: http://userwww.sfsu.edu/efc/classes/biol710/discrim/discrim.pdf

Rakkolainen, I. & Vainio, T. 2001. 'A 3D city info for mobile users'. *Computers & Graphics*, 25, 619–25.

Reilly, D., Rodgers, M., Argue, R., Nunes, M. & Inkpen, K. 2006. 'Marked-up maps: combining paper maps and electronic information resources'. *Personal and Ubiquitous Computing*, 10, 215–26.

Reiner, A., Yekutieli, D. & Benjamini, Y. 2003. 'Identifying differentially expressed genes using false discovery rate controlling procedures'. *Bioinformatics*, 19, 368–75.

Rossano, M. J. & Moak, J. 1998. 'Spatial representations acquired from computer models: Cognitive load, orientation specificity and the acquisition of survey knowledge'. *British Journal of Psychology*, 89, 481–97.

Sandelowski, M. 2000. 'Focus on research methods combining qualitative and quantitative sampling, data collection, and analysis techniques'. *Research in Nursing & Health*, 23, 246–55.

Sarabia-Sánchez, F. J., Rodríguez-Sánchez, C. & Hyder, A. 2014. 'The role of personal involvement, credibility and efficacy of conduct in reported water conservation behaviour'. *Journal of Environmental Psychology*, 38, 206–16.

Siegel, A. W. & White, S. H. 1975. 'The development of spatial representations of large-scale environments'. *Advances in Child Development and Behavior*, 10, 9–55.

Slone, E., Burles, F., Robinson, K., Levy, R. M. & Iaria, G. 2015. 'Floor plan connectivity influences wayfinding performance in virtual environments'. *Environment and Behavior*, 47, 1024–53.

Speake, J. 2015. '"I've got my Sat Nav, it's alright|": users' attitudes towards, and engagements with, technologies of navigation. *The Cartographic Journal*, 52, 345–55.

Spiers, H. J. & Maguire, E. A. 2008. 'The dynamic nature of cognition during wayfinding'. *Journal of Environmental Psychology*, 28, 232–49.

Stankiewicz, B. J. & Kalia, A. A. 2007. Acquistion of structural versus object landmark knowledge. *Journal of Experimental Psychology: Human Perception and Performance*, 33, 378.

Stern, E. & Leiser, D. 1988. 'Levels of spatial knowledge and urban travel modeling'. *Geographical Analysis*, 20, 140–55.

Tabachnick, B.G., Fidell, L.S. and Osterlind, S.J. 2001. *Using Multivariate Statistics*. Boston, MA: Allyn and Bacon. Available at: https://trove.nla.gov.au/work/7185329

Thorndyke, P. W. & Hayes-Roth, B. 1982. 'Differences in spatial knowledge acquired from maps and navigation'. *Cognitive Psychology*, 14, 560–89.

Tom, A. & Denis, M. 2003. 'Referring to landmark or street information in route directions: what difference does it make?' *International Conference on Spatial Information Theory*. Springer, 362–74.

Tom, A. C. & Tversky, B. 2012. 'Remembering routes: streets and landmarks'. *Applied Cognitive Psychology*, 26, 182–93.

Wasinger, R., Stahl, C. & Krüger, A. 2003. 'M3I in a pedestrian navigation & exploration system'. *International Conference on Mobile Human-Computer Interaction*, 2003. Springer, 481–85.

Weber, R. J., Brown, L. T. & Weldon, J. K. 1978. 'Cognitive maps of environmental knowledge and preference in nursing home patients'. *Experimental Aging Research*, 4, 157–74.

Wen, W., Ishikawa, T. & Sato, T. 2011. 'Working memory in spatial knowledge acquisition: differences in encoding processes and sense of direction'. *Applied Cognitive Psychology*, 25, 654–62.

Westerbeek, H. & Maes, A. 2013. 'Route-external and route-internal landmarks in route descriptions: effects of route length and map design'. *Applied Cognitive Psychology*, 27, 297–305.

Willis, K. S., Hölscher, C., Wilbertz, G. & Li, C. 2009. 'A comparison of spatial knowledge acquisition with maps and mobile maps'. *Computers, Environment and Urban Systems*, 33, 100–10.

Zimmer, H. D. 2004. 'The construction of mental maps based on a fragmentary view of physical maps'. *Journal of Educational Psychology*, 96, 603.

10

DATA AND EMOTIONS

Mapping of Beirut Central District through physiological emotions

Roua Ghosh and Samer El Sayary

Introduction

Human response to architecture is usually based on subjective emotions: '*I like that building, I hate this space; this room is so open, this office is oppressive*'. But something more nuanced is happening to elicit these responses (Berg, 2014). Neuroscientists have found that distinctive processes occur in our brains – consciously and subconsciously, cognitively and physiologically. These processes affect our emotions, our health, and the development of memory. They argue that buildings can shape our brains. This chapter raises the problematic of sensory depreciation in spaces, which creates a "non-existent area," an environment without a clear meaning, negatively affecting the user's emotions and behavior. This will be examined through a case study conducted in the urban area of Beirut Central District – BCD, Lebanon.

This research will focus on overlaying people's senses and emotions in a geographical map of a selected zone of Beirut, to evaluate the urban environment and its influence on the human experience. A new type of map of physiological emotions will be produced. The users' evaluation and perception of places is recorded and related to sensuous stimuli. The research experiment involves a group of 30 participants equipped with GPS and cameras, walking along a route in the city and responding to a questionnaire designed by the researchers. A positive association is observed between sensuous stimuli and positive human experience. The urban areas with higher stimuli for the human senses lead to positive feedback, a positive human experience, and attachment to the environment.

Our daily urban experience is the result of our perceptions and senses (Quercia, Pesce & Almeida, 2014), and the significance of this is raised by several researchers and theorists. Cedric Price (1966) proposed that "mental, physical and sensory well-being is required in our environment," suggested that the full spectrum of our sensory system should be taken into consideration, and introduced the new approach and idea of "the sensorial urbanism." Although sight has been historically considered as an important sense and criterion in urban planning, the other senses have been extensively discussed. For Lynch "[n]early every sense is in operation, and the image is the composite of them all" (Lynch, 1960) whereas for Kaiser "visual quality may be the most important influence on how people experience and respond to urban areas and planning initiatives" (Kaiser et al., 1995). A considerable number of architects extended, recently, their interest toward the complete sensorial spectrum, addressing sound, odors and touch in their design.

For this specific case study, Beirut Central District – BCD in Lebanon was selected because of its financial, commercial, historical, and administrative significance. This area hosts the Lebanese Parliament, the Governmental Palace, Beirut Municipality, the Beirut Stock Exchange, the regional offices of the United Nations, International Labor Organization, and UNESCO, as well as the headquarters of the ESCWA and the Union of Arab Banks, and is a focal point for both locals and tourists. Parts of this area have been under reconstruction since 1990, following the disastrous Lebanese Civil War. The reconstruction is being done by private developers following government guidelines.

For Libeskind, it takes a long time for a public space to shape itself. No matter how sad, how tragic, a site might be, or how abused by history, architecture can point to the future. In major cities, the great buildings tell you things you don't know and "remember" things that you've forgotten. For Libeskind, architecture is the biggest unwritten document of history (Libeskind, 2015)

Scope and research questions

The urban environment of the BCD affects the human senses and emotions; this chapter will develop a new way of mapping this area through examining the human experience, and will offer a starting point for possible future planning guidelines. The objective of this study is to examine people's perception of urban space, and gain an understanding as to how sensuous stimuli lead to specific cognitive and psychological responses and states. The long-term aim is to create guidelines for reducing the human "anger" and "fear" and enhancing "enjoyment" in urban environments.

What is sensing a place, and why is it becoming a need in our city planning strategies? How do users perceive their urban surrounding, and what are the senses and emotions that can be associated with each place? How can the interrelation between the human emotions and the architecture be used in the future as guidance, for revitalizing some urban spots and giving visitors a positive experience?

In order to establish the framework for this study, the following section presents a review of the relevant literature on the human senses and emotions, aspects and classifications, and the importance of using these data in mapping the city. Following this, the specific experiment and its outputs will be presented.

Senses and emotions as mapping data of a city

This project is an attempt to map the un-mappable; to map/record/analyze emotions and experiences and to link these to the physical attributes of a place. This is a big, ongoing, complex question in architectural studies – a complex matter addressed in different ways and through different philosophical threads.

The "sense of place" is a concept raised by several researchers and practitioners in architecture and urban design. The sense of place has been associated with a sense of satisfaction, identity, and attachment to a place and to the local communities. In general, the notion of a sense of place has been used to describe our relationship with places, expressed in different aspects of human life: biographies, imagination, stories, and personal experiences (Basso, 1996). In the context of psychology, sense of place is associated with how we perceive a place (Kudryavtsev, Stedman, and Krasny, 2012). It is for Adams "the lens through which people experience and make meaning of their experiences in and with place" (Adams and Gupta, 2013). The sense of place is reintroduced in a different light through the development of crossovers between architecture and neuroscience.

To analyze the case study of BCD, human senses and human emotions are two key elements that will be looked at. These two elements and the different types of their classifications will be discussed in relation to the writings of designers, planners, and anthropologists. The same two elements will inform the case study.

According to Lynch, "Nothing is experienced by itself, but in relation to its surroundings, the sequences of events leading up to it" (Lynch, 1960). The creation of the image of a city is the result of the interaction between the observer and the surrounding environment. The physical elements can be classified into different categories, such as: natural (river, garden, etc.) and man-made (buildings, streets, bridges, vehicles, etc.). For Lynch, physical elements determine the Urban Design Qualities of the city (*imageability, legibility enclosure, etc.).* They are also the main attributes that constitute the Lynch's Five Elements (path, edge, district, node, and landmark).

The environmental physical attributes affecting the human senses and emotions could be described, for the purposes of this study, as shown in Table 10.1.

Definition of senses and classifications

From a psychological and biological perspective, sensation is the process of receiving a stimulus from the external environment and transforming it into neural energy. "Whatever the source of stimulation, its energy must be converted into nerve impulses, the only language the nervous system understands" (Liedtke, 2006). Physical energy such as light, sound, and heat is detected by specialized receptor cells in the sense organs – eyes, ears, skin, nose, and tongue. When the receptor cells register a stimulus, the energy is converted to an electrochemical impulse or action potential that relays information about the stimulus through the nervous system to the brain (Sani et al., 2009; Wang and Hatton, 2009).

TABLE 10.1 Physical elements/attributes of an urban area

Attributes of an urban area			
Buildings	*Public space*	*Streets and transportation*	*Landscape*
– Historical – Modern – Damaged – Vandalized	– Urban Furniture – Clean/dirty – People interaction – Enclosure – Safety – Planning	– Narrow – Wide – Pedestrian – Vehicular – Crowded/calm – Pollution – Clean/dirty – Safety – Guidelines and signage	– Vegetation – Natural made – Man-made landscape – Clean/dirty

The senses are frequently divided into exteroceptive and interoceptive. Interoceptive senses are related to the perception of sensations in internal organs. Exteroceptive senses are those that perceive the body's own position, motion, and state. External senses (exteroceptive) include the traditional five: sight, hearing, touch, smell, and taste, as well as other types of senses such as thermoception (temperature differences) and possibly an additional weak magnetoception (direction). Other senses, or ways of describing sensations, include: equilibrioception, associated with balance, and proprioception, associated with the perception of the relevant position and movement of the parts of one's own body. Table 10.2 illustrates the physiological mechanisms that are responsible for processing a stimulus, perceived by a sense organ and analyzed in our brain and body into a type of sensation. For this table, the categorization of the five traditional senses is used.

TABLE 10.2 Summary table analyzing the sensation process

	Sense	*Stimulus*	*Sense Organ*	*Receptor*	*Sensation*
Traditional Senses	Vision	Light waves	Eye	Rods and cones of retina	Colors, brightness, patterns, motion, textures
	Hearing	Sound waves	Ear	Hair cells of the basilar membrane	Pitch, loudness, timbre
	Skin senses	External contact	Skin	Nerve endings in skin	Touch, warmth, cold
	Smell	Volatile substances	Nose	Hair cells of olfactory epithelium	Odors
	Taste	Soluble substances	Tongue	Taste buds of tongue	Flavors

The increasing interest in the notion of senses is a catalyst for new methods and tools to be developed for the analysis and design of the built environment. For Alvar Aalto, "[t]he best way to acquaint oneself with architecture is not to read about it: it is to look, touch, smell, and listen to it - a building only gains meaning when it becomes part of human life." For Pallasmaa, "[e]xperiencing architecture is multi-sensory; qualities of space, matter and scale are measured together by the eye, ear, nose, skin, tongue, skeleton and muscle." (Pallasmaa, 2005). Zardini points out the evolution in the way in which senses are studied and discussed: "In recent years, the human and social sciences, from anthropology to geography, have undergone a 'sensorial revolution' in which the 'senses' constitute not so much a new field of study as a fundamental shift in the mode and media we employ to observe and define our own fields of study" (Zardini, 2006).

In this study we will focus on three traditional senses; vision, smell, and hearing. Sight or vision is considered a principal element in architectural design, and is related to light, color, texture, etc. According to Le Corbusier, the visual sense is key to architecture, and he claims: "Architecture is the masterly, correct, and magnificent play of masses brought together in light" (Corbusier and Etchells, 1970). The importance of hearing is raised by Blesser and Salter (2007) in their book *Spaces Speak, Are You Listening? Experiencing Aural Architecture*, where they explore the auditory spatial awareness and its relationship to architecture. They develop the hypothesis that listeners can learn to "see" the space with their ears by recognizing the spatial geometry of a room with low or high ceiling, or open doors, or even the emptiness of a house without furniture. Finally, the sense of smell is very important, and several studies have revealed the effects of odors on cognition, emotion, mood, and memory (Ehrlichman and Bastone, 1992). An individual's experience of a space is informed by all the senses. Additionally, according to Lynch (1960), the interaction with a space depends also on the cultural background, temperament, status, and purpose of the observer. Table 10.3 illustrates a number of physical attributes existing in the urban environment (selected by the researchers) and the human sense each one addresses.

TABLE 10.3 Correlation between the senses and certain urban physical attributes

Senses	*Sensations in urban areas – physical attributes*
Vision	Natural and landscaping areas, historical buildings, modern/historical/damages/vandalized buildings, unplanned zones, clean/dirty places or streets, enclosure, signage, wide/narrow paths
Smell	Car pollution combustions, landscaping and natural odors, food odors, bad odors from unclean zones,
Hearing	Loud sounds and car horns, music, crowded/calm places, etc.

Definition of emotional aspects and classifications

"Emotion" is a notion used to describe a range of phenomena, such as sentiments, moods, and passions. For Reeve (2009) "Emotions" can be described through four categories of elements: Feelings, Bodily Arousal, Cognitive Process, and Behavior. Different theories discuss emotions and attempt to explain how they are created; for James and Lange (1884), the emotional experience is a way of making sense of bodily changes. The Cannon–Bard Theory of emotion, of 1920, interprets the emergence of emotions differently from James and Lange, and claims that people can experience physiological changes linked to emotions without feeling those emotions. They suggest that physical and psychological experiences happen at the same time and that one does not cause the other. In 1962, the Schachter–Singer theory of emotion, known also as the two-factor theory, argues that similar physiological responses can produce – or be related to – various emotions. The Cognitive Appraisal Theory (Lazarus, 1991) came as an expansion of the Cannon–Bard Theory, and clarified that the development of our emotions is determined by our appraisal of stimuli, which affects our physiological arousal and the emotional experience itself. Facial feedback theory, introduced by Charles Darwin and William James, claims that physiological responses have a direct impact on emotion, rather than being simply a consequence of it.

In addition to the different theories for how emotions are generated, there are different theories for grouping emotions of different nature. Robert Plutchik's theory (1980) presents eight basic groups of human emotions. He claims that our primary emotions, and their various combinations in different intensities, lead to the broader spectrum of human emotions. His model organized emotional expressions in a wheel, according to eight types and four degrees of intensity. Parrott (2001), influenced by Shaver et al. (1987), developed a list of emotions, categorized into three phases: primary, secondary, and tertiary. Recently, Lovheim (2011) proposed a three-dimensional model, following the three main axes – substances: dopamine, noradrenaline, and serotonin, which are considered by several researchers

TABLE 10.4 Theories of emotions

Theories of Emotions			
James–Lange Theory	Cannon–Bard Theory	Schachter–Singer Theory	Cognitive Appraisal Theory
Arousal	Arousal	Arousal	Arousal
↓	↙ ↘	↙ ↘	↓
Bodily Changes	Bodily Changes Emotions	Bodily Changes	Appraisal
↓		↖ ↗	↓
Emotions		Cognitive Label Emotions	Emotions/Bodily changes

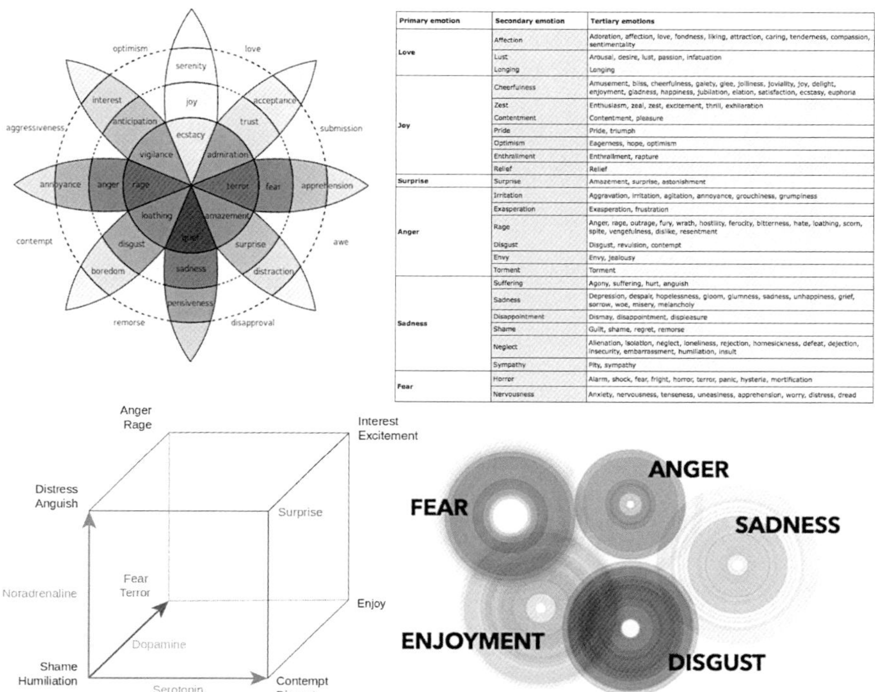

Primary emotion	Secondary emotion	Tertiary emotions
Love	Affection	Adoration, affection, love, fondness, liking, attraction, caring, tenderness, compassion, sentimentality
	Lust	Arousal, desire, lust, passion, infatuation
	Longing	Longing
Joy	Cheerfulness	Amusement, bliss, cheerfulness, gaiety, glee, jolliness, joviality, joy, delight, enjoyment, gladness, happiness, jubilation, elation, satisfaction, ecstasy, euphoria
	Zest	Enthusiasm, zeal, zest, excitement, thrill, exhilaration
	Contentment	Contentment, pleasure
	Pride	Pride, triumph
	Optimism	Eagerness, hope, optimism
	Enthrallment	Enthrallment, rapture
	Relief	Relief
Surprise	Surprise	Amazement, surprise, astonishment
Anger	Irritation	Aggravation, irritation, agitation, annoyance, grouchiness, grumpiness
	Exasperation	Exasperation, frustration
	Rage	Anger, rage, outrage, fury, wrath, hostility, ferocity, bitterness, hate, loathing, scorn, spite, vengefulness, dislike, resentment
	Disgust	Disgust, revulsion, contempt
	Envy	Envy, jealousy
	Torment	Torment
Sadness	Suffering	Agony, suffering, hurt, anguish
	Sadness	Depression, despair, hopelessness, gloom, glumness, sadness, unhappiness, grief, sorrow, woe, misery, melancholy
	Disappointment	Dismay, disappointment, displeasure
	Shame	Guilt, shame, regret, remorse
	Neglect	Alienation, isolation, neglect, loneliness, rejection, homesickness, defeat, dejection, insecurity, embarrassment, humiliation, insult
	Sympathy	Pity, sympathy
Fear	Horror	Alarm, shock, fear, fright, horror, terror, panic, hysteria, mortification
	Nervousness	Anxiety, nervousness, tenseness, uneasiness, apprehension, worry, distress, dread

FIGURE 10.1 Top left: Plutchik emotional Wheel; top right: Parrot emotional list; bottom left: Lovheim emotional 3d model; bottom right: "Atlas of Emotion" by Ekman.

to be the essential controllers of behaviors and emotions. Later on, in 2016, Paul Ekman and his daughter, Eve Ekman, created the "Atlas of emotions," identifying five "Universal Emotions" that all humans have in common.

As a summary of the above, Table 10.5 compares the four listed theories through their primary emotions, to show similarities and differences between them. The first three types of emotions, appearing in all four theories, are used for the Beirut case study. Table 10.6 illustrates a correlation between the random physical attributes existing in the urban realm and human emotions, selected by the researcher.

Beirut Central District as case study: sensory and emotional mapping survey

This section presents the method for data collection and analysis. This can be regarded as opinion and emotional feedback captured by the participants about the built environment. The results can be used for follow-up studies to evaluate the relationship between physical attributes of places and the emotions invoked.

TABLE 10.5 Emotional classifications

		Emotional Classifications			
		Plutchik (1980)	*Parrott (2001)*	*Lovheim (2011)*	*Ekman (2016)*
Primary Emotions	Anger/Rage	x	x	x	x
	Enjoyment/Joy	x	x	x	x
	Fear	x	x	x	x
	Disgust	x		x	x
	Sadness	x	x		x
	Surprise	x	x	x	
	Love		x		
	Shame/Humiliation			x	
	Interest/Excitement			x	
	Distress/Anguish			x	
	Admiration	x			
	Vigilance	x			

TABLE 10.6 Correlation between emotions and urban physical attributes

Emotions	*Excitements in urban areas – physical attributes*
Anger	Unplanned zones, traffic jam, unclean areas, crowded zones, damaged/vandalized/etc. buildings
Enjoyment	Landscaping and natural zones, defined pedestrian and car paths, Interesting urban fixtures and sites, modern/etc. buildings, enclosed areas, clean zones, people interaction
Fear	Unsafe and unsecured zones, undefined area, calm areas, damaged/vandalized/etc. buildings, narrow/wide streets, vehicular roads, unguided paths

As was mentioned in the beginning of this chapter, the selected area for this study is the Beirut Central District–BCD, and more specifically a defined path of 2.5 km length. The path passes through several nodes of different types, as shown below:

- Piazzas and historical spots: Martyrs Square, Nijmeh Square, Roman Baths, Beirut Souks, Zaytuna Bay
- Civic buildings: Governmental Palace, Lebanese Parliament, ESCWA, Beirut Municipality Arab Bank
- Commercial Buildings or zones: Beirut Souks, Zaytuna Bay

Furthermore, the path allows the participant a general overview of the BCD and to feel the different faces of Beirut city center, as it passes through diverse building types, modern and refurbished, different types of roads and pathways (vehicular or pedestrian), etc. Two possible paths were considered, surveyed and

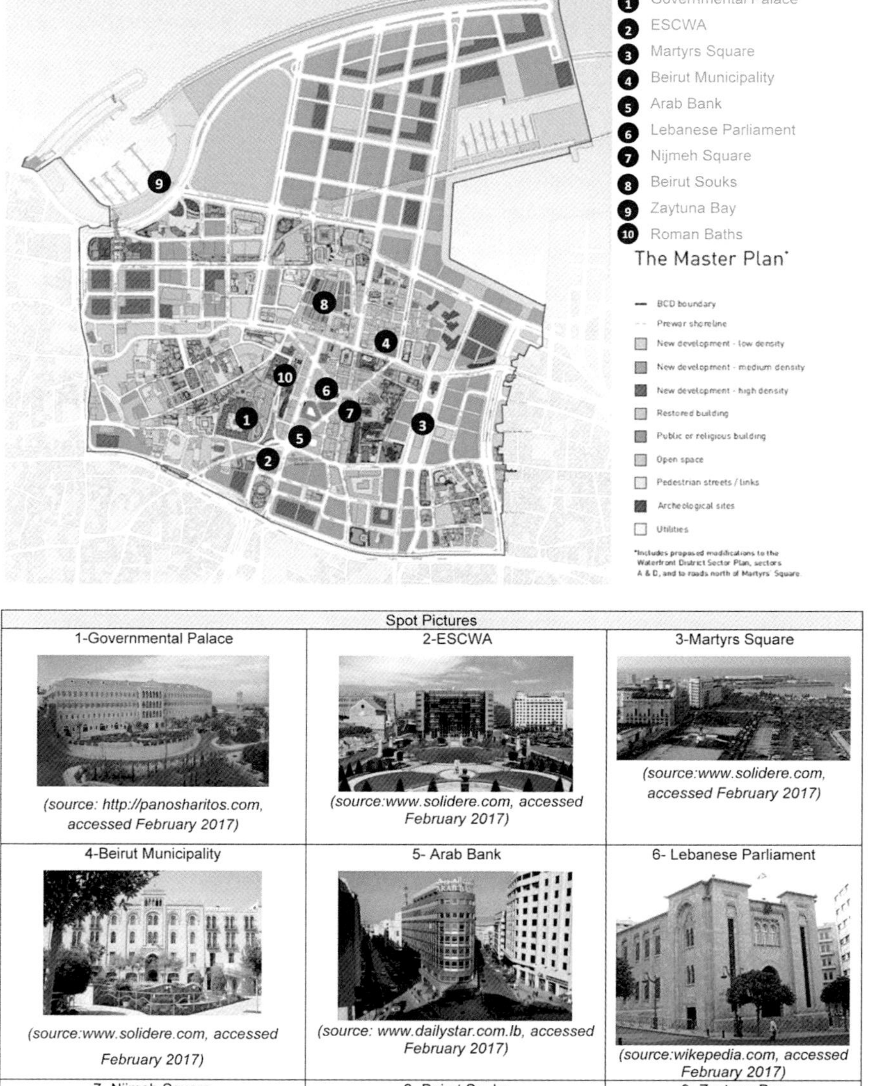

FIGURE 10.2 Top: BCD diagrammatical map (source: map edited by the author, based on a map of the Lebanese Urban Planning); Bottom: Pictures of the selected spots.

analyzed, and the path shown on Figure 10.3 was selected as more appropriate for the purposes of this research.

The 30 volunteers who participated in this study consisted of 15 females and 15 males, from Beirut, aged between 18 and 30, who have visited this area several times before and were familiar with the buildings and streets. The participants were asked to complete a questionnaire developed by the researchers regarding their sensations and emotions while perceiving and moving along the specified path of the study, and recorded by each one of them for reliability of data, using the mobile application 'My tracks' (to define the line through the map) and by photographs. The recordings and data collected will have both subjective and objective qualities. For each spot specified on the map, each participant was asked to evaluate first their senses (vision, smell and hearing) on a scale from 1 to 5 (from very bad to very good), mentioning the physical reasons behind their answers in relation to the surrounding urban area. The second component of the evaluation is related to their emotions (anger, enjoyment and fear), on a scale from low to high. The combination of these two parameters allowed the researchers to examine the relationship between the two for each 'node' of the path.

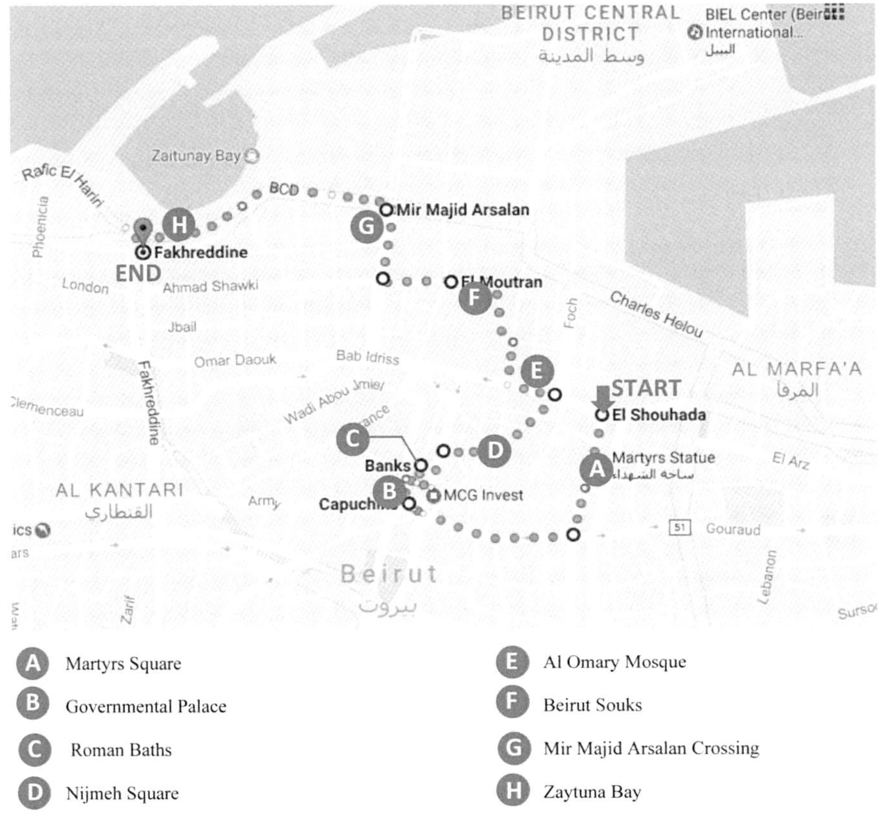

FIGURE 10.3 Path followed by the experiment participants.

TABLE 10.7 Extract from the questionnaire given to the participants to fill in. A set of these two tables (shown in Table 10.7) was used for each one of the 'nodes' – key points of the path. On the left-hand table, the numbers 1–5 correspond to negative – positive. On the right-hand table, the numbers 1–5 correspond to low-high

The questionnaire also included other questions, such as age group, gender, etc.

SENSES	*Scale*	*Reasons*			
		Buildings	*Public space*	*Streets and transportation*	*Landscape*
Vision	1				
	2				
	3				
	4				
	5				
Sound	1				
	2				
	3				
	4				
	5				
Odors	1				
	2				
	3				
	4				
	5				

EMOTIONS	*Scale*	*Reasons*			
		Buildings	*Public space*	*Streets and transportation*	*Landscape*
Anger	1				
	2				
	3				
	4				
	5				
Enjoyment	1				
	2				
	3				
	4				
	5				
Fear	1				
	2				
	3				
	4				
	5				

The participants were asked to walk along the specified path at rush hour; the duration of their walk was approximately 30 minutes. The studied area and path will be assessed on two levels, by means of the questionnaire: sensorial and emotional, where the evaluation of the latter is essential. Processing the sensory input data will enable us to recognize surrounding objects. For the first level, the city identity will be evaluated by its visual aspects, odors, and soundscapes; for the second, an emotional analysis will be the outcome, specifying the levels of anger, fear, and enjoyment. The overlaying the sensorial and the emotional layers will give a new type of mapping for the BCD and an assessment of the presented built environment, plotting the different analyzed spots, highlighting the stimulated sense in each area and recording emotions.

To summarize the answers to the questionnaire, charts were created to visualize the results. Averages of the outcomes surveyed were calculated and introduced in charts of Figure 10.4. Moreover, during the survey, participants took several photographs for the different spots, illustrated in form of a journey map.

Results analysis: overlaying the people outcome

To analyze the results of the study, each surveyed spot was examined and the average of the participants' responses was used to create the relevant graphs. The graph and map of Figure 10.5 present the link between the senses–stimuli and the emotions of the participants.

Starting from Martyrs Square – Spot A – the hearts of downtown, representing a significant historical area from the Ottoman rule, through to the Lebanese Civil War, and on to our present time, caused high levels of anger for the participants; it was accompanied by a lack of visual stimuli and high levels of noise. Toward the Governmental Palace and the ESCWA – Spot B – high levels of fear were recorded, associated mainly with the vandalism observed and the security fencing. The areas of the Roman Baths, Nijmeh Square, Beirut Municipality, and Beirut Souks – Spots C, D, E and F – include designed landscapes with planned areas, kids' activity areas, pedestrian walkways, etc. Participants recorded high levels of sensuous stimuli, accompanied by high levels of enjoyments and low levels of anger and fear. The design characteristics of these zones should be monitored and looked into as precedents that could inform the design of other areas of the BCD. Spot G is considered the link between the old city and the Cornice, and does not include any safe or guided pedestrian paths. Participants recorded high levels of anger and fear, and did not record any particular sensuous stimuli. This area was devoid of the physical characteristics that could enhance the interaction between the user and its environment. The final spot of the surveyed path was Zaytuna Bay, where, as was predicted, participants' recordings showed that a mix of urban elements, landscape and social areas lead to a positive emotional experience, accompanied by high levels of sensuous stimuli.

The outcome for some regions was unexpected, specifically the Martyrs Square, and should be more closely examined in future studies. After calculating the

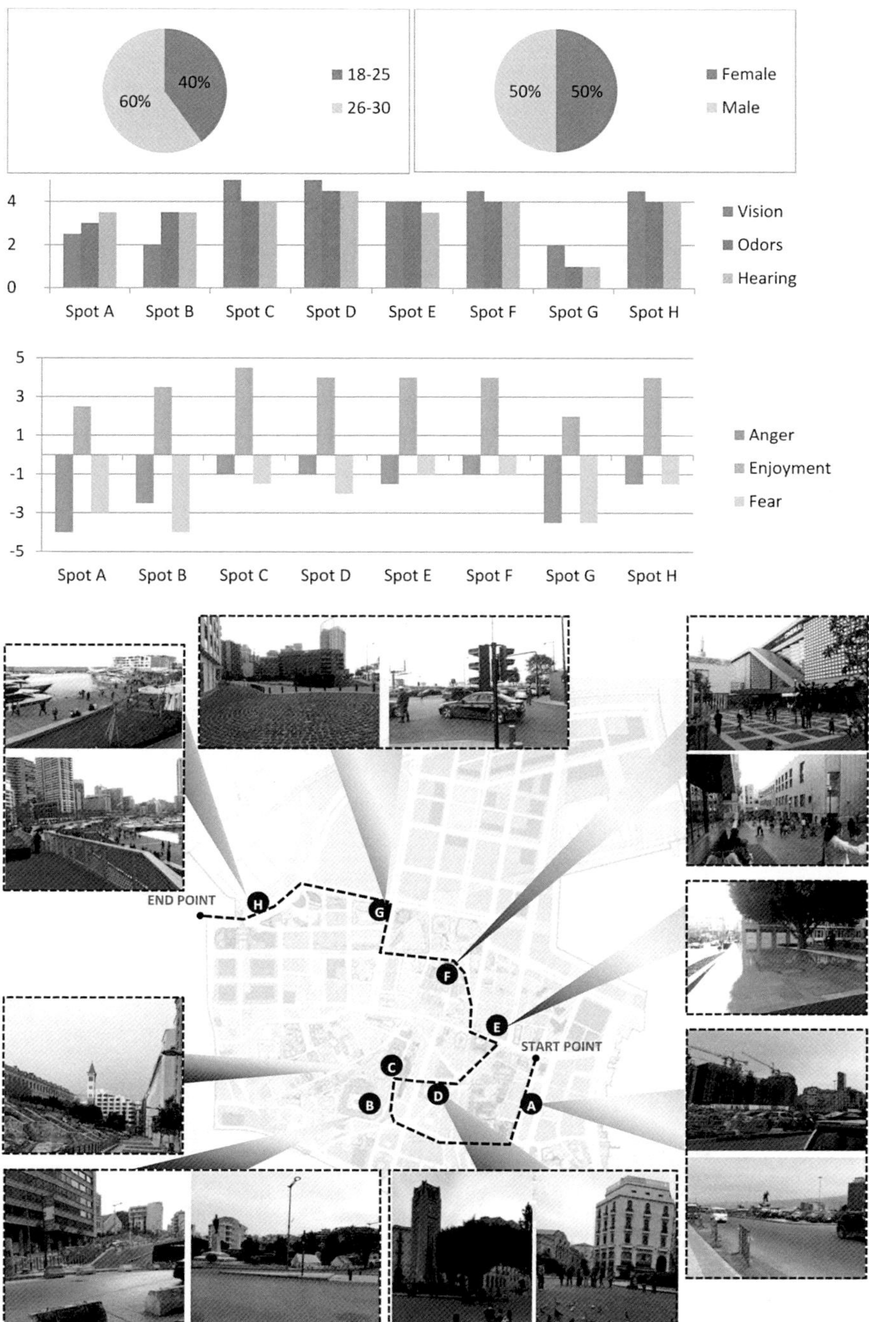

FIGURE 10.4 Top left chart: participants age range; top right chart: gender; middle first chart: evaluation of human senses; bottom second chart: evaluation of human emotions; bottom map: journey map of the surveyed path.

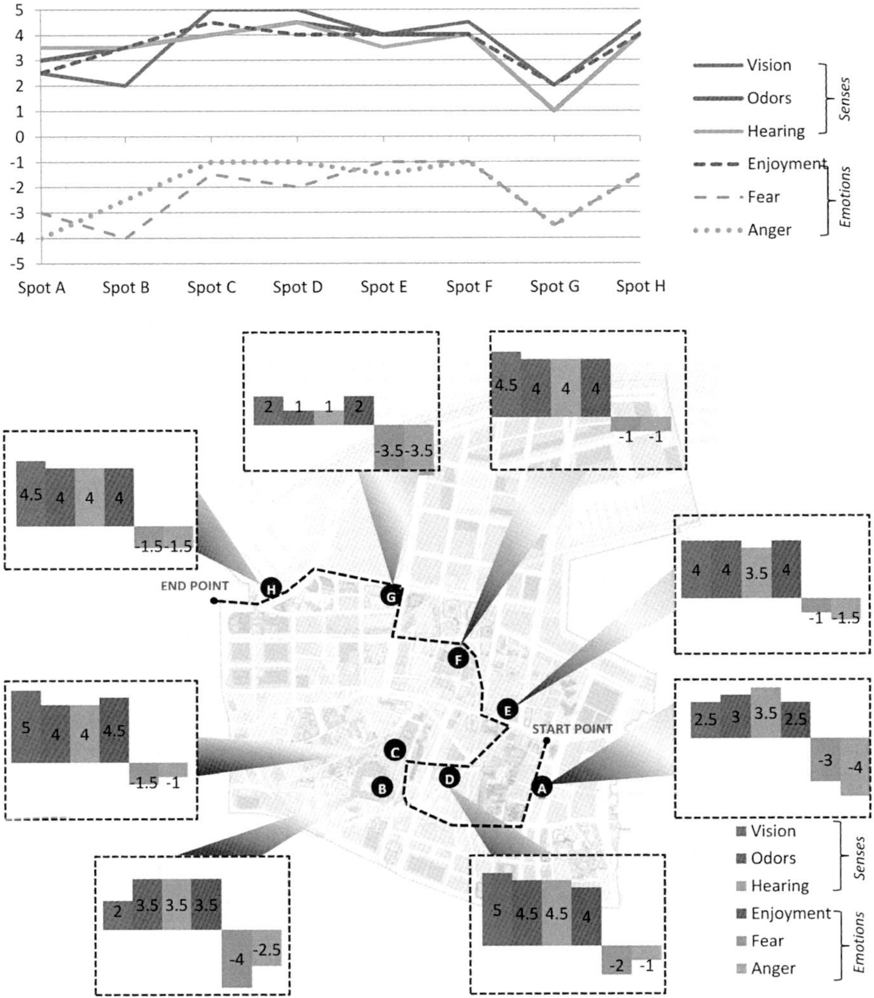

FIGURE 10.5 Top chart: overlaying the people outcome; bottom map: overlaying the people outcome on the map of the surveyed path.

average scale for each point, the spots having scale averages below 7.5 for senses, and below −2.5 for emotions, must be reconsidered to enhance the human experience. Spots A, B & G are locations identified in this study as having remarkable architectural buildings and landmarks, but not giving the visitors the best reflection of this historic and special city through the senses. Reconsideration of the physical attributes of these three cited spots should be in the next plan to revitalize them. For these reasons, a map reflecting human emotions, not only the geographical places, will be a useful guide for experiencing and feeling the whole environment

TABLE 10.8 Emotional and sensual scale averages surveyed for each spot and physical attributes reasons

	Senses	*Emotions*	*Physical attributes*			
			Buildings	*Public space*	*Streets and transportation*	*Landscape*
Spot A	9	−4.5	Some are under construction	Unplanned zones Empty spaces Unsafe area	Traffic jam Crowded zones Vehicular roads High sound and odor pollution	Poor landscape
Spot B	9	−3	Scary buildings	Vandalized zones Protest tents	Crowded zones	Poor landscape
Spot C	13	2	Historical spot	Birds around Enclosed and Calm area	No cars	Relaxing, refreshing landscape
Spot D	14	1	Historical spot	Kids playing area Enclosed and Calm area	No cars	Birds around
Spot E	11.5	1.5	Historical and commercial spot		Slow car drive on cobblestone road	Water feature
Spot F	12.5	2	Mix of historical and modern buildings Mixed use area	Social interaction Kids playing area Enclosed area Food odors	No cars Pedestrian Piazzas and walkways	Modern landscape
Spot G	4	−5	Modern buildings	Undefined zone	Crowded zone Wide vehicular roads	
Spot H	12.5	1	Modern buildings Mixed use area	Social interaction Food odors	Safe and wide pedestrian sidewalk	Sea view

through senses, body, and interactions. Moreover, the analysis showed a clear relationship between positive feelings and historical, safe, pedestrian areas.

Conclusions and findings

Throughout this study, the main source of data was the field survey of emotions and sensations, as perceived by the participants, in several spots in Beirut Central District.

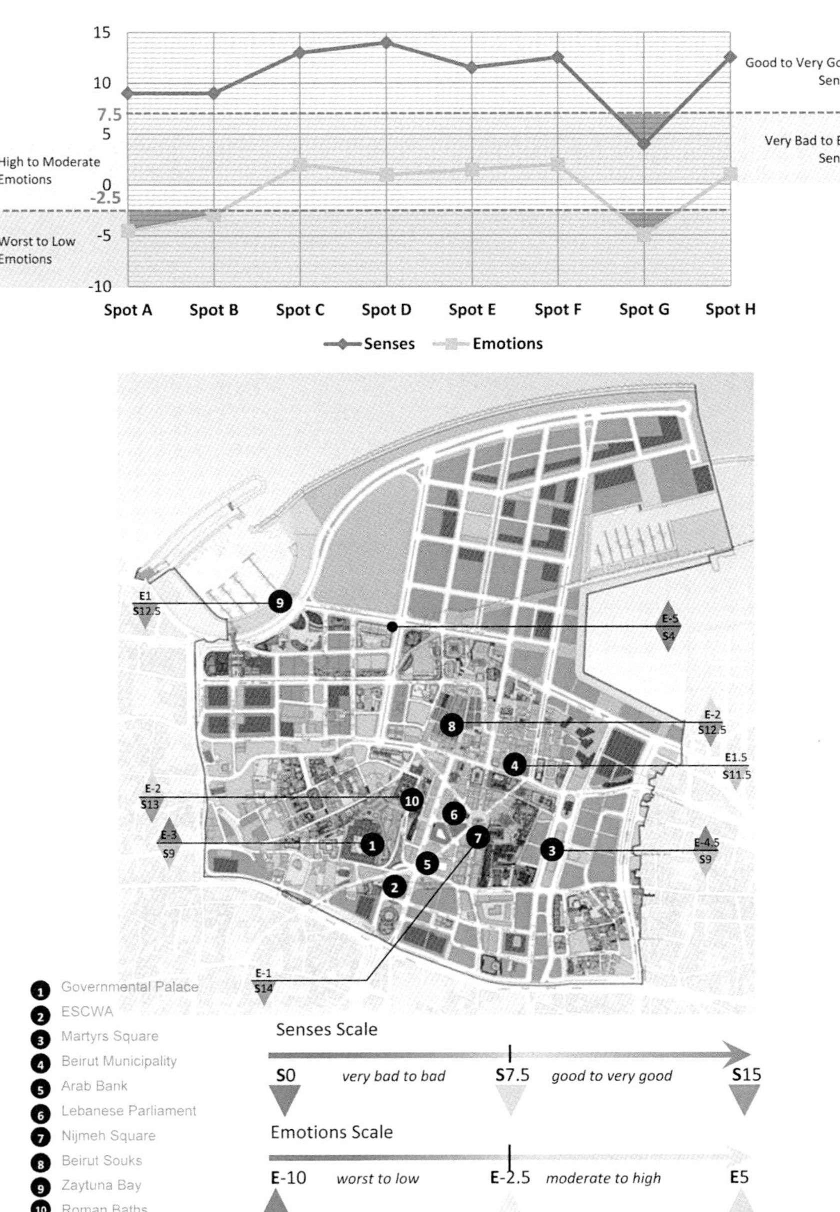

FIGURE 10.6 Top chart: emotional and sensual scale averages surveyed for each spot (source: researcher); bottom map: geographical, emotional and sensual Map of the BCD.

This study gives architects, landscapers, and urban designers a more complete image of the human experience and aims to explore ways for integrating people's feedback into urban understanding and planning. It was clear from this study that there is a strong relation between the sensuous stimuli and the level of human emotions, and it was concluded that the more pleasant places are those stimulating different senses – visual, hearing and smell sensations – in a positive way. Future studies could address Beirut Central District as a multisensory city, capturing whole streets and districts, not only specific spots, and using new techniques for gathering information, such as sensors, microphones for sonic properties, etc. Architecture comes with a character and a personality that cannot be captured by a pixilated photograph or an image on a computer screen (Rasmussen, 1964). The Danish architectural theorist Steen Rasmussen once chastised an art historian for his description of a town that he had gleaned through photographs. Rasmussen knew that we do not experience a city in the same way that we experience images. When we physically come to a town we observe and feel its overall character, atmosphere, topography, sounds, colors, scale, odors and fragrances, and material presence. As Juhani Pallasmaa wrote in his book *The Eyes of the Skin*, "Architecture is the art of reconciliation between us and the world, and this mediation takes place through the senses" (2005).

Note: All tables are created by the chapter authors.

References

Adams, J., & Gupta, P. (2013). 'I learn more here than I do in school. Honestly, I wouldn't lie about that': Creating a space for agency and identity around science. *International Journal of Critical Pedagogy 4*(2). Available at: www.partnershipsjournal.org/index.php/ijcp/article/download/401/369

Basso, Keith (1996). *Sense of Place*. School of American Research

Berg, Nate (2014). The science of design; three ways Neuroscience can inform and improve architecture. *Architect: The Journal of the American Institute of Architects*, Sept.2014. Available at: https://www.architectmagazine.com/technology/three-ways-neuroscience-can-inform-and-improve-architecture_o (Accessed Sept 2018).

Blesser, B. & Salter, L. R. (2007). *Spaces Speak, Are You Listening? Experiencing Aural Architecture*. Cambridge, MA: MIT Press.

Cannon, W. B. (1927). The James-Lange theory of emotions: A critical examination and an alternative theory. *The American Journal of Psychology*.

Corbusier, L. & Etchells, F. (1970). *Towards a New Architecture*. London: The Architectural Press.

Darwin, C. R. (1872). *The Expression of the |Emotions in Man and Animals*. London: John Murray.

Ehrlichman, H. & Bastone, L. (1992). *Olfaction and emotion*. In Serby, M.J. and Chobor, K.L. (eds), *Science of Olfaction*. Springer-Verlag, New York, Vol., *1*

Ekman, P & Ekman, E. (2016). *Atlas of Emotions*. Available at: www.atlasofemotions.org

James, W. (1884). What is an emotion? *Mind, 9*, 188– 205

Kaiser, E. J., Chapin, F. S., & Godschalk, D. R. (1995). *Urban Land Use Planning* (4th ed). Chicago, IL: University of Illinois Press.

Kudryavtsev, A., Krasny, M. E. & Stedman, R. C. (2012). The impact of environmental education on sense of place among urban youth. *Ecosphere 3*(4), 29.

Lazarus, Richard S, (1991). Progress on a cognitive-motivational-relational theory of emotion. *American Psychologist*.

Libeskind, D. (2015). Architecture that touches the heart and soul. *CNN interview*. Available at: https://edition.cnn.com/style/article.daniel-libeskind-architecture-emotions/index.htm

Liedtke, W, (2006). Transient receptor potential vanilloid channels functioning in transduction of osmotic stimuli. *J. Endocrinal* 191.

Lovheim, H. (2011). *A New Three-Dimensional Model for Emotions and Monoamine Neurotransmitters*. Elsevier.

Lynch, K. (1960). *The Image of the City*. MIT Press.

Mosso, L. (2009). Rationalisation of Manniskan. In: *Alvar Alto: Architecture, Modernity, and Geopolitics*, Eeva-Liisa Pelkonnen (ed) Yale University Press p. 185

Pallasmaa, J. (2005). *The Eyes of the Skin: Architecture and the Senses*. Chichester: Wiley-Academy.

Parrott, W. G. (ed), (2001). *Emotions in Social Psychology. Essential Readings*. New York: Psychology Press.

Plutchik, R. (1980). Emotion: Theory, Research, and Experience. *Theories of Emotion* Vol *1*. New York: Academic

Price, C. (1966), *A Lung for Midtown Manhattan*. In Exhibition catalogue: CCA Competition for the Design of Cities (Montreal: Canadian Centre for Architecture).

Quercia, D., Schifanella, R., & Aiello, L. M. (2014). The Shortest Path to Happiness: Recommending Beautiful, Quiet, and Happy Routes in the City. In: *Proceedings of the 25*th *ACM Conference on Hypertext and Social Media*, pp. 116–25. Available at: https://dl.acm.org/citation.cfm?id=2631799

Rasmussen, S. E. (1964). *Experiencing Architecture* (illustrated). London: Chapman & Hall.

Reeve, J. (2009). *Understanding Motivation and Emotion* (5th ed.). Hoboken, NJ: Wiley.

Schachter, S. & Singer, J. (1982). Cognitive, social, and psychological determinants of emotional state. *Psychological Review 69*(5) 373–399. Availavle at: http://dx.doi.org/10.1037/h0046234

Shaver, P., Kirson, J. & O'Connor, C. (1987). Emotion knowledge: Further exploration of a prototype approach. *Journalof Personality and Social Psychology*.

Wang Y. F. & Hatton G. I. (2009). Astrocytic plasticity and patterned oxytocin neuronal activity: dynamic interactions. *J. Neurosci*. 29, 1743–1754.

Zardini, M. (2006). *Sense of the City – An Alternate Approach to Urbanism*. Las Muller Publishers.

11

DATA AND 'SOCIAL'/'SEXUAL' ENCOUNTERS IN THE CITY

Mappings of potential embodied experiences through geolocative dating apps

Phevos Kallitsis

Introduction

Taking Portsmouth, UK, as a case study, the chapter aims to contribute to the wider discourse about mapping sexuality, by overlaying mappings of the city's more traditionally advertised and experienced gay activity and the representation of data provided by the dating/hook-up app, Grindr. The overall perception about dating apps, such as Grindr, is that they are 'just for sex'; however, this is usually contested by the claim that the app offers newcomers or visitors to a city the opportunity to connect with the city and the local community, 'competing' with the promoted LGBT social spaces advertised in printed and online guides. So how different is the map constituted by Grindr from that promoted by the LGBT press? Do the solid data hidden in private mobile screens – screens that exist within the public realm – alter the traditional perception of public and private? What new opportunities arise for those who carry these 'screens' to meet physically through the mediation of the digital apps? The chapter focuses on the different ways of experiencing urban space offered by smart phones and dating apps. In order to discuss these issues, I have introduced a series of maps that capture the density of users of Grindr in different moments and places, overlaid on a conventional map of activities within the city, including information about LGBT life retrieved from local guides and press. Data collected from the app allow for the comparison of the two ways men seeking sex with men can experience a city's LGBT life and/or meet partners.

Sexuality is traditionally linked to an embodied encounter, a meeting of bodies, this meeting happening in a place, and that place of the sexual encounter and/or affection, being the driving question of the literature on geographies of sexuality (Blidon, 2008). However, mapping sexualities has always been a challenge, because of the fluidity of the subject and its constant displacement in time and space (Pile and Thrift, 1995; Bell and Valentine, 1995a). For a long time, mappings have concentrated on recording spaces of LGBT socialisation or sexual meetings (Castells, 1983; Cattan and Leroy, 2013), and how they were spread out in cities – with some relatively recent and limited works focusing on rural areas (Bell and Valentine, 1995b). In the digital age the nature of these meetings may remain physical but their arrangement may happen through different means, and the gay community – or to be more accurate, men who have sex with men (MSM) – have proven their ability to quickly seize upon the channels of communication and information provided (Ashford, 2006; Miller, 2015).

As digital tools and the internet have evolved, they have offered new ways for the meeting between two – or more – persons, which means that they have unavoidably transformed the spatial manifestation of these meetings. PCs and laptops offer a more private way of networking and meeting people. The introduction of the smartphone, in 2007, and especially the 2009 launch of the geolocative application, Grindr, are argued to have completely transformed the way that users perceive space and the way offline meetings are sought (Blackwell, Birnholtz & Abbott, 2015). On the one hand mobiles, as more personal gadgets, offer 'extended privacy', while on the other hand Grindr signals a displacement from the 'home' and offers the notion that bodies represented by the digital profiles are on the streets, 'somewhere near you'. Mobile phones offer the ability to the bodies behind the profile to be moving around in cafes, bars and shops. Grindr offers an imagined easier access to possible partners – for a variety of purposes. The Grindr user becomes the centre and enters the space of other users.

In the beginning of 2015, a TV series triptych started being broadcast on British TV attempting to present a contemporary record of LGBT life in the twenty-first century through Cucumber, Banana and Tofu (Davis, 2015). In the first episode of *Banana*, which focuses on LGBT youth in Manchester, Dean Monroe, a twenty-something man, receives a message on Grindr from someone and automatically suspends whatever he is doing in order to go and meet him. The reason for the young man's contact is revealed a bit later. Dean had located the guy on Grindr some time ago and had added him to his list, but then realises that the guy is constantly moving, as a result of which he appears at different distances. In a very brief way, Dean maps out the stranger's life, possible cities he has visited, possible professions. For Dean, a mobile app becomes a geographical tool that provides him with quantitative (distance) and qualitative (profession, lifestyle) data about a complete unknown. What if Dean's approach was applied outside the TV universe? What would the hard data retrieved from the public profiles of Grindr users reveal about the way they use the urban space?

The app creates a type of map, but once an embodied experience is sought, the geographical realities have to be taken into account. As a result, the simplistic grid of the interface doesn't always deliver the promised proximity. While Grindr allows MSMs move freely in the public space while communicating, it has been accused of leading to a return to invisibility and 'discrete fun'. The chapter attributes to the discourse of mapping sexuality, by examining a way to map the LGBT community beyond the traditional meeting spaces, the mapping of legislation, or people who are out of the closet. Grindr is an everyday technology that uses data, willingly provided by various subjects, who not only function outside the heterosexual matrix, but sometimes are also alienated from the 'LGBT scene'; in other words, they avoid traditional LGBT socialisation spaces, such as cafes, clubs and centres. This is a why people claim that the online perspectives open up to a wider number of people.

So, can Grindr and similar geolocative apps offer a different view of MSM communities in the city? Especially in the case of non-metropolitan areas with limited LGBT venues, the online world looks like a one-way street for any offline gratification (Ashford, 2006). What can the hard data retrieved from recordings of the available users within a medium scale city reveal about the geographical distribution and activities of these users?

This chapter, by looking into the case of MSMs within a medium-sized city, tries to reconnect the digital data to the physical space and the embodied experience. Through analysis of the data, the chapter questions whether geolocative apps can actually become the new gay bars or cruising areas (Miller, 2015), myths around the app's target audience being young people. Moreover, the maps show that the space of the closet (Brown, 2000) and issues of sexuality and the public are repeated within the digital world.

Introducing the sexual grid and the data it provides

In 2009, Grindr was launched: the first mobile app designed for MSMs using the global positioning system (GPS) in order to 'help bi and curious guys looking for dating or friends', bring one '0 feet away' with the guy they are chatting to; in other words, aiming to take people from the virtual space into the physical one. Privacy is an extremely important element: 'How much of your info they see is entirely your call' (Grindr, 2015). The application's interface has a public and a private side. The public one consists of a grid where the user can see thumbnail tiles of user profiles, with a no-nudity policy in the public realm, with the upper left tile being the mobile owner's profile. From left to right one can find the user closest to him and as one scrolls further right and down, the distance augments. The second part of the public side of the app provides more information about the distance, physical characteristics (age, height, ethnicity, etc.), relationship status, a 'Looking for' section and the Grindr Tribes. The 'Distance' indication is based on a radius, which measures per metre (or foot depending on the metric system the user has set up) up to 1km (or mile) and then the scale used is per km/mile. The application also suggests the time you need in order to reach the user on foot (up to 15 minutes' walk) or driving. The 'Looking for' section creates a categorisation of the users based on the predefined categories: 'Chat', 'Friends', and 'Networking' indicate the social aspect of the app, 'Dates' and 'Relationship' show the search for a partner, while 'Right Now' indicates the direct sexual nature of the possible meeting. Furthermore, the various categories of Tribes are based on elements that have to do with the body type and appearance (Bear, Otter, Rugged, Jock, Clean-cut), the age (Daddy, Twink), sexual practices (Leather), hobbies (Geek), health (Poz) or whether the user is in the closet and has no intention of coming out soon (Discreet). The choice of a Tribe in the beginning sounds a way of self-identification to specific categories of the gay world. Out of these Tribes the chapter examines only the case of the Discreet Tribe, because of the interesting geographical implications of the space of the closet (Brown, 2000). Moreover, there are two fields where the user can freely express and present himself outside the typified elements – a brief 'Headline' and then an 'About me' section.

The private side includes a one-to-one chat channel, through which the user can start direct negotiating and exchange additional information with a specific user. Apart from the exchange of text, the chat allows for the exchange of photos (where the no-nudity policy doesn't apply as it is private), as well as their exact location, through the use of maps that transform the generic distance information into a specific point in the city. Finally, blocking allows the user to make somebody's profile disappear from his grid (customisation of the grid), and him not appearing on the other user's grid. The favourite button is a little star that allows the user to easily trace back another user, even when not within the app's range.

The app sets its geographical limits by the number of profiles presented to the user (100 or 300 depending on whether one uses the free or the paid membership version) in a 'man by man' exploration of the world. So, depending on the density of the users in the specific area, the app changes the range of people who will be located. Grindr's simple interface, in contrast to older web-based relevant platforms, offers tools for a brief exchange of information before deciding to meet or not, bringing back the focus on the physical space (Robinson and Moskowitz, 2013).

In 2014, a report in *The Washington Post* described a major security 'glitch' in the app's system (Mowlabocus, 2014). An unknown started sending messages warning users that through the data in the app their exact location has been revealed (Avari, 2014; Dupere, 2014). The unknown user's rationale was to expose and create pressure on Grindr's lack of sensitivity on the issue of privacy, and how it could lead to possible 'outings' (Grindrmap). Furthermore, Grindrmap raised the issue of users living or travelling in countries where homosexual activities are illegal, and cases where information provided by Grindr was used by the police to arrest and harass. Mowlabocus (2014) raised also the issue of homonormative Western thinking in the initial response by Grindr that it is not a 'flaw but a feature'. Finally, Grindr started issuing warnings in such countries and took 'the proactive step to hide distance information' within countries 'with a history of violence against the gay community' (Grindr, 2014). In a way, Grindr as an enterprise thought that people who wanted to hide their identity shouldn't be using the app, but this excludes a large number of users who use Grindr and similar apps exactly because they don't want to be spotted in gay areas.

Portsmouth's topography and the LGBT scene

Portsmouth, being the only island city in the UK, and one of the few in Europe, provides an interesting geographical set-up, while the limited gay-life choices make cyberspace an important channel of interaction among MSMs. Portsmouth is one of the most densely populated cities in the UK (ONS, 2014; Hampshire County Council, 2014), with 5141 persons/km^2, while the areas of Landport, Portsea and North End are among the 20% most deprived areas in the UK (Hampshire County Council, 2015). Portsmouth is a rather fragmented city, with various barriers, creating difficulties in navigating. The voids created by the bombings during the Second World War were used for housing estates, which ignored the existing urban grid and created barriers or restricted access between parts of the city. These boundaries are also reflected in social levels, with the higher incomes being concentrated in the south part.

Contrary to the developing tendencies of the city, traditional gay entertainment seems to be shrinking. In 2011, two of the most popular gay bars closed. During the time of this research, there were three venues addressed to the LGBT community, but today they are reduced to one. Cruising areas in Portsmouth are infamous also outside the gay community, and there have been incidents of gay bashing and robberies: for example, websites warn about the proximity of the Rock Gardens cruising area to a straight club and of the danger of drunken males being aggressive to gay cruisers. Moreover, in 2009 a man was arrested for blackmailing people in the cruising areas of Rock Gardens and Portsdown Hill, taking money by pretending to be a policeman (TheNews, 2009). These incidents, in combination with the limited gay venues, create a rather unwelcome environment for LGBT people. In this gloomy picture, the reincarnation of *Portsmouth Pride*, after a 13 years hiatus, shows that the city hosts a vibrant LGBT community that tries to change things. So, do LGBT people go for a night out, and where do they meet? Portsmouth is a case where the idea of using Grindr as a way to meet locals could be very practical, as traditional mappings do not seem to reflect the reality of the community. Grindr's marketing constantly refers to locality, so can it really be a tool for a different mapping of gay life?

Methodology

For the purposes of the research, a blank Grindr profile was created. The app offers geographical instances of the geographical distribution of bodies around a specific reference point. Data were recorded in three different locations in the City of Portsmouth: Commercial Road next to the Civic Centre, Gunwharf Quays and Palmerston Road.

Recordings took place at eight different times during two weeks in spring 2014. For every point in the city, a list of the first 100 profiles appearing on the app was created, excluding the researcher. No interaction with users was sought and no information was collected through private channels of communication.

The researcher recorded information provided only on the public profiles, with no collection of user photos, respecting the privacy of the users. The information collected was: the headline, the age, the distance (using the metric system) and, finally, if the profile included a face picture or not. The age allowed to test the myth that Grindr is for young males, while the photo raises the question about how open people feel within the app environment. It is important to mention that the app displays a profile in a specific location in two cases: the user is online, or the user was online at that location within the last hour.

For the visualisation of data space was divided into the following zones for each point of reference: A (0–99m), B (100–499m), C (500–999m), D (1,000–2,000m) and E (2,000–3,000m). These zones were put on a map in order to calculate their surface area as, at times, part of the area was sea or inaccessible territory. One could argue that a user maybe on boat, but the technology of Grindr, in practice, cannot be accurate when one is on the move and usually shows someone at the point he was before starting moving. As a result, it is safe to exclude the areas of sea when calculating the area of each zone. The number of users in a specific zone, divided by the surface area of the zone, formed the maps of densities on specific times and dates.

Looking into the maps

Even before looking into the maps, just by looking at the raw data (an example of which one can see in Table 11.1) shows that the number of Grindr users in the city is minimal compared to national data of LGBT population (Knipe, 2017; Chalabi, 2013), with the densities remaining at a maximum of 0.7% in a dense urban background of 2,050 men per km^2 of Portsmouth (The Guardian, 2012). Zone A is the area of actual proximity where the other user is just around the corner, in this perimeter in no moment and place, more than three users were recorded. Also, as an average of the number of users, it appears that for every 500m of extending the radius, 23 users are located. This is also indicated by the relatively equal spread of users in the city, with zones appearing to have similar numbers of users during the day, with the higher densities being recorded during working times around the zones that include commercial uses.

The Commercial Road maps (Figure 11.2) show that as long as the shops and offices are open a lot of users are around that area and the maximum radius recorded was of Zone D (>1km, <2km). Outside the shopping and working hours, the radius expands, but the density of Zone D remains more or less the same. The all-male sauna near Commercial Road doesn't seem to alter the density of profiles in the area. On the contrary, the area around Gunwharf seems to attract a larger number of users, especially during the working day. While one would expect this to link to the university and the students, the age average of the users recorded is slightly higher than that in other areas (Figure 11.1). Even in Zone C (500–1,000m), where most university buildings and student residences are located, the average age is 27.1 years, similar to the general average of the other reference points.

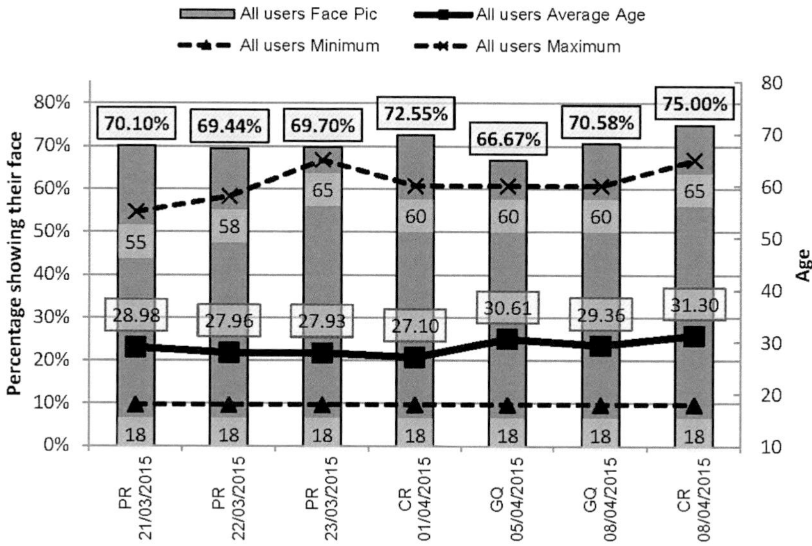

FIGURE 11.1 Average age of the 100 users recorded according to date and point of recording (indication of the minimum and the maximum age for every recording) and the percentage of users showing a clear indication of their face. PR Palmerston Road, CR Commercial Road, GQ Gunwharf Quays.

So, while one would expect the average age of this area to be lower, it doesn't differ. Moreover, this observation indicates that app users' average age grows as the app gets older, contrary to popular belief that Grindr 'is mainly a thing for the younger'. It might also mean that students avoid using it while on campus (Ahlm, 2017).

Finally, the data recorded from the last point of reference – Palmerston Road – show higher concentration on Sunday evening than Saturday. Possible explanations are that people on Saturday are already out, so they do not bother using the app, or that the users spread among different entertainment venues. When one would expect that there would be a higher number of users in Zone D, where the two more popular gay bars are located, the data do not alter much during the times the gay bars are open, compared with the times that they are not. This is an indication that despite the belief that gay men check the app even when in gay bars, this may not be the case here, or that people use alternative social media.

Overall, the maps show that the concentration of Grindr users is equivalent to the concentration of people in general, at the equivalent time and place. As a result, there is a higher number of users in the commercial zones during opening, and in residential areas in evening hours.

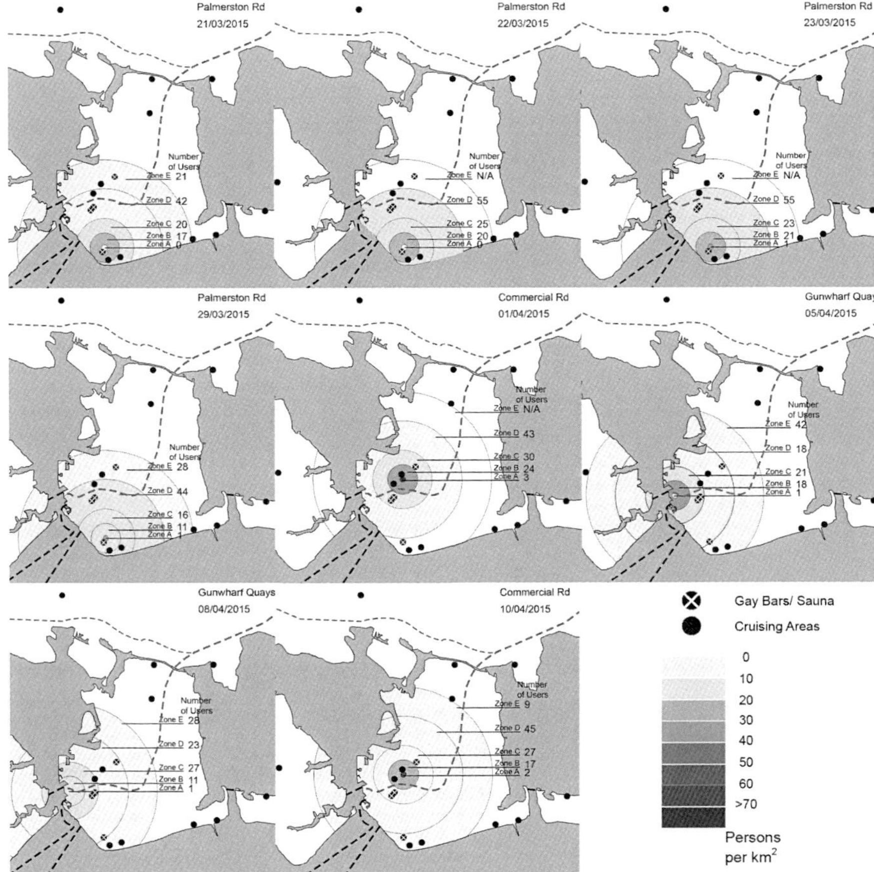

FIGURE 11.2 Density maps of the recorded users in the various points of reference on specific dates compared with the areas of traditional gay interactions (Gay bars, Saunas and Cruising Areas). On each map, apart from the density the actual number of users is indicated for each zone.

TABLE 11.1 Example of user densities in the three different points of recording.

Zone	*1. PR 23.03.15*			*2. CR 10.04.15*			*3. GQ 08.04.15*		
	Area (km^2)	*Users/ no*	*Density users/km^2*	*Area (km^2)*	*Users/ no*	*Density users/km^2*	*Area (km^2)*	*Users/ no*	*Density users/km^2*
A (0–99)	0.03	1	32	0.03	2	64	0.03	1	32
B (100–499)	0.76	21	28	0.76	17	22	0.57	11	19
C (500–999)	1.52	23	15	2.34	27	12	1.46	27	19
D (1000–1999)	4.26	55	13*	7.26	45	6	6.23	23	4
E (2000–2999)	6.68	N/A	N/A	9.42	9	1*	9.38	38	4*

PR: Palmerston Road Point, CR: Commercial Road Point, GQ: Gunwharf Quays Point

*Density for this zone is incomplete as more users may exist within the same boundaries but not visible because of the app's limit of maximum 100 users

Proximity and accessibility: topography vs grid

During the process of placing the information on a map, a contradiction appears between the representation of proximity in the application and the physical space of the city. The innovation of geolocative apps had to do with the distance indicator that is added to the profile. Grindr translates the distance into travel-time between the users. However, this feature is fairly inaccurate, as it doesn't take into consideration the urban fabric and its complexities. Portsmouth, and its particular geography, constitutes a complex example of distances for the app to map effectively. Several areas are close to one another geographically, but it takes longer to travel between them; the journey between Old Portsmouth and Gosport, for example, involves a 5-minute ferry ride. Moreover, the Portsmouth city plan consists of various edges and barriers, because of unplanned development, and this leads to difficulty in navigating the city, whether driving and walking. The various detours and roundabouts may lead to increasing the time needed to move between different points in the city (Verenini, 2011). An example from this research would be the Grindr indication of 3km between the Palmerston Road point of recording and a user in Baffins Pond in the mid-east of Portsmouth. The 3km indication equals, according to the app, to a 3-minute car drive, while according to Google maps, which takes into consideration the actual route, the distance is almost double (5.5km) and takes five times longer to get there (14 minutes) not taking traffic into account. Portsmouth's geography and urban conditions – especially when moving on a north-south axis – makes Grindr's promise of the 'guy closest to you' not equal to the 'guy more accessible to you'.

'Out of the scene' but inside the grid

Cyber space is regarded as a way of communication for people who feel excluded from the gay scene, especially the closeted ones. In a way, the apps put these people on the gay map, while offering a specific kind of privacy. Grindr allows users to self-identify as 'Discreet', giving them at the same time the option to show or not a photo of their face, but even so, it is not perceived as a safe space. As seen in Figure 11.1, 60–70% of the users display a recognisable picture of their face; however, among the profiles that categorise themselves as being 'Discreet', the percentage drops to almost half (Figure 11.4). Even among the 40% who show their faces, one can argue that despite identifying as 'Discreet' they are not always closeted men; some users may add 'Discreet' as a promise of not revealing the secret of closeted men. In a similar approach, a lot of profiles hide their face and information, despite not categorising themselves as 'Discreet'.

Despite these possible inaccuracies, it is interesting to examine how this particular category is placed on the map. Parallel to the recordings of the users at any of the three points of reference, I recorded the closest 50 profiles that appeared once a filter was used to show only the 'Discreet' profiles. As expected, as we refer to a subset of the profiles, the densities of 'Discreet' users are much lower.

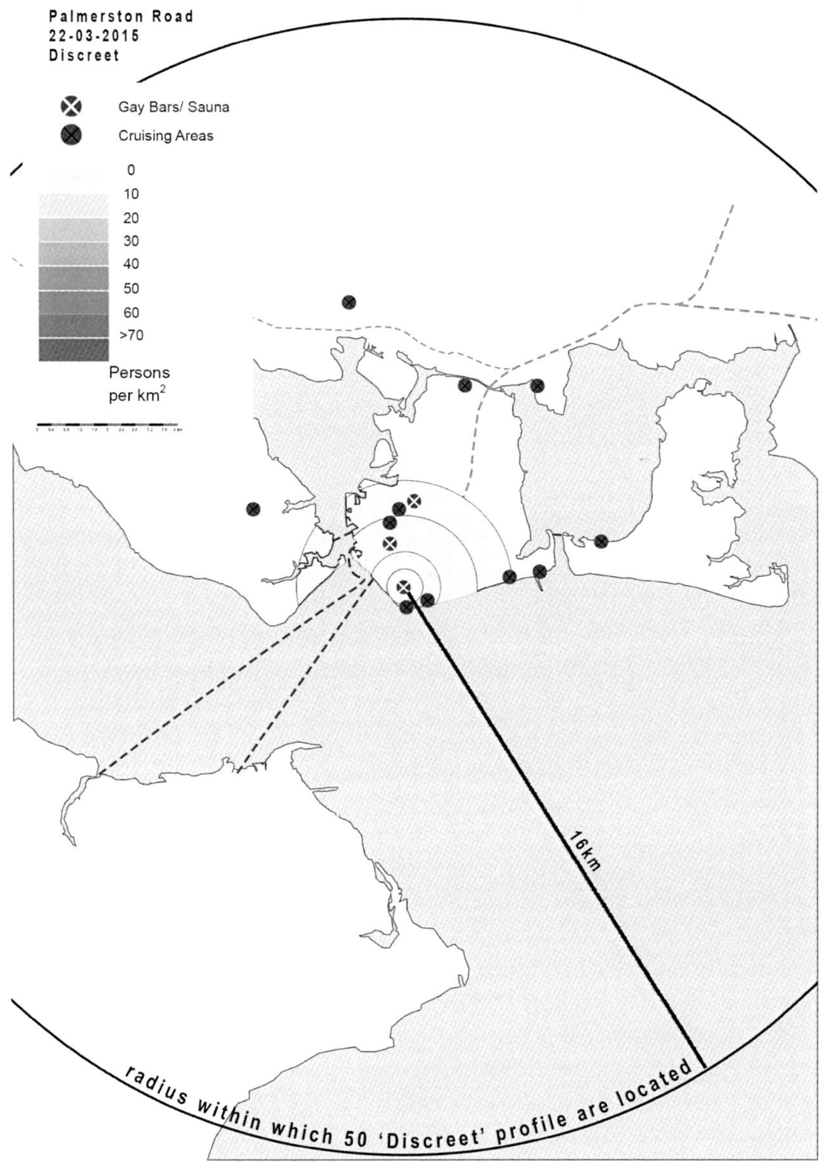

FIGURE 11.3 Density and maximum radius of the 50 closest users who identify themselves as discreet.

While the maximum radius of 3km within which one could locate 100 Grindr users, the maximum radius of the 'Discreet' profiles increased 4–6 times, depending on the day. This means that the geography of the app expands beyond Gosport and Hayling Island (which happens with the general search), two areas that at least can be accessed by car, as the radius of 16km indicates that many

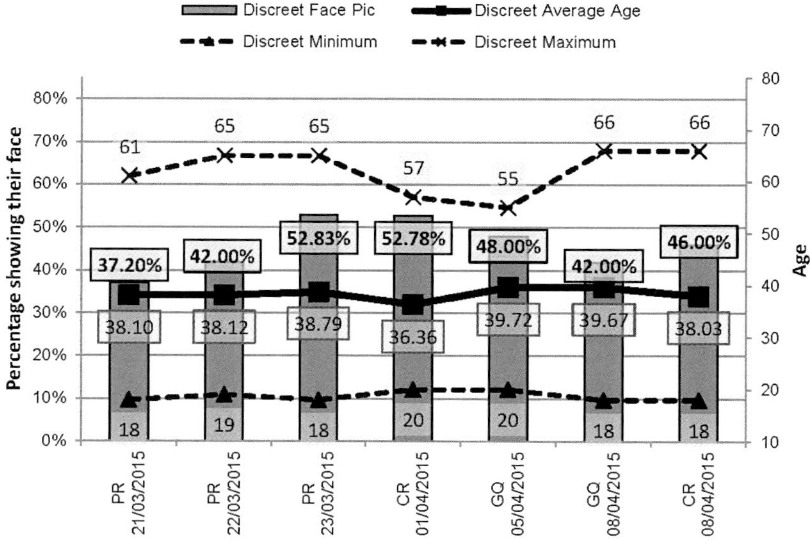

FIGURE 11.4 Average age of the 50 'Discreet' users recorded according to date and point of recording (indication of the minimum and the maximum age for every recording) and the percentage of users showing a clear indication of their face. PR Palmerston Road, CR Commercial Road, GQ Gunwharf Quays.

of the 'Discreet' users are probably located on the Isle of Wight (Figure 11.3). Automatically, the possible encounter becomes expensive and limited to specific times, when ferries and the hovercraft are available. Geolocative apps retain this sense of locality only as long as there are high concentrations of users, otherwise they expand the radius they map, assuming that the user can travel further – as they would as well do without the app, to reach conventional 'gay-places'.

The subversion of the 'Right Now' hook-up

Finally, it is interesting to examine the relation between the Grindr users and the cruising areas of the city – areas that remain active and known also to people outside the LGBT community. As Miller (2015) underlines, apps like Grindr respond to the gratification of the safety factor. The recorded attacks and blackmails in Portsmouth create a rather unsafe image for the city's non-commercial cruising spots; however, MSMs still use them and these areas are part of the gay guides. One reason is that even if the majority of gay men have a smartphone and Grindr has its free version, not everybody has access to a smartphone, not everyone has access to internet anytime-anywhere or, for various reasons, people do not want to have their app installed on their phones i.e. partnered, married, people afraid of the 'digital panopticon'. As a result, there is a chance that in the cruising areas there will be bodies who do not have an online presence for financial, class or personal reasons. Another reason that MSMs may visit the cruising areas is the spatiotemporal gap in the 'Right Now' indication in Grindr and the promise of a possible 'right now' encounter in the cruising areas. Gavin Brown comments that communication in these sites is achieved through minor details 'the cheeky, lustful vitality in the man's eyes, the sly smile and the enticing raising of his eyebrow' (Brown, 2008: 920). Cruisers are interested in the physical bodies in actual proximity, and they focus on these bodies. Despite the dangers of being in these public areas and the various strategies by city councils to eliminate such activities (Andersson, 2012) proposing the alternative of commercialised cruising venues, cruising in public spaces remains active. Negotiations on Grindr take time, without having a clear image of the other user. But even after the chat has started and photos have been exchanged, there is a negotiation about who between the two users 'can accommodate' and who 'can travel', sometimes ending up in a dead end.

The cyber world may seem safer but it doesn't provide a 'right here', a place, while rarely both communicating parts have a clear image of the actual space that the encounter will take place. Despite the fact that cruising is not always the celebration of democracy through sexuality (Qian, 2014), as cruising areas have their social structures and divisions, cruising puts bodies into a specific space and time; once a connection is made there is limited space for postponing or realising that the virtual distance is not actually as approachable as it seemed. The research revealed some post-digital practices, such as various users including in the names of specific cruising spots in the city in their online profile title. This inclusion seems to function as an indirect invitation of a meeting in a cruising area, where an actual space for the sexual encounter is provided. Contrary to dating apps, meeting in a cruising spot gives limited room for negotiation and postponing invites for a 'yes' or 'no' response to the 'right now' sought encounter. As a result, there are users who appear online in specific moments, while being in a cruising area. Instead of using Grindr as an alternative to cruising, they actually use the app while cruising in order to assure that cruising will be successful.

A similar pattern – the use of invitation to a public space – has been recorded during the busy days of the gay bars – Friday, Saturday and Monday – and in the area of the all-male-sauna in Commercial Street. Grindr doesn't always function as an alternative to the traditional LGBT spaces; on the contrary, it is a tool for an open invitation. Hence these users create – and move within – this hybrid of digital and physical space, willingly revealing their actual location. In a way, these places provide a different sense of safety. If the overall perception is that the meeting will take place in a private area, skipping the public meeting, the data show that users are not always ready for an isolated meeting with one of the possible 'too many weird guys in this app' – as many users state in their profiles. The user leaves a digital trace for his physical location without any

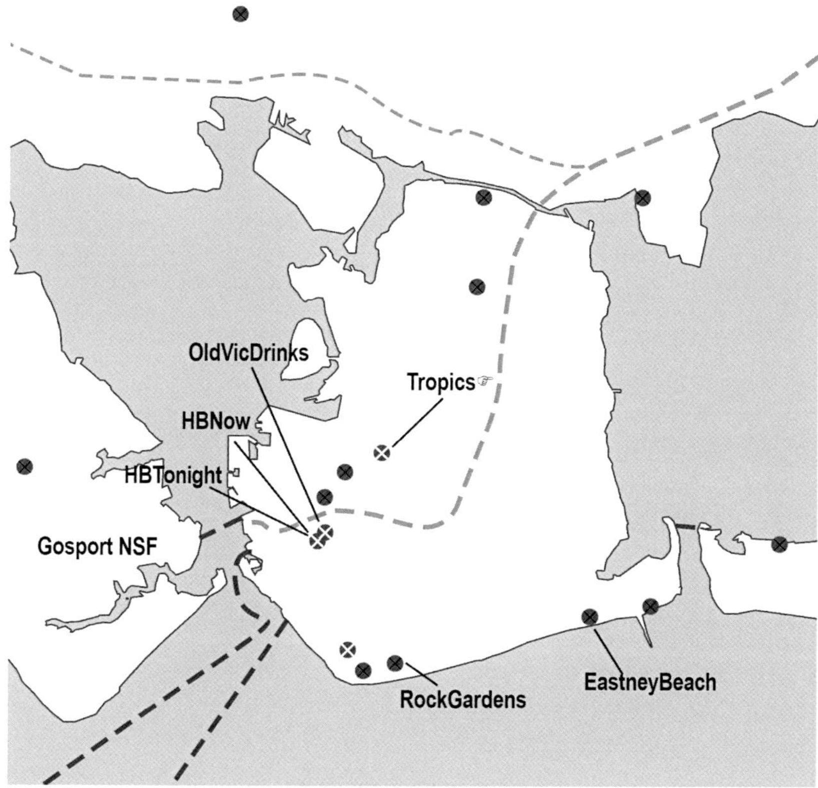

FIGURE 11.5 Grindr Data beyond the distance info: The generic map created by Grindr, based only on the radius factor and various areas of interest that start appearing through the titles the users choose to give to their profiles, introducing more specific geographical information.

negotiations or promises. As a result, the map created by Grindr starts including geographical information beyond the spaceless grid. When someone mentions that he is in Gosport, or Isle of Wight, it becomes obvious that there are various possible obstacles, or when the title is HBNow, it clarifies that the user is in the local gay bar (Figure 11.5). Subverting the Grindr approach of the radius, these users transfer the negotiation of possible encounter from the digital to an offline meeting and discussion over a drink, wearing a towel, on a nudist beach or a dark park.

Conclusion

Literature on cyber space and sexuality provides evidence of an increasing number of MSMs using technology for meeting sexual partners, while various research projects show an increase of gay men using smart phones and the internet. The GPS information of Grindr and other similar apps, promises a return to locality. The digital, in this context, is not related to something abstract or remote, but supports actual meetings in physical places. A major condition for two users to start interacting is a relative proximity. The simple format of the interface, Grindr's lack of means for cyber sexual gratification – such as video or voice chats – and the marketing of the app, underlines that the main aim of the app is to facilitate the offline encounter (sexual or not). However, the app is not complex or refined enough to address the complexities of the physical geography of a place. It is using actual distances as an approximation or indication of degree of proximity, which, however, at times differs from the actual reality.

The app makes a variety of data available in its public interface: age, photos, sexual orientations and preferences, body measurements and desires. Breaking away from other means of encounter, these data are connected to specific bodies that are expected to be 'somewhere near'. But the question remains, how near are they and what type of people are they? The effort to study the use of Grindr in a city like Portsmouth, with an active but limited LGBT community, subverts various myths around the app. First of all, it is not 'a thing of the twenty-something', as the average age range is 27–30 years and includes people up to 66 years old; as the app gets older, the average age is growing. Additionally, the fact that the average age of users declaring being closeted is 10 years older than the average age of the general users, shows – as expected – that younger generations are more open, even in a not-so-welcome environment like Portsmouth. At the same time, the perception of the cyber space as a safe environment is subverted by the fact that the majority of closeted users still hide their faces on their public online profile and try to attract users through text or photos of fragments of their bodies.

As discussed earlier, although online apps such as Grindr show the proximity between users, this can sometimes be misleading. When the user moves from the digital grid (approximating physical distances) to the actual physical space, the indicated degree of proximity may seem distorted. As a result, users who use the 'Right Now' feature or chat, or negotiate over a meeting, may end up being too far to travel to one another, when location is revealed. In metropolitan areas, where the radius may remain below the 1km range, one may claim that the correlation between the actual distance and its representation in the app is more accurate. Masking the exact location – for reasons of privacy and safety – is causing the above-mentioned challenge, leading some users to joke with the Grindr interface, putting on their profile title an arrow pointing left saying 'This guy is closer' (Figure 11.5).

One could say that Grindr works also as post-digital device for users who, instead of interacting within the digital world, they just advertise their location within the city's gay map. They do not replace bars or cruising with the app, but rather use the medium to show their availability in a traditional gay spot – spaces where these users feel safer than going to an unknown place or inviting an unchecked stranger in their private space. In a way, if someone wants to meet guys when in the city, there is a great possibility of ending up where the traditional gay guides will point them out, showing the crossover between the physical and digital mediums for initiating interaction.

Within the discussion of cyber versus physical space, the Portsmouth experience shows that the digital and physical cannot be addressed as two separate worlds but are multiple and occasionally interrelating layers. As Jason Farman (2012) states, the material world coexists with the virtual world, in hybrid of 'old' and 'new media'. Geolocative apps reveal how the various bodies move within urban space, as they appear, disappear and then reappear in different locations.

Data revealed through dating apps such as Grindr allow for different types of mapping of the urban space – of density, movement, activity, demographics, within a self-selected group of people (who use a particular app). Overlaying this data set on the conventional map of the city and correlating the data to the discussions and practices developing within the relevant groups allows for interesting narratives of the experience of place to emerge.

References

Ahlm J. (2017). 'Respectable promiscuity: digital cruising in an era of queer liberalism'. *Sexualities* 20: 364.

Andersson J. (2012). 'Heritage discourse and the desexualisation of public space: The "historical restorations" of Bloomsbury's squares'. *Antipode* 44: 1081–98.

Ashford C. (2006). Only gay in the village: Sexuality and the set. https://www.tandfonline.com/doi/full/10.1080/13600830600961202?scroll=top&needAccess=true

Avari, J. (2014). 'Alleged Grindr security flaw exposes exact location data, endangers users'. *N-DTV Gadgets*, 20 August. Available at: http://gadgets.ndtv.com/apps/news/alleged-grindr-security-flaw-exposes-exact-location-data-endangers-users-1-579031 [Accessed 03 March 2015].

Bell D and Valentine G. (1995a). *Mapping Desire: Geographies of Sexualities*: London: Routledge.

Bell D and Valentine G. (1995b). 'Queer country: rural lesbian and gay lives'. *Journal of Rural Studies* 11: 113–22.

Blackwell C, Birnholtz J and Abbott C. (2015). 'Seeing and being seen: co-situation and impression formation using Grindr, a location-aware gay dating app'. *New Media and Society* 17: 1117–36.

Blidon M. (2008). 'Jalons pour une géographie des homosexualités'. *L'Espace géographique* 37: 175–89.

Brown G. (2008). 'Ceramics, clothing and other bodies: affective geographies of homo-erotic cruising encounters'. *Social & Cultural Geography* 9: 915–32.

Brown M. P. (2000). *Closet Space: Geographies of Metaphor from the Body to the Globe*, London: Routledge.

Burgin V. (1996). *In/different Spaces: Place and Memory in Visual Culture*: Berkeley, CA: University of California Press.

Burrell E. R., Pines H. A., Robbie E., Coleman L., Murphy R. D., Hess K. L., Anton P. and Gorbach P. M. (2012). 'Use of the location-based social networking application GRINDR as a recruitment tool in rectal microbicide development research'. *AIDS and Behavior* 16: 1816–20.

Castells M. (1983). *The City and the Grassroots : A Cross-Cultural Theory of Urban Social Movements*: London: Edward Arnold.

Cattan N and Leroy S. (2013). *Atlas Mondial des Sexualités: Libertés, Plaisirs et Interdits*, Paris: Editions Autrement.

Chalabi M. (2013). 'Gay Britain: what do the statistics say?' *The Guardian*. Available at: www.theguardian.com/politics/reality-check/2013/oct/03/gay-britain-what-do-statistics-say (accessed 11 November 2017).

Crooks R. N. (2013). *The Rainbow Flag and the Green Carnation: Grindr in the Gay Village*. Available at: http://firstmonday.org/ojs/index.php/fm/article/view/4958/3790 (accessed 20 November 1977).

CruisingGays. (n.d.). *Portsmouth Gay Cruisng Areas*. Available at: http://www.cruisinggays.com/portsmouth/c/areas/.

Davis R. T. (2015). *Banana* (TV series). UK: E4.

Dupere K. (2014). '*Tipster alerts Grindr users of location-based security breach*'. Available at: http://www.pinknews.co.uk/2014/08/22/tipster-alerts-grindr-users-of-location-based-security-breech/ (accessed 03 March 2015).

Farman J. (2012) *Mobile Interface Theory: Embodied Space and Locative Media*. New York: Routledge.

Grindr (2014). *Grindr's Location Security Update*. Available at: http://grindr.com/blog/grindrs-location-security-update.

Grindr (2015). *User Information*. Available at: http://grindr.com/learn-more.

Grindrmap (n.d.) *Grindr: A Chronicle of Negligence and Irresponsibility*. Available at: https://grindrmap.neocities.org/

Hampshire County Council (2014). *Portsmouth Key Facts*. Available at: http://www3.hants.gov.uk/factsandfigures/keyfactsandfigures/key-facts/kf-portsmouth.htm#pay (accessed 1 September 2015).

Hampshire County Council (2015). *2015 IMD Deprivation Factsheets*. Available at: http://www3.hants.gov.uk/factsandfigures/figures economics/deprivation_indices.htm (accessed 15 September 2017).

Knipe E. (2017). *Sexual Identity, UK*: 2016. 4 October 2017 ed.: Office for National Statistics. Available at: https://www.ons.gov.uk/peoplepopulationandcommunity/culturalidentity/sexuality/bulletins/sexualidentityuk/2016 (accessed 3 March 2015).

Miller B. (2015). '"They're the modern-day gay bar": exploring the uses and gratifications of social networks for men who have sex with men'. *Computers in Human Behavior* 51, Part A: 476–82.

Mowlabocus S. (2014). 'Grindr's locator "glitch" was a major fail. *It revealed the company's lack of empathy for its gay users'*. Available at: www.washingtonpost.com/posteverything/wp/2014/09/08/grindrs-locator-glitch-was-a-major-fail-it-revealed-the-companys-lack-of-empathy-for-its-gay-users/ (accessed 3 March 2015).

Newswire PR. (2012). '"Grindr for Equality" initiative debuts to spur action for GLBT issues'. *Grindr-for-Equality*. Available at: https://www.prnewswire.com/news-releases/grindr-for-equality-initiative-debuts-to-spur-action-for-glbt-issues-140131833.html (accessed 3 March 2015).

ONS (2014). Population. London: Office for National Statistics. Available at: http://www.ons.gov.uk/ons/about-ons/business-transparency/freedom-of-information/what-can-i-request/published-ad-hoc-data/pop/july-2014/index.html (accessed 17 November 2017).

Pile S. and Thrift N. (1995). *Mapping the Subject: Geographies of Cultural Transformation*: London : Routledge.

PinkUK. (n.d.). *Hampshire Gay Cruisings*. Available at: https://pinkuk.com/gay-cruising/hampshire.

Qian J. (2014). 'Narrating the trope of abnormality: The making of closeted experiences in gay public cruising'. *Geoforum* 52: 157–66.

Robinson BA and Moskowitz DA. (2013). 'The eroticism of Internet cruising as a self-contained behaviour: a multivariate analysis of men seeking men demographics and getting off online'. *Culture, Health & Sexuality* 15: 555–69.

The Guardian (2012). '2011 census results: how many people live in your local authority?' in *DATAblog: Facts are Sacred*. 12 July 2012 ed. Available at: https://www.theguardian.com/uk/datablog/2012/jul/16/2011-census-results-data (accessed 17 November 2017).

TheNews (2009). 'Conman admits blackmailing men at city gay sex hotspots'. Available at: https://www.portsmouth.co.uk/news/conman-admits-blackmailing-men-at-city-gay-sex-hotspots-1-1241899 (accessed 18 August 2015).

TheNews (2011). 'Last orders called at city's gay nightclub'. *The News Centre*. Available at: https://www.portsmouth.co.uk/news/last-orders-called-at-city-s-gay-nightclub-1-2720487 (accessed 18 August 2015).

UpNorthDownSouth. *Up North Down South: Portsmouth*. Available at: http://www.upnorthdownsouth.co.uk/portsmouth.php.

Verenini A. (2011). 'Living on the edge: Portsmouth's urban metamorphosis through the effect of edges'. *Spaces & Flows: An International Journal of Urban & Extra Urban Studies* 1: 145–66.

Winetrobe H. (2014). 'Associations of unprotected anal intercourse with Grindr-met partners among Grindr-using young men who have sex with men in Los Angeles'. *AIDS Care* 26: 1303–8.

12

TOWARDS A COMPUTER-AIDED EPISTEMOLOGY OF ARCHITECTURE

Alejandro Mieses Castellanos

Introduction

This research is an ongoing software development effort that uses neural networks to map word relations, hierarchies, gaps, and foci of terms within large data sets of architecture theory and public opinion, as they are graphed geographically and by epoch. It seeks to develop a set of digital tools capable of engaging with the massive amounts of public opinions, debates, and beliefs that compose our ideological landscapes, as they become topics relevant to the built environment. It is meant as a higher resolution layer of analysis in order to increase our capacity to map and understand urban experiences and occupation patterns, with the purpose of modulating struggles between environmental and human forces in culturally sensitive ways.

Computational complexity within architecture- and design-related fields has been largely oriented towards the research of spatial data in its numerically manifest forms: structural, infrastructural, material, procedural, or geometrical. These current efforts as an industry have been aimed at the development of technological processes for the construction of space in recognizable forms, such as modeling processes, forms, and spatial relations in numerical ways. However, numerical relations represent a carefully curated body of work around a limited series of subjects or conditions, whether they are site-related, visitor- or occupation-related, energy-, structural-, schedule-, or economic/budget related. Buildings in data-substantiated ways represent a certain degree of democratization, which still hinges on an interpreting eye; a collective produces a certain information set, which is then interpreted by the builder or designer. The process of building, however, is still reliant on limited forms of outside influence, such as: public hearings, protests, or community interviews in the best of cases. The growing toolset of algorithms meant to measure environmental, energy-efficiency, occupation-load, among other uses of a building, while generating a second coming of massively produced energy-efficient box-like structures founded on the principles of modernity, seems inadequate to withstand future increases in population growth. The tensions induced by struggles with migration, labor, policy, rights, minorities and at-risk communities, and wealth-gaps or differentials can scarcely be attended to with our current toolset, for all the benefit they may bring in terms of the economy. Furthermore, treating collective problems within the built environment as uniform has been a shortcoming of the International Style we may hinge on repeating. Instead of relying on manufacturing processes that were meant to bring forward certain freedoms for a middle class, we are now relying on certain algorithms to aid our designs prior, during, and after construction to sustain an urban fabric, made of the limited relations we can measure through BIM-substantiated ways.

Within our collective efforts towards a radical redefinition of what the built environment should be, it is important to question the role our data have in propelling us towards certain aims, and more so, what are the data-types we are discarding? – as these may involve hidden branchings that challenge our design and practice orthodoxies.

The fundamental question – What are we computing? – brings forth the lines of questioning, research, and the accelerated growth that have been enabled by our tools – the rapid customization, manufacturing, and analysis of complex building processes. However, should we ask: What isn't computed? – we would open a wider range of questioning around topics of social relevance, such as: poverty, economic fluctuations, and politics; topics that, due to their reliance on narrative (word-based) data-types, are perceived as incomputable and, thus, too complex to understand in mass.

What is not computed incurs the risk of obsolescence due to the comparatively slow evolution of its study. The measure of our collective explorations into material systems, form-finding, advanced structural design, manufacturing, spatial analysis and occupation patterns, far surpasses the rate of growth of our studies into poverty, gentrification, theory, social unrest, cultural impact, city growth, religion and spirituality, and the assimilation of economic flows throughout the urban fabric. These are topics that are often carried by the social sciences at a far slower pace, due to an inexistent framework for comparative synthesis of these narrative data-types that is capable of keeping pace with the rate of data creation in which they are submerged. The combination of these two approaches could form a basis for research that is not only numerically substantiated in known statistical or quantified forms, but one that can also coalesce the writings and ideas of a large number of authors into a unified graph that can express collective beliefs by using the same words and phrased combinations of the writings sampled.

Humans think and express themselves primarily through narrative (representation- or symbol-based), not mathematical means. The amount of data produced by the vast majority of the world's population is very predominantly narrative, in all its manifest forms: text, audio, or video. It is the most direct form of expression, ranging from individuals to mass populations. Failure to engage with these primary forms of expression results in a lower resolution understanding of the cultural implications of building and the social/environmental repercussions in that given region.

Of the staggering amount of 2.5 quintillion (2.5 x 108) bytes of data produced daily, a vast percentage of these are narrative in essence. This is more so the case when we limit that body of data to those produced by citizens and individuals, where the primary form of expression and thought processes are non-numerical narrative forms that shape themselves into opinions, stories, wishes, regrets, celebrations, emails, SMS, chats, videos, audio, posts, and so forth. In the academic sphere, when taking into account the number of papers, books, articles, assignments, and reports done, they are invariably narrative based, whether they are of a scientific, economic, social, artistic, or psychological bend. A methodology to synthesize, analyze, and make sense of the growing number of stories, news, opinions, and repercussions that influence our daily lives is essential, in order to make sense of the data overload we are subjected to at every minute.

This research employs many of the algorithms present in natural language processing and computational linguistics for the purposes of understanding context, relations of meaning, and predictive analysis of subsequent words or topics, but diverges from the common purpose of deriving meaning from a single body of work – a book, article, sentence, or paragraph – to generate subsequent words or content. While it draws from many of the same algorithms meant to synthesize large amounts of language-based data through artificial intelligence (AI), it does not carry the same aims as the fields of study shared under Natural Language Processing and Machine Learning. It is primarily concerned with representing and forming a structure capable of tracing words/terms as they have been related regionally and across time. The product is not a single sentence, meaning, or the capacity for a machine to reply, but an interactive graph where users can document, implement, and analyze changes across large volumes of narrative data, and find their connecting points, how they vary culturally, by institution, author, or work.

These may take the form of analysis of migration patterns, globalization, historical invasions or civilization changes, gaps between governments and people, gaps between regions, as well as complementarities, and the effects of knowledge migrations on civilizations, due to causes such as labor force re-allocation, economic or industry changes, social or civil rights struggles, among others.

This research seeks to extend our set of available tools to enable an architecture that can engage with the massive amounts of public opinions, debates, and ideological forces that compose our noetic landscapes. It is meant as a higher resolution layer of analysis, with the purpose of increasing our capacity to modulate struggles between environmental and human forces in culturally sensitive ways. (In this context, the notion 'Noetic' is used to describe the following: of or relating to mental activity or the intellect. It refers to the ideological environment involving the population of a region, around a defined set of terms.)

Methods

The methods employed by the software in order to achieve this relies on each term being stored according to its contextual relations (words directly surrounding the term in a sentence) that are referenced according to their place in multiple texts and occurrences within the same text. While this context is dynamic, as dependent upon the weighted relations traced through texts loaded upon the data set, it is balanced against a static or fixed context – the definition of these words, their author, place, and date. Relying upon the information acquired, each term behaves as an active agent, seeking out relations based upon new contexts and visually graphing them, according to place, author, and date, as opposed to abstract or empty space. This comes with the purpose of visually revealing the movement of architectural

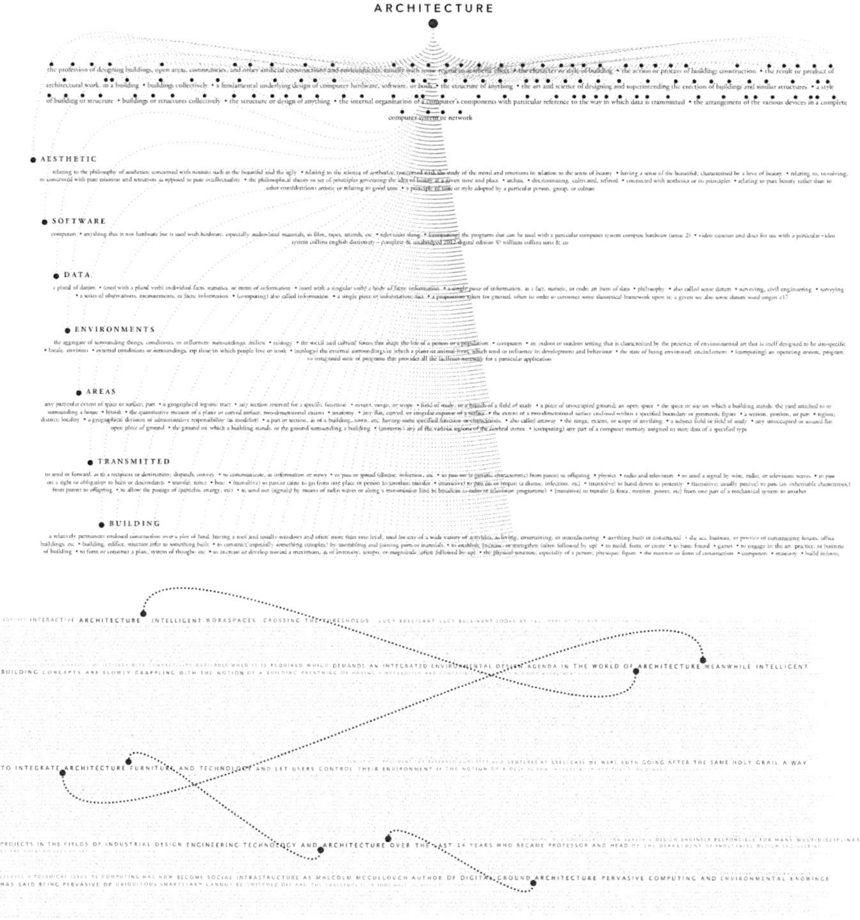

FIGURE 12.1 Definition of term 'architecture'. Branching arrangement between all the words used to define 'architecture'.

thought through the terrain, while describing how it converges and diverges from certain concerns locally, as compared to global currents across time, as a computer-aided epistemology of theory.

All words used to define the term architecture are indexed according to the words contained in those definitions. All words contained in the definition of the term are also subsequently defined, thus creating a branching pattern where all words are recursively linked by their definitions to all other words used in the database.Extraction of words surrounding the term 'architecture', indexed according to proximity.Words preceding and following the term 'architecture' are also indexed according to their proximity to this initial user query – 'architecture'. This allows the system to understand common word relations, as well as extracting all the common uses and citations involving the term 'architecture'. This process is done for every single term sampled in all the bodies of text incorporated in the database, not solely 'architecture'. © 2017 Alejandro Mieses Castellanos.

Storing the immediate contexts of each word allows us to generate a collective registry of the uses given to each term, a collection of all the words necessary for describing a certain condition related to the term in question. The term[1] 'architecture', for example, is syntactically enveloped, in any body of text, by the words deemed by the different authors to be necessary for conveying the variety of ideas related to this term. While a single citation containing the term "architecture," is not enough to convey the vast variety of terms that can be combined with this term, a large collection of them will. Each citation containing "architecture" is compared to all others containing the same term, in order to extract all other words which are repeated across the complete body of citations used by the authors to describe a certain condition related to "architecture." Words that precede and supersede the term "architecture" are indexed according to their proximity to this term, as the source data to produce any computation (see Figure 12.1). The addition of these indexed proximity values across all citations reveals a hierarchy of terms that rely on their use and proximity, by each occurrence, called a hierarchy map – propensity of words with which the term in question seeks to relate. It is an algorithm reliant on massive amounts of redundant data – citations – to extract the common words used to describe the term in question, as an indexed registry of words related to this term. This process is done for every single word, in every written sample (essay, book, article, etc.) – not only for the term "architecture." This hierarchy map is the primary set of values stored in the database and weighed against a fixed set of word sequences – definitions, antonyms, synonyms – by a multiplier effect.

Each term used in the narrative bodies of texts scanned are stored alongside two weighted types of data: their dictionary definitions, synonyms and antonyms, and their context – words that precede and supersede each term, along with the article, author, dates, and author's affiliated institutions. In this case, a dictionary is not a passive reference to be visited but an active generator of word combinations. Weighting the values given to each type of data allows a measured outcome whereby words are connected by their proximity to each other, taking into account their universal usage, but giving precedence to the context in order to exhibit common combinations and articulations based on the usage of each author, culture, or region, according to the scope within which we analyze these texts. Redefining what a word is – that which in our minds recalls the uses given to it, according to that which we have previously heard or read – as an accent of ideas, not phonetically, as that inclination to link words together according to how we have heard them combined across cultures, and across time.

Neural Networks play an important role in searching through and deriving the correct word to be chosen from all the possibilities of combinations in each term's hierarchy map. When a user enters a single-term query, two words are automatically chosen to generate an initial triangle of words – the two words that have the highest proximity values to the term entered. Deriving this triangle is the first step in generating a knowledge seed – a lattice of primary relations between terms. This process is used later on to derive all other relations between words.

The weighted value derived from fixed and variable data is used to triangulate those terms associated to the terms queried by the user. The triangulated product uses the most associated term to the terms queried by the user to derive a lattice of primary relationships between words – a lattice of primary relations to terms in a branching arrangement, where the original term is submitted by the user. Previous words generated also carry a weight upon which the next word will be derived to assure that words are placed in conformity with complementarity of relations according to the set of authors' writings.

From this initial lattice, referred to as a knowledge seed, each term is attracted according to the weights derived from their use in their different contexts to attract and repel each other, as agents gravitating towards each other and clustering according to the relations traced in the original text. All weights are influenced by a constant that assures that the overall knowledge map achieves a certain level of dynamic stasis or entropy, where each word is in perfect balance with those surrounding it in the map. In this way, the system is auto-regulated by each node's (word's) proximity to all other nodes in the map, taking into account not only their distance from the original terms entered, but their distance from all others.

From this lattice of primary relations, a third step follows to derive the correct proximities to all other terms on the lattice, not solely based on the highest proximity, but that also weighs the proximities of all other words, from the highest to the lowest. In this step, each word, based on their hierarchy map, seeks out the words generated from the previous step, attracted by the measure of proximity in its hierarchy map. This process allows for clustering of terms that are most related, deriving densities of topics and relations across separated clusters of words. This is what is called a knowledge map – a balanced dynamic of words attracted to each other to find the optimal placement where each word is in relation to all others in the map. This is done for every single word in the knowledge map, assuring a balanced clustering of terms based not only on each of the author's use of that term, but on their dictionary definition, synonyms and antonyms. (see Figure 12.2).

Within these structures one can see various branchings generated from the word "Computer." Since the database involves solely writings pertaining to architecture,

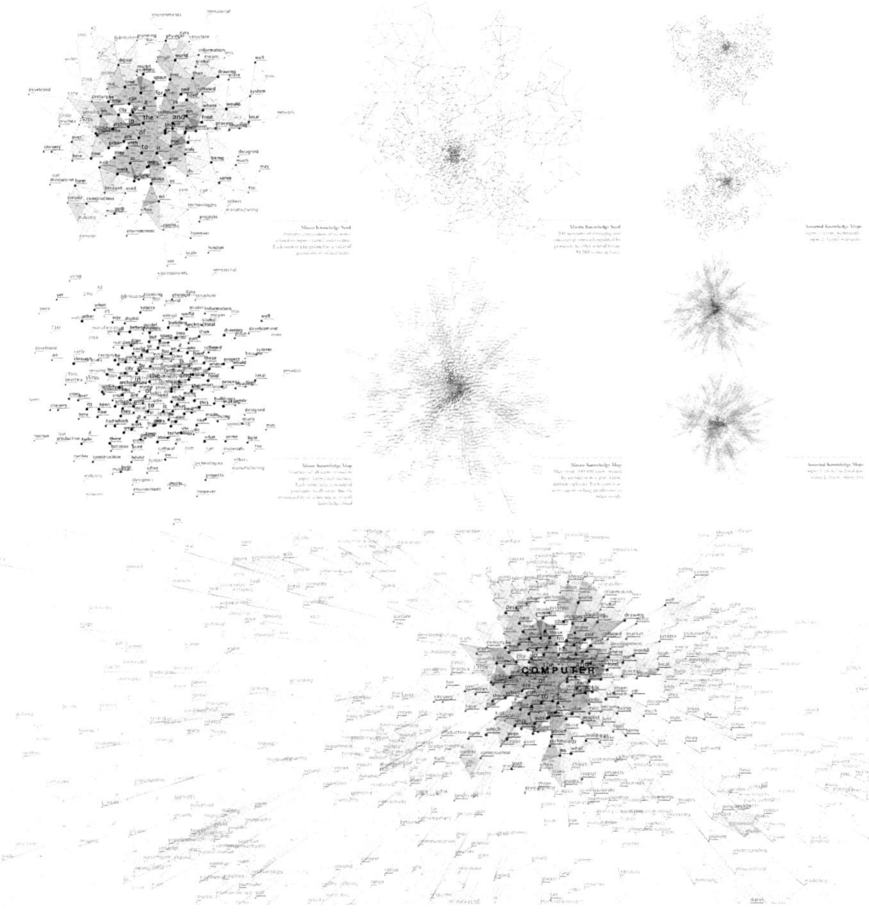

FIGURE 12.2 Taxonomy of structures surrounding user queries. The taxonomy of structures above shows the primary lattice of immediate relations generated between words queried. The words most closely used to the initial term queried by the user are built as an initial triangle that is recursively branched according to its associated terms (upper left figure). This initial lattice is called a knowledge seed, whose words are attracted to each other according to proximity values derived from their use within the texts in the database. These values serve to create a dynamic balance of words that is generated as each word is attracted to all others. The resulting graph (figure in lower part of the image) is called a knowledge map. The number of words per knowledge map hinge on the computing power – these may range from 100 words (Micro Knowledge Map), to 10,000 words (Macro Knowledge Map) Macro Knowledge Map: Approximately 2,000 terms related to "computer," by proximity clusters. Zoomed in view showing proximity clusters of words relating to the user input: 'Computer'. © 2017 Alejandro Mieses Castellanos.

the resulting graphs reveal ideas connected to "Computer" from the point of view of architecture or related professions. Within these branchings one may see common terms such as: "CAD," "CAM," "technologies," and "manufacturing" as they self-assemble to form their own cluster. Other clusters contain words such as "virtual," "physical," "world," "data," "structure," "global," and "environments," which further branch into clusters that contain "housing," "process," "system," "place," "local," and, surprisingly, "food," which may be a term one wouldn't associate with computation but which some of the authors have linked to food production and data assessment of food quantities in urban environments. Other clusters self-assemble according to criteria of time, such as: "20th," "century," "developed," "1990s," "1970s," and "sensing," which anchor ideas pertaining to the periods of time during which ideas relating to this term saw accelerated growth. Within these self-assembled clusters of words one can get a glimpse of the common branchings and spheres of knowledge related to those queried by the user. It is a purely generative process, assisted by common combinations of words and reliant on the intelligence derived from the writings sampled in the database. This visual map of ideas is the primary product of the research – referred to as abstract mode – where all words used throughout all bodies of text are put in relation to one another in abstract space, a space defined solely by the proximity between all words.

In terrain mode, as opposed to abstract mode, words are geo-referenced. This is done by taking into account the authors writing the bodies of text and their affiliated institutions. This approach parts from two simple premises: a) that an institution is a collection of ideas embodied through a set of words that are used in higher frequency than others, i.e. keywords; and b) that the authors who articulate those ideas do not have to be physically present in such places to attract other authors that will be, and that are able to influence the territory with those ideas.

Through the author's affiliated institutions and the places referenced within the work, we can derive real vectors of ideas and opinions, from one location to another (see Figure 12.3). These vectors can be self-referential (a collection of vector points of associated terms) – which exhibit a sequence of proximity relations to terms queried by the user which represent a single geographic point, or they can be other-referential (a collection of vector lines of associated terms) – which can be abstracted when one work refers to other places, authors, or times, as a line where one set of terms in a geographical point refers to another set in other latitudes. Currently, the software uses a 1GB database (2.25 billion words) of architecture theory taken from assorted periodicals (mainly Architectural Design Magazine and Architectural Record), for proof-of-concept purposes.

Research premises

This algorithmic process is not concerned specifically with meaning – it is primarily concerned with proximities of words, i.e. context, and the sets of words included

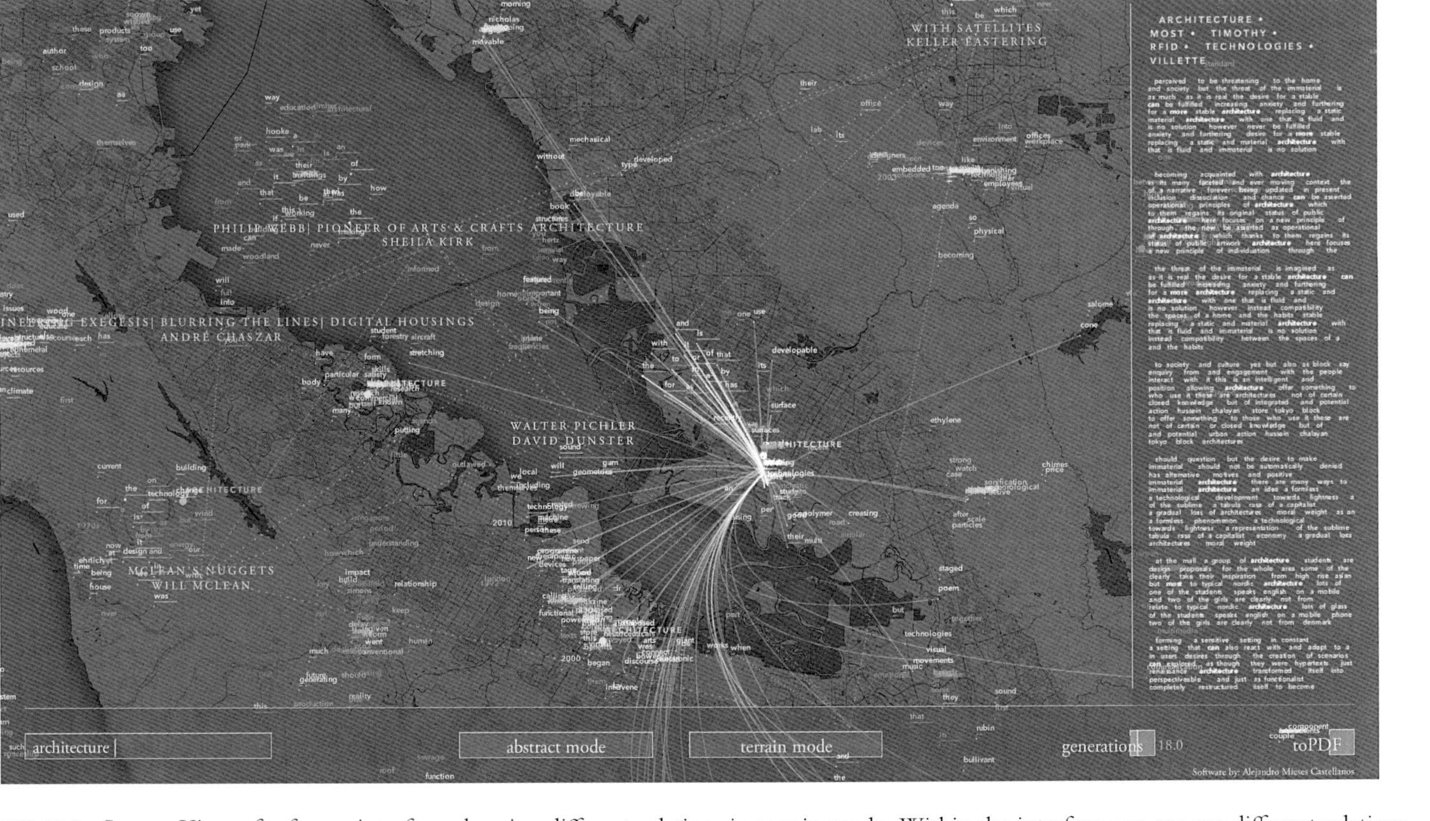

FIGURE 12.3 Screen-View of software interface, showing different relations in terrain mode. Within the interface one can see different relations of essays having complementary content, as well as the right panel containing all citations where the sequence of words queried by the user occurs in the texts within the database, sorted by relevance. Controls showed in lower part of the image have a query section for user input, abstract mode – where graphics only show words in relation to others as they are used by the authors in the database (similar to image 2), and terrain mode – where all words are referenced according to the affiliated institutions of the authors sampled in the database. © 2017 Alejandro Mieses Castellanos.

in their definition, synonyms, and antonyms. The computer does not need to "learn" the meaning of a word in the same way a human does – it only needs to know to which other words it is commonly related. Those rules of relation are extracted from human intelligence writing patterns put forth by the authors, and the meaning derived from the maps is not inherently in the algorithms or graphs, but belongs to the beholder of the knowledge map – the human eye. In this way, the intelligence in the system is distributed between human and computer, where humans dictate combination patterns based on their collectively natural or socially accorded ways of writing, and carry the last view through which to interpret the final knowledge maps. Due to this approach to language as units of proximity whose meaning is dependent on a fixed set of definitions, synonyms and antonyms, and a plethora of contextual relations, the system can compute any language dependent on alphanumeric characters that are read sequentially, whether left to right or right to left, and top to bottom. Special characters, such as those of Asian languages, haven't been tested within the system. It can also be applied to any topic, not merely architecture or urbanism, although all examples have been limited to those subjects due to the nature of the topics in this chapter.

This approach to language is borrowed from Leibnizian concepts of Monadology, and while this is primarily concerned with substances, ideas, or entities that are "pre-programmed" to interact with one another in certain ways, I would state that the language representations of these entities – words/concepts – are also preprogrammed, a view that is shared with L. Wittgenstein in *The Big Typescript: TS 213*:

> "Irregular infinite decimal number." We always have the idea that all we have to do is to put together the words of our everyday language, and that in so doing the combination has a sense that we now just have to explore – if it happens not to be completely clear to us right away. It's as if words were ingredients of a chemical compound, which we pour together and allow to combine with each other; and now we simply have to investigate the properties of the (respective) compound. Someone who said that he didn't understand the expression "irregular infinite decimal number" would get the answer "That's not true, you understand it perfectly well: don't you know what the words 'irregular', 'infinite', and 'decimal number' mean? – Well, then, you understand their combination as well." And what is meant by "understanding" here is that he knows how to apply these words in certain cases, and say connects a mental image with them. In fact, someone who puts these words together and asks "What does that mean?" is doing something similar to what small children do when they cover a piece of paper with random scribbles, show it to a grown-up, and ask "What's that?"".
>
> *(Wittgenstein, 2005, p.504)*

This view of words as ingredients in a chemical compound is especially appealing to illustrate this point, not only as the role of words within language in abstract terms, but as an instrument through which we learn and relate entities (tangible or intangible) to describe our constructed and inherited reality. This preprogramming or chemical reactiveness, however, is not fixed or eternal. Its interactions are (re)written by the cultural environment they are in. In this sense, because a word exists for an entity, we become aware of it, and it can branch out into other words by analogies, or into its own field of study, if the topic is sufficiently dense and sustained by ideas – or relations of concepts, manifested in language, as relations of words.

This topic is especially pertinent to the study of buzzwords, and the effects they may have upon industry, research, and steering our collective knowledge towards certain directions versus others. The term "sustainability" may be considered a somewhat recent example of this, where it entered into our collective consciousness following a trend towards massive manufacturing, customization, and tailoring to a set of market-defined consumers, characteristic of the first half of the 20th century, which those in themselves were of course buzzwords, and have become commonly accepted and studied terms. "Sustainability" as a response to earlier material consumption provided by industrial manufacturing, and an embodiment of environmental conscience, was collectively accorded to become this body of ideas. It did not have to become exactly this set of ideas, as opposed to others, but by repetition and addition of terms, some connections have become prevalent, such as the connection "sustainability" has to: environment, waste, logistical processes, environmental protection, species conservation, construction, cars, suburbia, urbanism, and landscape. The weight in any body of ideas, of each of those concepts in relation to "sustainability" is unmeasured, whether in: positive impacts – environmental protection, species conservation, environmental hazard mitigation, or landscape; negative impacts – waste, cars, suburbia; or neutral – logistical processes, construction, and regulation. The term "sustainability" has become pollinated to become accompanied by these terms and many others, and when mentioning the first word, the others come to mind at varying rates, dependent upon the amount of literature on the subject we have read, and the cultural set of ideas (geography) we are immersed in.

That for which we don't have a word, we don't see, we don't understand. It doesn't participate within the networks of meanings and culturally assigned values that we have deemed important. These gaps of information, of words least touched upon, words that do not connect, are an important part of culture, as the antithesis to that which receives more attention – that which we call buzzwords. Buzzwords represent an alignment of cultural values where collectively we seek to expand a defined field of knowledge and incremental depth that is accreted by the enormous amounts of effort dedicated by experts into developing certain topics, while not touching upon others. They provide space for the accretion of topics within a certain sphere of our collective knowledge and expand them in certain directions.

Buzzwords, in whichever form they take, in architecture or any profession, serve as a collectively accorded set of ideas that are primed to be expanded in certain directions by future intellectual efforts. In this sense, words behave in accord with monadic canons, as entities which are preprogrammed to combine, although this combination is not natural, it is humanly defined, in a collective way. This "collective" way can and should be challenged in the capacity to study - Who produces these ideas? Who propels them and gives them access to a wider population? In this sense, "collective" is not meant in any way as egalitarian or democratic – not everyone or every institution who produces knowledge produces it at the same rate, nor has the capacity to propel it forward to the same territorial extent, and repetitive frequency through time, which are factors that were very much taken into account while quantifying words to reveal these relays of information.

This approach is also embedded above certain concepts of Kantian Transcendentalism, or that which he termed a priori. Kant's treatment of conditions that precede human perception and cognition, such as: three-dimensionality (everything that takes place and is visible to us, takes place in three dimensions), linearity of time (everything we experience is linear in time, and time moves forward), and causality (everything we experience is involved in a chain of reactions of cause and effect), form hard examples of that which gives form to our cognition. However, language, by the principles stated previously, has a more tacit and malleable set of conditions that precedes our cognition. Though it may change, the language into which we are born defines a set of very different relations to the environment, society, each other, spirituality, and the material world, dependent upon the language. The connections of ideas afforded by any one language is in itself a biased set of propensity growths for ideas and topics to be expanded in certain directions – as that which is "preprogrammed" to combine and grow in certain measures.

This is a fact highlighted by M. Halliday in his *Towards a Language-Based Theory of Learning* (1993), while stating the capacity for language to shape how concepts are joined since a very early stage, and the role of cultural context in shaping language:

> When children learn language, they are not simply engaging in one kind of learning among many; rather, they are learning the foundation of learning itself. The distinctive characteristic of human learning is that it is a process of making meaning-a semiotic process; and the prototypical form of human semiotic is language. Hence the ontogenesis of language is at the same time the ontogenesis of learning.
>
> Whatever the culture they are born into, in learning to speak children are learning a semiotic that has been evolving for at least ten thousand generations. But in some cultures, including those comprising the Eurasian culture band, during the past hundred generations or so the nature of this semiotic has been changing: A new form of expression has evolved, that we call writing, and following on from this a new, institutionalized form of learning that we call education. Children now learn language not only in home and neighbourhood but also in school; and with new modes of language development come new forms of knowledge, educational knowledge as distinct from what we call common sense.
>
> *(Halliday, 1993, p. 93)*

It is a common theme threading many ideas, also supported by other 20th century linguists and philosophers, such as N. Chomsky, W. Laboy, L. Wittgenstein and J. Derrida. Hidden within these writings is not only that language could be taken as a whole, but that it is also fragmented into social institutions, where, for example, a school would carry a very different set of words, a different language, and teachings from what a home does, or a civic center, or a court of law. Similarly, every profession or other forms of social collectivity has its own language hierarchies, or sets of words upon which their concerns have hinged on historically, that builds itself into institutions or spaces, where one recognizes their lineage or importance. They entail different spheres of knowledge, which we sense tacitly or immanently, whenever we enter into these buildings, and the behavior they exert upon us. It is part of the assumed behavior one may feel within a library, around historical monuments, or in religious institutions, regardless if one is participant of their creed. The silent behavior of respect, awe, and gravitas within these spaces, is very different from the collective behavior one feels at sporting events, for example, where there is a common acceptance of the historical importance of a team, accompanied by similar sentiments of pride, loyalty, and respect; however, the space entails a certain vociferous behavior to recognize their importance. This becomes an event where our individual knowledge is rewired according to the expected norms of the environment we are in, where these norms are not written, they are immanent, and traceable by common linguistic combinations of ideas. The capacity to bring these common linguistic combinations to the fore can afford us a conscious knowledge of that which takes place reflexively or subconsciously.

Software capacities

Language in this sense becomes a map of ideas with differentiated densities, expanded as needed, due to our collective volition – social, spiritual, economic, military, or intellectual. Words in language behave in much the same way as neurons in brain tissue. A word that is more widely used, will carry more connections of variated strength to other concepts. This is what allows a person to say "sustainability" and the receiver's brain to automatically connect it with a set of concepts, images, and opinions, related to his previous experiences, readings, and thoughts, which are refined collectively – experiences, readings, and thoughts – may be individual, but are formed through communication collectively. This set of concepts the receiver generates is not in the emitter's message necessarily; they pertain to our collective understanding of the term, manifested instantaneously through the receiver. If that concept is repeated sufficiently, the connections grow stronger; if it is connected to a new concept/word, the set of connections expand as "new ideas" – the combination of two or more concepts in previously unforeseen ways. A cluster of words, which are reinforced to connect through time, will warp language to become almost synonymous or irremediably linked in our collective mind, in much the same way that the brain's tissue folds to allow for stronger synaptic connections. More so, a cluster of words/concepts will relay information within itself, as well as outside itself, to other regions, which can manifest themselves as civic, educational, or organizational transformations, as a sort of collective plasticity of our language, in much the same way our brains undergo varying rates of neuroplasticity.

This process is based on certain biological processes present in the development of neuron clusters within the brain due to neuroplasticity. A set of neurons dedicated to a certain task will grow more connections between them, but also their proximity to each other will increase over time, while those pathways that aren't used during a certain time range will become weaker or will disappear. This model is based on a view of language as a repository of words as neurons, as entities that are capable of articulating and branching between themselves to achieve a certain reality – a balanced or reliable correspondence of meanings that are sustained during a certain period of time. A word that is most commonly used will allow for certain thoughts or guide certain concepts, or influence certain realities, more so than that which is not used. It will link to other regions of speech or collectives as neurons do. The role of buzzwords in our society allows for the differentiated development of our cognition – where are our efforts to expand our knowledge concentrated on? – a condition which allows for our vocabulary to be expanded in certain directions versus others.

A body of ideas is not solely the ideas. They may become synonymous with authors, places, cultures, and social arrangements that produced such ideas. This is why in occidental cultures we can say "Ancient Greece" and a set of ideas comes to mind, primary characters or philosophers, and a social arrangement (democracy mainly). It is the similar reason we can say "Silicon Valley" and the same happens, with a completely different set of ideas, that nonetheless hold their integrity to become an "identity" accepted by their integrands and representative of that geographical extent.

The knowledge maps derived from this process enable us to provide a variety of analyses that trace not only how ideas or connections of terms move throughout the terrain but how they change through time. By registering the date of production of that body of text – academic paper, newspaper article, blog entry, book, website, magazine article, or social media post – we can map changes in usage of terms and their connections through the dates belonging to these sources. In order for the process to purvey an adequate representation of connecting concepts, the amount of texts must be constant throughout all periods of time. For example, in any given body of texts divided through ten years, the amount of texts in the first year shouldn't be larger or smaller than those that are subsequent. The amount of texts for any period of time should be above a critical threshold of 30 texts by unit of time – decade, year, month, depending on the time-comparison range desired by the user.

If the texts in the database are composed of a larger set of authors and larger amounts of texts, the resulting knowledge map will reveal concept connections across the collectivity of authors included in the database. However, the process can also be useful to study concept connections within one author's body of work, if that is all that is included in the source database. The same would be true if one wanted to study works from a single epoch, a single region, culture, source or institution, allowing for that which we term modularity – the capacity to integrate words and ideas across wider or narrower ranges in topics of text. However, the process still requires a level of curation – of specifying the sources – in order to allow for a desired amount of integrity within the topics discussed by the different authors. Through this process, the system can become a comparative analysis tool, in addition to a collective synthesis tool, where through a process similar to terrain mode, it would not show the affiliated institutions, but the names of the authors distributed in abstract space.

If it is taken solely from the writings of one author, we can gage the common associations that author has with the term. If it is taken from all the writings an institution has produced, it is reflective of that institution's authors views on that given subject. And through this same manner, if we incorporate larger, more wide-ranging bodies of text, we can have a glimpse into regional approximations or cultural approximations to the terms queried.

Conclusions and applications

Knowing the reach of a certain collection of ideas can serve to analyze how they propel, epidemiologically speaking, how they interbreed with those that were present. The spread of ideas carries subjacent consequences upon topics such as segregation, migration, poverty, and the ideological environments, which we may sense immanently, but that imply real changes in collective behaviors.

Within this visual analysis of terms, it is possible to explore in greater depth what are the areas of knowledge have grown more. Towards which other ideas or concepts have they grown or coalesced with? What are the wide-ranging impacts of the spread of this knowledge and how has it frozen into built form? How many people has this affected and what has been the growth curve of this idea, supported by which other ideas, and in support of which other concepts? What is the reach of this set of ideas, in demographics, space, and longevity? How do we measure this? What are the topics that we concentrate on or are most cited? Which are less cited? A view into the sphere of influence of any term, where "sphere" is not the exact word that should be used in this context, since it is not always an even spread in all directions. This analysis is a measure for visualizing that which we build together, that abstract set of criteria which we sense tacitly and to a limited degree, but have a limited view of how it comes to be, yet carries a very real set of influences upon our collective growth.

A higher-level view of the gaps within the body of knowledge we produce collectively can also help to further identify topics of value that have scarcely been attended to. A time-dependent map of how our efforts and topics change can also help to identify trends in the past that we may have forgotten, or revisit studies that have fallen out of public view. A spatial view of how knowledge changes can help to identify a variety of power relations on the ground, regarding who provides knowledge and who receives it. It can also help to identify complementarities within populations or groups of people, which may not have thought of themselves as collaborators or having sharing mutually beneficial interests.

Applications for this can span various scenarios, such as:

a) An interface for exploring our collective knowledge, the most pressing stimuli upon our profession and our obscured topics as they are hierarchized through time. This higher-level view affords us the capacity to not only know how we fit within a larger body of practice, but to also question these beliefs and accelerate the production of theory to assume its traditional role of articulating collective concerns within certain contemporary realities. These realities, along with our modes of practice (our collective responses), can be evaluated collectively.
b) A synthesis of the diversity of public opinions upon the built/urban environment, whether a single building or regionally, without sacrificing variables, or channeling opinions through surveys. The forces that shape our cities are inevitably top-down, dependent upon clients, permits, zoning, politics, and investors, among other agents. A tool that coalesces a collectivity of voices from visitors, citizens, and those that work and surround buildings, could not only balance these equations of power, but also raise a higher level of consciousness from the public regarding their role in the built environment, and their capacity of challenging our modes of praxis.
c) A map of ideological or economic movements through the terrain, such as protests, gentrification, and educational inequalities, in data-substantiated ways, that can give further insight into other statistical analysis. It is usual for this data to travel through narratives – documentaries, pictures, editorials, stories. We've all seen the pictures of Martin Luther King Jr. in protest and countless others. One wouldn't dream of discussing those topics solely in statistical terms, it would seem insulting. However, a way of surveying how concepts were connected, with what populations, and which heroes, could give our historical trajectories a more vivid light.
d) A dynamic graph that can connect the user's interest with particular places, authors, or historical facts, of the subjects he or she has queried. A large part of that which we seek when traveling or moving is the people, not the city. We want to make sure we fit in, that the place we are moving to or visiting provides us insight, growth, human contact, and cultural knowledge, in whatever form – practical, monetary, spiritual, or social. The capacity to reflect collective or cultural concerns can give us a clearer picture of our complementarity of beliefs.
e) Population growth in cities will need a direct form of collective engagement to voice the needs of populations in non-numerical or direct ways. Projections on growth of urban density will put a strain in the expected interactions between local governance and occupants. A large part of voicing opinions is that they are heard, and have the necessary documentation or mechanisms to travel

and sum up to a critical mass of voices that a government can reflect or react to. This entails not only a communication between individuals and government, but individuals and communities, and between communities and other communities, to decipher points of convergence.

f) The need for aid in traumatized regions due to war and natural disasters, where acquiring/organizing information from the ground can give a clearer and more rapid picture of the necessities of the people affected, as these are instantaneously built into a database sourced from social-media feeds, newspapers, or other periodicals. These case-scenarios depend upon a series of logistical hurdles during the first weeks since the event occurs, where the capacity of acquiring a veritable map of needs from the ground is limited due to time and resources. This situation usually leads to supplies and aid efforts being allocated homogeneously over vast terrains due to a lack of specificity in knowledge about the conditions of sites and communities most in need.

What this method provides in conclusion is a graphical interface through which to see and weigh, analyze and measure, the changes and current state of our collective knowledge, whichever "our" that is, regional, cultural, political, academic, public, or private, at any scale, interdepartmental, to university, to wide-ranging media, and cultural opinions. What it provides is a first set of tools for a science capable of conducting studies upon changes, striations, and oscillations in our collective beliefs.

The statement made by the Pritzker Prize Selection Committee of 2017, has voiced these concerns in a succinct manner:

> In this day and age, there is an important question that people all over the world are asking, and it is not just about architecture; it is about law, politics and government as well. We live in a globalized world where we must rely on international influences, trade, discussion, transactions, etc. But more and more people fear that, because of this international influence, we will lose our local values, our local art, and our local customs. They are concerned and sometimes frightened.
>
> *(Pritzker Prize Committee, 2017)*

A statement such as this, that due to its nature as the highest accolade in our profession requires a response to our wider set of concerns, is in large measure reflective of the needs we should meet in the future, in our capacity to not only respond to physical forms, processes, and technologies, but our capacity to engage with social realities, community concerns, and the human within that which we've built.

Note

1 Term(s) here, means the first set of words queried by the user, as opposed to Word, which are all the words associated to the first term(s) according to the information extracted from the source writings and stored in the database.

References

Byrne, D. and Callaghan, G. (2013). *Complexity Theory and the Social Sciences*. London, UK: Routledge.

Chomsky, N. (2015). *Syntactic Structures*. Eastford, CT: Martino Fine Books.

Copeland, Jack, Posy, C. and Shagrir, O. (2013). *Computability: Turing, Gödel, Church, and Beyond*. Cambridge, MA: MIT Press.

Derrida, J. (1998). *Of Grammatology*. Baltimore, MD: Johns Hopkins University Press.

Halliday, M. (1993). *Towards a Language-Based Theory of Learning*. University of Sydney and Macquarie University. http://lchc.ucsd.edu/mca/Paper/JuneJuly05/HallidayLangBased.pdf. Retrieved on February 15, 2017.

Hight, C. and Perry, C. (2006). 'Collective Intelligence in Design.' *Architectural Design, 76*: 5–9. Hoboken, NJ: John Wiley & Sons Publishing Design.

Kant, I., (1999). *Critique of Pure Reason (The Cambridge Edition of the Works of Immanuel Kant)*. Ed. Guyer, P. and Wood, A. Cambridge, UK: Cambridge University Press.

Leibniz, G. (1991). *Discourse on Metaphysics and Other Essays*. Trans. Garber, D. and Ariew, R. Indianapolis, IN: Hackett Publishing Company, Inc.

Pritzker Prize Committee (2017). 'Announcement: Rafael Aranda, Carme Pigem and Ramon Villa receive the 2017 Pritzker Architecture prize'. http://www.pritzkerprize.com/2017/announcement. Retrieved on, March 24, 2017.

Railsback, S. and Grimm, V. (2011). *Agent-Based and Individual-Based Modeling: A Practical Introduction*. Princeton, NJ: Princeton University Press.

Wittgenstein, L. (2005). *The Big Typescript: TS 213*. Ed. Luckhardt, G. and Aue, M. Malden, MA: Blackwell Publishing.

13

DATA AND POLITICS OF INFORMATION

Rezoning New York City through Big Data

Pablo Lorenzo-Eiroa

Introduction

In the neoliberal model of urban development, policy makers have displaced architects and urbanists in planning and designing cities, or at least, one could argue, architects and urbanists have been removed from key decisions. In many cases, the implicit claim is that the market decides the form of the city. Architects have been criticised for designing cities from top-down structuring visions, apparently proposing autonomous, unrealistic ideas. But the result of this process perhaps escapes the personal agendas of policy makers, who often end up following autonomous, managerial real-estate parameters, which, by default, arrive at defining land ownership rights, zoning regulations, parks, infrastructure, transportation, the city fabric, the city block, and predominant building typologies. Moreover, financial parameters ended up defining urban uses without addressing architecture and urbanism as a field of study and disregarding previous revolutions in urbanism such as health, public space, and the integral relationship of cities with the environment. While this neoliberal ideology pressures public space, parks, and the environment, turning them into commodities, it seems that a clear, politically active urban position today would be to activate and expand urban voids and promote latent ecologies.

These issues are discussed through an academic-studio research that aims to understand the contemporary city as a topologically continuous space-environment, proposing overall transformations of the structure of New York City by specific accumulative interventions, gathering, processing, and transforming Big Data including fluid-dynamic information.

By mapping and representing the city and its flows, Alphabet Inc. has been organizing urban information top down, with a transformative empowerment, more effective than any architect would ever imagine and further than the neoliberal model, commodifying public space, domain, flows, and information access, among other issues. But the typologies of our cities have not been challenged through the information technologies used to disrupt reality, nor by addressing radical innovation, nor by addressing any potential ecologies that may become active by understanding the city as a space-environment. At the same time, while architects increasingly recognize the transformative empowerment of working with data and complex-information systems, citizens surrender commodified data continuously and architects precariously use data gathered through political and corporate biases. In the best scenario, architects originate, gather, and process data but, admittedly, through predetermined conventional algorithms. Standardized predetermination can be an advantage, but also quite problematic. Since information does not exist without a form of representation, a politics of representation can be traced across information technologies. This question opens further issues in representing an apparently inert reality that is more malleable to data measurement and representation through information processes. Perhaps architects should be more aware of the transformative aspect of information technologies in cities as they are in a position to consider these as they deal with the growth of its fabric, morphology, and space.

The neoliberal model of private development, for instance "the corporate skyline," replaced the policies based on the interests of the commons of public state development for the motto that urban growth follows finance, informing the overall structure of cities, including their infrastructure (Willis, 1995). While a large percentage of developed apartments are kept empty to pressure the market in search for a continuous economic gain, the homeless population grows and public space shrinks. At the same time, taxation holds up the failures of an economic system pressuring mostly middle and lower classes, and irrational outputs become naturalized by a manipulated, top-down market economy. In this model, the critique of centralized planning and design by an authoritative state through architects was replaced by apparently free market forces, naturalizing, formatting, and displacing parameters to suit corporate interests who lobbied for and informed urban development measured by economic profit, leaving behind, for instance, common welfare, public space, and urban, architectural, and environmental interests. Enclosed, out-of-context building typologies fostered by the autonomy of a consumerist system have been proven to be some of the most dangerous threats to the environment, and the current limit of the neoliberal model is the consumption of its own environment. Clusters of detached buildings developed by large, concentrated capital went against the balance of cities at multiple levels, all the way from the social to the environmental, affecting even their own interests, such as sustainable long term economic models.

Among the multiple layers that constitute cities, the recognition of a collective social project has marked their advancement, a utopian project of cultural and technological advancement, related, for instance to the uniqueness of the city's location, ecologies, site specificity, social, cultural, and geopolitical qualities. If until the 1970s architecture was able to construct utopias enabled by idealistic, visionary, top-down agendas executed exclusively by strong top-down state policies, today governments would not be able to provide the minimal parameters for these types of projects to be even conceived. Simply substituting common state interests, urban planning, and the architecture of public spaces with real estate interests through corporate development, just gave place to a different kind of indexed autonomy, that of a global economic system. This system develops cities through marketing strategies, promoting object-buildings by star architects, disengaged from any potential to activate the urban fabric, working through contrast by concentrating large capital investment and disengaging the city from building up a diversified space-environment. Rather than dealing with such problems at a structural level, architecture has been relegated to a superfluous aesthetic role, addressing a marketing object-oriented logic by decorating a given building shell, promoting visual photogenic impact, without the possibility of real, structural, aesthetic innovation, not at the level of public space, nor at the level of building development strategies, nor at the level of the city. Instead, with this system, architecture is complicit in developing ideal city-containers through large, enclosed, artificial building-environments, blocking mostly any relationship to the logic of the site, disengaged from the environment and the social diversity of a city.

New technological models seem to start to address the necessary distribution demanded by democracy for transparency by empowering populations through bottom-up participatory processes. It seems that the contemporary city should aim for a complex, non-deterministic, differentiated space in which citizens would be able to continuously update and redirect the development of the city. But the negative aspect of such transformative power may be that popular non-professional real-time decisions may not always be the best reflection of the real, long-term interest of an informed society. At the same time, while this process may seem to distribute decisions horizontally, it relies on authoritative deterministic top-down, centralized algorithms that organize data, problematically building up power. In a real-time, digitally-informed society, the development of systems of representation and interfaces that structure information, produces content. Moreover, one of the issues is that data gathering may reveal biases in the politics of centralized power by defining the categories through which data are gathered. The apparently neutral processes of objective measurement of reality often index its method of measurement. For instance, data frequently index the categories used to understand reality and that overall often determine social behaviour, normalizing models in a society being progressively engineered through feedback processes of measurement, representation, and optimization.

The typical conventional information visualization strategies represent different data through identical strategies, thereby separating form and content, or method of representation from the data gathered, without considering emerging cross-relationships once data are represented. By addressing representation as a problem of empowerment over reality, data representation informs the same reality it is indexing. The city is not only structured by its own information measurement and processing mechanisms and systems, but also by the aesthetic and ideological agendas implicit within the cultural projects underlying the technology being implemented to index reality.

Informed space-environments

Today, algorithms form a certain type of common origination in the way we structure relationships. Digital signs represent information, and in linguistic terms software languages determine how we currently understand, categorize, organize, and reference reality. By representing reality through codified computer signs, computation has been creating new objects that produce signification in advance independently from the reality they are representing, therefore informing reality by the simple implementation of a predetermined system of measurement and reference. Jacques Derrida's critique of Saussure's (de Saussure, 1916) equation (sign=signifier/signified) is that structuralism disseminates categorical thought (Derrida, 1978). Derrida pointed out that language creates signifiers, meaning that each time we name something we are creating an independent entity, an artificial construction independent from what it is being named (a sign at a certain point, becomes a signifier). Alain Badiou, points out that this does not happen with mathematics, which resolved the question of *being* that philosophy raised, since it is the only autonomous system able to support its own validation (Badiou, 2005). One could reference architecture's relationship to language (Tafuri, 1974). One could also reference computation as an algorithmic solution to a mathematical problem. But computation used for data gathering may not validate an underlying mathematical problem. A data-gathering algorithmic process needs mathematical verification before data are processed to make sure the results are valid. Mathematical problems based on statistics models in data gathering arise when computing results.

One could then reveal problematic relationships in how architecture, as a form of language, is structured digitally through computational languages including how computational digital signs become architecture signifiers by how they determine meaning in advance of what they are representing, sometimes indexing the mathematics of the algorithmic process implemented. Although these may be known communication linguistic problems, they have not been critically understood and implemented by design professionals who deal with data gathering and processing.

The promise of Big Data as a new form of a diversified structuralism is to build up large sources of information statistically, avoiding categorical preconceptions to interpret emerging relationships. Since there are no data without representation, there is a critical political dimension in the representation of data. Additionally, there are the technologies for measurement and surveying reality that then may or may not activate political categories in the gathering and categorization of data. Before data mining, data are inputted through problematic cultural and political categories that may reflect certain biases. There is a politics of data classification that actively uses this differential for civic representation, displacing the science of data measurement to activate ideological agendas, including, whether consciously or not, the implementation of linguistic structures to force signification through categories activating certain political agendas. The issue is not in the flow of data that emerge through computation, but rather in the politically charged set of parameters that define data output. Often, the single data-entry-point person does not develop such algorithms responsible for the categories that are input to collect and represent data. Categories confirm linguistic, cultural, and ideological biases that need to be addressed and critiqued. Nowadays, the problem has expanded, since data sets are often developed by a centralized authority with either access to large amounts of data or with sufficient funds to develop mechanisms for data gathering, even able to develop a data-gathering technology. Such centralized authorities are no longer exclusively governmental, but large corporations more powerful than governments have replaced their role accumulating power by creating their own systems of measurement and projecting value index to reality. The commonly imposed top-down *authority* of data generation, data gathering, and data ownership, also becomes an issue. The centralized authority of a single control mechanism to categorize, measure, represent, and communicate a field of information is quite problematic. The challenge resides in addressing how design parameters are originated in data gathering and the instruments used for that purpose. Usually, a single mono-dimensional algorithm based on a simple mathematical model gathers large quantities of data. Through machine learning, or algorithms that search for algorithms, higher dimensional meta-processing environments have advanced data gathering. For instance, image recognition has enabled a different means to understand processing of information through statistics, from the outside in, a reverse-engineering mechanical learning that emerges through processing large sources of data, displacing the typical processing by which reality was understood in discrete means and coded. In the context of the material used for this research, image recognition is being implemented to process information in urban environments to be able to retrieve data from, for instance, satellite images for the architecture studios that will be explained below. Another means to displace or critique conventional algorithms, is to critique the emergent technological positivism and top-down processing of information systems through a cryptographically secured blockchain as a distributed, decentralized system. Blockchain technology could be used, as explained further below, to administrate large sources of information requiring validation through a series of control points without a centralized, top-down, managerial organization in administrating and informing the form of the city, its coding, and its zoning.

Common generic visualizing strategies tend to structure data in determined simplistic terms, homogenizing reality in the same way government categories create types of citizens. Furthermore, recognizing the simplicity of current algorithms and the structuring, homogenizing force of computation, what happens is that data will match the system of reference for measurement, meaning that one would only be able to find through data mining what the system allows, engaging in a looping, enclosed system in which the results would be only possible within the spectrum of the system. This is the reason why Big Data becomes the subject matter of current design agendas, expanding any project to the measurement system that validates it. Any system of measurement distorts reality to confirm the reference, and this tends to validate enclosed systems such as numeric systems or mathematical models that are misused to model and confirm assumptions. This is a common problem that cities are facing by confirming their own assumptions in developing systems of measurement that instead of addressing issues, create problems and independent objects as signifiers.

Problematically, Big Data is usually understood as a *visualization* problem, for instance, separating an apparently inert content from the form of the media used to represent it (Grosswiller, 1999; McLuhan, 1967). There is no such non-media specific content. This old paradigm of translation of content among different media has been proven obsolete by the current empowerment and autonomy of new media as media of communication. New media understand the origination of content given by the simple systems of representing and administrating communication, such as, in social media, the case of Facebook Inc, which evolved its algorithms to generate profit by engineering social behavior, taking over public space in a new form of digital urbanism. Rather than analyzing media through problems of perception, the argument focusses on disclosing through deep structure the ideological projects implicit in protocols and algorithms that structure information. These issues present an interesting conflict in an apparently post-structuralist society, arguing a disjunction between a perception-based society in class conflict with undisclosed authoritative corporate interests, currently extensive to governments and nations displaced as public organizations to larger economic private conglomerate powers.

Additional to this issue is that if one were able to identify an interesting measurable problem, creating critical categories and an interesting data-mining relational system, one still would have to work out how to displace the common systems of representation in relation to the emerging content, almost to the point at which for each identified measurable problem one would have to develop a measuring methodology and an intrinsic-to-the-problem representational system. This representational strategy would have such autonomy that would be able to formalize the relationships necessary to advance and disclose the questions being researched by the emergent relational content in the crossing between the data processed and their representation. Once data are "visualized" they will infer signification beyond their initial condition, challenging the same data they are indexing. In a new form of representation of data, if autonomous and powerful enough in its new relational potential, this new form of information would produce readings that could not be anticipated. In an artistic sense, an aesthetic value based on visual logic becomes active once form is constituted, a new state of being no longer reversible. Such autonomy may be proportional to its capacity to induce further signification, dependent of course on potential socio-cultural readings, subject–object relationships, perception, affection, and any other conditions that may emerge. These issues activate a reflexive loop between representation, aesthetics, the senses, and an implicit Gestalt process between the data being represented and an apparently inert objective reality. A Gestalt of information representation also expands to continuously perceptive change in the subject that engages with these issues relative to the situation, extending the problematic relation between data and the senses relative to representation and into semiotics. This is the definition of the expansion of authorship in an *architecture of information* (Lorenzo-Eiroa and Sprecher, 2013).

New emergent disciplines

Computation has now become a new cognitive plateau across any subject of study, making computer science relevant to all disciplines. New technologies enable new means to understand reality, which therefore inform reality as well. Disciplines are expanding more than ever to the point that boundary divisions may no longer be relevant, opening new forms of transdiciplinarity content or entirely new disciplines or cognitive paradigms. An *architecture of information* implies that it may be more relevant today to address architecture through the development of new informational systems. Rather than understanding architecture through designing objects, buildings, spaces, environments, urbanism, an architecture of information implies shifting cognition to a different information level, redefining the epistemology of architecture.

As an expanded discipline, architecture is now dealing with the design of *space-environments*. But this expansion has not yet influenced the way of practicing urbanism or landscape urbanism, leaving the discipline potentially open to another expansion: *the architecture of environments*. Moreover, such expansion is now more influenced by a representation shift activated by Big Data processing. Increasingly information processes define new means to read, map, represent, and project reality, activating an *architecture of information*. This is one of the most relevant conditions today: to understand the implicit relationships between information processes and the city as space-environment.

The *ecological crisis* has initially been questioning architecture from an efficiency point of view, a technological problem that did not influence the cultural project of the discipline. But more recently, the ecological discourse has been able to enter architecture's cultural project through representation. Fluid-dynamics and energy modelling through dynamic, real-time simulation has been able to consolidate a new aesthetic, a new envision of an integrated space-environment. New means of representation has presented the possibility to directly manipulate energy, a new way to enable a discourse on ecology relative to architecture, shifting many of its means to address spatial boundaries, and by extension, architectural tectonics. This emergent quality through representation was instrumented into a new discipline, which understands spatial boundaries as energy boundaries. Fluid-dynamic simulation in administrating real time Big Data influenced a growing necessity to understand the decoding of environmental systems. This process, which is revolutionizing architecture representation, is also recoding architecture's matter, shifting the discipline to artificially structure environmental processes. Architecture is changing its internal coding and can now be understood as a meta-organizational system that can activate at a structural level dynamic forces latent in natural systems. Architecture has therefore shifted from structuring space to structuring environments.

While architecture expanded the definition of containment by blurring boundaries between space and environment, this expansion was not applied to the city. Instead of understanding continuous ecological systems that dismiss differentiations between center and periphery, the way we are currently organizing life, services, and production in cities, suburbs, and rural areas is set mainly to satisfy corporate conglomerate production models. The current ideological–political understanding of the city relative to policy making, spatial division, and land ownership in urban codes offers measurement parameters and tools for understanding the territory that cap the understanding and potential transformation of the city as a space-environment. While information technologies altered the way inhabitants interact with the city, these technologies did not challenge the city's development. Necessarily, the typology of the city, the blocks, and the buildings, would not only have to address ecological concerns, but themselves would have to be displaced and structurally transformed to engage in a topological, informed architecture of space-environments. The *anthropocene* (Crutzen and Stoermer, 2000) defines the geology and environment of the planet as informed, not exclusively, by human action. Since the planet can now be understood as artificially informed by humanity, the previously defined paradigm of separation between humans and their ecosystem, between ecology and "nature" must be thought as integrated built ecosystems and environments understanding a topological continuity between humans, cities, energy harvesting, industrial production, and the environment.

These issues are discussed through academic research that aims to activate the city as a space-environment gathering and modeling information displacing conventional technologies, proposing a rezoning of New York City in relation to environmental forces.

Rezoning the city in relation to environmental processes

Among the many different ways to process Big Data, in architecture and urbanism two kinds of data processing seem to have become more relevant: on one side, fluid-dynamic computer simulation to model environmental dynamic processes; and on the other, the different, large geospatial and social data sets (environmental, geographical, topographical, social, economic, etc.) that architects may use, or at best create, to inform the city and its design.

An architecture of informed space-environments defies the current role of the state and private media corporations in measuring and informing the city and its ecosystems to activate the voids as public space and latent ecologies for planetary welfare. Private ownership of land relative to capital gain is today in direct opposition to public environmental-protection interests. While above-ground resources often pertain to land ownership (Figure 13.1), the current environmental crisis cannot dismiss the building-up of common interests in regard to the environment that go across discrete land subdivision, which dismisses center from periphery and cities from farmland or even natural ecologies. Clear examples are not only above-ground pollution but also the harvesting of below-grade natural resources such as fresh water reservoirs polluted through private gain, such as is the case with biochemical land fertilizers, oil extraction, and gas fracking, among others. New zoning strategies and systems must be based not exclusively on promoting environmental balance, but also foster the activation of an *architecture of environments*, since environmental preservation seems not only problematic but also no longer possible. These issues require a comprehensive new law and zoning strategy necessarily following common interests that consider continuities across land ownership and lot rights. In this sense, the Viele, Egrebert L. Sanitary and Topographic Map of the City and Island of New York 1865 is an interesting representation of the tension between the projected abstract Manhattan Grid in New York City as real estate speculation repressing existing topography and ecologies (Figure 13.2, Project 6 and 7).

For instance, climate imbalance can also be related to social inequality. There is a form of urban imbalance in the development of social housing by the state in landfill, non-desirable wetlands' propensity to flooding in New York City (Figure 13.2 Project 4). Robert Caro makes several analyses of the conflicts of interest between state-sponsored infrastructure segregating private development from lower-income areas and social housing in New York City (Caro, 1974). A similar analysis is traced in relating environmental fragile areas and lower-income development. In the private speculation of real-estate waterfront, this equation

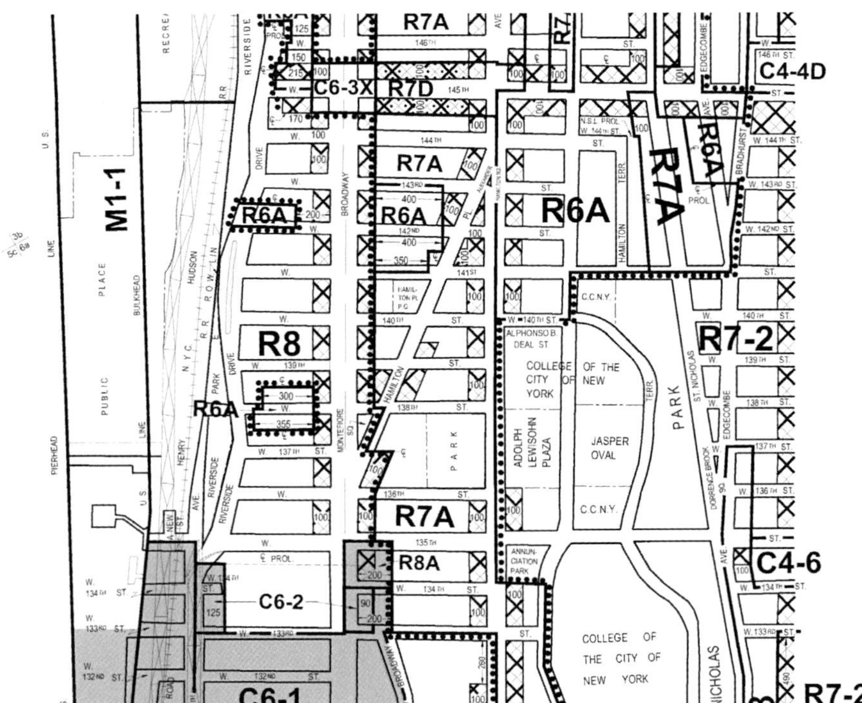

FIGURE 13.1 City Planning Commission, City of New York, Diagram showing zoning change on sectional map 3b & 6a, Borough of Manhattan. Rezoning effective November 13th, 2012; C.C. Reso #1583. Excerpt.

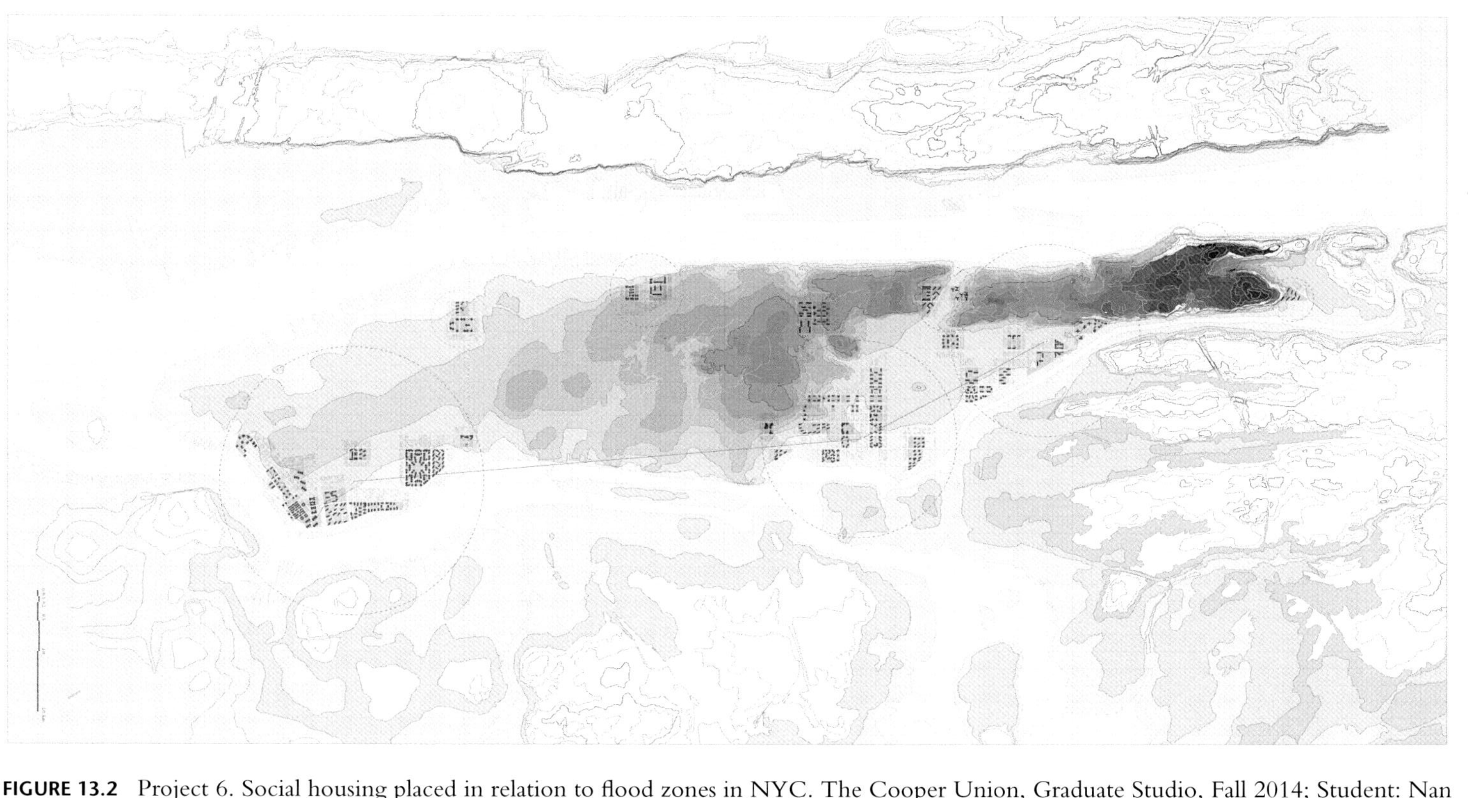

FIGURE 13.2 Project 6. Social housing placed in relation to flood zones in NYC. The Cooper Union, Graduate Studio, Fall 2014; Student: Nan Lei; Professors: Pablo Lorenzo-Eiroa (coordinator), Lydia Xynogala, and Will Shapiro.

is inversed, to the point of blocking public access. While the landfill of wetlands represses ecological balance, the seclusion to peripheral, less-desirable areas of the city fragments social continuity.

At a regional level, the entire typology of cities and their relation to the regional ecosystems should be critiqued and displaced in addressing the environmental crisis. For instance, the function of Central Park in New York City could now be critiqued and displaced to activate environmental continuity, creating, for instance, balanced relationships between center and periphery in Manhattan, as well as activating an ecosystem across parks or between parks (Figures 13.2, 13.9, 13.13; projects 3, 6, 7). The public welfare, setting up healthier conditions for cities, derived from the development of parks in the 19th century. It seems evident that this project should be actualized to integrate environmental conditions for the cities for the 21st and 22nd centuries, anticipating and planning phases for the next five hundred years.

The following research understands architecture to organize space-environments across New York City, valuing voids and latent ecologies. The research method follows a critical sequence in studying the city – reading, recognizing, measuring – to then raise questions and disclose urban problems, and ultimately displace revealed structures to open territorial and architecture possibilities through computation, Big Data processing, and fluid-dynamic simulation. The exposed problems are not speculations but conclusions after experimental applied research on the subject for over twenty years, explored through specific research experiments and academic architecture studios. The following architecture projects identify and activate an emerging architecture problem in the City of New York by means of creating data categories, mapping information, and reading the city as a mediated process of representation.

First, the projects of the research studio aim for a transfiguration of the city, a transfiguration of the existing, "naturalized" reality by activating a displacement of a revealed structure and typology of the city (Figure 13.2, Project 6).

Second, some projects of the research studio read, analyze, and disclose the tension between the repressed geological ground formations and the grid that orders the City of New York. Project 1 maps and design-specific building zoning envelops defining variability in height, indexing a diversified geological below-grade ground-density condition. Project 1 works with latent conditions previously categorized in simpler terms as the proximity of the bedrock to the ground surface that has historically informed the skyline height variation of New York City (Figure 13.3; Project 1). This project studies the architectural potential to displace conventional boundaries and spatial definitions in the variation of the sectional relationships between the Manhattan grid grade level and below-grade and above-grade topography. The below-grade geological soil density composition can now be studied with a different degree of specificity. This variable soil density below grade, for instance bedrock, clay, silt, sand, and other types of soil sediments and conditions, can inform a more precise variable economic ratio for building heights, defining a more precise zoning envelope (see Figure 13.3). While cities become

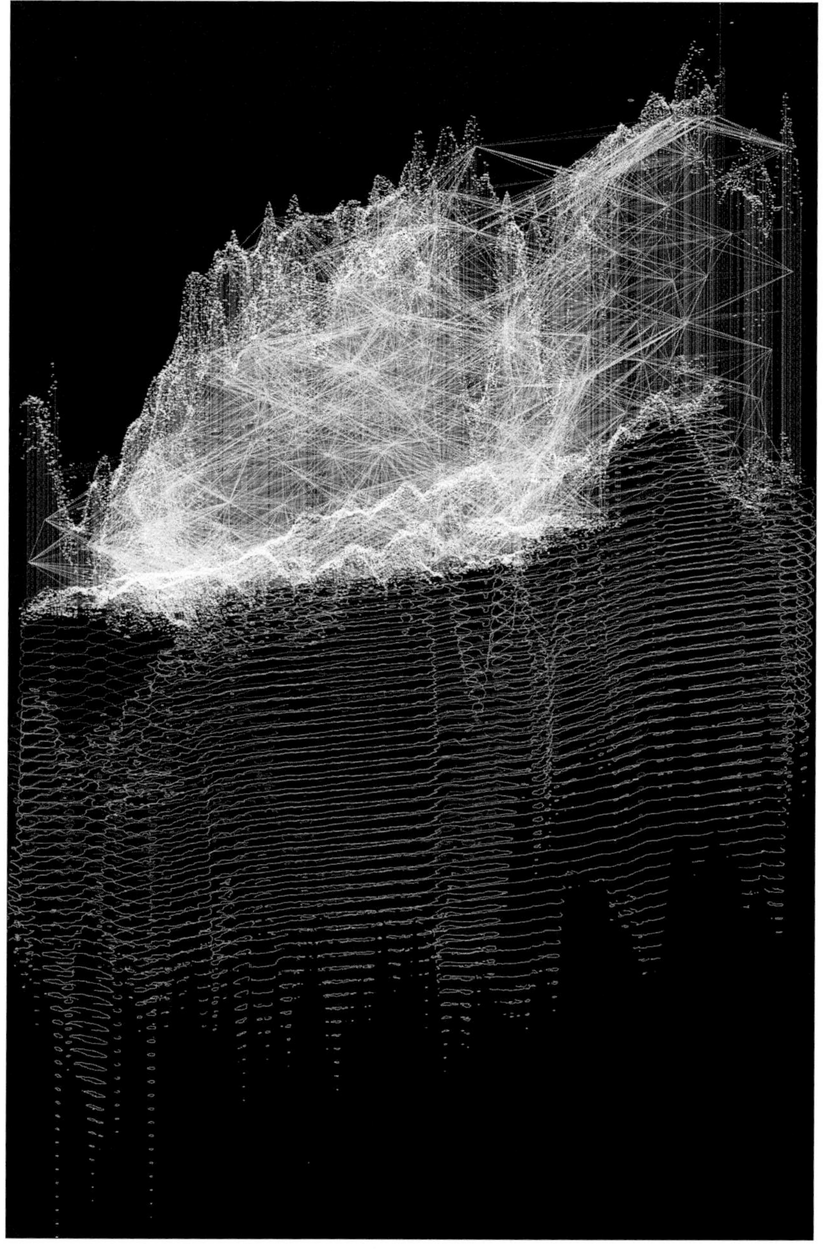

FIGURE 13.3 Project 1. Sectional relationships between the Manhattan grid and below-grade and above-grade topography. Geological soil-density composition below grade (not just bedrock) and variable proposed zoning building height. The Cooper Union, Graduate Studio, Fall 2015; Student: Bing Dai; Professors: Pablo Lorenzo-Eiroa (coordinator), Dorit Aviv, and Will Shapiro.

progressively overcrowded, the previous experiments that failed in the 1970s, proposing multilevel cities through skywalks, have a different potential today, presenting possibilities to explore a multilevel city by layering ecologies at multiple urban levels.

Third, other projects displace the fluid territories and emerging spatial patterns created through Big Data processing in simulating environmental forces in the city. By formalizing fluid-dynamic processes, these techniques allow to represent, analyze, and manipulate fluid-dynamic energy, organizing the increasingly complex space-environments of a city like New York (Figures 13.4, 13.6, 13.7, 13.9, 13.10, 13.12; Projects 2, 3, 4, 5). Project 2 maps conflicts in the relationship between the Manhattan grid and a possible extension across the East River (Figures 13.4a, b, 13.5). To do so, this project first develops an algorithm calculating increasing bifurcations as the typology of Manhattan grid is displaced by encountering different topographic levels (flood areas) and the bathymetry of the East River (Figure 13.4a). Then, the project develops a fluid-dynamic simulation program for sedimentation deposition in floating aggregates (Figure 13.4b explains the digital simulation of sediment deposition). The combination of these two algorithms is then related to the site-specific topographic data and bathymetry of New York City (see white background Figure 13.5a and black background Figure 13.5b). The form of the project is defined by its dynamic shifting ecology, which emerges by combining deterministic algorithmic operations with non-deterministic topographies based on Big Data processing. The shifting dynamic organization of a landscape urbanism

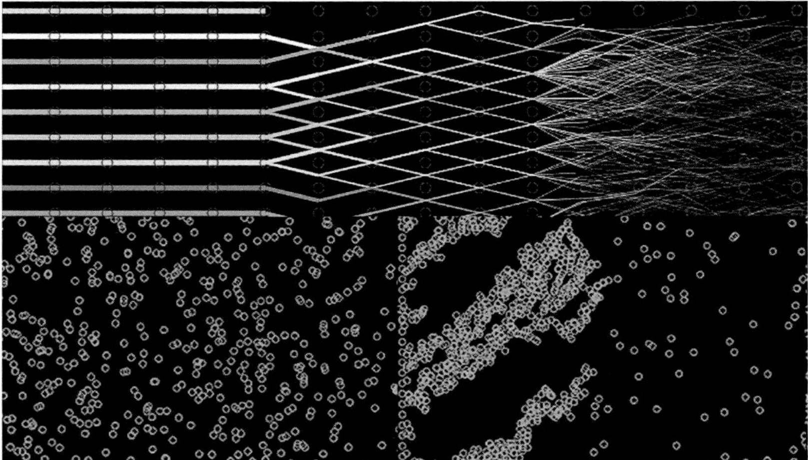

FIGURE 13.4A AND 13.4B Project 2. Algorithm calculating increasing bifurcations and fluid dynamic simulation program of sedimentation deposition in floating aggregates. The Cooper Union, ARCH 177/482B computation seminar S2013; students: Katheryn Bajo and Gregory Schikman; Professor Pablo Lorenzo-Eiroa.

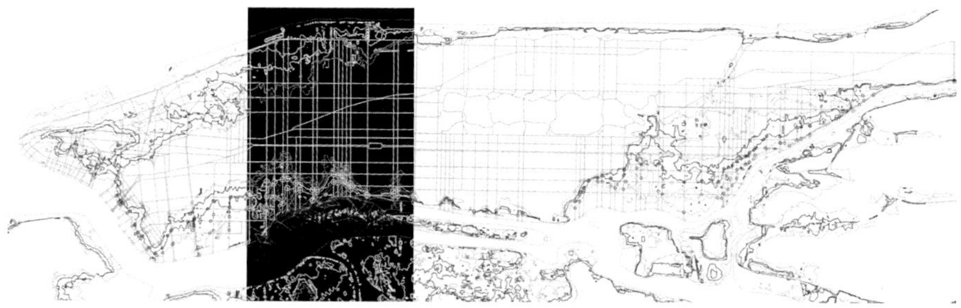

FIGURE 13.5A AND 13.5B Project 2. FEMA Flood Zones 1,2,3 but in relation to real below-grade topography and Manhattan Grid's main streets and avenues. The shifting dynamic organization of a landscape urbanism is activated by promoting natural side effects exchanging information and energy. The Cooper Union, ARCH 177/482B computation seminar S2013; students: Katheryn Bajo and Gregory Schikman; Professor Pablo Lorenzo-Eiroa.

is activated by promoting natural side effects exchanging information and energy. This project gathered its own data set, developing quantitative calculations as well as developing its own code and program to simulate the sedimentation process.

Fourth, other projects work more frontally on the relationship between spatial containment, urban morphology, and the architecture of environments, addressing urbanism as space-environment. One project initially maps the actual existing dissociation between Manhattan density building massing and the existing open green areas and how these two conditions contribute to the heat-island effect or feedback temperature gain in New York City (Figures 13.6, 13.7a, b, 13.8a, b, 13.9: Project 3). This urban reading considers the city as a space-environment by relating urban massing and building typologies to the environment that they inform. This project reads and renders visible the heat-island effect or temperature gain in relation to urban massing, reading NYC as layered space-environments. Considering the city as space-environment, the project relates the city's skyline to its explicit non-visible but perceptible environmental skyline (Figure 13.6 plan, 13.7a and 13.7b axonometric and sections, 13.8a). Urban massing, urban clusters, and building typologies and their relationship to urban voids create artificial micro-environments in which the measuring of the heat-island effect can be more relevant (Figure 13.8b). To activate a critical reading of the city and a potential addressing of such reading, the project proposes a series of interrelated urban interventions that aim to balance through fluid-dynamic simulation the previously mapped heat-island effect produced by urban massing. The project expands and interconnects key specific open spaces and corridors in the city, activating artificial environmental continuity through the activation of specific wind patterns (Figures 13.9a and 13.9b; Project 3), which a different project takes forward (see Figure 13.10; Project 4). This second project renders visible the complex network of fluid-dynamic simulation of

New York City in relation to multiple wind patterns, directions, and vortexes (Figure 13.10). By opening public spaces to create larger urban corridors, both Projects 3 and 4 progressively activate an ecology of wind patterns to balance the high temperatures created by building massing and building up inertia by adding continuity between existing green areas (Figures 13.6, 13.8b, 13.9a, 13.9b, 13.10).

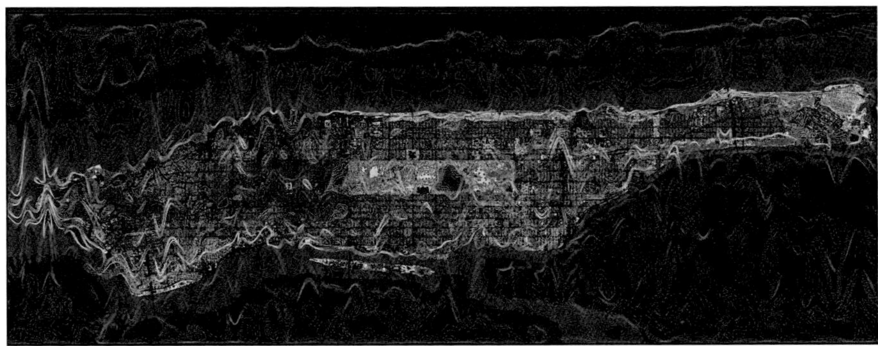

FIGURE 13.6 Project 3. Manhattan urban massing and open Green Areas in relation to their heat-island effect/temperature gain. The Cooper Union, Graduate Studio, Fall 2015; Student: Yuan Gao; Professors: Pablo Lorenzo-Eiroa (coordinator), Dorit Aviv, and Will Shapiro.

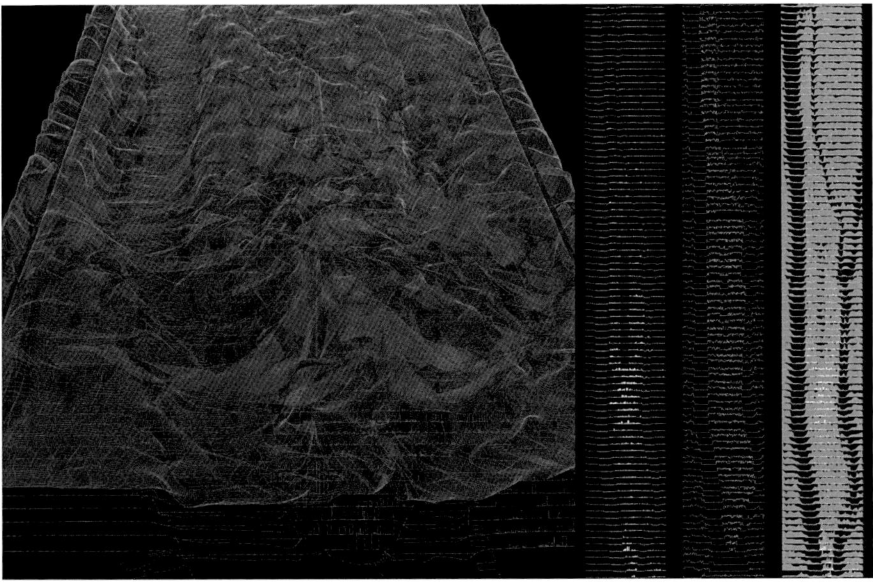

FIGURE 13.7A AND 13.7B Project 3. Heat-island effect/temperature cloud (13.7a) and skyline (13.7b). The Cooper Union, Graduate Studio, Fall 2015; Student: Yuan Gao; Professors: Pablo Lorenzo-Eiroa (coordinator), Dorit Aviv, and Will Shapiro.

Some buildings open public spaces, increasing the available urban voids in such way as to activate wind vortexes at corners, activating an artificial ecology conditioning the city as a space-environment (Figure 13.9a and 13.9b, 13.10).

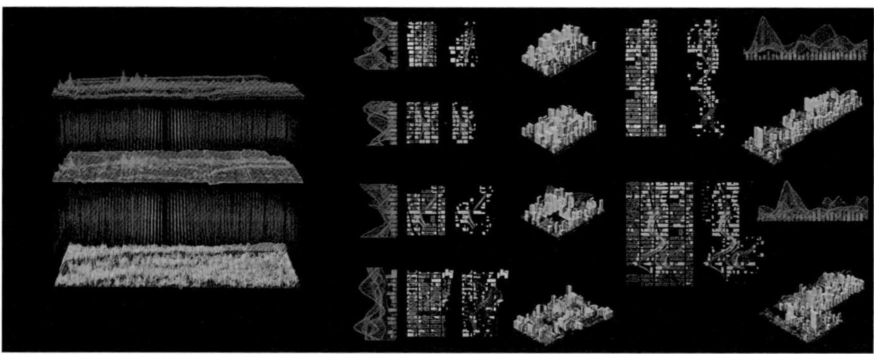

FIGURES 13.8A AND 13.8B Project 3. Heat-island effect/temperature gain in relation to urban massing, reading NYC as layered space-environments. The Cooper Union, Graduate Studio, Fall 2015; Student: Yuan Gao; Professors: Pablo Lorenzo-Eiroa (coordinator), Dorit Aviv, and Will Shapiro.

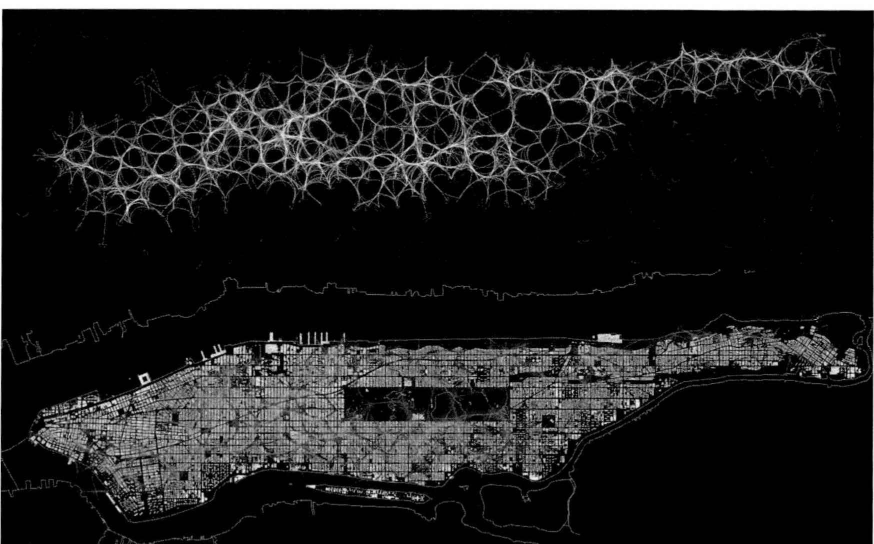

FIGURES 13.9A AND 13.9B Project 3. This urban project balances through fluid dynamic simulation the previously mapped heat island effect produced by urban massing (see images 6, 7, 8). The Cooper Union, Graduate Studio, Fall 2015; Student: Yuan Gao; Professors: Pablo Lorenzo-Eiroa (coordinator), Dorit Aviv, and Will Shapiro.

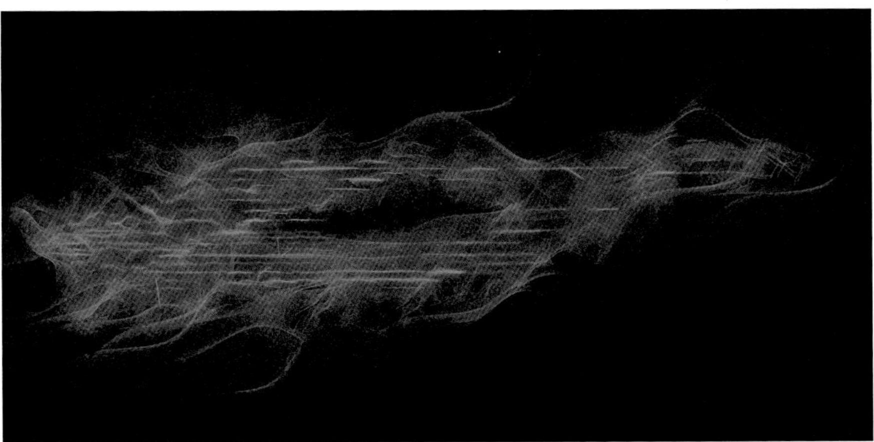

FIGURE 13.10 Project 4. Multiple wind direction, fluid-dynamic simulation of NYC. The Cooper Union, Graduate Studio, Fall 2015; Student: Seung Hwang Kim; Professors: Pablo Lorenzo-Eiroa (coordinator), Dorit Aviv, and Will Shapiro.

Fifth, other projects work out rather invisible and intangible environmental conditions, such as a project that develops a rezoning of NYC by reorganizing sound (Figures 13.11, 13.12a, and 13.12b; Project 5). This project creates a sound mapping strategy by identifying means to collect crowd-sourced data. By accessing portable cell-phone microphones as measuring devices of participating individuals that provided access to their portable devices, this project aimed, to a certain extent, to displace the typical authority structures in data gathering, frequently filtered by communication protocols and corporate interfaces. But, apart from mapping sound and identifying different levels of feedback and frequencies, the project then goes beyond an indexed mapping to develop a critical reading of the city as an environment. The architecture of data becomes then a new diversified territory, a plateau for the architecture of the project. The first tests are developed in a NYC block, developing sequential street-sound simulations retrieving different data sets and then studying relationships between building typologies and the soundscapes they inform (see Figures 13.12a and 13.12b). The project develops different studies, identifying the local sound conditions relative to building setbacks in plan and section, facade thresholds and folds, and building heights and density (Figure 13.11). The project then develops systematic readings of the collected data and studies how different spatial conditions and boundaries propel different sound patterns. The project also studied how different façade-rugosity and materiality affect each of the studied conditions. After these local studies, different block densities and street alignments are studied at a neighborhood level, engaging with clusters of city blocks and defining an urban morphology relative to sound. After these studies combining local and regional readings, the project proposes an overall mapping of the city identifying statistically the measurement through time of certain sound-density areas, with the hope of developing a comprehensive mapping of the sound of the city (Figure 13.12a). Ultimately, the project questions the city and its environment to develop a reorganization of sound patterns, proposing a rezoning for New York City through Big Data sound-simulation displacing block typologies to architecturally organize sound space-environments (Figure 13.12b).

By developing Big Data processing mechanisms, this project aims to engage ideologically with the disclosing and definition of the politically and culturally charged conditions of these territories.

Sixth, other projects of the research studio work by reading, analyzing, and disclosing the tension between repressed, hidden, latent ecologies and the grid that originally organized the city. The existing zoning mechanisms by which the city is structured – such as the city grid, blocks, blocks backyards, setbacks, building

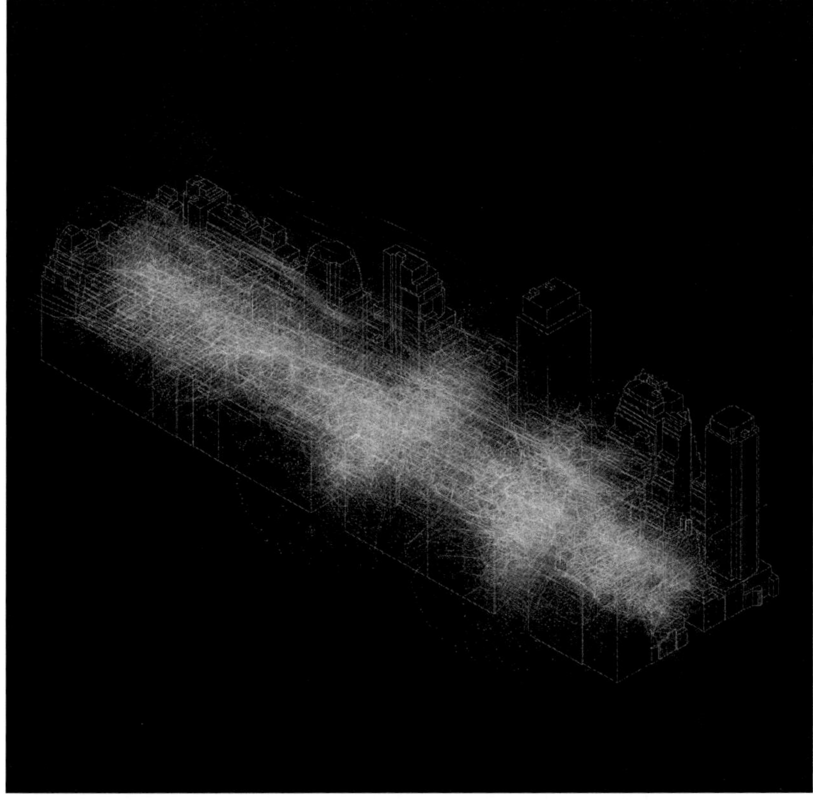

FIGURE 13.11 Project 5. NYC block, street sound simulation. The Cooper Union, Graduate Studio, Fall 2015; Student: Jin Woo Lee; Professors: Pablo Lorenzo-Eiroa (coordinator), Dorit Aviv, and Will Shapiro.

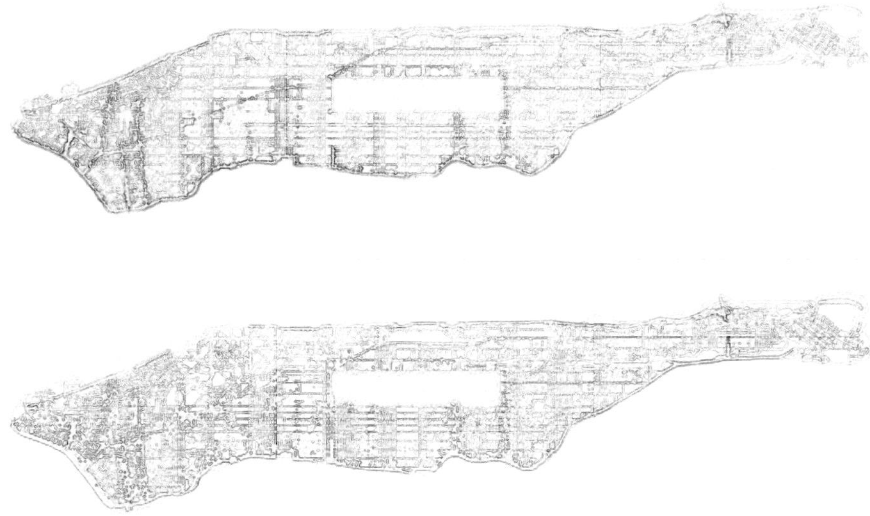

FIGURES 13.12A AND 13.12B Project 5. Soundscape simulation of NYC. Master Program Studio, The Cooper Union, Graduate Studio, Fall 2015; Student: Jin Woo Lee; Professors: Pablo Lorenzo-Eiroa (coordinator), Dorit Aviv, and Will Shapiro.

envelopes, orientation, public space, voids, and parks – create prototypical solutions to the multiple forces that inform the city, including real-estate speculation and civic functions. These prototypical solutions form urban typologies at multiple levels, for instance: the overall morphology of the city and its structure, urban fragments, urban block, streets, and the city's buildings. The interesting architectural problem is how these various typologies not only inform the environment, but how they are themselves transformed as systems in relation to their organization, to each other, and to the overall form and structure of the city.

Latent ecologies, environments, and other parameters are recoded to make sense of the mapped conditions. But this act of design avoids any linearity between the analyzed data, the systems, and the algorithms used to gather data and process environmental simulations and the proposed rezoning of the city, including urban typologies. Implementing a critical reading, the projects expand design to a recoding of the parameters that formalize the city. By understanding the differential between the creation of data, data gathering, and mapping acknowledging signification beyond its original understanding through actualization and representation, an informed reading of the city then becomes a design project, which inevitably will challenge the data that are indexing the project. This process would necessarily engage in a displacement of the common systems that gather and process information, including the emerging typologies of how information is processed. And, as described, this representation process necessarily relates to the emerging design and the form of the urban projects in terms of the architecture that results from the representational method and systems implemented. These readings and transformations would necessarily have to engage in a topological displacement and transfiguration of the urban typologies and the city themselves by addressing environmental processes to the point that new building typologies, new urban typologies, and new city typologies would emerge by addressing an informed, synthetic space-environment. This topological continuity between built environments and emerging environmental forces would engage in a reconsideration of the relationship between center and periphery, the city and "nature," the artificial and the natural, or thinking nature and the environment as the other.

Two projects make sense of these problems complementing each other. A final project (Figure 13.13; Project 7) outlines a sectional rezoning of New York City blocks to propose water-infrastructure mechanisms for environmental balance. Instead of keeping water off the city, a sort of complex, networked aqueduct for New York City works out at multiple grade levels: from flooding reservoirs to water alleviation through open-water canals (see Figure 13.13). This project proposes topological displacements of city-block typologies altering the relationships between urban fabric, contained backyards, and public and private space. By inverting the fabric of the city, the project enables a parallel, continuous ecological system. This project proposes a displacement of New York City block typologies in terms of spatial containment. Internal blocks create first reservoirs to contain flooding by which they then become interconnected and function as water-alleviation canals across different blocks. These canals interconnect while they reactivate hidden underground canals, developing a larger, hybrid, artificial and natural waterway system. The affected blocks progressively open their interior containment while they activate larger ecologies. The overall project starts activating latent ecologies of different scales from swamps to rivers (more clearly represented in Figure 13.2: Project 6). The block's typologies are displaced by activating a topological space-environment (Figure 13.13). NYC blocks' interiors spatial containment becomes interconnected to develop a parallel, negative city. By interconnecting the city's interior blocks' courtyards, the project activates latent suppressed ecologies hidden by the grid, inverting the city's structure. The city, as an artificial, imposed system produces latent counter systems that may build up on each other, producing a synthesis of contrasts between a planned Cartesian space and an existing site-specific topographic and environmental condition, displacing the typology of the city. The city must acknowledge the same conditions it creates by default of its logical system, by critiquing and opening its structure to the latent ecological counter-cities-systems that may be implicit.

Lastly, a certain deconstruction of the single data-gathering mechanism and design proposal is placed in motion when all participants of the research studio build up information layers to place back together a new reading of the city, integrated and synthesized at a higher cognitive level. In complex-system theory, isolating problems to study them may feedback negatively in an apparently sound isolated solution. Once the complexity of the system builds up out of the accumulation of

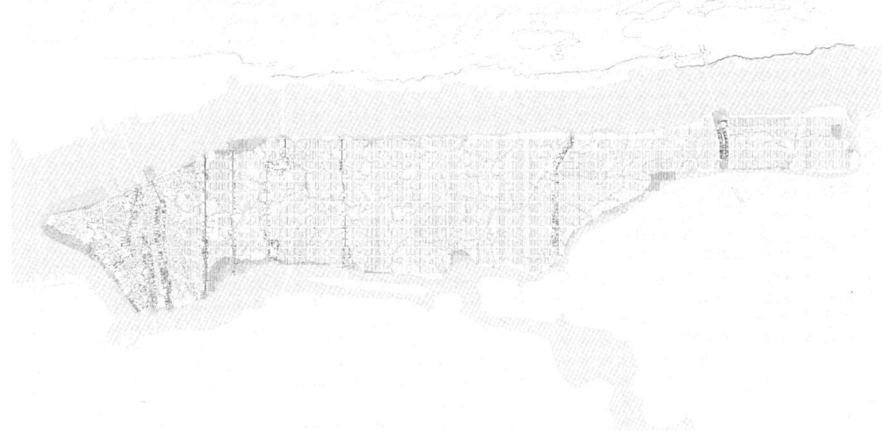

FIGURE 13.13 Project 7. Topological displacements of city blocks typologies altering relationships. The Cooper Union, Graduate Studio, Fall 2014; Student: Jaebong Jean; Professors: Pablo Lorenzo-Eiroa (coordinator), Lydia Xynogala, and Will Shapiro.

different aspects, it builds up feedback, reflective information through the totality building up complex non-linear emergent interaction among the different conditions that become active. Eventually, complexity becomes topological, recursive, and reflective. The objective here is to develop a continuously expanding platform, a multidimensional open-sourced design platform in which designers, as well as different professionals and citizens, could continuously enter data democratically and affect the measuring methodology, the processing system, and the representational strategies that inform a continuous modeling of the environment of which they are part. Blockchain technology is being implemented as a work in progress to develop a platform in which a self-regulating system without a centralized authorial organization (nor corporate interests, nor governmental agencies) may administrate a zoning for the city based on professional, accredited peer-review experts, through a voting mechanism with a certain governmental base control. The final proposal would be a dynamic open platform in which the form of the city would be continuous flux, since each time the city adds to its density, the measurement would change, and the model would be reassessed in relation to its new information. Multiple means to automate this platform are being studied, both at an experimental academic level as well as at a professional level. For instance, a dynamic model would not necessarily work as an optimizing machine, but rather the aim is to understand tendencies, inertias, and potential confluence of information, which may lead to a different kind of non-linear, indexical architecture optimization that would open up to multidimensional levels of authorship in its process of formation.

To avoid a linear indexing relationship between data and a proposed design-solution, a critical reading becomes a means to address the accumulative potential effect given by recognizing latent opportunities to transform the entire structure of the city. This topological project becomes active each time there is a reading of implicit latent realities.

References

Badiou, Alain (2005). *Being and Event* (trans. Oliver Felthan). London: Continuum.

Caro, A. Robert (1974). *The Power Broker*. New York: Robert A. Knof.

Crutzen, Paul J., and Stoermer, Eugene F., (2000). 'The Anthropocene'. *Global Change Newsletter*, *41*, 17–18.

Derrida, Jacques (1978). 'Force and signification' in *Writing and Difference*. Chicago: The University of Chicago Press.

De Saussure, Ferdinand (1977). *Course in Central Linguistics* (orig. 1916, trans. W. Baskin). Glasgow: Fontana/Collins.

Grosswiller, Paul (1999). 'The method is the message: rethinking Mc Luhan through critical theory'. *Canadian Journal of Communication*, *24*(1). Available at https://www.cjc-online.ca/index.php/journal/article/view/1087/993

Lorenzo-Eiroa, Pablo and Sprecher, Aaron (eds) (2013). *Architecture in Formation*, London: Routledge/Taylor & Francis.

McLuhan, Marshall (1967). *The Medium Is the Message: An Inventory of Effects*. Harmondsworth: Penguin Group.

Tafuri, Manfredo (1974). 'L'architecture dans le boudoir: The language of criticism and the criticism of language. *Oppositions 3*, New York.

Willis, Carol (1995). Form Follows Finance, Skyscrapers and Skylines in New York and Chicago. New York: Princeton Architectural Press.

INDEX